ROAPE AFRICAN READERS
Edited by Giles Mohan & Tunde Zack-Williams

THE POLITICS OF TRANSITION IN AFRICA
State. Democracy

Villiams

DATE DUE

Demco, Inc. 38-293

ROAPE AFRICAN READERS
Edited by Giles Mohan & Tunde Zack-Williams

THE POLITICS OF TRANSITION IN AFRICA
State, Democracy
& Economic Development
Edited by Giles Mohan & Tunde Zack-Williams

Forthcoming titles
GENDER RELATIONS IN AFRICA
Edited by Lynne Brydon

THE ENVIRONMENT IN AFRICA
Edited by Phil O'Keefe & Chris Howarth

ROAPE AFRICAN READERS
Edited by Giles Mohan & Tunde Zack-Williams

THE POLITICS OF TRANSITION IN AFRICA
State, Democracy
& Economic Development
Edited by Giles Mohan & Tunde Zack-Williams

REVIEW OF
African
Political Economy

IN ASSOCIATION WITH

James Currey
OXFORD

Africa World Press
TRENTON, N.J.

ROAPE Publications Ltd
Box 678 Sheffield S1 1BF
in association with

James Currey
73 Botley Road
Oxford OX2 0BS

Africa World Press
PO Box 1892
Trenton, NJ
08607

British Library Cataloguing in Publication Data
The politics of transition in Africa : state, democracy & economic
development. - (ROAPE African readers)
1. Africa - Politics and government - 1960 - 2. Africa -
Economic policy
I. Mohan, Giles, 1966 - II. Zack-Williams, Tunde III. review of
African political economy
320 . 9'6

ISBN 0-85255-822-8 (James Currey paper)

**Library of Congress Cataloging-in-Publication Data
is available**

Typeset in 10/11 pt Times New Roman
by Long House Publishing Services, Cumbria, UK
Printed and bound in the United States of America

CONTENTS

Section Two
THE POLITICS OF VIOLENCE
Imperialism, Militarism & Warlordism

Section Three
THE POLITICS OF CULTURAL PLURALISM
Gender, Culture & Participation

Section Four
THE POLITICS OF NEOLIBERALISM
Democratisation, Civil Society & the Developmental State

LIST OF CONTRIBUTORS

Hussaina Abdullah   Independent Researcher
Jocelyn Alexander   University of Bristol, England
Chris Allen   University of Edinburgh, Scotland
Yusuf Bangura   United Nations Institute for Social Development, Geneva,
                         Switzerland

Carolyn Baylies*   University of Leeds, England
Björn Beckman   University of Uppsala, Sweden
Roger Charlton   University of Coventry, England
Craig Charney   Yale University, USA
Jacklyn Cock   University of the Witwatersrand, South Africa
Jean Copans   L'Université René Descartes, Paris, France
Basil Davidson   Bath, England
Joshua B. Forrest   University of Vermont, USA
Rafael Kaplinsky   Institute of Development Studies, University of Sussex,
                         England

Colin Leys   Queens University, Kingston, Canada
John Markakis   University of Crete, Greece
Roy May   University of Coventry, England
Morris Morley   SUNY, Binghamton, USA
Barry Munslow   University of Liverpool, England
James Petras   SUNY, Binghamton, USA
John Rapley   University of the West Indies, Mona, Jamaica
Lars Rudebeck   University of Uppsala, Sweden
John S. Saul   York University, Toronto, Canada
Eiichi Shindo   Tsukuba University, Japan
Morris Szeftel   University of Leeds, England

Editors
Giles Mohan   Lecturer, Open University, England
Tunde Zack-Williams   Professor in Sociology, Department of Education and Social
                         Science, University of Central Lancashire, England

* (1946–2003)

SERIES INTRODUCTION

This series of Readers on Africa has been put together in response to requests from colleagues and activists working within and beyond the continent. Subscribers to the *Review of African Political Economy* (ROAPE) were increasingly requesting not only that specific articles in the journal be used for teaching but that themes running through many of the issues be used as a classroom text. This niche is continuing to expand. These Readers will ensure that there is continued access to relevant material not just for students and teachers but for grassroots activists not able to participate in any formal teaching structure. The object is accessibility which will be reflected in the cost and style of the books.

Unlike most Readers we are not seeking to present a comprehensive overview of a disciplinary sub-field. Rather we have brought together articles which reflect the way that contributors to ROAPE have interpreted and transformed these debates. The journal which began in 1974 was committed to a practical politics which was not simply tied to the more rarefied world of academic debates. To this day, despite changes in editorship and a publication agreement with Carfax, the journal has maintained its identity and remained true to its founding goals. Hence, the Readers which will be derived from ROAPE material will have a coherence which is not usually found in other more all-encompassing readers.

Giles Mohan
Tunde Zack-Williams

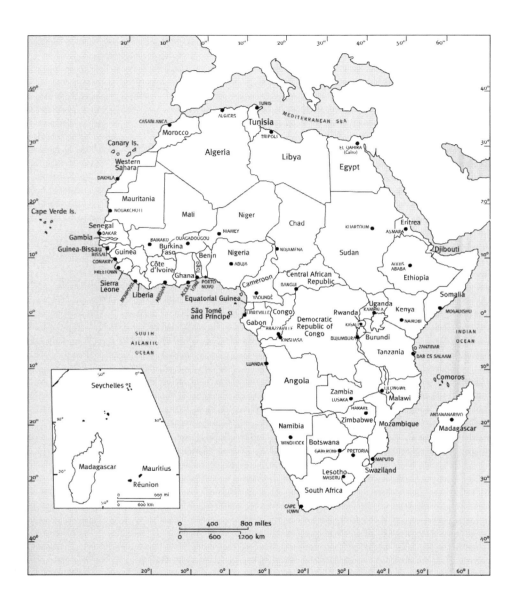

Contemporary Africa

1 TUNDE ZACK-WILLIAMS & GILES MOHAN
INTRODUCTION
Theories of the State / The State of the Theories

This book is divided into four sections. Section One, which seeks to situate the politics of underdevelopment, sets out to answer the question about the nature of the post-colonial state and the class interests that it serves. Section Two looks at issues of political violence, militarism and warlordism, which, by the late 1980s, had become features of politics in Africa. Section Three addresses issues of culture, political power, gender and political participation. As Africa continues to react to the neo-liberal agenda, the final section focuses on the politics of neo-liberalism, democratisation and the question of the role of the state in fostering development.

SECTION ONE THE POLITICS OF UNDERDEVELOPMENT
Dependency, Bureaucracy & the Bourgeoisie

Debates on the state and political transitions in Africa have always assumed a dynamic form, reflecting social, economic and political struggles within Africa, as well as the dominant ideology in the hegemonic centres. These changes will be reflected in the discussions below. The aim of this introductory chapter is to situate the debates running through this collection in relation to wider issues concerning the state in general, in particular, political and economic transition in Africa. In this chapter we hope to point to the theoretical influences, which came to bear on the debates in ROAPE, and how contributors to the journal adapted or rejected such approaches. Discourses on the state are strewn with paradoxes. Thus as Ralph Miliband has observed:

> While the vast inflation of the state's power and activity in the advanced capitalist societies … has become one of the merest commonplaces of political analysis, the remarkable paradox is that the state itself, as a subject of political study, has long been very unfashionable. (Miliband, 1969: 1)

The African paradox is premised on the fact that whilst the power and areas of activities of the state have grown (the African Leviathan) in the post-independence era, for most Africans the state continues to have little meaning, as many people continue to operate outside of its ambit. Analysis of the state in Africa was equally slow to develop largely because of the perceived alien and bifurcated nature of the post-colonial state (Mamdani, 1996); the voguish position held by pluralist ideology (Miliband, 1969) and the obsession with 'tribalism' – that product of colonial 'other-ness' sui generis – as a heuristic category in African studies. The proliferation of 'elites theories' and the dominance of African socialism did not help the situation, which at best tended to obfuscate the debate, and at worst inclined to deny the class nature of African societies.

If the 'right' failed to grasp the nettle of the state, then Marxist political analysis of the nature and function of the state 'has long seemed stuck in its own groove,' whilst waiting for an intellectual renewal (ibid. p. 5). This is in spite of the fact that Marx (*Capital* Vol. 1; *Communist Manifesto*); and Lenin (*State and Revolution*) had laid the foundation for such a project. Indeed, notwithstanding Gramsci's invaluable contribution to Marxist analysis with the concept of 'hegemony', the orthodox position prior to Miliband's work was condensed in the maxim set out in the *Communist Manifesto*: 'The executive of the modern state is but a committee for managing the common affairs of the whole bourgeoisie'. This notion of the (bourgeois) state as essentially the instrument of the (ruling class) bourgeoisie, is seen as Marx's 'predominant view' of the state (Miliband, 1969; Pierson, 1996). Whilst there are occasions when the state might work against certain fractions of capital, the state's monopoly of violence is utilised in class conflicts to subsume the enemies of the bourgeoisie to its interests. Another perspective of Marx's analysis of the state ('the secondary view') is that which is often referred to as the relative autonomy thesis. This asserts that at certain moments, the state can act independently of the desire of the ruling class, and is often referred to as Bonapartism (Pierson, 1996). We shall return to the Marxist position presently; however, a comment on Weber's perception of the state is in place.

Like Marx, Weber accorded control over the means of violence as a defining characteristic of the state, though this is not the only means of administering political organisations (Pierson, 1996). In tune with Weber's ideal typologies, a number of features have been identified as collectively providing the ingredients of the modern state, and their alleged absence of these has led a number of writers from both left (Mamdani, 1996) and right (Chabal & Daloz, 1999) persuasions to question the efficacy of conventional state theory in comprehending political actors in Africa. These typologies include territoriality, sovereignty, constitutionality, impersonal power, the public bureaucracy, authority/legitimacy and citizenship (ibid.). The absence of these 'ideal types' in African political praxis has led to the centralisation of patrimonialism and clientelism as major theoretical tools in analysing the African State and political actors. We shall return to these debates presently, for now we want to trace the chronology of debate on the state in Africa.

Analysis on the state in capitalist society was given a fillip by Miliband's *The State in Capitalist Society*. It provided the intellectual renewal, which Miliband himself felt Marxist investigation needed. Above all it provided an intellectual challenge for further reworking of Marx's work to explicate the situation in non-capitalist formations.[1] This task was taken up by Hamza Alavi in his pioneering work, 'The State in Post-Colonial Societies: Pakistan and Bangladesh', *New Left Review*, No.74, July/August, 1972. Alavi's point of departure was a rejection of Miliband's conclusion that:

> For Marx, the Bonapartist State, however independent it may have been politically from any given class, remains, and cannot in a class society but remain, the protector of an economically and socially dominant class. (Alavi, 1972: 40)

He noted that in post-colonial society the relationship between the state and the underlying economic structure is more complex than the trajectory of the Bonapartist State. This complexity is premised on the fact that the state in post-colonial society is not the creation of indigenous classes, but that of the metropolitan bourgeoisie, who in addition to replicating bourgeois structures in the colony, also instituted 'state apparatus through which it can exercise dominion over all the indigenous social classes in the colony'.

The problem of a state created by a foreign bourgeoisie who constitute the ruling class, and an ascendant indigenous governing class,[2] Alavi observed, rendered the class basis of such societies a complex one: on the one hand the state is not subordinate to the indigenous bourgeoisie since they do not control the destiny of the formation, that being the raison d'être of the ruling class, the metropolitan bourgeoisie. On the other hand, the post-colonial state is no longer a simple instrument in the hands of the neo-colonial bourgeoisie. Here lies Alavi's central thesis:

> (T)hat the state in post-colonial society is not the instrument of a single class. It is relatively autonomous and it mediates between the competing interests of the three propertied classes, namely the metropolitan bourgeoisie, the indigenous bourgeoisie and the landed classes, while at the same time acting on behalf of them all to preserve the social order in which their interests are embedded, namely the institution of private property and the capitalist mode as the dominant mode of production. (ibid.: 42)

Though Alavi's work was concerned with state and society in South Asia, nonetheless, it was meant as a grand theory incorporating other post-colonial societies. It was his theme of relative autonomy that impelled Africanist contributions initially by Colin Leys and later by John Saul (both in this volume). In his initial work on the politics of neo-colonialism in Kenya, Leys noted that though the parallel with Kenya was not exact, yet he found similarity in the situation in post-colonial Kenya and that which Marx described of the politics in France in the 1850s. In the case of the latter, whilst the bureaucracy and the state apparatus were independent of any single class,

> it could not do without class support, and could not prevent its policies fostering the interests of certain classes, and so undermine its own independence of action; therefore it also worked constantly to counteract the political power of the classes whose economic power it was simultaneously building up. (Leys, 1975:207)

In the case of Kenya, Leys produced a caricature of the Kenyan bourgeoisie, which later led to a volte-face and a quick auto-critique. Initially, he characterised the Kenyan regime as even more Bonapartist than the regime in 1850s France, for no sooner had it proffered populist rhetoric on African Socialism and 'rural development' than it progressively curtailed the power of peasants and urban workers. In his view, the Kenyan bourgeoisie was dependent, non-innovative and comprador, which cannot distinguish its interests from those of the neo-colonial bourgeoisie.

The fieldwork for this 1975 work was undertaken in 1971; however, upon his return to Kenya in 1977, Leys claimed to have experienced a resolute desire on the part of the indigenous bourgeoisie to supplant the neo-colonial bourgeoisie. His findings on his 1977 visit led to a fierce debate with critics, which is often referred to as the Kenyan debate (see Kaplinsky in this volume). The significance of the debate goes beyond an analysis of the Kenyan economy per se (Leys, 1978), as contributors sought to situate the Kenyan experience within a wider discourse of underdevelopment theories. Leys' 1978 thesis, which seemed more in tune with the position of more orthodox marxists such as Bill Warren, questioned some of the gloom of the by now voguish dependency perspective, which argued that Africa, like other Third World formations, because of the manner of their incorporation within the global capitalist economy, were doomed to stagnation and underdevelopment. For these theorists, the only way out of the morass of underdevelopment was through a 'socialist break'. Thus Gavin Kitching observed:

I believe that a socialist alternative to capitalism in Africa can be constructed by a sophisticated socialist movement created among the working classes of Africa as they slowly expand through time … I believe, however, that the formation of a sophisticated socialist working class in Africa will take a long time and that a prolonged period of struggle against the developing capitalism here is one of the important prerequisites of its creation. (Kitching, 1985)

By contrast, critics of the dependencia, such as Warren, argued that not only was capitalist transformation occurring in these societies, but that a significant number of these countries were now at a stage of capitalist development which the now developed countries once occupied. As far as the more substantive issue of the state is concerned, Leys (1978) argues:[3]

- That the Kenyan economy has experienced substantial growth since independence;

- That an independent autochthonous bourgeoisie has now emerged;

- That there has been a significant shift in ownership away from the neo-colonial bourgeoisie, in favour of the domestic bourgeoisie;

- That the state has become a significant instrument in enhancing the process of control over foreign capital by the indigenous bourgeoisie;

- Kenya will continue to experience sustainable capitalist development as capitalist accumulation continues.

Kaplinsky challenged Leys' conclusions by pointing to the fact that structural change of the economy was limited, as the share of manufacturing to GDP grew rather sluggishly in almost a decade and a half after independence. Furthermore, using empirical data, Kaplinsky concluded that there has not been any significant shift of ownership from foreign capital to an indigenous bourgeoisie, though the bureaucracy was making substantial headway within the parastatals. Whilst pointing out that Leys had failed to disprove the dependency school, Kaplinsky rejected what he called 'the cruder formulations of dependency theory'; instead he concluded that,

although an indigenous capitalist class has managed to carve out a slice of the benefits arising from accumulating in large scale industry, this has arisen from an alliance between this class and foreign capital. (p. 43)

For Leys and Nicola Swainson (1980) the state is not only a major instrument in emancipating the indigenous bourgeoisie as seen from the various economic measures taken, but they went on to argue that the state is controlled by this class. Leys abandoned his earlier position of a state mediating between the interests of a weak domestic bourgeoisie and that of a powerful international bourgeoisie. In short, the specific class project is the entrenchment of the domestic bourgeoisie, and as Beckman has pointed out this assumed that the interests of both the neo-colonial and domestic bourgeoisies were incompatible. As such their position tends to obscure 'the nature of the contradiction and the degree to which foreign capital depends on domestic class forces for its penetration' (p. 54).

Kaplinsky and Steven Langdon (1980) noted that the neo-colonial state would side with foreign capital in disputes with domestic local capital. Langdon maintained that the state's 'relative autonomy' is based on a perception of mutual interests between a quartet: senior state bureaucrats; the political class; the domestic bourgeoisie and the foreign bourgeoisie. However, Beckman has argued that both sides of the debate have put an unwarranted significance 'on the state as an instrument of "fractional" interests at the expense of its function as determined by the general, "non-functional" requirements of capital accumulation' (p. 54). Furthermore, the counter blast of the debate has tended to lose sight of the imperative for a 'scientific support for the ongoing revolutionary struggles of the oppressed people of the Third World' (p. 55).

Beckman, in his 'Imperialism and the "National Bourgeoisie"', tried to relate the Kenya situation to that of the politics of black Africa's most populous nation, Nigeria, by using an article by the Nigerian marxist Segun Osoba, who had argued for the need to transcend the bourgeois stage, as he perceived the Nigerian bourgeoisie as inefficient and dysfunctional to the developmental needs of the nation, as they continue to act out their role as comprador commission agents of imperialism. Osoba argued that if the national bourgeoisie pursued its objective class role, then it would be able to bring legitimacy and stability to society, which in the end would benefit the mass of the people. In short, for it to foster its historic role, it will have to abandon its comprador status. However, Beckman questioned Osoba's position suggesting that it would be in the interests of foreign capital if the Nigerian bourgeoisie were efficient, since at least this would reduce the cost of operations in Nigeria. For Beckman both sides of the Kenyan debate fail to visualise the state as an organ of capital. Thus the fundamental contradictions of imperialism are those between the hegemonic classes and the politically fragmented workers and peasants.

By the middle of the 1980s (the lost decade of African development), as the problems of peripheral capitalism took their toll on the people of Africa, and as the dependency model came under increasing scrutiny, theorists concentrated their attention on internal factors for the parlous state of African development. In particular, attention was beginning to be focussed on the conspicuous consumption and the role of 'graft' in African politics. Szeftel's article was one of the first to draw attention to this phenomenon in the case of Zambia. This article points to the legal and moral difficulties in trying to define corruption. For Szeftel, graft is only one element of a wider mode of political legitimisation; that of clientelism. Through patron-client networks, the state is used as a vehicle to distribute resources for private ends. Attention is drawn to the detrimental impact of graft and corruption (defined as the transfer of resources from one class to another) on the state and developmental efforts, leading to structured inefficiency, as well as the undermining of the legitimacy of the state. Joshua Forrest's contribution is a brief review of the literature, stating the major positions in the debate, whilst at the same time calling for greater fluidity in class analysis.

SECTION TWO THE POLITICS OF VIOLENCE
Imperialism, Militarism & Warlordism

The 1980s saw various critiques of Marxist theorising, which attacked its reductionism and Eurocentricism. Some aspects of these criticisms were not specifically directed at Marxism as such, but at all grand theories. This was particularly true of the onslaught from post-modernists who reacted

> to the 'monotony' of universal modernism's view of the world ... (Particularly) the belief in linear progress, absolute truths, the rational planning of ideal social orders, and the standardisation of knowledge and production. (Harvey, 1993: 9)

Postmodernists clearly show an aversion for universal or 'totalising' discourses, as well as rejecting all meta-narratives. The 'postmodernist supremacy' led to a disinclination for 'theory', and a retreat to empiricism. Thus Geoffrey Kay's work

(1975) marked a watershed in 'meta-narratives', and was followed by an impasse in theoretical work on development and underdevelopment (Booth, 1994). This retreat into empiricism in development thinking was influenced by the poor performance of African states in comparison to other underdeveloped areas such as Southeast Asia. The question was constantly posed why other areas that experienced colonial and imperialist exploitations were able to breach the yoke of underdevelopment, and in many cases to embark on capitalist industrial development. Thus there were demands for theoretical self-reflection, in order to incorporate the role of human agency in the development process (ibid.).

Meanwhile, the 1980s witnessed two important factors that had far-reaching effects on the developmental efforts in Africa. The first was the sharp growth in indebtedness of African countries. Though these figures (Table 1) seem small in comparison to other regions such as Latin America, Africa's ability to service debts has been called into question. The ratio of debt to GDP is averaging 62 per cent in Africa as compared with 58 per cent for Latin America over the period of time in question (Assiri et al., 1990: 118). The figures point to both a rapid growth in Africa's debt, but also a sharp rise in debt service ratio. The other factor was the decline in Africa's share of the world market, as the continent entered a prolonged crisis. As one contemporary observer noted:

> In the 1970s, the state of African economies was decidedly mixed. Many countries were suffering from a decline of the agricultural commodities that they sold to the world while many of the post-colonial elected governments had given way to military regimes or degenerated into corrupt dictatorial systems ... From the end of the decade, however, the situation deteriorated very substantially. The 1980s were marked by a decline in production and income per capita in most African countries, a declining share in world trade participation and an impending crisis. At the material heart of this lay the rising African Debt. Before 1980, few African states were significantly indebted (Freund, 1998: 253).

Table 1: The Growth in Africa's Indebtedness

Year	Total (in $ billion)	Debt Service Ratio
1970	4.5	5.4
1971	41.7	7.2
1985	60.7	21.3
1987	71.9	31.0

Source: A.M. Assiri, R. A. Parsons, N. Perdikis, 'A Comparative Analysis of Debt Rescheduling in Latin America and Sub-Saharan Africa', *Scandinavian Journal of African Alternatives*, Vol. IX, No. 2 & 3, 1990, p.118.

In essence this was a crisis of the nation state, 'as much a crisis of politics and institutions as it is a crisis of the economy and society itself' (Olukoshi & Laakso, 1996: 20). This crisis materialised in the 1980s as the value of exports fell, whilst imports continued to rise, resulting in a drastic fall in government revenue, though this was not reflected in a fall in expenditure. This period saw African governments trooping to the International Finance Institutions (IFIs) for aid packages in order to halt deteriorating balance of payment problems. In many cases, the medication almost killed the patient, as African states came out of the decade of structural adjustment programmes very battered and weak, marking the end of the 'developmentalist' state.

These cutbacks were so devastating that observers have noted that in several countries there emerged a clear trend towards 'the reversal of the entire "modernisation" process … as people moved from the formal to the informal sector and as school enrolment dropped sharply and attendance at poorly provisioned health facilities rapidly declined in the face of rising user charges' (Olukoshi & Laakso, 1996: 19). This too impacted on studies of the politics of economic decline, as these 'moved very rapidly from generalities about the post-colonial state towards more or less serious efforts to specify characteristics of politics and the state in *Africa*' (Booth, 1994: 8).

Whilst many contributors to ROAPE focused on the politics and economic process within specific states, there were a number who began the task of reformulating theories in the face of pressing practical problems relating to the end of the Cold War, the triumph of neo-liberalism and structural adjustments, and the political conflicts which these engendered. Within Africa, the 1980s witnessed various political, economic and ecological crises, and the contributions in the journal showed how these complex processes were unfolding as well as debating solutions. In particular, there was a focus on the increasing role of violence in politics as social movements sprang up to contest the state. As war and famine continued, contributors such as Eiichi Shindo drew attention to the relationship between hunger in the Third World and nuclear militarism in the developed world. He argued that the increasing militarisation of the Third World is directly related to famine-induced hunger suffered by its population. He showed how militarisation tends to increase indebtedness, ensure capital's flight and deprive agriculture of much needed investible resources (through the 'crowding out' effect) by creating distortion in the rest of the economy and strengthening the ties of dependence with advanced industrial economies.

Markakis' work on Ethiopia is both an attempt to analyse the events leading to military dictatorship in Addis Ababa, as well as to examine the possibility of 'garrison socialism' effecting a badly needed transformation in that country. The article points to the events leading to the military seizing power, as well as the role played by popular forces, whose activities were treated in ambiguous manner by the soldiers who led the 'February Revolution'. He drew attention to the petty bourgeois aspirations of the junior officers in the Dergue, which ran contrary to the wishes of the majority of radicals who called for a 'people's government' as a sine qua non for the transition to socialism. Petras and Morley's contribution continues with the theme of social transformation from the top. They posed a question to those who argued that Ethiopia has experienced a social revolution:

> The question that proponents of the notion that Ethiopia has experienced a social revolution must answer is whether there can be a revolutionary class in the modern world that is neither peasant nor worker and that also acts in a systematic and violent fashion to exploit and destroy the independent organisations of urban and rural labour. (p. 130)

They also drew attention to the superpower involvement in this area of Africa, noting that in the case of Ethiopia, there seemed to be a coincidence of interests between, on the one hand, the Dergue's need for weapons to prosecute various internal class and nationalities wars, as well as a threat from Somalia, and on the other, the Soviet Union's need to have a foothold in the region to counter America's hegemony.

Charlton and May's contribution seeks conceptual tools and approaches to explain the endemic nature of violence within the Chadian state, which renders the latter as the site of both 'state collapse' and 'upward trajectory'. Whilst trying to problematise concepts such as 'militarism' and 'militarisation', using Chad as a case study, they argued that an alternative approach of analysing violence in Africa could be the approach that

Sinologists have perfected, namely the theory of warlordism. Pointing to the growing militarisation and militarised nature of the continent, these authors argued that the 'warlord model' was quite appropriate as an analytical tool to explain political violence in Africa. This meant that in Chad at least there was 'personalisation of politico-military leadership and its regionalisation' (p. 153). Furthermore, these warlords (Hissene Habre, Quaddafi, and Wedde) fulfil Chiang Kai-shek's five essential characteristics for a warlord:

- lack of political principle;

- occupation of an area;

- insatiable need for money and property;

- dependence on imperialist support;

- love of his own skin.

Jacklyn Cock took up the theme of militarism and militarisation in her work on 'Militarism and Women in South Africa'. This connection she argued is obscured because most analyses perceived war as a male affair and the military as a patriarchal institution par excellence from which women are excluded, and by whom they are often victimised. She observed that white women in Apartheid South Africa contributed to the militarisation of the society in both ideological and material terms. At the same time a minority of white women acted as a major source of opposition to the conscription efforts of the apartheid state. She noted that the 'politics of gender', the power relations between men and women, which are structured around the dialectics of masculinity and femininity, determine the process whereby women are either resisting apartheid or contributing to militarisation. Though apartheid is seen as an aberration, some theorists have recently argued that it is only a peculiar form of indirect rule (Mamdani, 1996). As such, Cock's analysis can be applied to other polities on the continent.

SECTION THREE   THE POLITICS OF CULTURAL PLURALISM
Gender, Culture & Participation

The question of democratic participation is one that has dogged Africanists. Indeed, many writers from the left have agonised on the problem of the 'nation state', which Basil Davidson has characterised as a 'curse'(Davidson, 1992), as the 'nation' triumphs over the 'social' (ibid., p. 138) from a struggle between the elites who wanted power and the 'lower orders' who were desirous of the 'social'. It was not long after the departure of the colonial masters than the liberator soon turned oppressor, and the one-party system of government was the vehicle for this new autocracy (Davidson, 1992; Mamdani, 1996; Ekeh, 1997). The dictatorship of the party soon superseded the dictatorship of the proletariat as the party became identified with the state. In the case of Africa's most populous nation, it has been argued that

> the military has succeeded in destroying Nigerian Federalism (and that) ... Nigeria thus finds itself now with a so-called Federation that is for all practical purposes a unitary state with some limited devolution of power to the states. (Ibrahim, 1997: 163)

These themes of empowerment of the rural masses, democratic participation, accountability and political transparency were all central in the dialogue between Basil

Davidson and Barry Munslow. For the former, the way out of the curse of nation-statism is through:

> Decentralisation of power from the stiffly centralised bureaucratic kinds of state which have been created in Africa. Decentralising down to local government, whilst on a larger scale moving towards regional constellations and confederations of power. (p. 189)

Decentralisation of power and regional integration will not only bring development to the mass of rural inhabitants, but it will guarantee that they have a say in the type of governance being undertaken in their name. Furthermore, this policy will ensure that pre-colonial trade routes, now being patronised by peasant producers and 'smugglers', be accorded legitimacy. It is argued that this is one way of ensuring increasing food production, by attacking the growth of parallel economies at their foundation, and putting an end to the phenomenon, nation-state, which has by now become synonymous with the old colonial state. However, the major obstacle in the drive to decentralisation is the ruling elite, whose welfare is tied up to the nation-state. The absence of a national bourgeoisie that can impose its power, pending a constituted hegemony, which will transform the mass of the people from subject to citizens (Mamdani), as well as the fragmentation of the public sphere (Ekeh), are all signs of the torpid nature of the nation-state in Africa.

The theme of good governance through decentralisation is also central in Lars Rudebeck's contribution, which points to the growing gap between state and society in post-colonial Guinea, and the demise of hopes and optimism surrounding the liberation from Portuguese rule as state power continued to lose its legitimacy. Similarly, Jocelyn Alexander points to the obstacles to decentralisation strategies and land redistribution policies in Zimbabwe, arguing that the policy of decentralisation left the local authorities with some of the principal weaknesses of the *ancien regime*, of the white minority. Alexander concludes by noting that much of the land that was distributed went not to the 'land hungry', but was leased to members of the ruling elite.

Hussaina Abdullah's contribution examines gender challenges to the politics of what Beckett and Young have called 'permanent transition' in Nigeria (Beckett and Young, 1997). She drew attention to how state policies such as the Better Life Programme (BLP) for rural women, designed to raise women's consciousness and bring them together, in fact turn out to be nothing more than policies to bring 'rural women directly into the arena of capitalist exploitation' (p. 160). The military regime of Babangida rejected affirmative programmes recommended by the political bureau (which he set up), notwithstanding the fact that these are provided for in the Nigerian constitution. In her survey of state organisations such as the BLP and the National Commission for Women, she concluded that 'these BLP organisations cannot be expected to work for the elimination of gender subordination because their structure, objectives and constitution negate the need for the mobilisation of the majority of women in Nigeria' (p. 161). We are told that these organisations consist of women who are concerned with 'improving the provision of services rather than changing the consciousness of women' (p. 161). In her view a necessary condition for the genuine liberation of women and men in Nigeria is that a democratic trade union movement must embrace the feminist slogan 'the personal is political' as a first step, in order to ensure issues of private and domestic patriarchy are incorporated into the democratic and trade union discourse.

Craig Charney's analysis of the neo-colonial state serves a dual purpose: an attempt to contextualise the neo-colonial state as well as to explore the class basis of this type of state using a marxist theoretical framework, noting that the neo-colonial state, as a variant of the capitalist state, is one where 'foreign capital retains its hegemony through contradictory alliance with local dominant classes' (p. 179). This class alliance which itself is the product of the articulation (or interpenetration) of capitalist and domestic modes of production permits class hegemony and state legitimisation through 'lineage-type discourses' which increasingly sanctify capitalist reality. In other words, since commodity production is not universal in Africa, bourgeois hegemony and state legitimisation are not exclusively situated in the realm of exchange relations. Thus whilst there are the nuclei of bourgeois rationality, such as a legal system and early signs of proletarianisation, these are interspersed with patrimonial or lineage-type discourse. Charney argues that in a neo-colonial state, 'the dominant classes maintain their hegemony and the capitalist state its legitimacy by reproducing relations of dependence organised on the basis of lineage-type discourse' (p. 180). Lineage-type strategies continue to have an economic function, but continue to maintain the ideological conditions for the subjugation of dominated classes, as they draw upon shared symbols of history.

In a return to the class nature and interests, which the neo-colonial state serves, Charney argues that since independence did not mark a qualitative change in the form of the state, but only in the form of the regime, with multinational capital still dominant, the petty bourgeois in the state apparatus (the 'reigning' or 'governing' class) has a relative autonomy with respect to foreign capital. On the question of transformation, Charney warns that the neo-colonial state is neither invulnerable nor immortal. Its transformation could start as a result of an economic crisis, the collapse of lineage-type relations of subordination, and with the rise of organic intellectuals who are ready to contest the state.

Jean Copans' 'no short cut' thesis, reminiscent of Göran Hyden's work of the same title, is an attempt to situate Africa within the project of modernity. A distinction between 'modernity' and 'modernisation' is the starting point of his analysis, in order to argue that, 'in Africa, modernity has taken the form of mere modernisation, of an imposed acquisition of various disorganised and disembodied traits of modernity'. Whilst in the West modernity and modernisation occurred simultaneously, in Africa the two are separated, and modernity is more 'an imitation,' and modernisation has now become 'a permanent process to abort modernity', as the hegemonic groups continuously seek to eliminate ideas and action which constitute the double process of modernity: the social and the scientific. Thus he concluded:

> ... [T]he long and slow path of African history, the predominance of extra-African mechanisms for the production of social theoretical thought, and the absence of any kind of positive and dialectical relation between the groups in power and the 'modern' producers of such thinking have together impeded the making of modernity. (p. 165)

Copans concluded by pointing to the crucial role of the intellectual in the production of modernity and therefore the transition to democracy. However, in Africa the condition of the intellectual is quite bleak as universities and research centres are overcrowded and starved of resources, while repression and anti-intellectualism are rampant.

SECTION FOUR THE POLITICS OF NEO-LIBERALISM
Democratisation, Civil Society & the Developmental State

By the late 1980s structural adjustment programmes (SAPs) had come to dominate Third World, and in particular, African development,[4] in the global wave of economic liberalisation. Indeed, SAPs had become the mechanism through which African countries were 'hemmed in' the global economy (Callaghy & Ravenhill, 1993), rather than 'through the self-propelling power or rationality of the market' (Rugumamu, 1991: 4). Initially, this was premised upon a rejection of state dirigisme in favour of free market forces. The raison d'être for SAPs was to correct macroeconomic imbalances (Mohan et al., 2000). These imbalances are the product of a litany of woes culminating in the 'African crisis', which is symptomatic of growing indebtedness; slow rate of growth, as reflected in falls in export earnings whilst the import bill continued to rise; deteriorating infrastructure; famine; food shortage; and Africa's growing marginalisation from the global economy, as its share of world trade continued to shrink (Zack-Williams et al., 2002). In 1980, 21 African states had been categorised as Least Developed Countries, and by 1995, this figure had risen to 32, as the human condition continued to deteriorate. The crisis resulted in African countries trooping to the International Monetary Fund (IMF) and the World Bank for assistance. In return for loan capital, African governments agreed to introduce draconian economic measures to balance their budgets. At the core of these policies was the need to liberalise economic activities, as well as the rolling back of the state. Thus African leaders were urged to abandon 'benign mercantilism',[5] which had been the mode of accumulation in the post-war capitalist economies, whilst the IFIs and other aid agencies 'have virtually usurped the policy management powers of African government ... (and) in the process, the sovereignty of most African states, has been badly eroded' (Rugumamu, p. 11). As Bangura (in this volume) reminds us, the most important consequence of SAPs is the promotion of the private sector by seeking 'to further weaken the limited strength of the working class and strengthen that of the bourgeoisie by its insistence on the market mechanism as the primary regulatory force for the allocation of resources' (p. 203). Thus such policy conditions as privatisation further 'enrich the monopolies, widen the gap between the rich and the poor, and force the workers to pay the new monopoly price of the goods and services' (p. 204).

By the late 1980s, economic growth had been patchy and it was the state in particular (and institutions in general) which were identified by the lenders as blocking reform. Consequently, neo-liberals sought to reduce the activity and scope of the state in Africa, as the foremost explanation for Africa's poor economic performance was 'attributed to its alleged state-centred approach to development' (Rugumamu, p. 10). Thus in one of the most important reports on the African condition (World Bank, 1981) in the 'wasted decade of the 1980s', the Bank argued that, whilst exogenous and structural factors played a part in the African crisis, a crucial role was played by 'excessive statism'. The African state has been characterised as an 'overburdened institution' (Callaghy & Ravenhill, 1993), a 'lame leviathan' (Sandbrook, 1990) and a vampire (Frimpong-Ansah, 1991). The neo-liberal agenda emphasised the need for economic efficiency by removing distortions to the market caused by the intervention of the predatory state. This efficiency would be achieved through the twin-track measure of stabilisation and structural change, which would trigger off a 'harsh withdrawal of the state' (Riddell, 1993).

Contributors to ROAPE have consistently been critical of the Bretton Woods initiated liberalisation process in general, its perception of the state in particular, as well as the consequences of adjustments on vulnerable groups. Bangura's contribution draws attention to the danger for democracy stemming from the various strands of authoritarian rule and the monetarist adjustment package, which has become the reality of SAPs. The question of democracy and governance is central to Carolyn Baylies' contribution, which examines 'the extension into the political realm of the conditionality that forms the basis of structural adjustment packages' (p. 215). The utilisation of aid to promote political change marked a substantial extension of donor intervention in reshaping the institutional frameworks of recipient countries. Baylies points to the quagmire of adjustment conditionalities: on the one hand, political conditionalities are seen as a catalyst for the development of democratic movements in Africa, whilst on the other structural adjustment tends to undermine state reforms. Similarly, democratisation may challenge the process of economic restructuring, the cure for Africa's ailment.

Perhaps the biggest re-discovery of neo-liberals is that of civil society, which together with governance ranks high in the neo-liberal agenda. As the authoritarian African state was demonised, neo-liberals re-visited classical political economy and stumbled upon civil society, which we are told is distinct from the state and acts not only as a restraining factor on the neo-absolutist state, but is also seen as the source of democratic values. As Chris Allen's devastating critique (in this volume) has shown, civil society is a vague concept that is poorly defined by those who seek to utilise it, analytically vacuous, empirically elusive, and is more useful as an ideological tool than a theoretical category. Thus he warns:

> The significant theses associated with the concept appear not to be derived from a body of empirical evidence and well-constructed theory but from a set of neo-liberal nostrums, incorporated into the argument as assumptions and then proudly presented as valid conclusions…. Thus apart from the grant-seeking NGOs and the academic, it is proponents of the 'liberal project' who need civil society: western governments, their associated agencies, multinationals, and IFIs. Africanists can dispense with it. (p. 267)

The theme of the raison d'être of civil society is central to Beckman's critique. He argues that the motive force of the neo-liberal project is to 'de-legitimise the state, the main locus of nationalist aspirations and resistance to the neo-liberal project, (and) in order to undercut the claims by the state to represent the nation its alien nature is emphasised. Its retrogressiveness is explained in terms of its separation from civil society' (p. 233). Beckman observes that the neo-liberal project conceals its own extensive use of state power both locally and internationally in the construction of civil society in its own image, whilst simultaneously repressing existing civil society which is now defined as 'vested interests'. In his view, the need to promote capitalist economic development in the absence of a domestic bourgeois class meant that the state now had to act as a 'trustee of a budding capitalism'.

Beckman rejects the neo-liberal dichotomy of state and society, by arguing that 'civil society does not exist independently of the state, (and that) it is situated in rules and transactions which connect state and society'. An example of this rooting of civil society within society is that of Chambers of Commerce, a locus for the organisation and defence of business interests. He points out that in the post-colonial world, those who seek to locate civil society, could do no better than to look at the 'public service nexus', where a plethora of community interests are located, contesting scarce resources. In his view, 'both state and society are formed in the process of this contestation.' Beckman ends his contribution by warning against the hypocrisy of 'neo-liberal ideology'. He writes:

> By pretending to be civil society's best friend and by assigning the state the role of the enemy of civil society, the neo-liberal project conceals its own massive use of state power, transnational and local, for the purpose of constructing a civil society according to its own image. In doing so, it is busy suppressing and disorganising much of civil society as it actually exists, with its aspirations and modes of organisation centred on influencing the use of state power. (p. 240)

John Rapley's contribution is a reminder that perhaps contrary to the triumphalism of some neo-liberal war-horses, development studies is not yet ready to celebrate the end of history (Fukuyama, 1992) as the critique of the 'new political economy' of neo-liberalism continues to gain ground. Rapley argues that the moral and political critique apart, the short-term nature of any benefits of SAPs which are achieved at the cost of social immiseration has forced a new subtler and more sophisticated view of the state than the traditional state vs. market dichotomy. Rapley points to an emerging consensus, based on the belief that: 'liberalisation works best in those economies which have first been through a phase of infant industry' (p. 245). Drawing evidence from both Africa and the Third World, Rapley argues that not only has state intervention been crucial in the industrial take-off in many of the Tiger economies, but citing examples from the work of Gibbon, he notes that these inefficiencies of African marketing boards resulted not from public mismanagement, but from external problems such as under-capitalisation. He also points to the growing awareness that many of the conditionalities inherent in SAPs, such as privatisation, do very little to raise money for cash-starved governments.

Clearly, these criticisms have not fallen on deaf ears, as the 1997 World Bank publication, *The State in a Changing World*, points to a fundamental shift in the role of the state within the new political economy. In rejecting calls for a minimalist state, the report asserts the need for a developmental state:

> Many have felt that the logical end point of all these reforms was a minimalist state. Such a state would do no harm, but neither could it do much good. ... Far from supporting a minimalist approach to the state ... development requires an effective state one that plays a catalytic, facilitating role, encouraging and complementing the activities of private business and individuals ... Without an effective state, sustainable development, both economic and social is impossible. (World Bank, 1997: iii)

The emphasis is not so much on the size of the state, but rather on quality in order to match the state's role to its capability. In order to achieve this goal of the state as a 'partner, catalyst and facilitator', public institutions it is argued will have to be invigorated by making them responsive to people's needs through decentralisation and broader participation. The report emphasises the complementary nature of market and governments, as well as the rehabilitation of the developmental state. The report observes:

> (The) state is essential for putting in place the appropriate institutional foundations for markets. And government credibility ... can be as important for attracting private investment as the content of those rules and policies ... (W)eak and arbitrary state institutions often compound the problem.. Far from assisting the growth of markets, such actions squander the state's credibility and hurt market development. (Ibid. p.4).

Endnotes

1   In a similar way, the work of 'the French Marxist anthropologists' such as Claude Meillassoux, Georges Dupré and Pierre Phillip-Rey could be seen as part of this neo-marxist challenge by using marxist analysis in order to explicate socio-economic and political phenomena in pre-capitalist formations.
2   On the concept of 'governing' and 'ruling' classes see Nicos Poulantzas, *Political Power and Social Classes,* London: New Left Books, 1975.
3   Much of this summary is drawn from Kaplinsky's work in this volume.
4   Callaghy, T. M. & Ravenhill, J. (1993) *Hemmed In: Responses to Africa's Economic Decline,* New York: Columbia University Press; Gibbon, P. (ed.) (1993) *Social Change and Economic Reform in Africa,*

Uppsala: Scandinavian Institute of African Studies; Gibbon, P. Bangura, Y. & Ofstad, A. (eds) (1992) *Authoritarianism, Democracy and Adjustment: Politics ofEconomic reform in Africa,* Uppsala: Scandinavian Institute of Affican Studies; Onimode, B. (ed.) (1989) *IMF, 7he World Bank and Africa's Debt: 7he Economic Impact,* London: Zed Books.

5   By this, Rugumamu meant 'the use of extensive state power in the interest of state stability and well being on the one hand, and international adjustment on the other' (p.7).

References

Alavi, H. (1972), 'The State in Post-colonial Societies: Pakistan and Bangladesh', *New Left Review,* No. 74, July/August.

Allen, C. 'Who Needs Civil Society?' (in this volume).

Alexander, J. 'Decentralization, Planning and Agrarian Reform in Zimbabwe' (in this volume).

Assiri, A.M., Parsons, R.A. & Perdikis, N. (1990),'A Comparative Analysis of Debt Rescheduling in Latin America and Sub-Saharan Africa', *Scandinavian Journal of African Alternatives,* Vol. IX, No. 2&3.

Bangura, Y. 'Structural Adjustment and the Political Question', (in this volume).

Baylies, C. 'Political Conditionality and Democratisation' (in this volume).

Beckett, P. A. & Young, C. (1997), 'Beyond the Impasse of "Permanent Transition' in Nigeria', in Beckett, P. A. & Young, C. (eds) *Dilemmas of Democracy in Nigeria,* Rochester, NY: University of Rochester Press, pp. 1–14.

Beckman, B. (1980), 'Imperialism & Capitalist Transformation: Critique of a Kenyan Debate' (in this volume).

Beckman, B. (1981), 'Imperialism and the "National Bourgeoisie" ' (in this volume).

Beckman, B. (1982), 'Whose State? State and Capitalist Development in Nigeria' (in this volume).

Beckman, B. (1987), 'The Military as Revolutionary Vanguard: a Critique' (in this volume).

Beckman, B. (1993), 'The Liberation of Civil Society: Neo-Liberal Ideology and Political Theory' (in this volume).

Booth, D. (ed.) (1994), *Rethinking Social Development: Theory, Research and Practice,* London: Longman.

Callaghy, T. M. & Ravenhill, J. (1993), *HemmedIn: Responses to Africa's Economic Decline,'* New York: Columbia University Press.

Chabal, P. & Daloz, J. P. (1999), *Africa Works: Disorder as Political Instrument,* Oxford: James Currey.

Cock, J. 'Keeping the Fires Burning: Militarisation & the Politics of Gender in South Africa' (in this volume).

Davidson, B. & Munslow, B. 'The Crisis of the Nation State in Africa' (in this volume).

Davidson, B. (1992), *The Black Man's Burden: Africa and the Curse of Nation-State,* London: James Currey.

Ekeh, P. (1997), 'The Concept of Second Liberation and the Prospects for Democracy in Africa: A Nigerian Context' in Beckett, P. A. & Young, C. (eds) *Dilemmas* in *Democracy in Nigeria,* Rochester, NY: University of Rochester Press, pp. 83–110.

Freund, B. (1998), *The Making of Modern Africa: The Development of African Society since 1880,* Boulder, CO: Lynne Rienner.

Frimpong-Ansah, J. H. I. (1991), *The Vampire State: The Political Economy of Decline in Ghana,* London: James Currey & Trenton, NJ: Africa World Press.

Fukuyama, F. (1992), *The End of History and the Last Man,* London: Penguin.

Gibbon, P. (1992), 'A Failed Agenda? African Agriculture Under Structural Adjustment with Special Reference to Kenya and Ghana', *Journal of Peasant Studies,* No. 20, pp. 50–96.

Gibbon, P. (ed.) (1993), *Social Change and Economic Reform in Africa,* Uppsala: Scandinavian Institute of African Studies.

Gibbon, P., Bangura, Y. & Ofstad, A. (eds) (1992), *Authoritarianism, Democracy and Adjustment: Politics of Economic Reform in Africa,* Uppsala: Scandinavian Institute of African Studies.

Harvey, D. (1993), *The Condition of Postmodernity,* Oxford: Blackwell.

Ibrahim, J. (1997), 'Obstacles to Democratisation in Nigeria', in Beckett, P. A. & Young, C. (eds) *Dilemmas of Democracy in Nigeria,* Rochester, NY: University of Rochester Press, pp. 155–74.

Kaplinsky, R. & Langdon, S. (1980), *Multinational Corporations in the Political Economy of Kenya,* London: Macmillan.

Kay, G. (1975), *Development and Underdevelopment: A Marxist Analysis,* London: Macmillan.

Kitching, G. (1985), 'Politics, Method and Evidence in the "Kenyan debate"', in Bernstein, H. & Campbell, B. K. (eds) *Contradictions of Accumulation in Africa,* Beverly Hills, CA: Sage.

Langdon, S. (1980), 'The Invasion of the Kenyan Soap Industry,' *Review of African Political Economy,* No. 19 September–December.

Leys, C. (1975), *Underdevelopment in Kenya: The Political Economy of Neo-Colonialism,* London:

Heinemann Educational Books and James Currey.

Leys, C. (1978), 'Capital Accumulation, Class Formation and Dependency: The Significance of the Kenyan Case', *Socialist Register*, London.

Leys, C. (1996), *The Rise and Fall of Development Theory*, London: James Currey.

Leys, C. 'The "Overdeveloped" Post-colonial State' (in this volume).

Mamdani, M. (1996), *Citizen and Subject: Contemporary Africa and the Legacy of Late Colonialism*, London: James Currey.

Marx, K. (1973), 'The Eighteenth Brumaire of Louis Bonaparte', in Marx, K. & Engels, F., *Selected Works*, Lawrence and Wishart & Progress Publishers, Moscow.

Miliband, R. (1969), *The State in Capitalist Society*, London: Basic Books.

Mohan, G., Brown, E., Milward, B. & Zack-Williams, T, (2000), *Structural Adjustment: Theory, Practice and Impact*, London: Routledge.

Olukoshi, A. O. & Laakso, L. (eds) (1996), *Challenges to the Nation-State in Africa*, Uppsala: Nordiska. Africainstitutet & IDS, University of Helsinki.

Onimode, B. (ed.) (1989), IMF, *The World Bank and Africa's Debt. The Economic Impact*, London: Zed Books.

Pierson, C. (1996), *The Modern State*, London: Routledge.

Rapley, J. 'New Directions in the Political Economy of Development' (in this volume).

Riddell, R. (1993), 'The Future of the Manufacturing Sector in Sub-Saharan Africa', in Callaghy, T. M. & Ravenhill, I. (eds), *Hemmed In: Responses to Africa's Economic Decline*, New York: Columbia University Press, pp. 215–47.

Rugumamu, S. M. (1991), *Globalisation, Liberalisation and Africa's Marginalisation*, Occasional Paper Series, Vol. 3, No. 1, African Association of Political Science, South Africa.

Sandbrook, R. (1990), 'Taming the African Leviathan', *World Policy Journal* No. 4, pp. 673–701.

Sandbrook, R. (1993), *The Politics of Africa's Economic Recovery*, Cambridge: Cambridge University Press.

Saul, J. (1974), 'The state in Post-colonial Societies: Tanzania', *The Socialist Register*, London.

Saul, J. 'The Unsteady State: Uganda, Obote and Amin' (in this volume).

Schuurman, F. J. (1993), *Beyond the Impasse: New Direction in Development Theory*, London: Zed Books.

Swainson, N. (1980), *The Development of Corporate Capitalism in Kenya*, London: Heinemann.

Warren, W. (1982), *Imperialism: Pioneer of Capitalism*, London: Routledge.

Winrock International (1991), *African Development: Lessons from Asia*, Morrilton, AR: Winrock International.

World Bank (1981), *Accelerated Development in Sub-Saharan Africa: An Agenda for Action*, Washington, DC: World Bank.

World Bank (1997), *World Development Report 1997: The State in a Changing World*, Washington, DC: World Bank.

Zack-Williams, T., Frost, D., Thomson, A. (eds) (2002) *Africa in Crisis: New Possibilities and Challenges*, London: Pluto Press.

2

JOHN S. SAUL
The Unsteady State:
Uganda, Obote & General Amin

[1976]

It would be incorrect to see in the replacement of the colonial state by the post-colonial state merely a distinction without a difference. The colonial state provided imperialism with a quite direct and unmediated instrument for control in the interests of 'accumulation on a world scale' within the colonial social formation. The post-colonial state, while prone to play a similar role to that played by its predecessor, is something more of an unpredictable quantity in this regard. Unpredictable, because of the greater scope for expression given to indigenous elements who now find in the 'independent' state a much more apt target for their activities and a potential instrument for the advancement of their own interests and concerns.

In theory, such unpredictability might hold the threat of challenges to the structures of continuing imperial domination arising either from the left (socialism) or from the right (a burgeoning and competitive locally-based capitalism), with indigenous classes attempting to use the state in order to realize independent national projects of their own. However, under African conditions, these have been much less prominent than a third, more ironic, kind of 'threat' to imperial interests: the crystallization in many African settings of a state too weak and too internally compromised to stabilize society and economy and thereby effectively guarantee the on-going generation of surplus and accumulation of capital. Such weakness certainly reflects economic contradictions as well as specific attributes of the class forces at play in contemporary Africa. Nonetheless, it is a brand of weakness which finds its primary expression in the political sphere and, as we shall see, only a proper understanding of that sphere can shed real light on the problems involved. Unfortunately, it must also be noted that neither bourgeois political science (as exemplified in the work of countless 'Africanists') nor the work of those few marxists who have undertaken analyses of African politics, have yet taken us very far towards such an understanding.

The Nature of Petty-bourgeois Politics

Of course, it would be at least as incorrect to overestimate imperialism's difficulties in contemporary Africa as it would be to underestimate them. In this regard, Frantz Fanon's insight continues to serve us well since it is true that in post-colonial Africa,

> the national middle-class discovers its historic mission: that of intermediary. Seen through its eyes, its mission has nothing to do with transforming the nation; it consists, prosaically, of being the transmission line between the nation and a capitalism, rampant though camouflaged, which today puts on the masque of neo-colonialism.

The lines of neo-colonial dominance are etched deeply onto the economic structures of post-colonial society, the productive process having been cast over the years into a mould which continues to service the requirements of the imperialist system. Moreover, classes nurtured during the last years of the colonial presence tend to play their allotted roles as guarantors of that system. Consequently, the norm, for Fanon, was of a fairly smooth transition to the post-colonial phase and the absence of any very profound contradiction between the metropolitan bourgeoisie and the indigenously powerful.

This is, by now, familiar and convincing stuff, and many subsequent marxist writers on African decolonization have followed Fanon's lead. To be sure, the terminational middle class has tended to give way to the potentially more rigorous concept 'petty bourgeoisie' in characterizing the locally prominent – this shift further underscoring the point (which was nonetheless made by Fanon) that such a class is nothing like the fully-fledged (national) bourgeoisie familiar from western European development. In contrast to the latter this is a class of persons small in the scale of their economic operations and/or dependent upon and auxiliary to large-scale, particularly metropolitan-based, capital. Not that we can leave the question of definition even here. After all, this is the indigenous class which has gained the most direct and immediate access to the 'over-developed state' which Africa inherited from colonialism. It is obviously important that its nature be specified further.

Unfortunately, the attempt at further specification is not easy. Given that Poulantzas has argued that 'the definition of the class nature of the petty bourgeoisie is the focal point of a Marxist theory of social classes' this formulation will be challenging enough. However, it is made more challenging when features specific to Africa are added in. Fanon's own definition of what is, effectively, the petty bourgeoisie: 'an intellectual elite engaged in trade' hinted at one of the problems. In what ways and to what extent do 'the intellectual elite' and those engaged in 'trade' comprise one and the same social category? Another writer (Von Freyhold) has recently written that 'petty bourgeoisie' has a double meaning since it refers to small capitalists on the one hand and all those who look to the bourgeoisie as their model on the other. The petty bourgeoisie in this second sense refers in turn to that 'educated stratum … which is directly employed by colonialists or a national bourgeoisie' and remains 'subservient to those by whom it has been created'. In post-colonial Africa, the latter category defines, first and foremost, the salariat which staffs the machinery of the state.

As we shall see, some recent analyses of Africa have laid great stress on this distinction between the two wings of the petty bourgeoisie – small capitalists (traders and kulaks) on the one hand and bureaucratic salariat (especially the cadre of civil servants whose passports to rank and privilege have been their educational qualifications) on the other. Here it is necessary to confirm a prior point – that, whatever the reality and the implications of this distinction, both wings nonetheless may be conceived of as belonging to a single class.

The strongest statement of this argument, in general terms, is that presented by Nicos Poulantzas – though he also makes the distinction between what he calls the 'traditional' petty bourgeoisie (the small-scale producers and small traders) and the 'new' petty bourgeoisie (the nonproductive salaried employees including civil servants employed by the state and its various apparatuses). But what makes it appropriate to see these two elements as comprising a single class? For Poulantzas it is because 'these different positions in production and the economic sphere do, in fact, have the same effects at the political and ideological levels', viz. 'petty bourgeois individualism: attraction to the status quo and fear of revolution; the myth of 'social advancement' and aspirations to bourgeois status; belief in the 'neutral State' above classes; political instability and the tendency to support 'strong States' and Bonapartist regimes; revolts taking the form of 'petty bourgeois jacqueries'. Without accepting uncritically the relevance of all the items on this list, one can see that it does go some way towards defining the characteristics which the petty bourgeoisie displays in the post-colonial period.

Poulantzas suggests that there is something further which can be said about the political practice of a class so defined. For, in his judgment, it will manifest certain crucial weaknesses. Its intermediate position – strung out between bourgeoisie and proletariat – and its 'petty bourgeois individualism' make it 'very difficult for (the petty bourgeoisie) to organize politically into a specific party of (its) own'. Moreover, both of the groups which make up the petty bourgeoisie 'share a politically unstable nature. It is they who "swing" most often either to the side of the bourgeoisie or to the side of the working class, according to the conjuncture, since they are polarized around these two classes'.

In stressing the weakness of the petty bourgeoisie in this way, Poulantzas opens up an important perspective which can be brought to bear upon African realities, because it is this class which assumes formal political power in the post-colonial phase. And since, in turn, 'political power' in post-colonial Africa means manning a state at the very heart of the neo-colonial production process – a state which is at once overdeveloped and relatively autonomous[1] – this class's weaknesses are quite often clearly exposed in practice.

We thus find ourselves faced, in an ironic way, with a major qualification of Fanon's model. The middle class/petty bourgeoisie, too weak, in his searing description, to challenge imperialism or manifest any genuine historical creativity, threatens to be too weak even to carry out effectively its role as intermediary! In contrast to the more schematic versions of Fanon's approach, the coherence which the 'middle class' requires in order to play such a role is not present ab initio or by definition. It is, in itself, something which remains to be achieved and consolidated – and there are great obstacles in the way of any such consolidation. In consequence, what follows the winning of independence is a period of much greater uncertainty than Fanon sometimes seems to allow for.

The Definition & Coherence of Classes

This point appears particularly pressing if the petty bourgeoisie is now placed even more firmly in its specifically African context. Up to now, we have been advancing the argument as if the petty bourgeoisie, whatever its inherent weaknesses, were already a more or less fully formed class in Africa. In fact, this is far from the case. Such a class is still very much in the process of formation. This is even true, to a degree, of the petty bourgeoisie of the private sector. Its members in the agricultural sphere – the 'kulaks' as they are sometimes termed – have managed to distance themselves only very slowly and with some difficulty from the broader ranks of the peasantry, in which milieu many of their social relationships often continue to be embedded. Similarly, African traders have faced up-hill struggles against the competition of well-established alien trading communities (for example, Asians in East Africa) and as a result also have taken shape gradually as a coherent class fraction.

Even less straightforward has been any crystallization of the 'bureaucratic' fraction of the petty bourgeoisie. In an earlier article on the post-colonial state in Africa (Saul, 1974) I stressed this point, noting that the uncertainty of its predispositions led von

Freyhold to employ the term 'nizers' to conceptualize such a stratum. A stratum which is not yet unequivocally a class and one which might still 'commit suicide' by identifying downwards with the workers and peasants in the society. No wonder that Murray, in a seminal article, felt the necessity of 'refocussing class analysis' with reference to the decolonization and developmental process in sub-Saharan Africa by seeking the contradictions inherent in the accession to state power of unformed classes. To the extent that Murray's emphasis is correct, the provision of a steady hand at the helm of the post-colonial state will appear to be even more difficult an undertaking.

Focusing on the emergence of the petty bourgeoisie to positions of power in contemporary Africa is a crucial key to understanding them, but the ambiguity and incoherence of this process must not be underestimated. Mahmood Mamdani makes a similar distinction more sharply and draws from it implications which premise his interpretation of African development in general and the Ugandan situation in particular. Mamdani states,

> The ruling class in independent Uganda was the petit-bourgeoisie. What is central to understanding the 'underdeveloped' ruling class, in contradistinction to that in developed capitalism, is its weak economic base and its *fragmentation* at the level of politics. The 'underdeveloped' petit-bourgeoisie is *not a consolidated* class ...
> It is the struggle within the petit-bourgeoisie that determines the method of accumulation and the manner of appropriation of the surplus. Given that it is located both within the state (state bureaucracy) and outside of it (kulaks, traders), the petit-bourgeoisie has two alternative methods of accumulation open to it; either use the state to create public property which the petit-bourgeoisie would control indirectly through its control over the state, or use the state to expand private property which the petit-bourgeoisie would control directly through ownership.
> It is the economic base of the fraction that emerges victorious which defines the political character of the state. In Africa today, the petit-bourgeoisie regimes can be roughly divided into those that use the state to create public property (the so-called 'progressive' regimes) and those that do so to create private property (the 'reactionary' regimes). This difference in the manner of appropriation of surplus conditions the nature of future class formation. With the creation of state property, the dominant class that emerges is a bureaucratic bourgeoisie, whereas when the emphasis is on the use of the state to create private property, the petit-bourgeoisie transforms itself into a commercial bourgeoisie.

It is one of the contentions of the present essay that any such formulation, while obviously suggestive, goes much too far and has led, at least in Mamdani's case, to the creation of a stark and misleading dichotomy between entrepreneurial and bureaucratic 'fractions' of the petty bourgeoisie which obscures much more than it illuminates. There is an essential wisdom in Fanon's admittedly vague formula ('an intellectual elite engaged in trade') which allows us to conceptualise an interpenetration of the realms of petty bourgeois activity which substantially qualifies any such dichotomy. Once this interpenetration is lost from view, it is all too easy to misinterpret the role of the post-colonial state and to denature the essential features of post-colonial politics.

The Political Class

This argument becomes even more clear if we introduce one final element into the picture, an element which Roger Murray attempted to conceptualize by using the concept 'political class' – a somewhat unsatisfactory term for what is, nonetheless, a vitally important reality. The reference here is to those who staff the state at the most overtly political level – including, most obviously, the President/Prime Minister, his cabinet and immediate circle of advisers, senior officials of the ruling party (or politicized army), even the leaders and senior functionaries of the opposition party or parties. It is they who have the most immediate and potent access to the levers of the state. In consequence, they have a quite significant role to play in defining how that state will express itself. Yet they are certainly not to be elided straightforwardly with the 'bureaucrats' or civil service. Nor are they exactly co-terminous with the petty bourgeoisie of the private sector. Instead, this is a stratum which acts as a link between state and private sector, refracting and reconciling (when it can) the various pressures which spring from the production process. That is, they have a foot in both camps – bureaucratic and entrepreneurial – and comprise members with various interests of their own.[2]

What needs to be emphasized here is that this 'class' – this circle of political activists – is one which exemplifies particularly graphically the basic attributes of the African petty bourgeoisie identified above. Murray, in particular, has stressed this point, suggesting that such a stratum reflects 'the absence of a determinate class standpoint in the production process'. This may overstate the case somewhat. Obviously, the standpoint of the 'political class' will tend to be petty bourgeois. Moreover, insofar as its class character is 'partial and transitional' (in Murray's phrase) it will reflect attributes of the petty bourgeoisie as a whole, reflecting them in a manner which is, perhaps, merely an exaggerated version of the norm for such a class under post-colonial conditions. Nonetheless, this does mean that there is even less of an a priori reason why the elements who are closest to the state should express the 'determinate … standpoint' of any one particular fraction of the petty bourgeoisie. Nor is there any reason why they should underwrite exclusively either of the two policy thrusts which Mamdani has suggested as exhausting the options open to the post-colonial state. The elements are likely to be much too comingled for that! Perhaps enough has been said, however, to suggest that by adding the 'political class' into our equation we see even more clearly the dangers of fixing too schematically the nature of the petty bourgeoisie or of oversimplifying the likely characteristics of any fragmentation which it may manifest.

The Dynamics of the Petty Bourgeoisie

We must now say something more directly about the nature of these politics themselves. In doing this, we must consider the concept of the 'fraction', since it surfaced forcefully in recent attempts (by Poulantzas and Mamdani, for example) to understand the political dynamics of the petty bourgeoisie. For Mamdani, such fractions of the petty bourgeois class are fully defined by the different locations of groups within the production process – kulaks, traders, bureaucrats. He then interprets parties and other political formations in Uganda as quite direct expressions of one or another of the fractions so defined. Yet, in truth, this does not quite work. As Poulantzas correctly observes, 'the problem of fractions of a class is in fact rather complicated in Marx … (Indeed) … the effects of the political-instance … may produce fractions of a class in the field of political class practice alone.' For example, in the *Eighteenth Brumaire,* Marx writes that the 'republican fraction of the bourgeoisie' during that period was not a fraction of the bourgeoisie bound together by great common interest and demarcated from the rest by conditions peculiar to it; it was a coterie of republican-minded members of the bourgeoisie, writers, lawyers, officers and officials. Its influence rested on the personal antipathies of the country towards Louis Philippe, on memories of the old republic, on the republican faith of a number of enthusiasts, and, above all on French nationalism, for it constantly kept alive hatred of the Vienna Treaties and the alliance with England.

If this can be the case for the bourgeoisie how much more likely is it to be true of a class, like the African petty bourgeoisie, which is at once weak (as any petty bourgeoisie tends to be), relatively unformed (in the African context), and not yet divided, in any un-equivocal manner, into constituent elements diversely rooted in the production process? In the African petty bourgeoisie we find a whole range of 'fractions' which are produced 'in the field of political practice alone'. Such a perspective can lend to the diverse ethnic, religious, institutional and ideological alignments of Africa's petty-bourgeois politics the reality they so clearly possess in practice, while at the same time situating them in such a way as to validate the claims of class analysis to be the crucial key to an understanding of African social formations.

But what does such a class analysis look like? Here we must re-emphasize the role as interested 'intermediary': a junior but active partner with imperial interests whose role is more clearly enunciated, the more coherent and sharply defined such a class becomes. This, then, is the core of a realistic class analysis of contemporary Africa. What cannot be said with the same degree of certainty is who amongst the petty bourgeoisie in formation will achieve such control of the state. In fact, this will be decided officially by a struggle within the petty bourgeois stratum itself!

These fractions attempt to stitch together alliances and to rally constituencies in order to engage in such competition. Here the ethnic and/or regional card is a particularly tempting one to play, and for a number of reasons. At the level of alliances, the sharing of a common ethnic background (one which may actually be reinforced by direct ties of kinship) by certain members of the petty bourgeoisie can often serve as a kind of lowest common denominator of trust and communication on the basis of which negotiations towards formation of a political alliance may take place. After all, there do exist cultural differences between African peoples, differences which will have been underscored and exacerbated in many instances by the divide-and-rule tactics of the colonial powers.

Even more crucial is the fact of uneven development between regions and, by any easy transposition, between 'tribes'. Under these circumstances, it is relatively easy to induce the lower strata of any given ethnic group to interpret the essence of their backwardness as being the result of a zero-sum game over the distribution of scarce resources played out between tribes rather than being primarily a result of class division, both world-wide and local. Petty-bourgeois politicians can then present them-selves as their champions. Moreover, even members of the petty bourgeoisie can them-selves become mesmerized by this same kind of construction of social reality, resentful of the 'unfair' advantage (or, on the contrary, defensive of their own 'deserved' privilege) in terms of entrepreneurial/bureaucratic advancement, education, and the like, seen to have been bequeathed upon their class counterparts in another ethnic group by the unevenness of the development process. Upon these and other building blocks, tribalist ideologies and ethnic political groupings are developed, ideologies and groupings which take on a tangible and undeniable reality and resonance, however spurious some of their foundations may be.

Any student of African politics knows that ethnically and religiously-based fractions have been of great importance. Indeed, it is precisely along these lines that the petty bourgeoisie – and the countries which they lead – can crack wide open, failing, as suggested earlier, even to guarantee that minimum degree of stability necessary for the consolidation of a smoothly functioning neo-colonial system. In addition, fractions can sometimes crystallize around interests defined, for purposes of the competition for scarce resources, in narrowly institutional terms, the army being one obvious example of this in many African settings, the bureaucracy (narrowly, not broadly, defined) being another. Enough to note these three possible bases for fractions here.

But there is one final source of the kind of fractionalisation now under discussion which must also be noted. Even less familiar than the other three, it centres on the existence, within the petty-bourgeois class, of partisans of diverse developmental ideologies. To be sure, there is a conventional wisdom characteristic of the bulk of the African petty bourgeoisie which does serve, normally, as that class's ideological cement, both rationalizing its subordination to imperialism and crystallizing such internal unity as it possesses. It is a conventional wisdom which blends a fuzzy and opportunistic nationalism (of the sort so trenchantly demystified by Fanon) with its attendant elitism, 'capital scarcity' with its attendant 'requirements' of increased foreign investment (aid, expansion of the raw-material export sector, etc.). However, what must be emphasized here is that the mould of this ideology – like that of the class itself – is not firmly set. There is also room for ideological manoeuvre which can, upon occasion, introduce significantly new variables into the petty-bourgeois political equation.

Murray finds in such a milieu the seed-bed of the real (though severely limited) socialist departure which Nkrumahism represented. Elsewhere I have provided a parallel explanation for those progressive attributes which have been one dimension of Tanzania's experiment in Ujamaa. No doubt such left-leaning initiatives when undertaken by segments of the petty bourgeoisie also reflect other ambiguities of that class. We have seen that Poulantzas describes the petty bourgeoisie as being 'polarized' between classes above and below it, capable of 'swinging' one way or the other. Those who do identify downwards 'committing suicide', in Cabral's expression, and 'reincarnating' themselves 'in the condition of workers and peasants' also reflect this potentiality in the situation. Of course, it must also be recognized that even such left ideological expressions will tend to reveal their petty-bourgeois origins, exemplified most often by the absence of the clear perspective on class struggle and the dynamics of imperialism which Marxism might provide. Such ideologies all too easily collapse into a vague, even opportunistic, populism – one more ploy in building a broader popular constituency!

Of course, even this range of variation does move rather straightforwardly within the parameters defined by neo-colonialism – the petty bourgeoisie beginning to play, well or badly, the role it is best suited to play. Yet we have hinted that there may be somewhat greater leeway than this, that from the petty-bourgeois politics which swirl around the post-colonial state, something more unpredictable may emerge. The notion of the 'relative autonomy' of the state can be helpful here. Not that, for all its growing usage among Marxists in recent years, this concept is without real ambiguities. Thus, Miliband sharply criticizes Poulantzas for first establishing the relative autonomy of the state as a concept and then blandly and unjustifiably proceeding to subvert such a supposedly autonomous state (in Miliband's words) 'into the merest instrument of a determinate class – indeed all but conceptualizing it out of existence'. He continues

> The reason for that confusion, or at least one reason for it, is Poulantzas's failure to make the necessary distinction between class power and state power. State power is the main and ultimate – but not the only – means whereby class power is assured and maintained. But one

of the main reasons for stressing the importance of the notion of the relative autonomy of the state is that there is a basic distinction to be made between class power and state power, and that the analysis of the meaning and implications of that notion of relative autonomy must indeed focus on the forces which cause it to be greater or less, the circumstances in which it is exercised, and so on. The blurring of the distinction between class power and state power by Poulantzas makes any such analysis impossible: for all the denunciations of 'economism', politics does here assume an 'epiphenomenal' form.

Here Miliband points the way more clearly for us than does Poulantzas. Indeed, when the dominant class concerned is a relatively unformed one (as is the case with the African petty bourgeoisie) the possibility of state power assuming a particularly vital importance within the social formation is substantially enhanced. It is then that the fraction/s of the petty bourgeoisie which have managed to establish control over the state can hope to place their own stamp upon events. Needless to say, this does not mean that there are no limits upon their so doing, or that class determinants do not threaten to foreclose on such autonomy at every turn. What it does mean, for example, is that Tanzania or Ghana under Nkrumah, where the post-colonial state was used for a time for some novel and progressive purposes, are not to be construed glibly as being merely 'typical' neo-colonial regimes. Nor, for other reasons, is General Amin's Uganda to be so construed. A 'finer discrimination' is necessary here, too.

The Ugandan Case

In fact, Uganda offers a particularly illuminating case study, one which demonstrates clearly the possible contribution of the theoretical arguments advanced above. This is even apparent from a simple juxtaposition of writings already available on the country. On the one hand, there is a rich selection of analyses rooted in the conventional methodologies of western political science whose main contribution lies in documenting the diversity of ethnic, religious, institutional and ideological strands which have crisscrossed Ugandan political life.

However, what these analyses fail to illuminate is the broader setting of imperialism and the class struggle within which such in-fighting occurs. Glentworth and Hancock, for example, grace their analysis of the Obote period with the startling observation that 'the imperialists were absent', this with reference to what is, even by African standards, a parodically dependent economy and society. Obviously, it is here that a marxist approach shows its strength, a point at least partially demonstrated by the work of Mahmood Mamdani, cited earlier, which represented the first systematic analysis of Ugandan political economy from a marxist perspective. Mamdani begins to trace the process by which Uganda was incorporated into the global imperialist system and the seed sown from emergence of an indigenous petty bourgeoisie. And this, in turn, provides the context which alone situates and renders understandable the political realities pin-pointed by Twaddle and his colleagues!

Crucial long-term developments are identified by Mamdani: the enforced creation of a peasant-based, cash-crop economy designed, quite specifically, to service imperial requirements; the emergence of an intermediary Asian 'commercial bourgeoisie' in the economic sphere – their strategic position in the economy destined to become as much the target of African petty-bourgeois aspiration as the colonial state structure itself. Most graphically of all, the clear beginnings of crystallization of an African petty bourgeoisie, this latter being no mere casual by-product of colonialism but rather a class whose consolidation came to be considered by the British imperial strategists as vital to their long-term interests. Mamdani quotes Mr. Lennox-Boyd, when the (then) Colonial Secretary said in the House of Commons in London that an African property-owning middle-class would be 'one of the stabilizing factors of that continent'. He said he would regard himself as 'pretty inefficient' if, at the end of his period of office, he had not encouraged a sense of private profit and public service among Africans. Though the record of success was mixed, it is clear that a class ready to inherit power was to be created. And, of course, Africanization proceeded apace within the interstices of the state structure itself – in both bureaucratic and political spheres.

Given this strong and viable starting-point for analysis, it is all the more unfortunate that the closer Mamdani's account comes to the political realm – and the closer it comes to the present day – the more ineluctably it degenerates into an oppressive and overly schematic determinism. We have hinted at some of the terms of this analytical anti-climax in the preceding section. Substantively this means that, in spite of the overall vacuum within which their accounts proceed, Glentworth and Hancock, Twaddle and their ilk have at least as much to tell us about the terms of the political process under Obote and Amin as has Mamdani! A depressing admission if true, and one with which Marxist observers of the African reality must come fully to terms.

What does Mamdani have to say about petty-bourgeois politics in Uganda? As he quite correctly observes of the transition to independence, 'the nearness of the event, when state power was to be transferred to a class situated within the colony, brought to the fore the contradictions within the petty bourgeoisie. The question now was simply: Who was to control state power?' What were the terms of this competition for state power? In the first instance, he argues, the competitors crystallized into political parties, 'mass-based, petty-bourgeois parties (which) – whether ideologically nationalist, tribal or religious – were each based in a different section of the petty bourgeoisie'. In short, these parties derived their real meaning from their representing, variably, the 'trader', 'kulak' and 'bureaucratic' fractions of the petty bourgeoisie. But, surely, the overlap between kulak and trader in Baganda throughout this period was patent, with the interpenetration of African commercial petty bourgeoisie (kulaks and traders) and bureaucratic petty bourgeoisie almost equally so. Clearly, the history of party conflict in Uganda has to be accounted for in other terms.

A seeming impasse, then, between Twaddle and Co. on the one hand and Mamdani on the other. But, of course, we have already indicated the way out: the utilization of a concept of petty-bourgeois politics which refrains from boiling away the specificity and irreducibility of political fractions, while at the same time retaining the necessary bite of class analysis. By now it will be clear that this approach enables us to affirm, with Mamdani, the centrality of that broad process of the structuring of a dependent economy and policy in Uganda which he emphasizes, while also taking seriously the rich texture of petty-bourgeois politics illuminated by more conventional writers. What follows is merely the briefest of sketches of what such an analysis might begin to look like.

The Obote Era

The terms of politics in this period have already been suggested. Competition for power and resources within the petty bourgeoisie intertwined with what was an extreme form of uneven development even by African standards – characterized, in particular, by Buganda's dramatic historical head-start. And this in turn was overlaid with a highly-visible religious differentiation, the politicization of which provided a further building-block for petty-bourgeois politicians (the DP). Once the competition was cast in such tribal and religious categories – consolidated in party or factional affiliations and long-term strategic commitments for the petty bourgeoisie, crystallized in diverse fears and aspirations among the populace – this gave a much sharper political reality to these terms of reference than they might otherwise have had. Politics really was about tribe and religion, though it never ceased to be about the petty bourgeoisie as well! Moreover, as the energies released by this kind of competition burst out, it became apparent that the petty bourgeoisie in Uganda was not strong enough as a class to transcend the fragmentation which it had itself invoked. Indeed, the failure of the petty bourgeoisie to act effectively as a class defined the failure of conventional 'nation-building' in Uganda.

In such a context, as we have seen, further fragmentation and intensified intrigue (especially within the 'political class' itself) became the essential stuff of Uganda politics. Inside the UPC, groups now crystallized which also took on the attributes of fractions defined 'in the field of political practice alone'. One thinks here of the Southern, 'Bantu', politicians who banded together against Obote in 1966, but Obote found it difficult to avoid consolidating a Northern, 'Nilotic', and, towards the end of his reign, even a Langi 'fraction' as one crucial pillar of his own support. One sensed, of course, that Obote was never entirely happy with this seeming necessity forced upon him by the dynamics of petty-bourgeois politics and that he was constantly working to diversify and expand the ruling bloc over which he presided. In fact, one motivation behind his celebrated 'Move to the Left' was precisely his desire to escape from the 'Northern' corner (including strong reliance on the predominantly Northern-recruited army) into which he was being pushed.

What of his 'Move to the Left'? Unfortunately, it is all too easy to overstate its significance. It is true that towards the end of Obote's reign there began to surface a more marked diversity of perspective on the development problem, one such perspective (Obote's) becoming the aforementioned 'Move to the Left'. If this was not the bureaucracy's 'class project', as Mamdani would have us believe, what in fact was it? Again, the density and complexity of petty-bourgeois politics, as we have been describing them, determined that the 'Move' had several layers of significance. In Section I, we discussed the possibility of a petty-bourgeois fraction emerging which centred upon the ideological variable, with Nkrumahism and Tanzania's Arusha Declaration cited as cases in point. There may have been something of this in Obote's initiative as well, in his introduction of a more radical rhetoric and a form of nationalization into the political arena. Perhaps this was in part a spill-over from Nyerere's policy departures which Obote professed to admire, perhaps it also evidenced a dash of patriotism which caused Obote to look wistfully towards the image of a united and prosperous Uganda. Certainly, it seems difficult to account for Obote's increased militancy in foreign policy – his 'relative autonomy' from imperial dictate in that sphere – in any other terms.

Nevertheless, it is perfectly clear that Obote was no socialist; the manner in which he presided over the decimation of the UPC leftwing in the early 1960s and his stifling, throughout the years, of any possibility of genuine working-class militancy, offer proof of that. Nor was the 'Move to the Left' a particularly deep-cutting left initiative, demanding only marginal readjustments on the part of international capital and the domestic private sector, and in certain respects even servicing further the latter's interests. Much more clearly, the programme suggests a populist ploy in the petty-bourgeois political game, a calculated attempt to leap-frog the fragmentation inherent in that game in order to consolidate a more effective trans-tribal, popular, constituency. If this is so, the fact that the content of such an attempt remained far more rhetorical than real need not surprise us. Rare is the petty-bourgeois politician who can commit class suicide and turn to the full-fledged mobilization of a popular base of workers and peasants, as in the genuine African revolutions of Guinea or of Mozambique. Such an initiative in Uganda was unlikely to come from the top down, in any case. The story of Obote's last years was much more that of a sometime master of petty-bourgeois politics, the great coalition builder, trying now to add another string to his bow, that being a broader, more popular base. His main intention: to consolidate himself and his followers in power and in privilege.

The Amin Coup

Against this background it becomes possible to interpret the 1971 coup in something other than a one-dimensional manner. To be sure, the coup did represent a crisis of petty-bourgeois politics. But it was, at bottom, a familiar kind of crisis, one fully consistent with the overall pattern of such politics which we have been tracing, apparently just another turn of the wheel of petty-bourgeois coalition-building, despite its dramatic, military character. In this case, facilitating the coup was a kind of negative coalition of petty-bourgeois fractions, whose acquiescence at least ensured that the Obote government would have much too little support to enable it to resist the military's push. The initial positive response to the coup in many Baganda and other ethnic circles (at petty-bourgeois and mass levels) and in DP/Catholic circles must be accounted for as being, in significant part, the residue of previous historical battles. And such responses were continually being reinforced by the spectre of Obote's own apparent political schizophrenia. As noted earlier, even in the course of 'moving to the left' he was also falling back on a strategy of building up his own team of ethnic defenders: viz, the promotion of Acholi and (particularly) Langi military officers, as well as their prominence in his refurbished paramilitary General Service Unit, the latter apparently consolidated as a counterweight to the predominance of West Nilers in the army. But this, in turn, merely demonstrated that the unity of any prior 'Northern' component to Obote's coalition was disintegrating. The negative coalition which could align itself against Obote was becoming dangerously broad.

And then there was the military itself. Not unified, as we shall see, but an important institutional reality nonetheless, and one available for realizing the larger purposes of the senior command. Indeed, Twaddle and others have emphasized that it was precisely the army's interest *qua* army which most crucially determined the launching of the coup – whatever the other permissive conditions may have been. It became, in effect, the positive arm of a negative coalition!

Such an army becomes an institutionally-based fraction acting upon the competitive terrain of petty-bourgeois politics. Decalo applies his framework specifically to Uganda and there can be little doubt that his insight does illuminate one crucial dimension of the coup, that 'this was a classic example of the personalized takeover caused by a General's own fears and ambitions, within the context of a widespread civic malaise and a fissiparous fratricidal army rife with corporate grievances'.

Alternatively, Mamdani sees the coup as evidencing the resistance of the entrepreneurial petty bourgeoisie not to 'socialism', but to the aggrandizement of the governing bureaucracy which he takes the 'Move' to exemplify. Unfortunately, within his model there is no reason why the army should be expected to act as part of the entrepreneurial petty bourgeoisie, rather than as part of the governing bureaucracy; in fact, one would more readily expect the latter, not the former, to be the case. Once again, this lack of fit merely testifies to the weakness of the model itself and of the supposed juxtaposition of 'fractions' rooted in the production process which Mamdani continually emphasizes. In any case, the army's response was not monolithic, something which Mamdani himself must concede. His answer: 'factions within the army now reflected the fragmentation within the ruling class'.

Even this does not work, however. For the main expression of such fragmentation after the coup was the alacrity with which Amin's group within the army (mainly hailing from West Nile) set about killing Acholi and Langi officers and men – the latter suspected of 'subversive' loyalties to Obote on tribal grounds. Obviously, this was not a case of the entrepreneurial petty bourgeoisie locked in mortal combat with the governing bureaucracy. It evidenced a different kind of fragmentation of the petty bourgeoisie altogether, one with which Mamdani's model quite simply cannot cope. In fact, what was happening was that Amin, using the military as a necessary springboard and operating from within the bowels of the 'negative coalition' which united to permit the overthrow of Obote, had begun already to forge a new petty-bourgeois fraction – one built along ethnic and religious lines – in order to sustain himself in power!

The Post-Coup Period

The reality of the post-coup period could be interpreted differently. Was not the way now clear for the African entrepreneurial petty bourgeoisie to establish its hegemony unequivocally, without even the challenge which Obote's populist *etatisme* might have seemed to pose? It is tempting, perhaps, to see the expulsion of the Asians which came in the wake of the coup as that fraction's 'ultimate solution' to its contestation with the Asian commercial bourgeoisie. Certainly, the dramatic steps of 1972 and 1973 had something of this flavour (although the extent to which they represented any kind of sharp break with earlier trends could easily be overstated). Nonetheless, a great many other things were happening alongside this programmatic development which are too important to be bracketed off from the main line of the theoretical explanation. For example, the ethnic infighting mentioned in the preceding paragraph, and the reign of terror which Amin's army directed against broad segments of the African population, must not be considered phenomena secondary in importance to the anti-Asian measures. In fact, they have been, in certain respects, even more integral than the expulsions in defining the nature of Amin's regime.

For the killing did not stop with the Langi and Acholi. The weapon of terror was quickly turned against people from most ethnic groups in the country (including the Baganda, who had welcomed Amin with great enthusiasm) and from all the Christian denominations. More instructively, terror has been directed primarily against members of the petty bourgeoisie – and at least as often against those who might be deemed members of a commercial petty bourgeoisie as against those of the so-called governing bureaucracy. In short, what was taking place was the dismantling of the 'negative coalition' which had comprised the challenge to Obote. And it is another development which Mamdani has difficulty in explaining. For him, such developments become an expression of 'Amin's own individuality' and result, paradoxically, in 'a rapid erosion of Amin's social base'. As he puts it, 'the petty bourgeoisie advances as a class, but not necessarily the most advanced individuals within it'. The latter, it seems, are too busy being killed!

To be sure, Amin has carried intra-class competition to its logical (and most horrifying) conclusion: the unrestrained physical elimination of rivals, real or fancied.

But even if this is unprecedented, we need not be surprised at other aspects of his rule, the aggressive movement of army officers (those whose survival has been premised primarily on the ethnic and religious grounds described above) into the private sector, for example. Naturally enough, those members of the petty bourgeoisie who survive will sustain this project, their aspirations having been one force behind the move against the Asians and their present commercial activities being an obvious result of that move.[3] Not that this is the only explanation for the expulsion. The circumstances and timing of that move also suggest that it had an ironic parallel with the actions of Obote: Amin's attack on the Asian community seems to have been designed, as much as anything, for populist purposes, similar to those which inspired the 'Move to the Left'. Like the latter, the expulsion was aimed at broadening Amin's popular constituency and thereby further consolidating his position. Moreover, for all that it exploited a particularly racist formulation of the problem, it did build on a real popular grievance. Perhaps that is why, in the short run, it generated at least as much popular enthusiasm as had the 'Move to the Left' itself. At the same time, Amin, like Obote, was not one to mobilize the populace in any very fundamental way. Like Obote, too, he was prepared (albeit in a much more ruthless and paranoid manner) to subordinate his search for a populist legitimacy to the forging of a narrower, well-trusted, constituency and to the use of force. On these many fronts, therefore, the continuity with the Obote period is apparent. Perhaps Amin is a caricature (and a particularly frightening one) of petty-bourgeois politics, but he is an entirely recognizeable caricature nonetheless.

Having said this, it must also be affirmed that Amin's regime is unique in Uganda in certain important respects. There can be little doubt that developments there have been anything but satisfactory from the point of view of western imperialism. The sheer disruption caused by the kind of infighting we have been chronicling, particularly during the Amin period, has slowed the pace of economic activity, and hence of exploitation, to a crawl. This would be bad enough, an almost classic example of the kinds of difficulties imperialism has in establishing its hegemony efficiently in the context of petty-bourgeois rule at the periphery (even in the absence of any very serious revolutionary threat from the mass of the population). But Uganda also demonstrates another facet of the unpredictability, from the point of view of western capitalism, of petty-bourgeois regimes: the danger of their finding, in the degree of relative autonomy which is available for them, room for manoeuvre which can be further disruptive of any smooth and easy marriage between imperial and petty-bourgeois interests in the dependent social formation. By Uganda standards, Aminism has exemplified this possibility in an unprecedented manner.

But for Amin this 'possibility' has become virtually a full-time preoccupation; having knit together his own fraction and in reasonably firm control of the state, he has placed the stamp of his own (bizarre) personality upon events. Witness, for example, his very personalized manner of turning on the British and, after an initial round of denationalization, launching a fresh assault, one characterized by expropriation and by a steamy brand of anti-imperialist invective. Obviously, such initiatives have not been part of a socialist project, nor have they lifted any of the structural constraints upon Ugandan development. On the other hand, they have not serviced in any discernible way the interests of imperialism.

'Arbitrariness' is a good word to describe Amin's domestic activities as well, despite the fact that (as seen above) they are more broadly consistent with familiar patterns than is generally understood. For if the physical elimination of petty-bourgeois rivals is, in some sense, a 'logical' conclusion of the trajectory of petty-bourgeois politics, it is by no means an inevitable one. Amin's privileged access to the instruments of coercion – as spring-board to his ascendancy and as cornerstone of his dominant coalition – has rendered him even more 'autonomous' than most victors in the African political game. And here, too, that relative autonomy has enabled him to give much freer play to his personal motivations and personal style than might otherwise be the case. It is within some such a framework that Mamdani's reference to 'Amin's own individuality' makes most sense, for example. Because of that 'individuality', this latest turn of the wheel in Ugandan politics has been much more destructive than it need have been.

Mamdani sees signs that any such relative autonomy may be shortlived, however. He cites the consolidation of Amin's fellow army officers in entrepreneurial roles, and suggests that this will lead to a downplaying of arbitrariness and a relative stabilization of petty-bourgeois rule, all in the interests of a stable economic environment. In addition, Mamdani argues that peasant and worker protest is gaining increased focus and militancy, which, if true, provides not only a new revolutionary term for the Ugandan political equation, but also suggests a challenge which might force the petty bourgeoisie to unite more effectively in defence of their own project. Others have argued that the main lineaments of external dependency – those which run in the direction of the western imperial centres, with their markets for Uganda's crops and their seductive supplies of capital and technology – are also reasserting themselves, and that there are signs of a rapproachment with the United States and Britain. Even if Amin continues to evade assassination, it could be argued that Aminism is being dragged back into line by the determinants of dependency and class, and that it is on the road to stabilization – even if it be, as Mamdani insists, the stabilization before the revolutionary storm.

Such an analysis provides a clearer sense of the dynamics of petty-bourgeois politics in Uganda. It also presents the beginnings of an accurate portrait of the Ugandan state: dependent but not dependable, the unsteady state par excellence. Of course, it will be equally clear that in so short a space the Ugandan reality has not been probed at sufficient depth. But perhaps enough has been said to validate the strength of an approach to contemporary African politics structured along lines indicated in Section 1. If so, we might hope to avoid excessive reliance not only upon the bluff, common-sensical insights into day-to-day events provided by conventional political science but also upon the Procrustean, depoliticizing determinism – often illuminating almost in spite of itself – of various recent 'marxist' innovations in the field of Radical Africana. Certainly some kind of analytical way forward is necessary if we are to forge an approach to politics adequate to the tasks which face the African revolution.

Endnotes

1   See Leys' discussion in this volume.
2   This 'political class' is singularly absent from the analysis of Mamdani who tends to present the confrontation between bureaucratic and entrepreneurial 'fractions' of the petty bourgeoisie which he emphasizes as being virtually unmediated by politicians. Reference to such a stratum is also absent from the analyses of others, like Meillassoux and Shivji, whose frameworks parallel Mamdani's. In a previous paper ('The State in Post-Colonial Societies: Tanzania', *The Socialist Register*, London, 1974, esp. footnotes 17 and 22), I tended myself to underestimate the distinction between bureaucrat and politician, noting that Meillassoux merely elided the two in speaking of his 'bureaucrats' (while also overstating the cohesion of this group as a class) and suggesting that Murray could be interpreted as making such an elision (while correctly stressing the 'relative autonomy and plasticity' of such a class-in-formation). I see now that Murray was implicitly touching on an important distinction, despite the fact that he leaves the question of the class nature of the bureaucracy relatively unexplained.
3   Mamdani observes that 'unlike the pre-coup governing bureaucracy, the army officers are *not*

transforming themselves into a class, they are not developing an *independent* economic base. Quite the contrary: members of the officer corps are being integrated into the commercial bourgeoisie which is gradually emerging.' He does not explain why this should be the case, why the army officers do not beoming a governing bureaucracy. In fact, it can be repeated here that these activities are fully consistent with the activities of army personnel bureaucrats and members of the 'political class' in the pre-coup period. From the correct theoretical vantage-point they require no special explanation.

Bibliographic Notes

The work of Nicos Poulantzas and Ralph Miliband has been of obvious importance to the writing of this paper. Poulantzas' most interesting writing on the nature of the petty bourgeoisie is to be found in his *Fascism and Dictatorship* (London, 1974) and *Classes in Contemporary Capitalism* (London, 1975). Miliband's article 'Poulantzas and the Capitalist State', *New Left Review*, 82 (Nov./Dec., 1972) has been particularly helpful.

On the post-colonial state, see Hamza Alavi, 'The State in Post-Colonial Societies – Pakistan and Bangladesh', *New Left Review*, 74 (July/Aug, 1972) and John S. Saul, 'The State in Post-Colonial Societies – Tanzania', *The Socialist Register* (London, 1974).

Among general works on African politics, Roger Murray's 'Second Thoughts on Ghana', *New Left Review*, 42 (March/Apr., 1967) is cited on several occasions in the text and remains of seminal importance many years after its publication. Reference is also made to Michaela Von Freyhold, 'The Workers and the Nizers' (mimeo, University of Dar es Salaam, 1973), Samuel Decalo, 'Military Coups and Military Regimes in Africa', *The Journal of Modern African Studies*, 11, 1 (1973), and Colin Leys, *Underdevelopment in Kenya*, (London, 1975), ch. 6, 'Neo-colonial Society'.

The works of Mahmood Mamdani are 'Class Struggles in Uganda', *Review of African Political Economy*, 4 (November, 1975) and his book *Politics and Class Formation in Uganda* (Monthly Review Press, New York & Heinemann, London). The latter Mamdani was kind enough to let the present author read in manuscript form. Mamdani's work is closely linked to that of Issa Shivji, whose own book on Tanzania will soon be published by Monthly Review Press and Heinemann and whose article 'Peasants and Class Alliances' appeared in *Review of African Political Economy*, 3 (May/October, 1975). Mamdani's writings share many of the strengths – and many of the weaknesses – of those by Shivji.

3

COLIN LEYS
The 'Overdeveloped' Post-Colonial State:
A Re-evaluation   [1976]

At the end of his review of recent theorizing about the state in post-colonial societies and its application to Tanzania John Saul raises a critical question: is state power in Tanzania a force which defends and promotes the interests of workers and peasants, or should 'the independent political organization of progressive elements, already a (difficult) priority in most other one-party and military administrative regimes in Africa, become a priority for Tanzania as well?'.[1] John Saul does not presume to answer this question for his concern is to see whether current theory furnishes a valid framework within which Tanzanians themselves can try to answer it.

He starts out from Hamza Alavi's influential article on the state in post-colonial society, focused on Pakistan and Bangladesh. First, Alavi argued that the original base of the state apparatus inherited by a post-colonial society lay in the metropole and its task was to subordinate all the indigenous classes in the colony. Hence, it was said to be 'over-developed' in relation to the ex-colonial society possessing, in particular, a strong military-administrative apparatus. Second, the state directly appropriates a large part of the economic surplus and deploys it in bureaucratically directed 'development' activity. The 'centrality' of the post-colonial state, which evidently follows from these propositions, implies the 'centrality' of the state bureaucracy. Alavi suggested that this bureaucracy, which he called an 'oligarchy', was relatively independent of control by any social class, but Saul points out that Alavi's reasons for saying this are not clear. For one thing, as Saul notes, in East Africa there were no strong indigenous classes to be subordinated, so that the 'overdeveloped' nature of the state is not due to the need to subordinate such classes, but to the need to 'subordinate pre-capitalist social formations to the imperatives of colonial capitalism'. A corollary of this is that the absence of strong indigenous classes must affect the degree of independence of the state bureaucracy, although how this occurs is not clear. Saul does not underrate the pressures which operate to curtail and neutralize the influence of the progressive forces inside the state bureaucracy but he contends that their initiatives have been genuine, and that it is essential to understand the 'plasticity' of the state bureaucracy in terms of a real class struggle taking place between different elements inside it.

The Overdeveloped State?

It is not difficult to agree that the Arusha Declaration, *ujamaa vijijini, Mwongozo*, etc., have resulted from some kind of struggles within the state apparatus. But Saul himself is now pessimistic about the prospects of further such initiatives from that quarter, and there is mounting *prima facie* evidence of the weakness and/or neutralization in practice of several of those which were taken earlier. But what, then, is the class character of the state as given by this relationship? But the class interests of the state bureaucracy, whether they are congruent with those of the dominant class, or in conflict with them, are unlikely to be the determining factor in establishing or upsetting that dominance. In post-colonial societies in Africa there can be little doubt that the dominant class is still the foreign bourgeoisie and the question, for Saul, then is whether or not the Tanzanian state serves its interests, not whether the Tanzanian state bureaucracy has 'become a bureaucratic bourgeoisie' by virtue of its control over state-owned capital. So, to summarize, we cannot discover the class character of the state by inspecting the class interests of the state bureaucracy, even if these are clear.

The 'Petty-bourgeoisie'

In the debate about whether the state bureaucracy are a new class, or a class-in-the-making, it is generally taken for granted that the members of the state bureaucracy are drawn from the 'petty-bourgeoisie'. If this debate is misconceived anyway, it may seem unimportant whether or not their class origins are being correctly described. However, the rather casual way in which the term 'petty-bourgeois' is used corresponds to the lack of interest which some of these theorists have displayed (at least in their discussion of the state) in what I would call the historical tendencies of the capitalist mode of production in these 'post-colonial' societies; a question which seems to me fundamental for anyone attempting to answer the political question posed by Saul.

Briefly, Marx's use of the term 'petty-bourgeoisie' was historically fairly specific. It referred to small manufacturers, shopkeepers, peasants and artisans. By contrast the word 'petty-bourgeois' as used by the parties to the debate on the state bureaucracy in post-colonial Africa refers mainly to owners of small amounts of non-agricultural capital, such as small manufacturers, contractors, traders, etc., the richer peasants, white collar workers generally (mainly, of course, in state employment). This clearly means something different from Marx's concept. For one thing, the last category are not owners of capital at all, but the sort of people who Marx thought would replace the petty-bourgeoisie as he used the term, even though they may well have 'bourgeois' tastes, ideas and aspirations. The richer peasants are generally included, and other peasants excluded, because the former have distinct economic interests to defend against the latter and against the rural labourers. Further, all these categories are typically *expanding* in present-day Africa, and have gained both influence and wealth at the expense of the rest of the peasantry and the majority of wage workers.

The 'petty-bourgeoisie' so defined is thus a different concept from that of Marx. This does not necessarily mean it is inept, but it does mean that its political implications cannot be taken for granted. Whereas Marx's petty-bourgeoisie played an ambivalent political role corresponding to its contradictory class interests *vis-à-vis* the developing bourgeoisie and proletariat, this seems less likely to be true of the 'petty-bourgeoisie' as the term is used by both Murray and Shivji. In order to know the real significance of any statement about the 'petty-bourgeoisie' as they use it, we need a general analysis of the development of the capitalist mode of production and its relations with petty commodity production, and thus of the development of the relations of production and the class struggle. And this is also the essential starting point for an assessment of the role of the state and of the significance of the fact – if it is significant – that its personnel are recruited from one class rather than another.

Conclusion

The point of these comments has not been to disagree with Saul's interpretation of the situation in Tanzania, but to question whether the theory he has used in this instance really helps to illuminate that interpretation, or points the political way forward.

As far as the analysis of events in Tanzania is concerned, the distinctions I have tried to draw out most put a gloss on Saul's views, especially with regard to the *origins* and the *course* of the struggles inside the state apparatus. The origins of any such struggle evidently lie in the links – personal, organizational and ideological – with the workers and peasants which some of the party-recruited elements bring into the state apparatus with them. Individual career officials identify themselves with their outlook, but the impetus comes from the party elements, and it was in the party executive, by then largely composed of holders of state posts but still organizationally and ideologically distinct from the state, that the initiatives of 1967 and 1971 were taken. These initiatives reflected an appreciation of some of the class *implications* of the existing social and economic system, as revealed in a succession of policy contradictions (neutralism versus dependence on bilateral aid, egalitarianism versus the elitist educational system, etc.). This appreciation was very partial, however. In particular it was assumed that the dominance of a local bourgeois class, and of foreign bourgeoisies, could be prevented by legislative and administrative action taken by the existing state. This ignored both the bourgeois character of the existing state (its adaptation to the task of defending bourgeois interests) and the fact that the penetration of Tanzanian society in all its dimensions by capitalism was far too advanced to be checked, let alone prevented, by juridical measures.

Rosa Luxemburg's words apply as much to periphery capitalism as to capitalism in the metropoles: '… the fundamental relations of the domination of the capitalist class cannot be transformed by means of legislative reforms, on the basis of capitalist society, because these relations have not been introduced by bourgeois *laws*' (italics added). To check, let alone eliminate, the dominance of the capitalist class could only mean mobilizing the working class and the poorer peasants to struggle against it at all levels. This was excluded, partly by Nyerere's resistance to the idea that class struggle was involved in the 'building of socialism', and partly, one suspects, from a reasonable fear that mass struggle would involve the leadership in being outflanked on the 'left' by new leaders emerging in such struggles, while simultaneously running the risk of a reaction from the right within the state apparatus. Distortion and 'neutralization' of the initiatives taken by 'Nyerere and his supporters' within the state apparatus clearly played a part in reducing their impact – the clearest example being the open opposition to the urban workers' response to the TANU Guidelines by the economic bureaucracy – in other words state-company managers and directors, supported by the union bureaucracy and the police – in 1973-74. But it needs to be emphasized that this process itself reflects the limitations of the original initiatives taken. It was Nyerere who insisted in February 1967 that the nationalization measures were 'primarily nationalist' in purpose, and that the fact that ownership and control had to be transferred to the state, which made the measures 'socialist', was welcome (because 'we are socialists as well as nationalists') but incidental; in the interests of 'Tanzania' the firms affected 'should be efficiently run. Their management must be good, and their workers must play a full part in securing high production. Industrial discipline is an essential part of this process ...' (Economic Nationalism). These ideas mark the limits, not of one man's ideology, but of the broadly 'populist' form of consciousness of the wing of the original nationalist leadership most sensitive to its mass base. The 1973 decision to enforce 'villagization' need not necessarily be seen as completely inconsistent with Nyerere's earlier political position, either. His 1968 statement was that no-one could be forced into an ujamaa village; it could not be a *socialist* village if force was used. The villages into which people have since been forced are actually termed 'development villages'. While the President was obviously very reluctant to use force, for any purpose, he seems to have concluded that it was justified in order to improve the ability of the government to direct an increase in agricultural production. This is consistent with the conception of 'socialism' as something that can (if necessity requires) be 'introduced' later, when the material basis for it has been built.

Looking ahead, the theoretical considerations given earlier simply suggest that the concept of the 'bureaucratic bourgeoisie' as an entrenched ruling class is an unreliable starting point for further analysis. Most writers on Tanzania are impressed by the state bureaucracy's expansion and growing powers, and by the bureaucratization of the party and the trend towards authoritarianism in general. But the contradictions of the situation are obscured by this lumping together of different elements in the state apparatus with the idea of the dominant class and specifically also with the undifferentiated 'petty-bourgeoisie'. One illustration must suffice to indicate the sort of issue involved. The initiatives of the Arusha Declaration, etc., cannot be known to be 'progressive' *per se*, but only from an analysis of the class forces and contradictions of the situation as a whole. So the 'progressiveness' of the nationalization measures can be questioned: perhaps, as Aidan Foster-Carter suggests, they were really just 'the most up-to-date form of denationalization'. Conversely, can the enforced villagization be known automatically to be *retrogressive*? As Raikes points out, it does not obviously advance any class interest of the state bureaucracy and it could both raise peasant consciousness, and even stimulate organization among them. Or again, how well does the present power of the state bureaucracy cater to the material needs of the non-state petty-bourgeoisie-rich peasant (included in forced villagization?), traders, entrepreneurs of various kinds? These questions seem prejudged by the proposition that the state bureaucracy has now constituted itself a ruling class.

In general, I am not entirely convinced that the 'state bureaucracy' does now constitute a class, rather than having simply consolidated itself in its bureaucratic function, in however officious a manner, and with however bourgeois a mentality; or that the bourgeoisie proper (abroad) has been really, rather than juridically, expropriated, under the nationalization arrangements as these have been described by Shivji and others; in short, I am not sure that there has been a fundamental evolution in the relations between the different elements of the ruling class alliance, as the 'ruling bureaucratic bourgeoisie' thesis implies. Unless these issues are first clarified, the next phase of the class struggle cannot be clearly understood either; specifically, it is not a question of *deciding* whether the struggle between the 'progressive' 'nizers' and their opponents inside the state bureaucracy is over, but of reconsidering all the changes that have been made in terms *of their impact on the* development of the class struggle as a whole, and what that impact now implies for future strategy.

Endnote

1.   'The State in Post-colonial Societies – Tanzania', *The Socialist Register* (1974).

4 RAFAEL KAPLINSKY
Capitalist Accumulation in the Periphery:
The Kenyan Case Re-examined   [1980]

The original article contained a great deal of tabulated data covering a period from the mid-1960s to the mid-1970s. Since this Reader focuses on the state, class forces and accumulation, we have tended to remove this finer empirical detail in order to make the dimensions of the arguments clearer. As the reader will note, Kaplinsky posits five hypotheses, only some of which deal directly with the concerns of this collection. Hence, in our editing we have tended to retain the relevant sections and simply summarised the rest. For references see Bibliographic Note on p. 56.

Colin Leys, author of one of the most interesting books on underdevelopment in recent years, has caused considerable surprise by his 1978 article reassessing his pioneering study. The particular point of contention is the characterization of the indigenous industrial bourgeoisie. In the earlier study Leys argued that the indigenous bourgeoisie – which he termed an 'auxiliary bourgeoisie' – was largely defined by its relationship to foreign capital and that it saw its future in alliance with that of foreign capital. Langdon (1980) supported this, characterizing the 'insider bourgeoisie' as bargaining with foreign capital for a greater proportion of the surplus generated by foreign capital to be distributed to the Kenyan elite. But he, too, saw the interests between the indigenous bourgeoisie and foreign capital as being basically harmonious, rather than antagonistic.

Leys' recent assessment of the earlier analysis seems to have been influenced by two factors. The first is the research of Cowen tracing the roots of the indigenous bourgeoisie back to pre-colonial times. This, Leys argues, bears the lie to the characterization of the indigenous bourgeoisie solely in relation to foreign capital. The second factor underlying Leys' reassessment is the difference in the aspirations of the indigenous bourgeoisie between his earlier fieldwork (1971-73) and his visit to Kenya in 1977. In this latter period Leys encountered a very strong desire by the indigenous bourgeoisie to supplant foreign capital. For Leys the Kenya case poses perhaps the most basic question of all – is successful capitalist accumulation at the periphery of the global economy possible?

Leys argued that there 'is the need to study and theorise the conditions under which other periphery countries have, and others have not, experienced significant measures of growth' (p.244). He concludes that a

> plausible explanation of Kenyan economic growth since the 1940s lies, rather in the specific social relations of production developed before, during and since the colonial period, and particularly – but in no sense exclusively … in the key role of the class formed out of the process of indigenous capital accumulation. (p.247)

The control of this class over the state, Leys argues, originally largely through ethnic links, led to the accumulation of surplus through state-protected merchant, distribution and service activities. Increasingly this allowed the indigenous bourgeoisie to buy out foreign capital in farming, service and manufacturing sectors, helped in recent years by capital accumulated through the ivory, charcoal and coffee trade.

The move into the manufacturing sector has been aided by the development of appropriate skills and institutional forms, notably syndicates of individual investors, co-operatives, mass investment companies and parastatals. Moreover the state assists indigenous Kenyans in moving from the sphere of circulation to that of production. But, contrary to his earlier work, this does not imply a relatively autonomous state. He argued:

> Some such conception was at times implicit if not explicit in my own earlier work on Kenya. Instead of seeing the strength of the historical tendency lying behind the emergence of the African bourgeoisie I tended to see only the relatively small size and technical weakness of African capital in the face of international capital, and to envisage the state as little more than a register of this general imbalance; rather than seeing the barriers of capital state and technology as relative, and the state as the register of the leading edge of indigenous capital in its assault on those barriers (pp.251-3).

I have marshalled new data which can be brought to bear on five hypotheses which can be drawn out of Leys (1978) and the subsidiary analyses of Swainson:

1) the Kenyan economy has seen a successful period of economic growth since independence;

2) an independent indigenous industrial bourgeoisie now exists. The word 'independent' is taken in its relativist sense, implying an ability to maintain accumulation independently from foreign capital and with some significant measure of indigenous technological capability;

3) there has been a significant increase in ownership and control of industry by this indigenous bourgeoisie which has moved to supplant foreign capital holdings;

4) the state has moved from a mediating position to an instrument for increased indigenous control over foreign capital;

5) the Kenyan economy will see continued successful capitalist accumulation.

The dependency school, which these hypotheses challenge, argues that industrial development in small peripheral economies is conditioned, and moreover limited, by their relation to the global economy. The Cowen-Leys-Swainson school, as I understand it, challenges the 'dependistas' by (a) pointing to the indigenous roots of the capitalist class; (b) noting that they, in part by manipulating the state, have moved to supplant foreign capital; and (c) believing that such a momentum is sustainable. The remainder of the chapter examines these five hypotheses.

Economic Transformation in Kenya

It is often believed that the Kenyan economy has been a 'success story', witnessing high and sustained economic growth since independence. Indeed this appears to be the view of Leys (1978) who argues that not only has there been a significant increase in the penetration of the monetary economy (associated with an extension of capitalist relations of production), but that this has been accompanied by significant economic growth and structural change. Labour productivity is said to have grown, transfer pricing by multinational companies (MNCs) brought under control and new markets found, following the loss of markets in Tanzania and Uganda. In sum, economic growth is said to have resulted from structural transformation and both have occurred with the spread of capitalist production relations. Let us examine each of these assertions in turn.

Extension of capitalist relations of production
There is no doubt that capitalist relations of production have been extended significantly over the years, as measured in the relative growth of the monetised vis-à-vis the non-monetary economy. However, the extent of this transformation may be misleading since a proportion of this decline is accounted for by significant increases in government expenditure (and therefore revenue), particularly on education, health and (especially over the last two years) defence. Not all of this increase in government expenditure is reflected in the growth of monetised production since a significant proportion of this state expenditure has been financed by budgetary deficits, aid and foreign loans. Thus while Leys (1978) is correct in interpreting a significant extension in capitalist relations of production, the evidence used to support this contention is subject to qualification.

Changes in economic structure
Changes in the structure of the Kenyan economy have in fact been rather limited. Despite significant changes in the composition of imports which has occurred as a result of the policy of import substitution, the share of the manufacturing sector in GDP grew slowly in the first thirteen years of independence. Of course accumulation need not necessarily be limited to the industrial sector. But I draw these trends out since the analyses of Leys (1978) and Swainson lean heavily upon the emergence of an indigenous bourgeoisie in this sector, particularly in large-scale manufacturing. The slow growth of the manufacturing sector is reflected in the share of manufactures in exports where, despite repeated trumpeting of improved performance, their share remained essentially static over the time period.

In the same period there has been a steady worsening in the balance of payments and trade and additionally there has been little or no curbing of transfer pricing. In summary, therefore, there is little evidence of any profound change in economic structure. Kenya remains a predominantly agricultural economy exporting primary products and importing manufactures. Although import substitution has seen some change in the composition of imports, the underlying pattern is one of increasing balance of payments problems. Heavy new outflows of surpluses, largely arising from foreign investment, further exacerbate these balance of payments difficulties.

Economic growth
The growth of the Kenyan economy has not in fact been as rapid as has been believed. Additionally, industrialization has been of a heavily-protected nature and has been paid for by consumers of non-food products, particularly in the rural areas, who for most of the period have suffered adverse terms of trade with the industrial sector compared to those prevailing at independence in 1964. Such industrialization was thus financed by modest gains in agricultural productivity, particularly in the 1960s. However, as Leys (1978) points out, increases in agricultural productivity have begun to tail off. He sees the powerful place of 'middle peasant household production in agriculture' (p.261) as an obstacle to growth in agriculture.

The consequence of this discussion, therefore, is to place doubts upon the much vaunted past economic performance of the Kenyan economy. Some limited structural transformation occurred between Independence and the early 1970s, and was accompanied by a significant increase in per capita incomes. Since then real per capita incomes have stagnated and accumulation in industry has been financed by limited growth in agricultural productivity, balance of payments deficits and the temporary boom in coffee prices. However, now that coffee prices have fallen nearer to the long-run trend price and agricultural growth has begun to peter out, serious doubts must be placed on the long-run growth potential of the economy and the sustainable nature of protected industrialization and the consequent mode of accumulation. An indication of this has been the decreasing inflow of foreign investment, with most new projects being joint ventures between machinery and service suppliers (who extract their surpluses in forms other than dividends) in joint ventures with parastatal agencies and Development Banks.

The Indigenous Industrial Bourgeoisie in Kenya

Leys (1978) points to the failure of his earlier analysis to foresee the emergence of an indigenous industrial bourgeoisie. This failure was said to arise from an analysis preoccupied with what was currently in existence. But the works of Swainson and the impressions gained in a recent visit to Kenya seem to have led Leys to accept that even if the indigenous industrial bourgeoisie is not yet fully formed, its emergence – in contradistinction to an 'auxiliary bourgeoisie' in alliance with foreign capital – is only a matter of time.

There are two important origins of such an indigenous industrial bourgeoisie. The first is from the pool of small, petty accumulators amongst whom may emerge the large-scale independent industrialists of the future. Of this group we have little to say, but merely remark that my 1975 studies of such industrialists point to their very small-scale nature and their investment in technologies which show little scope for intensified accumulation, but expand extensively through replication. The second source of future industrialists is from the group which is currently engaged in large-scale accumulation, assisted through links with the state and/or foreign capital. My comments on the existence of an indigenous industrial bourgeoisie are based on an analysis of this latter group of industrialists.

Noting the dangers of linear extrapolation in a dynamic situation of class formation, we can proceed to an analysis of the characteristics of existing industrialists in large-scale enterprises.

In our study of these firms the names of some individuals recurred. Basically these people can be divided into three different groups, namely:

* those of settler origin (for example, the Block family, Madhavani, Chandaria, Sir Ernest Vasey, the Bellhouse family, M.W. Harley, etc.);

* indigenous Kenyans holding directorships purely on an ex-officio basis (for example, L. Kibinge, Permanent Secretary of the Ministry of Commerce and Industry);

* indigenous Kenyans holding directorships in firms in which they have an active interest, as well as in firms in which they acted on an ex-officio basis.

The following analysis is based upon the third group of individuals. First, we found that most indigenous accumulators have links with foreign capital, even if we only consider the firms in which they have a direct stake. But even some of the accumulators who are not in joint ventures with foreign capital are linked through licensing agreements. The restrictive relations with foreign capital can hardly be taken as a sign of an 'independent accumulator'. Second, the scale of these investments is modest. Third, less than half of these accumulators have investments in more than one manufacturing firm. Fourth, a small sub-group used close family relationships with Kenyatta to build their empires and these are still in very close alliance with foreign capital in a joint venture contracted in very recent years.

Although the argument for the pre-eminence of a 'national bourgeoisie' does not necessarily preclude any links with foreign capital, the extensive links which this group of industrialists have with foreign capital as well as their almost total reliance on foreign technology and market power, makes it difficult to see them in such a pre-eminent position. One further point needs to be made and this is that it is by no means certain that indigenous ownership will lead to local reinvestment, since there is an observed tendency for even local capitalists to repatriate surplus abroad. Furthermore, the evidence (see my article in No.14, 1979, pp. 90–6 of this *Review)* suggests that the types of investments made by local capitalists are often indistinguishable from those made by foreign capital.

However, there is no doubt, as any discussions with aspirant indigenous industrialists will rapidly show, that there exists a very strong *desire* to supplant foreign capital. Moreover there are pockets in the State (for example, the Central Bank and parts of the Ministry of Commerce and Industry) which offer clear support for these aspirations. What remains dubious is the extent to which such aspirations can be met. Although these are yet early days to reach a definitive viewpoint the discussion which follows below on ownership, control and the role of the state will provide the reader with further insights.

The Transfer of Ownership & Control from Foreign to Local Capital

In discussing the extent to which ownership has been transferred from foreign to local capital over the years, I shall draw upon the major conclusions of the study which I have undertaken for the NCCK.

Ownership
Data show that the share of total issued capital owned by foreign residents plummeted dramatically between 1966 and 1976 and although there were some exceptions (for example, in the wood, furniture, paper, printing and large tourist sectors), this pattern seemed to be common to most sectors and size groups of firms. From this we might be tempted to conclude that because Kenyan residents owned more of the economy in 1976 than in 1966, they therefore had greater control over it. However, a more detailed look at the data on ownership points to a different conclusion.

One of the main reasons why the overall share of foreign ownership declined was because there was a very marked tendency of the wholly-owned foreign subsidiaries to sell off a minority of their shares to local residents. Thus whereas over three-quarters of foreign capital was in wholly owned subsidiaries in 1966, this proportion fell to less than half by 1976. However, these firms seldom sold off more than fifty per cent of their shares so that they have been able to keep control over their subsidiaries despite the respectability gained by selling off shares to local residents. Against this some of the smaller foreign firms increased their holdings from majority – to wholly – foreign ownership in the same period.

Thus it appears as if the increased share of the large-scale industrial and the tourist economy owned by Kenyan residents seems to arise from the establishment of new (small) firms by Kenyan residents, because many of the larger wholly foreign-owned firms sold off a small proportion of their shares to local residents and because of advances in ownership by parastatals. While it is difficult to conclude that the share of foreign ownership has increased over the decade, it is equally difficult to concur with Leys and Swainson that there has been a significant transfer of ownership from foreign capital to the indigenous bourgeoisie in large-scale manufacturing and tourism. At best one can conclude that little overall change occurred in the time-period.

Control

Of course ownership is not identical to control. In fact there are many reasons to believe that control is of greater relevance than ownership, since it determines the rate and nature of accumulation and the distribution of surplus. My analysis suggests that foreign capital tends to command a greater degree of control over large-scale manufacturing and tourism than its share of ownership. If we consider the citizenship of the majority of directors as a proxy for control, almost a third of all large-scale manufacturing and service firms were majority controlled by foreign citizens despite being majority owned by Kenyan residents.

In summary, then, the evidence available does not appear to support the hypothesis that there has been a significant shift of ownership (let alone control) from foreign capital to an indigenous industrial bourgeoisie, although there seems to be a trend towards the establishment of new Kenyan-owned and controlled enterprises and an advance in parastatal participation.

The State as an Instrument of the Indigenous Industrial Bourgeoisie

The fourth hypothesis which can be drawn out of the re-evaluation of the Kenyan case by Leys and others concerns the role of the state. While Leys (1975) had characterised the state as harmonising the alliance between foreign capital and the 'auxiliary bourgeoisie', Langdon (1980), in particular, extends the argument to illustrate how this included an appropriation of part of the surplus by members of the state apparatus as well. The re-evaluation characterises the state as being an instrument used by the indigenous bourgeoisie to squeeze out foreign capital, thereby, in the view of Leys (1978), not falling into the trap of characterising the state as being relatively autonomous.

The state, of course, is not an homogenous entity. In my experience, the 'national' interest is most clearly articulated by the Central Bank and by middle-level officers in most ministries and parastatals (a subject to which we shall return later). But the important point is to note which faction prevails when conflicts arise in actions to be taken by the state. It is my contention that the state shows little evidence of taking an antagonistic stance to foreign capital in the post-1975 period, when it is argued that the capital acquired through primitive accumulation via charcoal and ivory, and latterly through coffee, removed the capital constraint faced by the indigenous bourgeoisie in supplanting foreign capital (see Leys, 1978, pp.253–4).

Leys (1978) identifies mass investment companies such as GEMA Holdings as being one instrument enabling the extension of the indigenous industrial bourgeoisie, and he points to a joint venture with Fiat as an example of this. In actual fact this example supports an entirely different conclusion. In the post-1973 period the state decided to encourage the local assembly of commercial vehicles and after considering a number of proposals, three projects were agreed. One was a joint venture between Leyland (45%), the Treasury (35%) and a local public company distributing these vehicles (20%). The second was between General Motors (49%) and the Industrial & Commercial Development Corporation (ICDC) (51%); and the third between the Treasury (26%), the IDB (25%) and Lonrho/Inchcape/Gecaga/Muigai – the latter group representing the distributors. Finding itself excluded from a market in which it had a significant share (and which showed the potential for future growth) Fiat selected what it thought to be a very powerful local partner (GEMA Holdings) in an attempt to press its right to assemble vehicles. However, despite the undoubtedly powerful support of GEMA Holdings, the three existing MNCs in alliance with equally powerful local interests allied to foreign capital (i.e. Gecaga and Muigai) eventually managed to crush the bid by Fiat-GEMA Holdings. In this case the alliance between foreign capital and the 'auxiliary bourgeoisie' managed to halt the bid by local capital, insofar as it was represented by GEMA Holdings, a group hitherto not in alliance with any foreign capital.

As mentioned earlier, the Central Bank repeatedly took a more 'national' line than other parts of the state system. In an attempt to increase the net foreign-exchange inflow from foreign investment, the Central Bank has over the past decade consistently attempted to limit the ability of foreign firms to borrow locally, although the precise percentages allowed have varied over the years. Evidence that the policy to limit loans to foreign capital has failed is reflected in data which show no evidence of decreased gearing as the share of foreign ownership increased.

No doubt these examples do not provide conclusive evidence that the state is closely allied with foreign capital. However, they do each illustrate that there is evidence that despite the representation of the 'national' position in some parts of the state apparatus, there are many cases of significance where the position of foreign capital has won out over that of local capital. Even if this segment of the state were to predominate, it is not clear whether this would reflect a tendency to supplant foreign capital, as Leys and Swainson argue, or to squeeze out a larger share of the surplus, perhaps for an 'insider faction' as Langdon argued. And, moreover, these examples are drawn from the most recent time period during which the state is supposed to have become more closely allied to the position of the indigenous bourgeoisie. Thus the state remains a 'soft-touch' as a joint venture partner.

Successful Capitalist Accumulation will Continue

Above I argued that the evidence suggests that the significant economic growth of the 1960s began to taper off in the 1970s. The accumulation which had occurred in large-scale industry had been 'inefficient' when compared to global standards and requires a very high protection. Although it is notoriously difficult to predict future rates of growth it is only possible to envisage continued accumulation of this type in Kenya if there is rapid growth in manufactured exports. This will not only ease the balance of payments problem, but by enabling fuller capacity utilisation and through the discipline of the international market, will allow for greater efficiency in production. Leys (1978) asserts that a successful breakthrough has been made, but the evidence certainly does not bear this out.

Conclusions

Let us return to the basic issue under discussion. At least two major and divergent viewpoints emerge from Marxist-inspired theories of underdevelopment. The first argues that the spread of the capitalist mode of production to the periphery is inevitable and that sustainable industrial accumulation will occur in much of the periphery as a consequence. The second, and opposing, view is that it is in the nature of capitalist accumulation at the world level that sustainable industrial accumulation in the periphery is most unlikely, if impossible.

Leys (1978) responds to these generalised positions by asserting that there is no *a priori* evidence that such accumulation at the periphery is impossible. I have tried to respond to Leys by examining the Kenyan case in great detail. The extension of capitalist relations of production is not challenged. But I am more sceptical as to the past performance and sustainable nature of accumulation and in the extent to which indigenous capitalists have been able to squeeze out foreign ones. In particular, I am drawn to the conclusion that Leys' reassessment is not supportable.

With respect to the existence of an indigenous bourgeoisie, I believe that Leys (1978), Swainson and others are reacting to an identifiable hostility to foreign capital, and some aspects of its 'culture', which is prevalent in Kenya. In my experience these views are predominantly held by middle-level civil servants and small-scale industrialists in competition with foreign subsidiaries. In both cases these two groups have not gained directly from the prominent position held by foreign capital in the Kenyan economy.

Insofar as the Kenyan case can be generalised, I believe it shows that the possibilities for successful accumulation in an open economy of this type are limited, whatever the historical roots of the accumulating class. While the subject obviously bears further extended discussion, it is my view that the pattern of accumulation in such economies is significantly conditioned by the nature of global accumulation and their interspersion in that global process. Economies of the first type may yet exhibit sustainable accumulation as they are able to insulate themselves from the global market. Moreover, because of the large size of their internal markets, the scale of production may be large enough to support the growth of an indigenous technological capability and even for the export of capital goods to other peripheral economies.

Finally to observe, as I believe we have, that the arguments of Leys (1978) and Swainson do not disprove the conclusions of the dependency school does not automatically lend credence to cruder formulations of dependency theory which argue, or imply, that classes in peripheral economies are solely formed through interaction with the global economy. Clearly this is incorrect. But, I believe, there is strong evidence to argue that, whatever the roots of such classes, their future development is circumscribed by the relation of the particular economy to the global economy. More specifically in relation to Kenya, I believe that the evidence shows that although an indigenous capitalist class has managed to carve out a slice of the benefits arising from accumulating in large-scale industry, this has arisen from an alliance between this class and foreign capital. Not only does little prospect emerge for indigenous capital to squeeze out foreign capital but the inbuilt contradictions of economies of this type make it difficult to foresee that such a pattern of accumulation – with or without foreign capital – can proceed in a viable form.

5 BJÖRN BECKMAN
Imperialism & Capitalist Transformation: Critique of a Kenyan Debate   [1980]

A question of whether or not a dependency model is applicable to Kenya has been subject to considerable debate. Beckman offers a critique of the overall terms in which the debate has been cast. He argues that the critics of underdevelopment theory have failed to transcend its problematic and its misdirected identification of contradictions. They have in consequence placed unjustified emphasis on the state as an instrument of 'factional' interests. Defenders of the dependency position have for their part been unable to place their analysis within the framework of the logic of capital accumulation, imperialism and class formation. But for Beckman, it is only in terms of the general requirements of capital accumulation that the relation of the state to underlying class forces can be adequately understood.

The Anti-Dependency Position

Colin Leys' 'Capital Accumulation, Class Formation and Dependency' (1978) is an attempt to assess current development in Kenya in the light of a theoretical reorientation since his main work *Underdevelopment in Kenya: The Political Economy of Neo-Colonialism* (1975). This reorientation reflects a widespread unease with some of the basic propositions of 'underdevelopment theory', including the notion of 'blocked capitalist development'. Attention has been drawn to the poor fit of such theory with Marxist analysis of the development of capitalism and imperialism. Partly the unease was prompted by the inability to predict the rapid changes in some parts of the Third World, particularly in industrialising Southeast Asia. Ad hoc revisions of the theory to accommodate such changes (for example, the shift in emphasis to technological dependence) have done little to appease the critics, as the revisions merely draw attention to the theoretical weaknesses of the positions.

Leys' observations on the advance of capitalism in Kenya, with the key role attributed to the domestic bourgeoisie supported by the state, are therefore clearly set within a theoretical debate which goes far beyond the empirical evaluation of the Kenyan case. This is despite Leys' (1978) insistence that each case should be examined on its own merits, as 'the debate about dependency and underdevelopment has not shown either that capitalist development cannot occur at the periphery ... or that it is eventually bound to'. Studies of individual cases according to Leys should be pursued at three principal levels: the level of the logic of capital, the level of capitalist geopolitics (imperialism), and the level of class relations and class struggles in particular social formations, each level determining and being determined by the others'. In his observations on Kenya, however, he only deals with the last one. As we shall see, this limitation is probably a major source of the weakness of Leys' argument.

Let me first summarise the main propositions and the critique they have met. Kenya, according to Leys, appears to have the prerequisites for a 'transition to the capitalist mode of production'. The principal force of this process is the emergent domestic bourgeoisie and the state apparatus under its control. The preconditions for this relative 'success' are thus the specific factors which led to the creation of this domestic class. Leys traces the dialectics of capital accumulation to the impact of settler capital and the way in which it radically undermined pre-capitalist relations of production, preparing the way for the take-over by an indigenous bourgeoisie. From its landed base, this class has assumed a dominant position in an economy which already was quite advanced in terms of the development of capitalist relations of production. It used its position to 'set about recovering from international capital a good part of the field of accumulation which it had succeeded in occupying'. Control of the state apparatus by this class has been central to the advances made in the post-independence period. Most recently, this control has been used for the purpose of establishing a significant and growing stake in the manufacturing industry. The indigenous bourgeoisie can therefore now be seen as playing a leading role in the transition to industrial capitalism. In his understanding of this historical process, Leys draws support in particular from Michael Cowen's work on agrarian class formation and on Nicola Swainson's studies of the relations between the state and the development of international and indigenous capital in Kenya. At the level of theory, Leys has been particularly impressed by Robert Brenner's emphasis on the critical role of local class relations and class struggles in understanding why capitalism emerged at some ends (England) but not in others (Poland) of the international trading system preceding this transition.

The Dependency Position Reasserted

Leys' identification of major qualitative changes in the Kenyan political economy and the theoretically oriented interpretation given to them constitute a challenge to basic stands in the dominant radical analysis of African neo-colonialism. To one defender of the dependency position, Steven Langdon, the implication seems to be that 'the indigenous bourgeoisie is dynamic and autonomous, in control of the Kenyan state, and consequently leading relatively successful capitalist development in the country'. Although Langdon admits that this is an oversimplification of the Leys-Swainson position, as he calls it, it is clearly in this vein that the challenge is perceived. Rafael Kaplinsky, another student of Kenyan capitalism, has similarly come out with a major critique of Leys (*ROAPE* 17) who, according to Kaplinsky, contends that:

> there has been sustained economic growth in Kenya; an indigenous industrial bourgeoisie exists; this bourgeoisie has squeezed out foreign capital in manufacturing and tourism; the state has assumed an antagonistic position to foreign capital; sustainable accumulation in large-scale industry will continue in the future at historic rates.

Now, this is clearly a caricature of Leys' position. My concern here, however, is less whether or not the two parties give each other a fair hearing, than with the underlying theoretical assumptions on both sides. For that purpose, the perception of the argument on the other side, however distorted, is also relevant.

Let us summarise the main elements of the established radical dependency position which seem to be under challenge. I am drawing here on the general 'neo-colonial' interpretation of state and bourgeoisie in Africa, especially as it has been formulated by radical critics of the Nigerian situation, returning to the specific points raised by Kaplinsky and Langdon below.

1) The indigenous bourgeoisie has not transcended its essentially petty-bourgeoisie or comprador character; it is largely unproductive, not capable of spearheading a transition to real capitalist development.

2) The principal source of this incapacity is the complete dependence of this indigenous bourgeoisie on foreign capital for which it operates either as an agent, a transmission link or as a junior, subordinate partner. This applies to the bureaucratic as well as to the private domestic bourgeoisie, although there are certain patriotic or technocratic elements among the former which seek to protect national interests. These, however, are likely to lose out in view of the overall balance of forces.

3) The unproductive, inefficient, corrupt and dependent nature of this domestic bourgeoisie is compounded by its extreme sectionalist tendencies, further diminishing its ability to generate the appropriate conditions for a successful capitalist transformation.

4) The nature of its relationship with foreign capital is therefore essentially one of harmony or 'symbiosis' (Langdon), a mutually profitable relationship, which the domestic bourgeoisie is very unlikely to challenge. Far from being a threat to foreign capital, this 'national' bourgeoisie, despite its occasional outburst of anti-foreign rhetoric, is firmly in the pocket of foreign capital, although its rampant sectionalism and other vices may at times render it a liability to the foreign masters and scare them away.

5) The state power in such a dependent neo-colonial context is either seen as a direct instrument of the foreign bourgeoisie, the only real ruling class, or as an organ of international capital in a more abstract sense. Alternatively, state power is defined as being in the service of the symbiotic relationship, performing an important mediating role within it. If and when disagreement arises between the unequal partners, the state either seeks appropriate compromise solutions, or, if any real interests of the foreign, senior partners are at stake, comes down firmly on the side of the latter.

6) This constellation of class forces is the basic source of underdevelopment as it ensures continued subordination to international capital. The domination of the latter obstructs any significant development in the direction of a more self-centred, more autonomous, capitalist development. The economy continues to be integrated internationally, blocking productive internal sector linkages. Whatever industry is established does little to change this pattern. It is highly inefficient and requires high levels of protection, it depends heavily on imports, which, in combination with the outflow of profits, leads to a deteriorating balance of payments. Little industrial employment and linkages are created. In the meantime, productivity in agriculture stagnates or declines. Foreign-exchange earnings from exports are undermined by their fluctuations, with destabilising switches between inflationary spells when the going is good and recessions when it is not.

Kaplinsky and Langdon may not agree with all the formulations ventured above. The purpose, however, is to outline the general analytical tradition in which their own more specific contributions are set. Let us now turn to these. In both cases, the argument is essentially empirical, not theoretical. Both marshal an impressive array of figures and other evidence in support of their rejection of Leys' position. As Leys' observations were rather impressionistic and preliminary and not based on any amount of current research of his own (which he also duly acknowledges), one may be easily impressed by the empirical strength of the critique. Occasionally the evidence is not very conclusive in lending support to the points made. But, again, my concern is not primarily with the accuracy of the evidence brought forward on each side, but more with the theoretical premises on which such evidence (whatever its quality) seems to be selected and thought to be supportive of a particular position.

Continued Dominance by Foreign Capital

Let me begin with Kaplinsky, whose 'Capitalist Accumulation in the Periphery – The Kenyan Case Re-examined' (1979) was first in the field. Kaplinsky has been following the Kenyan scene over a long period, monitoring foreign capital and the development of ownership and control in industry. In reasserting the dependency position, he points first of all to the limited achievements which, according to him, characterise Kenyan economic development in general and that of industry in particular. Manufacturing contribution to GDP had only moved from 10 to 13 per cent between 1964 and 1977 and the effort to move into export manufacturing has been unsuccessful. Productivity in manufacturing is very low and there is heavy protection. Outflow of dividends on past investments is greater than the inflow of new ones (this is not supported by Langdon) and a significant proportion of surplus generated seeps abroad. Industry has been financed largely from gains in agricultural productivity which can now be seen as tailing off. 'Kenya remains a predominantly agricultural economy exporting primary products and importing manufactures.' As can be expected, balance of payments difficulties are growing.

The bulk of Kaplinsky's presentation deals with much useful evidence to demonstrate, first, the great variety of links which most indigenous industrialists have with foreign capital and secondly, the extent of foreign domination and control in the industrial sector. He points out that indigenous ownership does not imply a change in the structure of industry. Types of investments are indistinguishable from those of foreign capital and have the same import reliance, tendencies to evade local reinvestment, manipulation of transfer pricing and so on. He sees no evidence in support of 'the hypothesis that there has been a significant shift in ownership (let alone control) from foreign capital to an indigenous industrial bourgeoisie'. However, he sees 'a trend towards the establishment of new Kenyan owned and controlled enterprise and an advance in parastatal participation', which somewhat undermines his critique of Leys on this central point.

The last piece of evidence forwarded by Kaplinsky is directed against the view that the state is controlled by the indigenous bourgeoisie. Kaplinsky quotes four cases, in some detail, which according to him show (not very clearly, though) that the state has sided with foreign capital when it has been in conflict with indigenous capital.

The empirical material presented by Kaplinsky is useful. However, as evidence, it is rather inconclusive and the argument becomes to a great extent one of differences in interpretation of quantitative changes and of whether they should be considered significant, either in qualitative or quantitative terms. Kaplinsky's limited aspiration to theorise and predict is underlined in some of his concluding observations. Essentially, he is sceptical about the performance of the Kenyan economy in the past and whether present rates of accumulation can be sustained. He is similarly sceptical about 'the extent to which indigenous capitalists have been able to squeeze out foreign ones'; while such scepticism may be justified it hardly solves the important theoretical issues raised by Leys' article.

Foreign Controlled Industrialisation & Stagnation

Steven Langdon's contribution, 'Industry and Capitalism in Kenya', is theoretically more ambitious. He places his critique of Leys more explicitly within the framework of the wider dependency/anti-dependency argument. He has also made major contributions to the study of foreign capital in Kenya and can draw on much significant research of his own in support of his critique.

The major part of Langdon's paper is devoted to a review of post-independence industrialisation in Kenya 'so as to test the extent of transformation to capitalist social relations which it is generating, and to prove the spread effects associated with the sector'. The first aspect is studied from the spread of wage employment. The critical relevance of this factor is assumed because it was 'at the heart of the new capitalist relations of production that emerged in Western Europe'. Langdon quotes figures indicating a slow-down in wage employment since 1974. But he attributes greater weight to the fact that manufacturing employment has not kept pace with the growth in manufacturing output. While the latter has grown at a pace of 10 per cent per annum during the 1970s, employment has increased by only 7.5 per cent. Dramatic increases in output 1976–78 (an average of 16 per cent p.a.) brought increases in employment at little more than half of this rate.

The second aspect relates to the domestic linkages of manufacturing industry where he sees no significant improvement when measured by the import content of industrial output. Both aspects, according to Langdon, underline the limited capacity of the current pattern of industrialisation to promote the expansion of capitalist relations of production and generate a more self-centred economy.

The pattern itself can be traced to the control exercised by the transnational corporations, with their 'product transfer' strategies, including 'developed-country product choices', and 'product-differentiation' efforts which heavily influence technological choice, employment generation and import-dependence. With examples from soap and shoe manufacturing he demonstrates how transnational penetration actually blocks and kills off smaller-scale domestic enterprises with a high employment-yielding capacity and strong local linkages. Using the relative rates of profitability of transnational subsidiaries and local capital Langdon shows that the transnational sector 'is growing from strength to strength'. Looking at some new major domestically controlled enterprises, no difference can be seen between them and the transnationals in terms of the 'employment-minimising, linkage-limiting style'. The overall conclusion is that 'growing industrialisation is having only limited effects on social transformation in Kenya, because of restricted employment and linkage effects'.

Langdon also reviews the general performance of the Kenyan economy in recent years. As does Kaplinsky, he emphasises growing balance-of-payment problems, import bills and debt service charges. The economy suffers from 'a stop-and-go cycle that makes sustained capital accumulation very difficult'. It lacks the 'export capacity to sustain the high level of imports which accelerated growth of investment set off, and this regularly chokes off the accumulation process'. This points to 'the fundamental fact that Kenya has not developed its own autonomous capacity to sustain capital accumulation through internal interaction among sectors of the economy'.

As does Kaplinsky, Langdon emphasises the declining ability of Kenyan agriculture to finance the present type of development (not to speak of the growing food deficit). So Kenya relies increasingly on external government borrowing. A familiar, Latin American, pattern emerges:

the interplay of dependence on a few export crops, agricultural stagnation, growing balance of payment pressures, rising external indebtedness and slow growth except in a highly-protected, inefficient and capital-intensive industrial sector (Langdon, 1980:39).

The result is 'explosive inequalities and imbalances'. The evidence suggests, according to Langdon, that Kenya is moving in the same direction.

He examines finally whether export manufacturing is a possible way out. He finds that it is not, mainly due to high cost structure. The 'optimistic view' of Kenyan capital accumulation taken by Leys and Swainson must therefore be questioned. Rather, Langdon concludes that Kenya is becoming *increasingly* dependent on external factors, commodity prices and international finance.

An Inconclusive Argument

Langdon and Kaplinsky have provided us with useful evidence on the continued domination of foreign capital in Kenya's industrial economy, on the dependent nature of the indigenous bourgeoisie and the state, and on the distorted pattern of industrial development which follows from this foreign domination. The evidence suggests that great caution must be adopted when evaluating the indices of quantitative and qualitative changes which have taken place within this overall pattern, such as the growing prominence of the domestic bourgeoisie and the state in industrial production, as documented and theorised by Swainson and Leys.

I believe that a wealth of *additional* evidence can be marshalled to highlight other aspects of the dependency syndrome, not touched on by Kaplinsky and Langdon. On the whole, I believe that the overall picture of a dependent, neo-colonial economy and its ruling class, as summarised above, can be sustained by contemporary Kenyan evidence more or less point by point, just as it could in the case of Nigeria. I also believe that the evidence summoned by Leys and Swainson to indicate new elements in the situation can be largely incorporated into the dependency perspective as changes which do not significantly alter the overall pattern of dependency and underdevelopment. It may even be shown, as ventured by Kaplinsky and Langdon, that some of these changes, such as indigenous private and state participation in industry, may in fact reinforce the underdevelopment syndrome as defined by the dependency line.

However, the opposite also seems true. It seems quite possible to integrate the empirical evidence quoted by Kaplinsky and Langdon into the anti-dependency pursued by Leys. The continued (or growing) presence of foreign capital, the close links between foreign and domestic capital (private and state), the low employment and linkage-generating capacity of the present pattern of industrial growth, are all compatible with an emphasis on the growing influence (power) of the domestic bourgeoisie, on its own and via the state apparatus. The figures clearly show a high rate of growth in both manufacturing output and employment, although the latter is lower. While the import dependence of manufacturing continues to be high (an average of 34 per cent in 1966-74, according to Langdon) there certainly are quantitatively significant domestic linkages which grow in absolute (if not relative) terms as industry expands.

The differences of emphasis in the interpretation of the overall growth performance and growth potential of the Kenyan economy are inconclusive. Both sides, in fact, see agricultural output and productivity as a major source of future weakness. But it is not clear, on either side, how this is related to the controversy over foreign dominance and the changing nature of domestic class forces. Similarly, the rising balance of payments difficulties (which we have no reason to doubt) may well lead to growing foreign borrowing (and dependency). But what conclusions can we draw about the performance of Leys' and Swainson's emerging class forces in this situation?

The evidence on its own is neither here nor there. Its significance depends on the interpretation given to it, which again is determined by the theoretical position taken. The inconclusive nature of the argument is caused not by contradictory or inconclusive evidence but by the weaknesses of the theoretical positions from which such evidence has been selected, ordered, and interpreted. So let us examine these positions.

The Notion of Successful Capitalist Development

> The most important question of all those which are at stake in the debate about 'dependency' is whether or not there are theoretical reasons for thinking that the ex-colonies cannot (as Marx put it) 'adopt the bourgeois mode of production' and develop their productive forces within it (Leys,1978).

This is how Colin Leys introduces the problematic of his article. Kaplinsky quotes it approvingly and it is within that problematic that his own response is set. While Leys sees such development taking place on a modest scale in Kenya, Kaplinsky and Langdon do not. Behind both positions, however, lingers an unspecified notion of the development of a real, national capitalism as being a precondition for such transformation. Ann Phillips has effectively demonstrated the ideological character of underdevelopment theory. It involves contrasting the present state of affairs in the third world with a notion of 'normal' capitalist development which draws partly on the historical experience of advanced capitalist countries and partly on an idealised conception of a rational system of utilisation of resources and allocation of surplus. This historically derived ideal-type picture of capitalism is then contrasted with underdeveloped capitalism. By demonstrating the impossibility of such normal, 'autocentric' capitalism under foreign economic domination, the case against the capitalist option can be established, and thus the case for a break with the world capitalist system and for socialism.

The relevance of much of this to the Kenya debate seems clear. Focusing on the low employment and linkage-generating capacity of the foreign-dominated manufacturing industry, Langdon concludes that 'Kenya has *not* developed its own autonomous capacity to sustain capital accumulation through internal interaction among sectors of the economy'. But which advanced capitalist countries, one may ask, have or ever had such an autonomous capacity? While Langdon perceives of the possibility of capitalist transformation through very close integration with Western Europe, this, according to him, could result in nothing but dependent development as distinct from broad, national capitalist development, including the rapid expansion of wage employment, characterising Western European capitalism in its early phases.

The point here is not to de-emphasise these historical differences, but to point to the absence of any effort to theorise them and thus specify the content of this 'broad capitalist transformation' on historical lines. One is left with the impression that such genuine transformation is not compatible, for example, with balance of payments crises, as if crises, stop-go, and stagnation were alien to the 'normal' behaviour of capitalism. 'Widening inequalities' are similarly quoted as evidence for the dependency position, implying that genuine capitalist transformation would not have such consequences. Inefficiency and a high degree of protection in the manufacturing industry, are identified by both Kaplinsky and Langdon as important aspects of the failure of capitalist transformation. It is by no means clear, however, why such protection and subsidies should be incompatible with capitalist transformation.

It may seem as if Leys seeks to avoid such idealist and ahistorical notions of capitalist development by speaking of the development of productive forces. We may also recall his own critique (1977) of the concept of development, meaning the capitalist development experienced by the metropoles. My impression is, however, that Leys is as committed as his critics to the underdevelopment problematic of whether or not real capitalist development is possible in the third world. As nobody denies, as far as I know, that *some* type of capitalist development takes place (however distorted or distorting), it must be a qualitative notion of such development which is the subject of their debate.

Leys fails, as do his critics, to provide a satisfactory theoretical basis for identifying *his* type of capitalist development. The choice of criteria and measurement for judging whether or not capitalist development takes place becomes subjective. This is, as I see it, a principal cause of the inconclusiveness of the Kenya debate. The way the problematic has been formulated is obstructive of an effort to analyse the nature of 'actually existing capitalism' and its consequences for class formation and political organisation. Let us examine some of the specific aspects of this false problematic.

The National Bourgeoisie as a Prerequisite for Real Capitalist Development

The principal expression of a faulty underdevelopment problematic, in Leys as well as in his critics, is the way in which the issue of the national bourgeoisie is handled. The question whether or not real capitalist transformation takes place becomes in this debate inseparably linked to the question of the emergence or not of a real indigenous bourgeoisie. This leads to a misdirection of attention from the nature of the process actually taking place and its principal contradictions, to a preoccupation with secondary issues without relating these in a systematic way to primary ones.

The position of underdevelopment theory has been, to put it crudely, that without a national bourgeoisie there cannot be a genuine transition to capitalism in the third world, the reason being the obstructive role of continued foreign domination. The way in which imperialism has moulded the domestic bourgeoisie, however, precludes it from becoming genuinely national. It is, in fact, the local bulwark of imperialist domination, and thus a source of continued underdevelopment. It is therefore necessary to fight both imperialism and the domestic bourgeoisie. As a political position this may be perfectly sound but it becomes easily vulnerable due to its weak theoretical base.

As the argument has been set, it is inevitable that any evidence of a domestic bourgeoisie growing in strength and independence is perceived as a challenge to the position of underdevelopment theory. It becomes necessary to prove that, despite everything, the domestic bourgeoisie is still weak and still dependent on foreign capital. While this may be true, the argument is gradually undermined as the position is poorly prepared for accommodation, analysing and theorising the changes in the relations between the sections of the bourgeoisie. On the other side, those dissatisfied with the ability of underdevelopment theory to explain the capitalist transformation that takes place, are encouraged to trace the roots of the changes to the rise of domestic class forces rather than in the wider process within which these local forces operate.

This, I believe, is what has happened in the case of Colin Leys. The growth of the indigenous bourgeoisie is treated as separate or even in contradiction to that of the development of international capital. It never becomes clear how the distinction between indigenous and foreign capital relates to the development or non-development of the capitalist mode of production. In what way does Kenyan ownership of industries, for example, alter the prospects for the generalisation of capitalist relations of production?

We learn about the high 'rate of penetration by African capital' in different sectors without being told how it relates to the simultaneous expansion of international capital. We learn that indigenous capital (with the help of the state) is engaged in an assault on the barriers of capital, scale and technology. The impression is given that in the process, the Kenyan economy emancipates itself from the domination of foreign capital. But what does such emancipation imply? Who is actually overcoming what barriers? Is the buying into foreign firms by local capital and the proliferation of partnerships with such increasing financially and politically strong local partners not as much related to the expansion of foreign capital, its domestic sources of finance and its need for political protection to expand its control over markets, to overcome its barriers of scale? If partnership is in fact the dominant strategy of penetration by foreign capital, how shall we understand this increasing African 'penetration' of the manufacturing sector? Who penetrates what?

The general impression given by Leys is that there exists an 'indigenous' as distinct from 'foreign' process of capital accumulation and that it is from the rise of the former, at the expense of or in contradiction to the latter, that Kenya's prospects for a capitalist transition must be understood. The period of decolonisation, he argues, was governed by the neo-colonial class project of international capital. The subsequent period, on the other hand, has been 'determined primarily on the class project of the indigenous bourgeoisie'. What, one wonders, has been the class project of international capital during this later period and, most specifically, in what way does the class project of the indigenous bourgeoisie distinguish itself from that of international capital?

As we have seen, Langdon and Kaplinsky emphasise the dependence of the African bourgeoisie and its integration with foreign capital. But their denying of 'autonomy' to indigenous capital does not stem from an understanding of the unity of the process of capital accumulation, but from their view of the complete subordination of one 'fraction' of capital to another. The preoccupation with the dichotomy indigenous-foreign is as fundamental to the perspective on the process of accumulation as to that of Leys. To them it is the dependent nature of the domestic bourgeoisie which blocks the road to 'autonomous' capitalist development. Underlying the positions on both sides are assumptions about the nature of the contradiction between this autonomous, self-centred development and imperialism.

Imperialism as Opposed to Real Capitalist Development

Behind the notion of real capitalist transformation requiring a national bourgeoisie (whose existence therefore must be proven/disproven) lies the fundamental assumption of a contradiction between imperialism and real capitalist development. I accept that there is a fundamental contradiction between national development and imperialism, but contend that the question of 'national' can only be defined in its articulation with the contradiction of class. My objection is to the structural definition given to this contradiction in the tradition of underdevelopment theory. By structural I mean a preoccupation with the manner in which the domination of international capital imposes constraints on the direction of production, for example, by favouring the mere extraction of primary commodities to their processing, the importation of goods to domestic production, assembly to real manufacturing, light consumer goods to capital goods, and so on. Langdon's concern with employment generation and domestic linkages is clearly an expression of this national, 'structuralist' view of the nature of the contradiction. But I believe that also behind Leys' focus on the rise of the indigenous bourgeoisie lies an assumption that this class, somehow, is the one likely to fight these structural barriers in opposition to international capital. While Kaplinsky and Langdon correctly draw attention to the identical structural features of indigenous and foreign investment in manufacturing industry, this is not being explained in terms of the *logic of capital* but merely by reference to the domination of *foreign* capital.

It seems quite correct to explain, as Langdon does, the backward structure of Kenyan industry, whether owned by foreigners or indigenes, as a logical outflow of the product strategies of the transnational subsidiaries. But this logic fails to relate to the dynamics of the process of capitalist industrialisation. It is as static as an earlier belief that *any* type of industrialisation could be achieved in opposition to imperialism.

It is not clear at all why manufacturing industry in Kenya must be expected to retain its present high level of imported inputs, why it is unlikely to go into increasing production of domestic inputs. It is easy to see that such a move may not be encouraged as long as it is possible to draw on readily available international supply lines. But what if the accessibility of such supply lines declines relative to domestic ones? This may be caused both by positive and negative factors, such as growing domestic industrial capacity and foreign-exchange scarcity. The balance of payments problem features prominently in Kaplinsky's and Langdon's argument as the ultimate obstacle to a continuation of the present pattern of industrialisation, which therefore will grind to a halt. But if excessive foreign-exchange utilisation becomes a threat to capital accumulation, is capital itself not going to seek solutions for overcoming such obstacles? There is clearly nothing inherently unprofitable in having a high level of local value-added!

We are told that manufacturing for exports is obstructed by the high level of protection and consequent inefficiency which goes with the import substitution pattern of industrialisation. But under what condition is foreign capital against export production? We have seen elsewhere how the 'right' conditions favoured such transformation. We are left with an impression that capital is committed to the upholding of its present uncompetitive cost structure and that any attempt at, for example, reduced protection would be 'deeply threatening' to transnationals as well as large-scale African capital. It is clear that the current conditions in individual countries favour particular strategies of accumulation by foreign capital, but these must be seen in a dynamic perspective. As one strategy is exhausted, others will be generated.

Most importantly, transnational capital does not represent one strategy, but a series of interacting and partly competing ones, which have very different consequences for linkages, both locally and externally. Alongside the direct investors we have a wide variety of pedlars of technology, management, consultancy services, and capital goods, none of whom have any necessary commitment to the interests of already established transnationals in a particular territory. On the contrary, there is intense competition between major and minor foreign firms, more or less aggressively backed by their respective home states.

These are forces pushing capitalist transformation. They will carry along new forms of 'dependence', probably more deeply rooted ones. So in that sense the dependency position still holds. But this is not sufficient to explain the nature of the transformation taking place, to predict the directions likely to be taken, and to guide political action.

The State

Before I attempt to spell out some of the political implications of this view of the contradiction between 'national' and 'dependent' capitalist development, there is a need to comment on the way it has been analysed at the level of the state.

Leys attributes a key role to the state in the emancipation of the domestic bourgeoisie. This role may be easily documented from various support measures taken. However, he goes further and argues that the state is *controlled* by the indigenous bourgeoisie. He criticises Langdon and his own earlier position for viewing it merely as a mediator between powerful international capital, on the one hand, and a weak and dependent local bourgeoisie, on the other. He now sees the state as the 'register of the leading edge of indigenous capital' in its assault on the barriers of capital, scale and technology of the inherited neo-colonial economy. The local bourgeoisie is said to have assumed an hegemonic place within the power-bloc controlling the state.

We are thus left with the impression that state support for the domestic bourgeoisie is the specific class project of that bourgeoisie itself, as distinct from the one of international capital. This assumes that the interests of domestic and foreign capital are significantly opposed, and that international capital has no interest in the creation of a domestic bourgeoisie. As I have tried to argue above, this position obscures the nature of the contradiction and the degree to which foreign capital depends on domestic class forces for its own penetration (partnerships and so on). How, for example, are we to understand the leading role of international finance capital (World Bank, IFC, CDC and so on) in state support schemes for domestic capital from such a perspective?

The position of Kaplinsky and Langdon is that, although the state 'is not an homogenous entity', it is likely to side with foreign capital in case of dispute with local capital. Kaplinsky goes on to demonstrate that this is so in four specific cases studied by him. Langdon argues that the state possesses relative autonomy from both local and foreign capital, based on a 'symbiosis' – or mutual interdependence among the senior state bureaucracy and political leadership, indigenous capital and foreign capital. State support for the formation of the local bourgeoisie is envisaged as long as it does not conflict with key foreign interests. While Langdon's concept of symbiosis seems more realistic than Leys' state of the local bourgeoisie, both have a conception of an hegemonic interest. In fact, Langdon's symbiosis is merely a function of the dependent nature of the domestic bourgeoisie, whether state or private. So the symbiosis is clearly internal to the structures of foreign domination. The unity of state power is thus defined in terms of this domination, not in terms of the process of capital accumulation as such.

On both sides, therefore, an unjustified emphasis is placed on the state as an instrument of 'fractional' interests at the expense of its functions as determined by the general, 'non-fractional' requirements of capital accumulation. It is only in relation to that general role, however, that we can understand its way of relating to various class forces in society, capitalist and anticapitalist, as defined by their relative strength of organisation. From such a perspective it may be easier to understand the manner in which the state is accommodating various 'fractional' pressures and demands, than from the perspective of fractional hegemony. This is, if you like, a position of 'capital logic', without, however, robbing social forces of their autonomy through class struggle and class organisation.

The weakness of Langdon's concept of symbiosis is clearly demonstrated in his inability to handle the phenomenon of the nationally-minded technocrats except from an idealist or, alternatively, very crude materialist perspective. Their progressive inclinations and potential for challenging the interest of both foreign capital and their local dependants, are seen partly as a result of their limited share in the loot derived from the symbiosis, partly as a matter of a commitment to a more genuine national development. While individual experiences and convictions no doubt will determine individual actions and commitments, we cannot understand the social role such inclinations will be allowed to play except from an understanding of their interaction with objective, materially based social forces.

Within the context of the overall logic of capital accumulation, however, the 'national' urges of these technocrats can be more easily grasped, but only, of course, if we are able to abandon a perspective where it is in the interest of capital to keep itself underdeveloped. Their bitter doses of cost-squeezing medicine may indeed be what heavily protected foreign and domestic capital require in order to be pushed over existing barriers of scale and technology. But who is actually pushing whom? Who is on what side of what contradiction? It is when we examine the political implications of this understanding of the state and the nature of the contradictions in which it is involved that the most disturbing aspects of this dependency perspective emerge.

Some Disturbing Political Implications of the Kenyan Debate

The appeal of radical underdevelopment theory to progressive intellectuals in the third world and elsewhere was the way it provided a theoretical basis for understanding the unity of the struggle against the two forces which could easily be identified as oppressing the people: imperialism, as represented by foreign capital and its military and political support system, on the one hand, and the domestic ruling class and its state institutions, on the other.

What are the political implications of the marxist-oriented critique of underdevelopment theory as well as the attempts to reassert the dependency position? The Kenyan debate can, I believe, be used to illustrate how in the course of such critique and counter critique theory is largely disarmed of its potential for providing scientific support for the ongoing revolutionary struggles of the oppressed people of the third world.

The implications of Leys' analysis seems to be that the African bourgeoisie is gradually overcoming, on its own and through its control over the state apparatus, the constraints on national capitalist development imposed by imperialism. What is the role of the revolutionary intellectual in this situation? To put his shoulder behind the wheels of 'progress' in the legitimate struggle against foreign domination? Or is it to disengage from the current struggle and wait for the real class contradictions of real capitalist development to unfold? (While perhaps in the meantime being a bit useful by monitoring these developments, for example, the growing differentiation of the peasantry or the various stages in the emergence of the African bourgeoisie.) I do not suggest that these are implications spelt out by Leys or informing his own position but merely that they may easily suggest themselves to others in this fashion.

Langdon is more explicit in his own reassertion of the dependency position. The deepening crisis of the present dependent mode of accumulation (foreign-exchange constraints, inefficiency, high costs and so on) will generate a political crisis. While it is hard to anticipate the dynamics of such a crisis, he suggests that

> It is not inconceivable that leaders of those technocrats [the progressive nationalist elements in the state apparatus] would be forced to try to widen their base of support by introducing redistribution policies that respond to urban workers and small-scale entrepreneurs, to peasants in less prosperous regions, and to the growing number of landless and unemployed in Kenya.

While this will not mean an end to international dependence, it would still be possible, according to Langdon, that such a strategy would accelerate capitalist transformation: redistribution would build a broader internal market which in turn could 'support more sustained local capital accumulation'.

The problem of this position is not its explicit reformism. Any strategy which seems to concern itself with the alleviation of the suffering of the oppressed classes must be seriously considered. The problem is its idealism, its failure to identify any objective forces which will push these 'progressive technocrats' into pursuing the interests of the oppressed classes. There are surely more logical strategies for expanding the markets for international and domestic capital as well as for increasing its efficiency and reducing its high cost structure. This could be done, for example, by increasing the rates of appropriation and exploitation in society, by pushing further its class differentiation, including the appropriation of peasants and petty producers for the purpose of expanding rural surplus and 'freeing' labour for direct subordination to capital – all consistent with the class logic of the capitalist state. It is 'progressive' only in the sense of the grim, destructive and oppressive logic of capitalist 'development'.

Any improvement in the material conditions of the oppressed classes within this process is not part of the logic of capital but as a result of the struggles of these classes to defend themselves in the face of this oppression. The preconditions and dynamics of such struggles can only be grasped from an understanding of the nature of the contradictions in which they are involved. The structuralist, dependency perspective with its preoccupation with sectoral imbalances and obstructed linkages is barren of any attempt to identify or relate to such contradictions.

While having dropped the idealism of this dependency position, the marxist-oriented anti-dependency stand has not succeeded in transcending this misplacement of contradiction. At the theoretical level (and I do not suggest that wrong theory is the ultimate cause) the principal expression of this failure is the misplaced preoccupation with the contradiction between national and international capital, without placing this contradiction within an attempt to understand the over-riding logic of capital accumulation and the nature of the class contradictions and class struggles which it generates. In my initial summary of Leys' position, I quoted his view that each national case must be examined at three levels: the level of the logic of capital; the level of capitalist geopolitics (imperialism); and the level of class relations and class struggles.

His decision to pursue the analysis, as he himself suggests, at the last level only, despite the explicit recognition of the interconnectedness of all of them, seems to be the main reason for Leys' inability to transcend an underdevelopment problematic, which he rejects in principle, and the political implications of which he is obviously concerned about. As a result, we get a class analysis which lacks foundation in either the analysis of the logic of capital or in an attempt to integrate 'capitalist geopolitics' (= imperialism) into such analysis. It is not surprising that such a method may result in misplaced identification of contradictions and inability to transcend the fixation of underdevelopment theory with the absence of a 'national' bourgeoisie.

Bibliographic Note

This paper is intended to be the first instalment of a three-way discussion of capitalist transformation in Africa. Subsequent sections will attempt to reconstruct an alternative theoretical approach out of the principal elements of the present critique and to apply this theoretical understanding to the case of Nigeria.

Works by Leys referred to are *Underdevelopment in Kenya, the Political-Economy of Neo-Colonialism*, (London, Heinemann, 1975) and 'Capital Accumulation, Class Formation and Dependency', *Socialist*

Register 1978. Works by Langdon are 'Industry and Capitalism in Kenya – Contributions to a Debate', paper presented to the Conference on the African Bourgeoisie, Dakar, December 1980 and *Multinational Corporations in the Political Economy of Kenya,* (Macmillan, 1980); and by Kaplinsky, 'Capitalist Accumulation in the Periphery: the Kenyan Case', *Review of African Political Economy*, No. 17, 1980. Other references include R. Brenner, 'The Origins of Capitalist Development – a Critique of Neo-Smithian Marxism', *New Left Review*, No. 104, 1977; A. Phillips, 'The Concept of "Development",' *Review of African Political Economy*, No.8, 1977; and N. Swainson, *The Development of Corporate Capitalism in Kenya,* (London, Heinemann, 1980).

Editors' Note: This paper was also presented at a conference in Dakar on 'The African Bourgeoisie: The Development of Capitalism in Nigeria, Kenya and the Ivory Coast', 2–4 December 1980, sponsored by the Joint Committee on African Studies of the SSRC(USA) and the American Council of Learned Societies, in conjunction with CODESRIA, Dakar. It was written before the publication of the debate between Kaplinsky, Henley and Leys in the *Review* No.17 and the author has not been able to revise it in the light of that debate. We believe that the argument pursued here goes beyond that debate and have therefore obtained the author's permission to publish it with only minor editorial changes.

6 BJÖRN BECKMAN
Imperialism &
the 'National Bourgeoisie'   [1981]

This article takes up some of the major issues surrounding the development/ underdevelopment debate, as taking place in Kenya and Nigeria in particular. While underdevelopment theory as exemplified in Amin and Frank has been found wanting, the 'return to Marx' via analyses of the internationalisation of capital and class formation in the periphery has not answered the questions raised by under-development theory because it has not made an adequate analysis of imperialism, one which integrates the study of class formation in the periphery with its effects on the system as a whole and vice versa. An analysis of the Nigerian case shows how this might be done. Most importantly it shows how imperialism protects local bourgeoisies from the demands of the oppressed classes, while local bourgeoisies through control of the state provide monopoly conditions for imperialist expansion.

This is a follow-up to my contribution to the Kenya debate (*ROAPE* 19). It is set within the framework of the argument between underdevelopment theory and its critics. The Kenyan debate revealed the basic weaknesses of the current dependency/anti-dependency polemic. Here I formulate some propositions which seem to follow out of the critique. They relate in particular to the relationship between imperialism and the domestic bourgeoisie. I argued that this was an area where both parties in the Kenyan debate tended to misconstrue the nature of contradictions. On the one side, we found the domestic bourgeoisie reduced to an appendage of imperialist-dominated stagnation. On the other side, we were shown the prospects of the domestic bourgeoisie asserting itself in opposition to imperialism and thereby allowing for some degree of 'real' capitalist development. Underlying both positions was an assumption that there will be no real capitalist development unless there is a national bourgeoisie. The basic difference was that one side saw evidence of such a class emerging and doing its job while the other saw nothing of the sort. I argued that the evidence was neither here nor there (it could be interpreted both ways) and the inconclusiveness was caused by the phantom of real capitalist development obscuring the capitalist development actually taking place.

Imperialist Lackeys or National Liberators?

Both the Kenyan and Nigerian debates relate to problems in the marxist tradition of evaluating the character of the domestic bourgeoisie in colonies, semi-colonies and ex-colonies in the epoch of imperialism. The issue at stake is whether the domestic bourgeoisie of this period is a progressive force capable of promoting the development of productive forces and opposing imperialism in the interest of national development or a reactionary force collaborating with imperialism for the oppression and retardation of development. Seen from the perspective of the struggle for national liberation and socialism there are two types of important implications. If the domestic bourgeoisie is an anti-imperialist force the struggle will be a two-staged one; first *with* this 'national' bourgeoisie against imperialism for national liberation; second, *against* the same class for socialism. On the other hand, if the domestic bourgeoisie is an agent of imperialism, the struggle for national liberation must be waged also against this class. The struggle for socialism and the struggle for national liberation thus coincide. Similarly, if the domestic bourgeoisie is capable of developing the productive forces, the class struggle would take on a character specific to the capitalist mode of production. If not, the anti-imperialist struggle would create conditions for bypassing the capitalist stage.

Concrete struggles have not, of course, been pursued in these abstract terms but from the evaluation of the balance of forces at work in a specific situation. The ambiguous character of the domestic bourgeoisie has often been stressed, distinguishing between comprador and national elements on objective as well as subjective grounds. Political strategies have aimed at linking up with patriotic or national democratic elements and isolating and combating those likely to collaborate with imperialism. However, the influence of theory and doctrine has no doubt been important in structuring the reading and interpretation of concrete situations.

In Nigeria, as in many other parts of Africa, a main source of theoretical influence in recent years has been underdevelopment theory as represented by Frank and Amin, popularised by Walter Rodney (1972) and reinforced in important respects by Fanon's earlier devastating exposure of a subservient, imitative, corrupt, parasitic and unproductive 'national bourgeoisie'. But, as the Nigerian debate demonstrates, such underdevelopment theory is selectively incorporated into the ideological arsenal of the aspiring domestic bourgeoisie itself. Its radical critics are threatened by co-optation onto the platform of bourgeois nationalism by which sections of the ruling class seek to legitimise their ascendancy.

The Domestic Bourgeoisie as a Leading Force

Bourgeois nationalism is a crucial political force in the third world today. It plays a central role in the structuring of the world capitalist economy, including the development of productive forces in the periphery. It is therefore vital to understand the class character of this social force, its relationship to imperialism, as well as the nature of national development it generates. It is a force in ascendancy, not in decay. It is growing in strength and independence.

In this situation, the notion of comprador, agent and lackey may obscure the independent sources of power and strength of this class in its own societies and in the world economy. It is often 'progressive' in traditional marxist terms of advancing productive forces. On the other hand, it is clearly not a class of national liberators, in the sense of being an anti-imperialist force capable of overcoming the injustices and oppression created by imperialism. On the contrary, this class continues to be part and parcel of imperialist domination and oppression directed against the masses of the third world. Its alliance with imperialism makes it in fact into one of the most brutally oppressive and unreforming capitalist ruling classes the world has seen so far.

The essence of continued underdevelopment in the third world is not the inability of imperialism and such 'national' bourgeoisies to develop productive forces, including capital goods industries, sectoral linkages, and the production of sophisticated goods for the world market. It is the ability of this transnational class alliance to protect its monopoly profits against popular pressures which may otherwise have forced the domestic ruling class to concede social and democratic reforms. This obstacle to reform is the source of sharpening cleavages and contradictions, but, for the same reason, also the source of revolutionary change. Let me try to indicate some of the main elements which constitute the basis of this position.

Marxism & Underdevelopment

The key role attributed to the presence or absence of a 'national' bourgeoisie in the dependency/anti-dependency polemic is closely related to assumptions about what imperialism is and what it is up to. A common misconception is that imperialism, as incarnated primarily in transnational corporations and foreign capital, is against capitalist development in the periphery. Historically, there is of course much evidence which shows how foreign economic and political domination has prevented the establishment of manufacturing industry despite the existence of large domestic markets. We know how colonial monopolists blocked the advance of indigenous trading houses by political means. Similarly, colonial settlers sought to block the development of commercial agriculture, not just be ousting indigenes from the land but by forbidding the cultivation of certain commercial crops. The destruction of domestic textile industry by state-supported foreign monopolists is of course common knowledge.

On the other hand, post-war industrialisation in the third world has been pioneered by foreign firms. Unilever's United Africa Company turned from produce buying to manufacturing in Nigeria well before there was any real nationalist pressure for such transition. Since independence, the Ivory Coast has experienced a significant capitalist development in both agriculture and industry under the auspices of French capital. So what is imperialism up to? What are the limits to capitalist transformation under imperialism?

Underdevelopment theory has provided a series of ad hoc positions which have had to be successively revised. The original position that imperialism was opposed to industrialisation in the third world, has to be abandoned. The next defence line was that only import-substituting industry was compatible with imperialist interests. Real industry (whatever that is) and capital goods industry in particular was the reserve of the metropoles, ensuring continued dependence and subservience. The emergence of aggressive export industrialisation in some parts of the third world was treated as exceptional or enclave phenomena. The final revision relates to the continued technological monopoly of the metropoles through patents, licensing agreements etc., ensuring an all-pervasive dependence. The constraints imposed on the development of capitalism by such dependence can be easily demonstrated as it affects choice of technology, product designs, etc. However, the constraints relate to the form and direction of this capitalist development rather than to the development as such.

A basic weakness of underdevelopment theory as a contribution to a marxist-oriented argument was its failure to relate systematically to the marxist theories of capitalist development and imperialism. The imperialism of underdevelopment theory is often either a general ideological category of no analytical consequence or something reduced to what some specific actors, foreign firms, the US government are doing.

There was little effort to root a discussion of the impact produced by foreign economic and political domination in studies of the laws of motion of capitalism on the world scale. The problem, of course, was that marxist political economy, being essentially a theory of the capitalist mode of production, had paid little attention to the manner in which 'peripheral' societies were incorporated and transformed by capitalism. A major exception is Lenin's *The Development of Capitalism in Russia.* It was primarily concerned, however, with demonstrating that capitalist relations of production were actually developing in the various sectors of the Russian economy and that a home market for large-scale industry (and thereby a modern working class) was being formed. He was certainly not out to show that capitalism did not develop in Russia because of the domination of foreign capital. His work on imperialism, on the other hand, paid little attention to the likely course of capitalist development in the semi-colonies and colonies being shared out between the major imperialist powers. The subsequent pronouncements and discussions in the Comintern were marked by the conjunctures of the political struggles. Standpoints were taken and abandoned without producing much of lasting value in terms of scientific analysis.

When underdevelopment theory emerged in response to the demand for radical theory created by the upsurge of anti-colonial and anti-imperialist struggles in the post-Second World War period it had thus little directly applicable theory to draw on. It shared this lack of solid basis in marxist theory with the simultaneous effort within Soviet marxism to articulate its own response to third world struggles. The effort to legitimise theories of non-capitalist development with reference to Lenin's pronouncements on developments in Soviet Asia did not strengthen their theoretical foundation and was essentially irrelevant to the problem of understanding imperialism and its relationship to development in the third world.

Underdevelopment theory and the theories of non-capitalist development (later 'socialist-oriented development') shared assumptions about imperialism blocking capitalist development and therefore creating the conditions for a transition to socialism on an anti-imperialist platform. The view of the domestic bourgeoisie, however, differed radically. While underdevelopment theory saw the domestic bourgeoisie as the lackeys of imperialism and a primary target for revolutionary struggle, Soviet marxists were more concerned with its progressive, anti-imperialist features. Patriotic or 'national democratic' elements were expected to link up with popular forces using state capital as a platform for industrialisation leading to the strengthening of the working class element in the anti-imperialist alliance. Support from socialist countries would facilitate gradual disengagement from the world capitalist system and thus enhance the prospects of a transition to socialism.

Both positions emphasise the deficiency of the domestic bourgeoisie, underdevelopment theory its total subservience to imperialism, Soviet marxism its weakness as a result of low development of productive forces consequent on imperialist domination. In the latter case, it is the combination of such weakness and the contradiction between national development and imperialism which makes the aspiring bourgeoisie into a potential anti-imperialist force. Underdevelopment theory arrives at the opposite conclusions from roughly the same definition of the situation.

From the point of view of marxist theory, the main weakness of the Soviet position is the subjective character of the 'patriotic' or 'national democratic' elements. The material basis for their readiness to oppose imperialism in any fundamental respect is not clear. As far as I can see, the underlying assumption must be that they are unable to realise their aspirations as a fully fledged bourgeoise because of imperialist domination. It is easy to see why this may encourage state capitalist solutions. It is less easy to see the socialist-oriented potential of such solutions. In this respect, underdevelopment theory appears to be more materialist in identifying the interests of the domestic bourgeoisie with imperialism. Both lines, however, fail to define the scope of national bourgeois emancipation within the framework of imperialism.

The rapid development of marxist scholarship in the universities of the capitalist countries in the 1970s has created a basis for overcoming the theoretical weaknesses of underdevelopment theory. Rethinking has also been encouraged by the way in which its positions have been co-opted by bourgeois nationalism for its own purposes. Similarly, the disappointing outcome of the 'non-capitalist' experiences of regimes such as those of Nasser, Nkrumah, Modibo Keita, and Sekou Touré, have encouraged Soviet marxists to study more closely the class basis of nationalist forces.

Great strides forward have been taken in the study of the restructuring of capitalism at the centre and much solid work has been produced on the internationalisation of capital, including the growth of export enclaves and industrial free zones. Similarly, in the spirit of Lenin's study of Russia, a growing number of solid empirical studies show the spread of capitalist relations of production in agriculture, the changing organic composition of capital, the growth of industry, the bourgeoisies and the proletariat.

To certain marxists this reorientation brings comfort. Things are back to normal. They can return to the task in which they are most skilled and where they can draw on the most authoritative models, that is, the study of capitalist development and the restructuring of social relations of production to which it gives rise. The confusion brought by underdevelopment theory with its lack of theoretical rigour and its ideological concept of development can be left behind.

But has underdevelopment theory really been transcended? Does the combination of these new studies of the internationalisation of capital and the study of class formation in third world countries really answer the questions posed by underdevelopment theory? I do not think so. A major problem is that they are not really combined. The studies of the internationalisation of capital are just as centro-centric as was Lenin's theory of imperialism. They suggest much about the laws of motion at the centre and the international movements of capital to which they give rise. They tell us less about the way such internationalisation interacts with the development of capitalism at the periphery, except in terms of penetration and imposition. The role of class struggles in the third world in structuring the preconditions for the development of the system as a whole is given little attention. On the other hand, students find it difficult to integrate into their studies of concrete third world societies an understanding of transformations at the world level. At that end, imperialism remains the external agents, the foreign firms.

The failure to locate contradictions and class struggles in a particular social formation in the context of the development of the mode of production, which is a global process, is clearly revealed in the Kenyan debate. It becomes particularly debilitating when the focus is on the relationship between the domestic bourgeoisie and foreign capital. Neither the new study of imperialism (as the internationalisation of capital) nor the new interest in accumulation and class formation in the periphery provide what underdevelopment theory seems to offer third world radicals: a theoretical platform for the combined struggle against imperialism and the domestic ruling class. The platform itself may have been undermined, its deficiencies exposed, but many will continue to cling to it, as long as the alternatives offered seem to be unable to address themselves to the strategic issues at stake.

Those issues are not defined by academics but by political forces to which academics can choose to relate or not relate. Let me first summarise what I believe are the issues.

Under growing marxist impact academic studies on imperialism and the third world have shifted the emphasis from underdevelopment to development. However, the new 'internationalisation of capital' and 'capital accumulation' seem embarrassingly weak in inspiring useful political analysis, as compared to less scientific notions of imperialism and national development. Some of the resentment against the ascendancy of marxist theory in this field is no doubt caused by those who have an interest in keeping the distinction between (petty) bourgeois nationalism and anti-imperialism blurred. But there is more to it than that.

In order to judge, we need to go back to the substantive political content of the underdevelopment position. Academics may have contributed in articulating it but the tremendous diffusion of its perspective can only be understood as a response to specific historical experiences and the development of social forces at the world level, including the realities of colonialism and neo-colonialism, the rise of socialist countries and armed liberation struggles. It is not a specific political line with a uniform theoretical basis. It is a position held by millions of anti-imperialist militants most of whom may never have heard of or read the works of André Gunder Frank or Samir Amin.

The position reads roughly as follows and I draw primarily on the prevailing radical view at Nigerian universities: the Nigerian people suffer from the continued and intensified domination by imperialism. Only a tiny minority benefit. Nothing substantial is done to change the backward conditions which characterise the material situation of the masses. Multinational corporations and other agents of imperialism aggravate the situation by distorting the use of national resources for the benefit of the imperialist countries and their local allies. The domestic bourgeoisie is essentially in the service of imperialism or is out to enrich itself at the expense of the people. Real national development, in the interest of the masses, can only come about through a combined struggle for socialism and national development. Socialism means in the first place socialist planning to direct the utilisation of national resources towards the eradication of mass poverty. National liberation means a radical restructuring of links with the world economy so as to allow for self-centred, nationally integrated development.

To my understanding, nothing in the recent marxist critique of underdevelopment theory justifies the revision or abandoning of such a position. The justified critique of the scientific basis on which such a position has drawn merely suggests the need to look for more adequate theory. It is in the context of that search that the present discussion of imperialism and national bourgeoisie is pursued. I suggest that marxism still provides an appropriate point of departure. The gap in marxist analysis which underdevelopment theory sought to fill is still there. Marxism has yet to provide a scientifically adequate and politically appropriate analysis of imperialism, capitalist development and underdevelopment, as it affects the third world. Why the gap came into being in the first place is easy to comprehend in view of the Eurocentred *political* horizon of classical marxism. There is nothing Eurocentred, however, as far as I can see, in the basic theory and methodology of marxism which could prevent it from becoming a powerful scientific tool in the struggle against imperialism and underdevelopment.

The Nigerian Debate

In the Nigerian context, a natural point of departure for discussing the domestic bourgeoisie and its relationship to imperialism is Segun Osoba's widely circulated lecture on 'The deepening crisis of the Nigerian national bourgeoisie', also published in this *Review* (No.13). It is a powerful formulation of an underdevelopment position. Its conclusions are revolutionary. The national bourgeoisie has to be stoutly opposed and overthrown because 'literally it is good for nothing' (except, of course, as a predatory agent of imperialism!). The manner in which Osoba arrives at this conclusion, however, suffers from some of the weakness endemic to this tradition, thereby undermining the conclusion itself.

This is what he proposes: 'It is objectively in the interest of our national bourgeoisie to be able to create a relatively independent and autonomous domestic capitalist economic order in Nigeria'. If they did so, 'they might be able to retain all, or at least most, of the surplus value generated in the Nigerian economy'. The bourgeoisie is well aware of the continued havoc caused by imperialism. Its leading members make the correct diagnosis. Osoba quotes Waziri Ibrahim, the millionaire politician, and the former head of state, General Obasanjo, at length. But they are incapable of changing themselves from mere agents of imperialism.

Why is this so? First, it is the international division of labour. 'In effect, the role predetermined for us within the framework of the global imperialist economy is that of an exporter of raw mineral and agricultural materials and an importer of finished or semi-finished manufactured goods.' To challenge this world order is highly dangerous and would involve sharp retaliatory measures. The bourgeoisie, despite its objective interests, does not have the guts ('revolutionary discipline and a self-sacrificing nobility') to mobilise the people to this end. The most Nigeria can count on is the multiplying of assembly-type industries, 'where nothing of consequence is fabricated locally and the inflated prices of whose inferior products are protected by high tariff walls'.

The sheer profitability of the role as a commission agent for international capital, also prevents the bourgeoisie from emancipating itself and the nation. It is also unable to unite within itself in defence of national interests because of rampant sectionalism. Its collaboration with imperialism places it in contradiction to the people of Nigeria. The end result is a disastrous failure to 'uphold and defend the genuine interests of their people, nothing, literally nothing, really works in the country'. Osoba paints a picture of urban congestion, scandalous opulence and stinking poverty,

> the chaos, misery and disaster that they, the leaders, have inflicted on their people through their intellectual and physical laziness, their lack of patriotism, their indiscipline and their moral and spiritual decadence...

Despite the strong condemnation of the Nigerian bourgeoisie and its despicable behaviour as an agent of imperialism, Osoba's position may easily provide an ideological platform for the rising Nigerian bourgeoisie which has no inhibitions in using nationalist and anti-imperialist rhetoric. First of all, the contradiction which he sees between the bourgeoisie and the oppressed classes in Nigeria is seen as a function of its role of imperialist agent, not of a bourgeoisie. In fact, we are given the impression that if the bourgeoisie pursued its objective interests as a national ruling class it would be able to gain in stability and legitimacy and the people would benefit from efficient government, less congestion, less squalor, more real industry, etc. Objectively, the bourgeoisie and the people are on the same side of the contradiction with imperialism.

The essence of Osoba's case against the bourgeoisie is that it is not national enough, that it is comprador. While this may be true, the case for an anti-bourgeois revolution hinges on the inability of the bourgeoisie to become more 'national' and on the relevance of the criteria used to measure the distinction.

The primary criterion in Osoba's argument is obviously the degree of subservience to imperialism, its significance being measured in terms of its effects on national development. Here two factors are particularly stressed, the siphoning off of national wealth and stunted industrialisation.

Osoba's argument is vulnerable on both counts. There is a heavy outflow of legal and illegal profits to foreign capital which a more efficient and nationalist government could reduce. Still, partly through nationalisations and partly through increases in oil prices the government has had exceptional resources at its disposal for national development. Yet this massive expenditure has done little to remove mass poverty. It is generally agreed that social injustices have been greatly enhanced. If the government had been able to retain more funds, would this situation have significantly changed?

Assuming that the government also had been more efficient, what could have been expected? Perhaps a more rapid development of new state capitals and the new federal capital, more efficient airports and telecommunications, less port congestion, better urban traffic systems, some more and better equipped universities and hospitals. In production, the steel works might have been completed much earlier, the plans for petro-chemical industries and gas liquifying plants, long on the drafting board, might actually have been realised, more Bakolori dams and irrigation projects established.

The point is that the profit outflow of the inefficiency argument does not really enter into a discussion of the nature of national development which actually takes place and its class character. What is it that a national bourgeoisie would like to do if it had more money (less profit outflow) and was less dependent on imperialism? Or the other way round, what is it that imperialism prevents the national bourgeoisie from doing by keeping it dependent?

Clearly, it would be in the interest of foreign capital if the Nigerian bourgeoisie was more efficient, if there was less congestion, and telephones worked. Surely, West German firms would not mind building more Delta Steel Works, and the Italian ones would similarly be happy to multiply the number of large irrigation schemes in the north.

This takes us to the question of industrial structure which is central to much under-development theory. The root cause, we learn, of why the Nigerian bourgeoisie is unprogressive is that it takes the side of imperialism in obstructing real industrial development. This point is argued, as we have seen, with reference to a global division of labour, where imperialism is against the development of petrochemical, chemical, steel, agro-allied industries, etc.

> It should be clear for all except the Nigerian political decision-makers to see that for Western capitalist entrepreneurs to respond to such demands by us would mean facing their lucrative export market in a wide array of products including processed food, petroleum products and synthetic fibres.

But if the absence of slow development of such industries is the essence of the contradiction with imperialism, where should the anti-imperialist intellectuals find themselves? I doubt that such analysis would prompt them to join the organised struggles of the masses to overthrow the 'national bourgeoisie'. A more rational (and certainly more comfortable) line would be to join ranks with the numerous Nigerian technocrats and administrators who are presently engaged in planning and negotiating for increasingly sophisticated industrial investments in the very lines argued by such scholars as being beyond the entitlement of Nigeria in the international division of labour.

Despite the overt anti-bourgeois orientation of this type of critique of the present order, it fails to transcend bourgeois nationalist thinking in important respects. This is because the barriers to national development which are identified, are not beyond the scope of bourgeois strategies. The implications are certainly not anti-imperialist in the sense that they confront the contradictions between imperialism and the oppressed classes in Nigeria. But even in bourgeois nationalist terms its anti-imperialism is undermined by the manner in which the contradiction between imperialism and national capitalist development is being misconstrued. Rather than being an anti-imperialist force, such radicalism may in fact contribute ideologically in preparing the conditions for further integration in the world capitalist economy and for further penetration by foreign capital.

The Ascendancy of the African Bourgeoisie

The bourgeoisie of the third world is coming of age. The material basis of this bourgeoisie is partly the sale of primary commodities in the world market, and to a much lesser but growing extent, the export of manufactured goods. But more important for the rise of this class is the growth of home markets for both domestic agriculture and manufacturing industry, sparked off and partly sustained by production for the world market but developing on its own momentum. The compradors who at an earlier point dominated the class outlook of the bourgeoisie are superseded by bourgeois elements with direct responsibility for owning, planning and managing capitalist production. State capital performs a leading role in this transition in many countries, including Nigeria.

Far from being a force in opposition to imperialism, this bourgeoisie is a product of imperialism. It continues to develop in close alliance with foreign capital. It seeks partnership in order to ensure access to technology and management. In return, it offers access to markets and investment opportunities as well as political protection.

Partnership does not imply harmony or identity out of interest. The parties struggle between themselves to get the most out of the bargain. Foreign firms capitalise on superior 'know-how' and resources. But they are not alone in the market. Competition restrains their bargaining power. The local partner capitalises on territorial political monopoly, its knowledge of local conditions. There is much cheating and subterfuge. But it is a profitable arrangement for both parties. Corruption may cause profits to disappear from official accounts. It does not mean that production is not profitable for the local bourgeoisie. The national, territorial and political basis of its bargaining power may justify that we speak of this bourgeoisie as 'national', as distinct from a foreign or international one. National or nationalist arguments are used to strengthen its bargaining position.

The national issue enters as well when it comes to competition between foreign and local firms, for market shares as well as for financial and state patronage. Domestically based firms will use national arguments to fend off competition or cut in on the markets of foreign firms. The national factor involved may be spurious. The 'Buy Nigerian'argument benefits firms like the Peugeot plant in Kaduna importing CKD cars ('completely knocked down') *by air* from France. However, the national factor is real in capitalist competition everywhere. Contradictions take on a national ideological form.

It is misleading to speak of a 'symbiotic' relationship between the domestic bourgeoisie and international capital. It obscures the way in which capital is fractionalised and the importance of fractional struggles and rivalries.

While recognising the existence of domestic capital and domestic bourgeois class interests in this sense, it is, however, a more serious mistake to assume that the emancipation of this class is in opposition to imperialism, despite the occasional anti-imperialist fervour of its agitation for better bargains or for national monopoly protection.

The basic misconception is that imperialism is opposed to capitalist development or that imperialist interests are served better by a weak and inefficient comprador-type bourgeoisie than by a strong, efficient domestic bourgeoisie.

Imperialism & Capitalist Development

It is time that we examine more closely what imperialism is and what it is doing, in order to be able to judge the way it relates to the domestic bourgeoisie. Imperialism, in the marxist tradition, refers to the international form of advanced capitalism. The central feature is the degree to which capital has been concentrated and centralised, the way finance capital has acquired a separate and leading role, the crucial importance of monopolistic arrangements to protect profits, and the increasing role of the state in providing the appropriate political (and military) conditions for such monopoly. The purpose of Lenin's analysis was to explain the material basis of the intra-imperialist rivalries which resulted in the First World War. It was a struggle for control over raw materials, markets and investment outlets. Struggle for colonies was one element in this but by no means the most important. Colonialism in this context served to bolster profits and thus strengthen the ability of the ruling class to pacify the working class at home by wage increases and social reforms. The relative contribution of colonies and other dependencies in this respect has been disputed but does not need to concern us here. The important thing is that this analysis had little to say directly about the impact of imperialism on the development of capitalism in the territories brought under its control.

The imperialism of underdevelopment theory, bent on blocking the development of capitalism in the periphery, has little basis either in Marx's analysis of capitalist development or in Lenin's analysis of imperialism. The underdevelopment version of the relationship between imperialism and capitalist development, on the other hand, drew on the concrete historical experiences of colonial or semi-colonial oppression and exploitation. There was little attempt to connect such interpretation with marxist theory.

If the summary of the 'Leninist' position given above is accepted we must ask how raw materials, markets and investment outlets are best secured by means of state-supported monopolistic arrangements (in the context of fierce intra-imperialist rivalry) at particular times and places, and the roles assigned for the domestic bourgeoisie. Take Nigeria. The securing of peasant produce and mineral exports under colonial military occupation was based on an alliance between a colonial bureaucracy and traditional or aristocratic elements. To protect such an alliance it was necessary to suppress the emergence of a domestic bourgeoisie. But there were limits to the usefulness of such suppression as accumulation in commercial agriculture proceeded. Commercial bourgeois elements rose to 'threaten' the monopolies of colonial firms. Old class allies were abandoned in favour of new ones.

Colonial monopoly was a temporary arrangement. Fortunes shifted in the continued intra-imperialist struggles. Imperialist relations were multilateralised. Rearrangements were speeded up by the interaction of such shifts at the international level and the emergence of bourgeois class forces within the colonial economy. The growing centralisation of peasant surplus under national control broadened radically the scope for accumulation by foreign and local capital. Imperialist competition made investment in local manufacturing a necessity in order to secure control over markets. The investments, in turn, required political protection to secure access to imported inputs and the outflow of profits. Partnership was sought with state institutions and private Nigerian businessmen. International finance institutions, acting as the state institutions of multilateralised imperialism, played an active role in supporting the state and the domestic bourgeoisie. Economic infrastructure expanded, a national banking system, a stock exchange, schools of management, market research institutes, financial newspapers, in all, the entire paraphernalia of the capitalist system emerge. The oil boom gives a powerful push. The market expands and the bargaining power of the bourgeoisie is greatly strengthened.

Foreign firms compete among themselves on several lines, first of all on the basis of individual firms in the same line of business; secondly on national lines as far as national monopoly protection can be secured from home countries (tied aid, state credits, trade agreements, economic unions etc.); thirdly on the basis of business sectors with different interests because of different positions in the production chain. Those, for example, who buy unprocessed commodities for the metropolitan processing industry have interests contradictory to those who trade in processing technology. Management consultancy firms compete with those who sell packages where ownership and control of management are closely tied.

It is within this competitive international environment that the domestic bourgeoisie pushes ahead, using its political monopoly to strike bargains with international capital. It is not a zero sum game where my gain is your loss. In pushing ahead it strengthens its own position but advances simultaneously the interests of international capital. Its own capacity to generate appropriate conditions for accumulation is enhanced to the benefit of capital in general.

The local bourgeoisie assists international capital to overcome contradictions which have been built into the imperialist system. Crude forms of imperialism, for example, may profit from extracting value from pre-capitalist forms of production. The political form of appropriation (e.g. alliance with feudal elements) may assist effectively in tapping this source of value. At a later point, however, such political arrangements may be obstructive of more advanced forms of appropriation and transformation on capitalist lines. Here bourgeois state intervention may assist in destroying social barriers (communal property relations, etc.) which shield the peasantry from such transformations.

Similarly, highly protected import-substituting industrialisation may provide adequate monopoly profits to a point. However, it easily hits market ceilings related to high costs and expensive products. A bourgeois state may perform the double service of depressing costs (e.g. by suppressing labour) and expanding markets (e.g. by raising the purchasing power of high income groups).

The more advanced the forms of appropriation by foreign capital, the greater the need for a strong domestic bourgeoisie capable of managing capitalist state institutions. Peasant produce can be appropriated under crude commercial and political arrangements. The production of manufactured goods for a highly competitive world market, on the other hand, may need more advanced capitalist class institutions.

In order to gain the territorial protection of a strong local bourgeoisie, foreign capital is prepared to make major concessions at the level where it finds itself in contradiction with this class. This, I believe, is the perspective from which to understand the politics of 'indigenisation' in Nigeria and elsewhere. It has been suggested that foreign firms were willing to tolerate a high degree of indigenisation because they knew how to dodge or circumvent the new regulations. While there may be much truth in this, the need to make real concessions does not only reflect the actual strength of the Nigerian bourgeoisie but also the need to strengthen it.

Imperialist concern with building up the domestic bourgeoisie is also reflected in the numerous schemes for training, financing and advising local 'entrepreneurs', first mostly private, but also increasingly state. The World Bank, including the International Finance Corporation, has played a crucial role in national 'development companies' which perform such functions (in Nigeria, the NIDB and the NNDC). Bilateral aid institutions are also active in this field of forging international class alliances.

Apart from building up the members and institutions of the bourgeoisie, such world development bodies concern themselves with wider political conditions necessary for the growth and survival of the class. The intense preoccupation of the World Bank with the Nigerian middle peasantry ('integrated rural development') should be understood not only in terms of the commercial potential of this stratum but also of the need to stabilise the rural class basis of an industrialising bourgeoisie at the national level.

Imperialism needs a domestic bourgeoisie. It does not mean that the latter always or mostly performs efficiently or to the liking of foreign capital. It may even develop into a major stumbling block. In its nationalist enthusiasm or greed it may greatly overestimate its own capacity and tax excessively the patience of its foreign partners. The fact that it does not perform well in the interest of foreign capital does not mean that it performs in the interest of the nation. It is not its nationalism as such which provides the stumbling block to imperialism but its inefficient performance as a capitalist ruling class. In such a situation, the domestic bourgeoisie, not imperialism, may be the obstacle to the development of productive forces. Imperialist intervention (e.g. IMF & Co. in Zaire) may thus be an attempt to reform such an obstructive and inefficient class and its state institutions.

Much inefficiency, on the other hand, is the result of the very mode of imperialist intervention. The way foreign firms, for example, bribe their way through Nigerian state institutions to overcome 'bottlenecks' leads to major irrationalities in the allocation of resources. The resulting disturbances in production may be harmful to the overall interests of foreign capital.

This takes us finally to the contradictory character of imperialism and the role of the national bourgeoisie within those contradictions. It is here we can reassert the link between imperialism and some of the backward features of third world capitalism associated with the notion of underdevelopment.

Imperialism, National Bourgeoisie & Underdevelopment: Conclusions

Imperialism is both reactionary and progressive. I am now speaking only of its role in the development of productive forces. Certain unprogressive features originate in monopoly. Monopoly gives the capitalist an escape route from the iron law of competition which forces him constantly to advance the productive forces in order to survive. But monopoly is rarely complete. Competition continues in monopolistic forms. Imperialism, however, means the backing of monopoly interests by the military and political power of advanced state institutions in a highly unevenly developed world capitalist system. The essence of imperialism is political:

> the policy of conquest which financial capital pursues in the struggles for markets, for the sources of raw material, and for places in which capital can be invested (Bukharin & Preobrazhensky 1919).

Imperialism is concerned with territorial monopoly through political (or military) means. The empirical study of imperialism in the third world today should therefore be the study of the manner in which state power is used to protect the monopoly interests of international capital. The relationship between imperialism and 'underdevelopment' is therefore the extent to which such state protection holds back the development of the productive forces. The domestic bourgeoisie through its control over state power plans a strategic role in providing the territorial monopoly conditions for imperialism and is therefore pivotal in the maintenance of such imperialist-generated aspects of underdevelopment.

But it is not only the domestic bourgeoisie which provides monopoly protection for international capital. It is also the other way round. The political monopoly of the former is reinforced and protected internationally by imperialism. This enhances the reactionary features of this class at the expense of its progressive ones. The advancement of productive forces is not just a result of the competition between capitalists. It is also the outcome of the class struggle. As workers struggle to improve their conditions capitalists are forced to introduce more efficient machines which can reduce the need for direct labour power. In this way the capitalist can either block improvements in the workers' conditions (the threat of redundancy) or he must reduce the damage to his competitive strength caused by concessions to the workers.

The reactionary character of imperialism in this respect comes from its way of protecting the local bourgeoisie and its state institutions from the demands of the oppressed classes. The repressive capacity of the state is enhanced. It is under less obligation to undertake social and political reforms to pacify popular forces which may threaten accumulation and class appropriation. The brutal, predatory, and oppressive aspects of capitalist development are intensified.

Bibliographic Note

This paper was originally read at the annual conference of the Nigerian Political Science Association, Kano, April 1981. It is a development of the argument presented in the *Review* No. l9 (Björn Beckman, 'Imperialism and Capitalist Transformation: A Critique of a Kenyan Debate') which in turn related to the debate on Kenya in the *Review* No. 17. For references to the contributions by Leys, Kaplinsky, Langdon and others to that debate, see No. 19, p. 62. See also A. Phillips, 'The Concept of Development', *Review of African Political Economy* No. 8, 1977. For references to the literature on 'non-capitalist development', see Mai Palmberg (ed.), *Problems of Socialist Orientation in Africa*, Uppsala, 1978. For a major radical Nigerian text see Ola Oni and Bade Onimode, *Economic Development of Nigeria: The Socialist Alternative*, Ibadan, 1975. Important contributions from a historical materialist perspective, avoiding the fallacies of the underdevelopment approach, have been made by Eskor Toyo, for example, in his 'National interest and structural contradictions in the Nigerian economy' (Paper read at ABU, Zaria, February 1980). Segun Osoba's paper discussed here was also originally read at ABU, in 1978.) Walter Rodney's influential book is *How Europe Underdeveloped Africa*, London, 1972.

7

BJÖRN BECKMAN
Whose State?
State & Capitalist Development in Nigeria   [1982–3]

General issues raised by the author's two previous contributions to *ROAPE* (in Nos.19 and 22), are here applied to an analysis of the character of the Nigerian state and the nature of its interrelationships with capital foreign, local and capital-in-general. Oversimplifications that blame 'underdevelopment' on international capital working through a straight neo-colonial state, and those that see a national bourgeoisie able to use state power against imperialism to promote national capitalist development, are rejected as at best part-truths. The state is seen as also and primarily an instrument for promoting the conditions for accumulation for capital in general. Further specification of the nature of the state depends on an analysis of the class struggle such activities inevitably involve, in their particular Nigerian context.

The Nigerian state is busily promoting capitalist development. While having important roots in colonial peasant production, this development is currently fed on oil. The state plays a key role in dispensing the oil wealth, and the way it is spent generates economic activity and incomes (not for all, though) in all sectors of the economy. It feeds into and transforms pre-existing social relations. It promotes capitalist accumulation and capitalist class formation.

It is obvious that foreign capital takes a leading part in this development, not only in the extraction of petroleum, but in all sectors: in commerce, banking, construction, and manufacturing. In agriculture, international capital is prominent through the World Bank.

There is also a large, growing class of Nigerian capitalists, some very substantial, the bigger ones usually allied to foreign capital. Further down the scale one finds a mass of small capitalists shading off into petty commodity producers. The state itself is a major owner of the means of production and finance capital. It invests in large-scale productive enterprises, on its own or in partnership with foreign and domestic private capital. It takes an active part in promoting Nigerian capitalists through state banks, development corporations and support schemes. It has introduced legislation which has significantly shifted the balance of ownership in the Nigerian economy from foreign to domestic capital. Heavy state investments in economic and social infrastructure clearly support further capitalist expansion.

The suggestion that the Nigerian state promotes capitalist development does not necessarily mean that it does so efficiently. Nor does it mean that such development provides a useful answer to the problems of mass poverty and deprivation facing the Nigerian people. As it is, however, business in Nigeria is profitable for many people,

Nigerians as well as foreigners. Nigeria has become an important part of the world capitalist system and more and more Nigerians are increasingly more closely 'integrated' into that system.

What kind of state is this? Presumably it is a capitalist state, but how can we understand its pre-eminence in the context of the development of capitalism in Nigeria? More specifically, how can we understand its role in the relationship between capitalist development locally and on the world scale? How does it structure the relation between domestic and international capital? In terms of state capital itself, how does it enter this relation? What are the consequences for accumulation and class formation? Answers to these questions need to be based on an understanding of how state forms and state actions are determined concretely and materially at the levels of production, class formation and political struggle in the Nigerian situation. It is also a question of how the state, through its mode of operating, itself intervenes in the organisation of production, its contradictions and struggles. The crux of the matter is of course the logic of the interaction between the two: the dialectical relationship between base and super-structure.

This is all very abstract. It can also be stated bluntly in class terms. In whose interest does the Nigerian state operate? Is it an organ of international capital, a neo-colonial and 'comprador' state? Is it an organ of an emerging bourgeoisie. Or is it both? If so, how does it serve two masters? Is it a contradictory relation? How is it mediated? What are the implications for the manner in which the anti-imperialist struggle and the class struggle relate to each other?

Imperialism & Capitalist Development

The questions raised above are dealt with in this article in the context of an ongoing discussion of imperialism, domestic class formation, and capitalist development in the Third World (see issues 19 and 22 of ROAPE).

Imperialism contributes to the prolonged, often deepening suffering and oppression of the peoples of the third world not so much by obstructing capitalist development but by pursuing specific forms of capitalist development as determined by specific class alliances and the related nature of the state. It is therefore not the absence of steel works and other desirable means of development which is the primary evidence of imperialist-generated underdevelopment. Instead, it is the manner in which such means (as well as the mines and plantations which preceded them) provide the material basis for oppression, thereby obstructing alternative strategies rooted in the material needs of the masses.

The essence of imperialism is the enforcement of monopoly profits by political and military means. Colonialism was monopoly by direct territorial conquest. The contemporary form is a transnational alliance of international capital backed at both ends by the power of the state. Such contemporary forms of imperialism need domestically rooted bourgeois class forces in order to establish the appropriate material and political conditions for their profits. The domestic bourgeoisie, on the other hand, uses the alliance with international capital to buttress its class rule and accumulation. Jointly, the two parties co-operate to hold back popular pressures for social and democratic reform. As a consequence, capitalism in the third world tends to take on a particularly oppressive, backward and predatory character. Struggles against imperialism are therefore inseparately linked to domestic class struggles.

The Nigerian State as an Organ of International Capital

A strong case exists for arguing that the Nigerian state is an organ of international capital. This is a common radical position and inspires much of the current critique of the state, (see, for example, T. Turner in No.5 and S. Osoba in No. 13 of *ROAPE*), both from a national bourgeois and from a socialist perspective. In fact, it serves as a meeting ground where such different and ultimately opposed political forces seek to establish a united front. The position is often argued within the context of neo-colonialism, where continuity with colonial domination is emphasised. Independence is seen as largely formal. Real control over the economy remains with foreign capital. Nationalist leaders have been co-opted by imperialism. They 'inherited' the colonial state, a state imposed by imperialism for its own purposes. The nature of the state itself therefore did not change fundamentally. The nationalists never really challenged the pervasive domination of the economy by imperialism. They were placed in a position where they were left to administer the state on behalf of foreign capital. The contemporary Nigerian state can therefore be described as a comprador state: state institutions and state officials operate as agents of imperialism. The real ruling class is the bourgeoisie of the metropolitan countries. It is not the indigenous businessmen and bureaucrats, who merely masquerade as a 'national bourgeoisie'. They are *allowed* to play this role by their foreign paymasters. In fact, they are performing a vital ideological function, as their nationalist rhetoric conceals the true class nature of the state. When they travel to international conferences attacking 'imperialism' and clamouring for a 'new international order', they simultaneously take the opportunity to check their international bank accounts which are regularly replenished by foreign friends. Corruption is not the failure to play the game according to the rules of the official ethic. It is a normal means whereby foreign firms compensate politicians and bureaucrats for their agency services. The methods are numerous. Co-operating ministers may be allowed, for example, to exercise patronage within the domain of the foreign firms. They nominate their own candidates to board memberships and management posts and when they themselves retire they will be taken care of appropriately.

There is ample evidence to support the view of the Nigerian state as a neo-colonial, comprador state, an organ of international capital in its continued exploitation and oppression of the Nigerian people. The continuous fractional rivalries of Nigerian politics, military and civilian, ensure that the corrupt transactions with foreign capital are repeatedly (although selectively) exposed and documented. Nor does radical Nigerian opinion need to wait to be informed by official commissions of inquiry or by documents released by one or other warring faction. Information about the forms, crude or subtle, in which international firms tie local leaders to themselves is common talk. [A list of some of the more famous public scandals of this type, including 'the Scandia Bus Scandal in which some crooked businessmen in Sweden and Nigeria ripped off the Lagos Municipal Transport Service', is offered by Osoba (*ROAPE*, No. 13). *The Daily Tribune* and *National Concorde* (party organs of the Unity Party of Nigeria and the Nigerian People's Party respectively) vie in exposing the shady deals of the businessmen-cum-politicians of the opposite camp.] Moreover, with 'partnership' increasingly becoming the official ethic and the prevailing institutional set-up for the relationship between the state and foreign capital there is less need for secrecy. It requires little ingenuity to expose the shallowness of such partnership arrangements in the many cases where 'state participation' means little more than the collection of fat allowances for state representatives on boards with little control over, or even information on, actual operations.

The Case of 'Indigenisation' of Foreign Enterprises

The policy of 'indigenisation' (see *ROAPE* No. 14) can in fact be seen as the institutionalisation of this sham partnership. Under the cover of a smoke-screen of nationalist ideology, foreign capital in Nigeria is now more securely entrenched than ever. The smaller foreign firms which were totally taken over by Nigerians did not constitute much of a sacrifice for international capital. They were mostly Lebanese anyway, who have their own mysterious ways (including double citizenship) of surviving in business. They certainly do not represent any of the dominant sections of international capital. For the latter it was a question of whether to have a 60 per cent or 40 per cent local partnership. There were certainly risks involved: that the new part owners were going to meddle in the business, pushing their nephews on to management, discriminating in favour of their own kin or home area in employment, and so on. But these 'risks' were also opportunities. The exchange of favours could be more open. No need any longer to send messengers through ministerial backdoors; business could now be settled between official partners. A big bonus, of course, was the handsome addition to the capital stock brought in by the local partner. There was no need to hand over existing assets as firms could expand through new issues of equity – witness the 'prospectuses' issued with these share offers, through the bank and press. Remember how foreign firms elsewhere are anxious to finance their expansion by mopping up domestic savings – while retaining, of course, their right to remit profits.

Indigenisation has meant that a significant amount of the oil earnings of the Nigerian government has been recycled into financing the expansion of firms which for all practical purposes remain firmly under the control of international capital. This is a plausible, radical interpretation of what has happened. It has nothing to do with whether or not this was an effect intended or desired by those technocrats and politicians who were pushing the idea. They may in fact have acted in good faith and inspired by the most laudable national sentiments. But neither is it primarily a question of cheating somebody.

It has been argued that the Nigerian government was outwitted by cunning foreigners. It has also been claimed that the policy was subverted by unpatriotic Nigerian individuals (officials and private businessmen) who colluded with the foreigners. From that perspective (for references see Notes at end), it is not the state itself which is neo-colonial or comprador but certain elements within the state or the local bourgeoisie. The state is too weak or inefficient to enforce its patriotic intentions. The political implications are that if the patriotic elements could be reinforced and the unpatriotic ones be weeded out, things would be alright.

While this could add to the bite of the indigenisation policies, it would hardly transform their subordination to the extended penetration by international capital. Certainly, there was a lot of manoeuvring and dodging by foreign firms seeking to have it both ways before settling for the new form of partnership. Why shouldn't they? It is a question of profit maximisation. There is nothing which is so good that it can't be better. The officials of the Nigerian Enterprises Promotion Board are undoubtedly justified in their concern with the evasiveness and unpartner-like behaviour of some of the foreign firms. The acrimonies on both sides, however, should not be misread as an expression of any fundamental antagonism. They should not be allowed to obscure the basic logic of the transformation, a transformation essentially in the interests of foreign capital, tightening rather than loosening its grip on the Nigerian economy.

Problems of the 'Neo-colonial' Model of the Nigerian State

It may be easy to support this radical interpretation of the Nigerian state on theoretical grounds. In addition, a wealth of documentation can be marshalled in support of the claim that the Nigerian political economy is dominated by international capital. It seems therefore also a plausible materialist position to assume that this domination is reflected at the level of the state. From such a position it is logical to identify the international bourgeoisie as the real ruling class, in the marxist sense of the term. Backed by such theoretical assumptions and empirical evidence, it is possible to make sense of indigenisation policies and other seemingly 'nationalist' features in the recent operations of the Nigerian state. They can be seen as objectively integrated into the logic of imperialist domination. They either spring from the requirements of international capital, are restructured to fit such needs, or are neutralised so as to be compatible with them.

The problem with such an approach is not that the conclusions are necessarily false. On the contrary, I believe that it makes good sense to assert that the Nigerian state is a product of imperialism and that it continues to serve the interests of international capital. The problem is that this explanatory model, by being very general, may fail to motivate useful theoretical work and concrete studies which allow us to see the specific economic and political forms of imperialist domination and how they link up with class struggle. If every aspect of the state is reduced to being ultimately determined by the needs of imperialism, very little may actually be explained, unless, of course, such conclusions are arrived at through an analysis of the way in which imperialism is articulated at all levels of the social formation. The supremacy of international capital may well be confirmed by such analysis but this would require an evaluation of the forces over which it dominates. To say that it ultimately comes out on top should not allow us to ignore the strength and organisation of the forces which it incorporates, co-opts or subdues. That strength will surely be decisive for the strategies chosen by international capital in each new phase. The danger of a simple neo-colonial model of the state is that it may rob domestic social forces of their own dynamic and give a false air of inevitability to the political outcome of class struggle.

How are we then to take account of the existence and rapid expansion of a large domestic bourgeoisie? How does it affect the material determination of the state? Is it compatible with a general theory of imperialist domination? I believe it is. But it requires a more developed understanding of what that domination means than is implicit in the radical position outlined above. Before we arrive at that let me outline a second 'explanatory' model of the Nigerian state which takes as its point of departure the growth of the Nigerian bourgeoisie.

The State as an Organ of the Domestic Bourgeoisie

The colonial state systematically obstructed the growth of a powerful domestic bourgeoisie. It sanctioned the monopolistic practices of the colonial commercial firms in their struggle to eliminate 'native' competition in the all-important import-export business. Politically, it allied itself with backward aristocratic elements blocking the demand for bourgeois forms of political representation. Colonial economic policies in the decolonisation phase centred on the restructuring of the colonial monopoly firms to ensure their access to markets after Independence. Under growing nationalist pressures, however, colonial regional development corporations were gradually geared to support Nigerian entrepreneurs, although at a very humble level. With the accession of bourgeois nationalists to state power, the resources of the state were increasingly used to promote their interests as an aspiring bourgeoisie. The methods used varied and involved intense sectional competition. The activities of state development corporations were greatly expanded, resulting in a wide range of enterprises, either sponsored or owned by the state. In the latter case it was normally stated that such enterprises in due course would be transferred into private Nigerian hands. The state thus took on the role of caretaker for the budding bourgeoisie. At first, all major investments were left to foreign firms, but Nigerian state institutions increasingly involved themselves in large-scale productive and commercial operations. While the economic contributions of such enterprises were frequently dissipated through corruption and *mis*appropriation, they were significant in providing a source for 'primitive accumulation' by an incipient capitalist class in society at large. They also generated a growing cadre of Nigerian administrators and managers engaged in state capitalist enterprises. Others acquired similar experiences while serving with foreign firms. The marketing boards, controlling the exports of peasant produce, promoted Nigerian 'Licensed Buying Agents' as another important contribution to bourgeois class formation under state monopoly protection.

The strength of the state as a national bourgeois class institution was greatly enhanced by the defeat of the separatists in the Civil War and the rise of the oil economy after it. I have outlined elsewhere how federal and non-federal state expenditure, sector by sector, contributed to bourgeois class formation (Paper on Oil, see Notes at end). State funds were systematically used to sponsor Nigerian firms often in competition with foreign ones. Despite the continued dominance of the latter in, for example, large-scale construction, it may be more significant, from the perspective of the class character of the state, to note the steadily growing proportion of contracts now handled by Nigerian firms. We can also note that these contracts have grown steadily in size and complexity.

The state itself has expanded its participation in all major sectors of the economy, often at the expense of foreign capital. Oil and banking may be mentioned as particularly strategic. There is still much complaint about the inefficiency of state supervision of the oil companies but national control has certainly been enhanced. Similarly, the Central Bank's direction of commercial bank operations has been tightened up. The state pushes ahead with strategic investments in the steel industry with Soviet partners, having failed to obtain Western support.

Generally, oil wealth has greatly enhanced Nigeria's bargaining position in the international economy. It can make demands and impose restrictions on the operations of foreign firms. The Nigerian market is very valuable, international competition is intense, and concessions by international capital to the national economic aspiration of the Nigerian state are necessary. We need only record the way Nigeria nationalised British Petroleum to put effective pressure on Britain in the Zimbabwean independence negotiations. Nationalism is a powerful political force in Nigeria. This is the context in which we can return to the question of Nigeria's policies of 'indigenising' foreign enterprises.

Indigenisation Reconsidered

Indigenisation offered a focal point for national self-assertion by the domestic bour-geoisie. It had consolidated its positions in the course of the Civil War, and oil provided funds and bargaining power to back up sweeping claims for the take-over, in whole or in part, of the assets of foreign firms. It was an accelerating process. Timidity and fumbling in the design and implementation of the first Decree (1972) subsequently generated fresh agitation, resulting in the revised Decree of 1977. Demands were drastically stepped up, this time for Nigerian *majority* ownership in most enterprises except the largest and technically most complex ones. It is true that in many cases the transfer of shares gave little effective control, but this in turn has generated a spate of fresh demands for the tightening of restrictions on foreign management ('expatriate quotas', etc.) and closer inspection by the Enterprises Promotion Board, including tougher reprisals against defaulting firms. The growing competence and business experience of those representing the Nigerian partners, state or private, must also be taken into account. The ability of the foreign partners to play tricks on the local ones was likely to diminish. 'Competence', of course, does not prevent people from being bought. But, combined with the latent threat of erratic nationalist outbursts, limits were thus set to the possibility of manipulations. If foreign firms were to survive in Nigeria, they must come to terms with the aspirations of the domestic bourgeoisie, in and out of the state apparatus.

The muted response of international *firms* to the successive waves of nationalisations (protests, if any, were timid) should therefore not be mistaken for complacency or as proof that nothing of significance really happened. The challenge was real. Strong reactions from individual firms or from their home governments, however, might have seriously endangered access to this strategic third world market for a long time to come.

The nationalism of indigenisation should not be equated with patriotism or a commitment to throw off foreign domination in any more fundamental sense. The Nigerian bourgeoisie, for its own class *reasons*, wanted a *bigger* share of the profitable, foreign-controlled business operations going on in 'its' territory. It wanted to be admitted on an equal basis to the exploitation of Nigerian resources and labour. It certainly did not *want to chase* out foreign capital. In fact, influential sections of the Nigerian bourgeoisie are seriously concerned that indigenisation policies have unduly frightened foreign capital, thereby undercutting the range of partnership which they, for their own purposes, wish to pursue. The 1977 Decree has recently been revised in order to permit foreign-majority ownership in agricultural ventures.

To sum up. The rising domestic bourgeoisie is emancipating itself in and through the state, either in the form of state support for private capital or through direct state participation in production and exchange. The indigenisation exercise is an example of both.

Problems of the 'Domestic Bourgeoisie' Model of the Nigerian State

There is much evidence to support the proposition that the Nigerian state operates as an organ of the rising domestic bourgeoisie. How is this compatible with the similarly plausible argument that it serves international capital? If, as we have already agreed, foreign capital continues to dominate directly or indirectly in the major sectors of the economy, how can we explain that the domestic bourgeoisie seems to be using the state successfully to strengthen its relative position vis-à-vis foreign capital? Is it the tail wagging the dog? The neo-colonial model of explanation has a ready answer: it is an optical illusion. Foreign capital dominates *as before*. It is just the form of domination which changes. The domestic bourgeoisie, whether state or private, is used by foreign capital for its own purposes. The 'national' character of this class and its state *institutions* is even necessary in order to maintain this illusion, under the cover of which foreign capital continues to undertake its exploits.

How can this riddle of who uses whom, who depends on whom, be solved in a way which is both consistent with the two sets of evidence which we have surveyed and which also makes sense theoretically? Is it the 'interdependence' or 'mutual dependence' which liberal development theorists have put forward as the answer to the radical view of dependence and underdevelopment?

To be able to solve the problem of how state power reflects the relative influence of various such national class segments, Nigerian and non-Nigerian, we must first ask more questions about the relationship of the Nigerian state to the process of internationalised capitalist production. The capitalist state is not above sectional contradictions. Still, its mode of functioning and the role of such sectional influences can only be understood if we assume the unity of capital vis-à-vis social forces which are opposed to it, either within the process of capital accumulation itself or in its confrontation with pre-capitalist or non-capitalist social relations of production, where the latter are gradually transformed and subordinated. Let us therefore outline a third perspective on the class determination of the Nigerian state: the state as the organ of capital in general.

The Nigerian State as an Organ of Capital in General

While the Nigerian state serves as an organ both for the penetration of international capital and for the emancipation of the domestic bourgeoisie, it cannot be reduced to either. Nor is it possible to comprehend the significance of either of the two aspects without examining such class functions of the Nigerian state for which the distinction between foreign and domestic is not relevant. The primary role of the Nigerian state is to establish, maintain, protect and expand the conditions of capitalist accumulation in general, without which neither foreign nor Nigerian capitalists can prosper.

When the lumpenproletariat of Kano stone the luxury cars and mansions of the propertied classes, inspired by a confused revolutionary opposition to the 'new order', it is bourgeois property and bourgeois class rule in general which need to be defended (on the 'Kano Rebellion' in December 1980 see *West Africa's* January 1981 issues as well as subsequent reports from the hearings of the Commission set up to inquire into the events). The massive shooting without trial of prisoners taken in this class war performs the same crude function as the bloody punitive expeditions by which the British state imposed its domination in the interest of colonial capitalism. The establishment and maintenance of 'law and order' is the crucial role of any state. But law and order is never abstract and classless. It is defined by the class character of the state. The particular form of repression demonstrated in this Maitasine rebellion shows the unconsolidated nature of the capitalist state and the partial manner in which production has at yet been subordinated to capital. The need to dispatch senior police officers to Thailand and other places in order to study what the Commissioner of Police termed, at the hearings, 'modern methods' of riot control is a sign of the way this class warfare is being stepped up.

But violent repression is only one aspect of law and order. More generally, it is a question of establishing and enforcing the complex pattern of rules which are necessary for capitalist accumulation. Bourgeois property relations must, on the one hand, be liberated from the bonds imposed by pre-capitalist relations of production. They must be protected, on the other hand, from challenges from within, that is, from the very forces which emerge within the new mode. The Land Use Decree may be taken as an example of the former. Private and state property in land is protected against the claims of traditional owners; simultaneously, the law facilitates the appropriation of *land for 'commercial'* use. Under this Decree large areas of land are currently being taken over by the emerging bourgeoisie.

Legislation relating to the organisation and control of labour is the prime example of the second type of condition. The regulation of the rights of labour to organise and the restrictions imposed on such rights are fundamental to the operations of any capitalist society. The Nigerian state has struggled hard, largely unsuccessfully, to establish its control over the organisation of the working class. When unions in the mid-1970s were dangerously close to forming a united organisation under radical leadership, the state stepped in, purged the leadership and set up a new organisation with state support, financed from deductions of union fees by employers. The state failed, however, to prevent the radical elements from gaining an upper hand in the new organisation. State support was therefore withdrawn. Employers refused to adhere to the check-off system, and attempts to establish unions in individual companies were resisted by the employers with impunity. The right of the Nigerian worker to unionise is still a fiction for a large section of the working class. Union leaders are sacked at will. Unions are banned from participating in politics and the state is now actively fostering alternative unions of a more co-operative kind (for details, see *West Africa* before and after the February 1981 Convention of the Nigerian Labour Congress in Kano).

The question of 'law and order' extends to the whole sphere of state rules and sanctions relating to the regulation of money, banking and trading in a capitalist society, including the protection of equity capital, the enforcement of the laws of contract, and so on, which we do not need to go into here.

The regulation of the procedures by which such rules are decided and altered, however, is the essence of bourgeois state formation itself. Civil war, military dictatorship and the elaborate constitutional regulation of the transition to civilian rule, were all successive stages in this process of bourgeois state formation in Nigeria, reflecting the changing conditions of accumulation. As I have elaborated elsewhere in a paper on this 'transition', it is one from a regionally fragmented state structure based on the appropriation of surplus from peasant production to a centralised state system based on the petroleum industry and a growing domestic market for agriculture and industry. The new constitution with its division of functions between numerous institutions and office holders is also an elaborate attempt to regulate the sectional competition of the bourgeoisie in such a way as to ensure the hegemony of the federal centre.

The massive direct investments by the state in the transport and processing of petroleum, in steel, cement, transport equipment, trunk roads, telecommunications, power generation and ports and airports cannot be reduced either to the sectional aspirations of the Nigerian bourgeoisie (although these may affect the physical locations of plants and roads) or to any division between foreign and Nigerian capital. It is a question of laying the physical foundations of a particular type of development based on accumulation within a world market context. The state undertakes these investments not because they are in any way unwanted by private capital, local or foreign, but because only the state itself is prepared to guarantee the profits of the private investors who struggle between themselves to participate as contractors, suppliers and managers. In the meantime, new productive forces are created which facilitate the expanded reproduction of capital.

But also labour must be produced and reproduced at new, higher levels required by accumulation. We have seen the rapid expansion of both general and specialised education, and its role in the recruitment of wage labour from below, the structuring and disciplining of labour (advancement by 'qualifications'), and the creation of a managerial class. Typically, the 'food and shelter' programmes of successive Nigerian regimes are firmly oriented towards the minority of Nigerians who earn salaries and wages. The World Bank is deeply involved in both fields, seeking to generate a commercial food surplus (rather than raising the general level of food consumption among the masses) and to provide 'modern housing' for those on fixed wages (rather than raising the housing standard of the mass of urban and rural poor).

Finally, in the sphere of ideology, state control over mass media as well as over education is used for the purpose of creating the ideological orientation necessary to support the bourgeois state and protect international accumulation.

The repressive, regulative, productive, reproductive and ideological activities of the state, indicated briefly above, cannot be understood in terms of the requirements of any particular segments of capital, domestic or foreign. The fact that foreign construction firms profit more from the big trunk road contracts, while Nigerian firms make more money from the smaller ones, has important consequences for accumulation and capitalist development (for example, in the way profits are invested). This is of secondary importance, however, to the fact that these roads, big or small, Nigerian-built or foreign-built, themselves feed into a particular mode of accumulation in society at large which is decisive when it comes to determine the class character of the state.

Indigenisation Reconsidered a Second Time

In an attempt to determine the class character of the Nigerian state, the 'national' divisions between foreign and Nigerian capital are not decisive. We need to place such secondary contradictions in the context of the basic problems facing capital in general, that is, in its relation to social forces opposed to capital or obstructing capital. It does not mean that secondary contradictions do not matter. On the contrary, they can occasionally disrupt and wreck capitalist accumulation and the operations of the capitalist state. Similarly, they may divide and paralyse social and political forces opposed to capital. Secondary contradictions are therefore intentionally manipulated by the ruling class for the purpose of managing and controlling primary ones. This is the context, for example, in which ruling class manipulation of regional, ethnic, and religious contradictions could be understood in contemporary Nigerian politics.

Secondary contradictions within the capitalist class on national, sectional and sectoral lines may threaten accumulation insofar as they undermine the capacity to face primary problems of subordinating labour or pre-capitalist social forces. The policy of indigenisation is an attempt to regulate competition between international firms and the rising Nigerian bourgeoisie. The need to do so does not arise, it seems, from the intensity of that competition as such. In fact, this may be much more intense between sections of foreign capital (on sectoral and national lines) and between sections of Nigerian capital with different foreign alliances (Beckman, 1981). We need to look elsewhere, to the role of indigenisation in the consolidation of bourgeois class rule and the management of primary contradictions. I wish to make the following propositions. Indigenisation contributed to the consolidation of the Nigerian ruling class by encouraging closer partnership between Nigerian and foreign capital. It propagated the national authenticity of the Nigerian state which was very much in doubt because of its place in international accumulation. This authenticity was officially asserted by subjecting international capital to its regulative powers. Simultaneously, indigenisation enhanced the national credentials of the foreign companies. ('Why do you attack us? We are Nigerian now'.) The scope for attacking capital on an anti-foreign platform was reduced, weakening the links between anti-imperialist and anti-capitalist agitation in the working class. It also diverted petty-bourgeois nationalist aspirations from potentially threatening link-ups with anti-imperialist and anti-capitalist social forces. More generally, indigenisation served to strengthen the domestic social and political basis of international accumulation in Nigeria. The advantages and disadvantages experienced by individual firms, foreign and Nigerian, in the course of the indigenisation exercise, should not distract from its wider usefulness in the development of capitalism in Nigeria.

International Accumulation & Domestic State Formation: Conclusions

I have so far tried to show three things. First, that the state serves as an organ of foreign capital in Nigeria as it expands its operations and entrenches itself more deeply. Second, I have also shown how the Nigerian state is simultaneously engaged in fostering a domestic bourgeoisie. Third, I have suggested that the most significant functions performed by the state in support of capitalist development cannot be reduced to the interests of such sections of capital, Nigerian or foreign. Instead, they need to be seen as performed in the interest of capital in general.

The next task is to discuss how these three aspects of the Nigerian state are dynamically linked together in a concrete type of capitalist state, as a target for concrete struggles. What assistance can the type of analysis ventured above be in understanding the position of the Nigerian state in the contradictions facing the Nigerian people and imperialism in particular? At this point, I can only suggest some elements of a wider discussion.

First of all, the Nigerian state must be examined in the context of the development of the world capitalist economy (the world market) as well as domestic social processes. Nigeria's position as a major oil producer, the constraints on world energy production, the recession in leading capitalist economies, the redistribution of income in favour of oil producers, these are all factors which have contributed to an intensified struggle on a world scale for control over energy resources and to heightened competition for markets and investment outlets. It should be remembered that Nigeria supplies some 40 per cent of US oil imports. It is Britain's leading export market outside the European Community. For the West as a whole, it has long passed South Africa as the principal market in Africa. Foreign investments have had one of the highest growth rates in the third world. Nigeria is very important to the world capitalist economy (see, for example reports in *West Africa* (23 March and 15 June 1981)). But its importance is not a function of oil alone. It also relates to the domestic production system into which oil revenue is fed. Its foundation in broadly-based petty commodity production, agricultural and non-agricultural, has major consequences for the development of capitalist accumulation and class formation.

Nigeria is in a stage of accelerated transition from a phase where accumulation was based on the appropriation of value from petty commodity producers, mostly peasants, to the direct subordination of labour to capital. However, the reproduction of labour (feeding, housing, clothing) continues to depend to a large extent on petty commodity production. The capitalist state faces the problem of overcoming the restraints imposed by pre-capitalist relations of production in agriculture without endangering the material basis provided by peasant-grown food for the present form of world-market-oriented accumulation.

The transition is simultaneously one from more direct to more indirect forms of foreign economic and political domination; that is, from direct domination by the colonial state, the big merchant firms, the mines etc., to more general forms of subordination of production to the laws of capital and the world market. At the level of the state, this transition can be traced from the colonial state and the neo-colonial state as direct agents of subordination to external class forces, to the state of the domestic bourgeoisie, which is the internationalisation at the level of state and class formation of an international mode of accumulation. The transition reflects the growing strength and organisational capacity of the domestic bourgeoisie in its management of the state apparatus. It is the outcome both of the systematic grooming of this class by international capital and its emergence in the process of accumulation itself. It corresponds to the requirements of international capital for a local support system capable of managing local contradictions, and provides the appropriate conditions for international accumulation.

The state is an organ of the domestic bourgeoisie, not because of the sectional rivalries between national and foreign capital (which do exist), but because of the strategic role of this class in bringing about the subordination of 'its' territory to the rules of international accumulation. It grows in strength in step with its success in internalising these rules. It is important to note the extent to which the bourgeoisie is constituted from above, in and through the state, rather than emerging through class struggle from below.

This reflects the manner in which the state is determined at the level of international accumulation and as such embodies a higher level of development of productive forces. The prominence of the state in capitalist development (state investments, etc.) needs to be understood in terms of this external determination and the huge gap between the level of productive forces locally and internationally.

Similarly, the state is an organ of international capital, not so much because state institutions are directly commandeered by international firms and their local agents (which is done), but because of the way in which international, world-market-oriented accumulation has been internalised into the Nigerian political economy. The state plays a crucial role in this process and attempts to overcome the resistance facing it from workers and petty commodity producers.

On the other hand, the Nigerian state is not a comprador state in the sense that it is primarily an agent of social forces external to the society. These forces have been internalised. Nor is it a 'national' state in the sense of being a carrier of national resistance to foreign domination. The relations of domination originating from outside have been built into the fabric of domestic class relations.

However, it is a state of imperialism: imperialist social relations of production have been domesticated and the state itself is the very linchpin around which the system of imperialist domination rotates. This is a new phase of imperialist domination: imperialist domination from within, with its specific contradictions, and its specific forms of resistance. Provisionally, we may call this state the 'state of internationally subordinated state monopoly capitalism' (One thousand Units of Account to the one who invents the best short name for this hydra!). It is international in the domination of production for the world market, in its integration into production and class formation (and class alliances) at that level. It takes a subordinated position in that wider system. State capital and state intervention perform strategic functions in organising production, class formation, and class alliances. The essence of its form of domination is monopolistic: state power is used to generate conditions for monopoly profits, including the suppression of anti-monopoly social and political forces (Beckman, 1981).

The resistance to internationally subordinated, state monopoly capital comes from many quarters: not only from the workers who are brought into direct confrontation with the state as the principal owner of large-scale capital in its partnership with private capital, foreign and domestic, but also from the workers whose efforts to organise in defence of their interests are suppressed by the state, or by management with the backing or tacit support of the state. Resistance comes from the peasants whose land is invaded and whose labour is appropriated by the state in co-operation with international capital and a rising rural bourgeoisie, and also from peasants and urban petty commodity producers whose access to basic production inputs and to market outlets is monopolised by the same forces. Also small Nigerian capitalists find that their conditions of survival are constantly circumscribed and threatened by state monopolistic arrangements.

This resistance is taking form in concrete struggles, from the militant actions of the Peugeot and Dunlop workers to the armed rebellion of the peasants at the Sokoto-Rima Basin Development Scheme (see Wallace in *ROAPE* No.17), to mention only some recent examples. But also the confused radical politics of Kano and the People's Redemption Party can be examined from the confluence of anti-feudal and anti-monopolistic social forces.

The state provides the unity and cohesion of the international alliance of monopolistic forces which are presently imposing themselves vigorously and brutally on the Nigerian people. Nigeria is waiting for the political organisations which will also give unity and cohesion to the emerging alliance of anti-monopolistic and anti-imperialist social forces, whose resistance is as yet scattered and fragmented.

Bibliographic Notes

This article further develops the more general arguments that I spelled out in two earlier pieces in *ROAPE*: 'Imperialism and capitalist transformation: critique of a Kenya debate', in No. 19, 1980, and 'Imperialism and the national bourgeoisie', in No. 22, 1981. Another paper, 'Oil, state expenditure and class formation in Nigeria', Conference of Nordic Political Scientists, Turku, Finland, 1981, also relates some of these issues to Nigeria and is referred to in the text. Examples of the 'radical', neo-colonial view of Nigeria can be found in: Segun Osoba, 'The deepening crisis of the Nigerian national bourgeoisie', *ROAPE* No. 13, 1978; T. Turner, 'Multinationals and the instability of the Nigerian State', *ROAPE* No. 5, 1976, and her contribution, 'Nigeria: Imperialism, oil technology and the comprador state', in P. Nore & T. Turner, eds., *Oil and Class Struggle* (London, Zed Books, 1980), and Ola Oni & Bade Onimode, *Economic Development of Nigeria: the Socialist Alternative* (Ibadan, 1975).

Material on indigenisation includes: A. Hoogvelt, 'Indigenisation and foreign capital: industrialisation in Nigeria', *ROAPE* No.14, 1979; and three works that argue the 'betrayal' thesis: P. Collins, 'Public Policy and the development of indigenous capitalism: the Nigerian case', *Journal of Commonwealth & Comparative Politics*, 15.2.1977; E. Akeredolu-Ale, 'Private foreign investment and the underdevelopment of indigenous entrepreneurship in Nigeria', in G. Williams, ed., *Nigeria, Economy and Society*; Nigerian Economics Society, *Nigeria's Indigenisation Policy*, Symposium Proceedings, Ibadan, 1974. A work that charts the sectional basis of politics is Okwundiba Nnoli, *Ethnic Politics in Nigeria* (Enugu, 1980).

On peasant resistance to state agricultural projects see T. Wallace, 'Agricultural project and land in Northern Nigeria', *ROAPE* No.17, 1980 and O. Oculi, 'Dependent Food Policy in Nigeria', *ROAPE* No.15/16, 1979.

8

MORRIS SZEFTEL
Political Graft & the Spoils System in Zambia:
the State as a Resource in Itself   [1982–3]

This article is concerned with graft in Zambian politics, its place in the political process and its contribution to class formation. No attempt is made, therefore, to treat it as a discrete phenomenon, in isolation from a wider pattern of social behaviour whereby state resources are diverted from public to private ends. Recent debates have focused, in different ways, on the importance of the state in fostering elements of an indigenous capitalist class. What is not clear in these accounts is just how this is done and what its consequences are for the political order.

Clearly, graft occupies varying levels of significance in different African cases. In Zambia it appears to be fairly common without being endemic, and the frequency of exposure and punishment indicates that it remains a risky undertaking. But still it has important implications for the way in which politics is acted out and for the process of class formation. It constitutes one way in which individuals appropriate the spoils of office or, more generally, of access to the state, and thus provides a valuable point of entry into the way in which the political process permits private accumulation.

I have used the term 'graft', rather than the more widely understood 'corruption', in order to avoid a construct at once bedevilled by conflicting definitions. More importantly, I thus avoid a term having a narrow and more or less precise legal meaning in particular countries (no judgment as to the legality of actions discussed is made here). In graft I include some broader phenomena – I mean any behaviour which deviates from the norms, rules and duties governing the exercise of a public office or role for purposes of private gain or influence. It may do this by ignoring prohibitions against certain actions, or by fulfilling obligations to act, or by exercising legitimate discretions to act, as long as it does so for private advantage or private motives. Such a definition would include, beyond formal corruption, such practices as theft of public resources, fraud, use of office as a business, nepotism, extortion, discrimination and even some cases of abuse of power where these involved personal or private enrichment in contravention of obligations surrounding the exercise of that power.

Clearly such a perspective indicates that graft involves practices which transfer public resources to private pockets by means of procedures which are not prescribed and which may even be specifically proscribed. But quite obviously, graft is not the only way in which state resources are so appropriated. Zambian politics are characterised by a clientelist form in which patronage constitutes an important mechanism through which political supporters often obtain access to state resources in return for helping patrons obtain access to public office itself. An understanding of the nature of graft should illustrate much about all the ways in which state resources are accumulated as political spoils. And, to the extent that clientelism involves the organisation of political factions, we would expect to find a relationship between the incidence of graft and the process of factional competition. What will seem to some groups legitimate pay-offs for political supporters, will appear as corrupt practices to critics and opponents.

Even so, there is clearly a difference between using clientelist links to obtain state contracts or public office, on the one hand, and stealing government funds or taking bribes, on the other. Most people recognise some kind of hierarchy of repugnance when considering misuse of public resources. The distinction made by one politician of New York's infamous Tammany Hall between 'honest graft' and 'dishonest graft' contains an element of truth about how people view the use of public office for personal advantage. In this context, it is important to retain some analytic distinction between graft and patronage despite their clear relationship and the blurring of distinctions in practice. It might perhaps be useful to consider patronage to involve the dispensing of state resources to third parties in return for political support of some kind, while graft would involve the use of state resources for personal advantage by officials.

The State as a Material Resource

The importance and pervasiveness of the spoils system in Zambia reflects the centrality of the state and the resources it commands in an underdeveloped economy. Indeed, the centrality is made more stark by the particularly uneven and distorted form which capital accumulation took in Zambia: an oppressive colonial state apparatus organised on behalf of vast copper mining multinationals, devastated labour reserves, settler racism excluding Africans not only from the petit bourgeoisie but from most skilled and semi-skilled labouring categories, and the concentration of commercial agriculture in settler hands. Thus the state became the focus of African aspirations, both for what it could do in the way of development policies to redress the deprivation of the population as a whole and (more significantly for our purposes here) as a resource in itself, an avenue of upward mobility and a source of wealth for entry into the private sector. Given the obstacles imposed by multinational and settler capital on entry into the market, members of an aspirant indigenous bourgeoisie were prone to look to the state for opportunities for consumption and for the initial capital stake for entry into the private sector.

From Independence in 1964, the Zambian government sought to respond to the many demands for resources from its supporters. After initial success in boosting urban social welfare, health, education, wages and infrastructural investment, by 1967 the system began to run into the inevitable problems of meeting investment needs. Where attempts were made to fund production by the mass of the population, such as through co-operatives, loans tended to benefit the better-off and not the average peasant producers. More success was achieved in expanding state employment opportunities. Thus, from 1963 to 1968 the number of Zambians in central government employment rose from 1,357 to 7,509 through Zambianisation of existing positions and the expansion of the civil service. The economic reforms after 1968 greatly increased state intervention in the economy and created a large parastatal sector, in the process opening up industrial jobs to political access.

The importance and value of public sector employment can hardly be overestimated. Between December 1975 and December 1977, a period of acute crisis for the economy, total employment of Zambians in the private sector fell from 120,320 to 98,730. In contrast, it increased from 124,760 to 126,260 in the government sector and from

116,150 to 128,350 in the parastatals. And average earnings were 60 per cent higher in the parastatal sector than in the private sector in 1977. At the top end of public employment, the rewards were indeed high, as the Mwanakatwe Report on public sector salaries observed in 1975:

> A top (parastatal) executive – in addition to receiving subsidised housing and furniture, an entertainment allowance, a free car with petrol provided, water, telephone and electricity bills paid, servants' wages, security guards provided day and night and the benefit of medical aid contributions – has generous leave and pension arrangements and may receive a bonus, can be individually supported by his employers to a value greater than that of the annual basic salary he earns ... it is apparent that there are parastatal bodies which have begun to extend generosity to the point of profligacy and are, moreover, using the tax-payers' money for the purpose.

All this would indicate that the state constituted an important resource as an employer and an attractive one for those with access to its upper echelon positions. In addition to salaries, subsidised housing, medical aid contributions and loans for the purchase of cars and refrigerators were available. Quite apart from such short-term additions to consumption, the state was essential as a source of capital for Zambians seeking entry into business and farming. A variety of loan organizations were created and loans were sometimes discovered to have been improperly dispensed. But even where this was not the case, political access appeared to have been extremely important. Political office was a crucially important resource for the acquisition of property. Sometimes this was the avenue to state resources; at other times it could be translated into private sector loans or positions with foreign capital.

And the insecurities of office ensure that there is pressure on those with access to the state to maximise the resources they appropriate from it. Few state salaries are sufficient to accumulate an investment stake, especially in circumstances where there are great pressures to consume and dispense patronage, and most official positions do not even provide a particularly luxurious level of consumption. Even subsidised housing, while sumptuous relative to that of the mass of society, is generally small for the size of Zambian families. The temptation to 'cut corners' and maximise the spoils of office while they are available is therefore clear. Graft occurs as a natural extension of the system, an unsurprising though neither inevitable or universal progression of the value placed on access to the state apparatus.

In the present conjuncture in Zambia, then, graft is a symptom of the peculiar conditions surrounding the process of class formation and a mechanism whereby some individuals appropriate state resources either to increase their consumption or, more fundamentally, to acquire property and change their class position. It is one strategy imposed on elements of an emerging indigenous capitalist class in the context of uneven development, as a result of which class formation is intimately dependent on access to the state apparatus or on the influence it brings. I would go further and suggest that graft is also an expression of class conflict in the peculiar conditions attending capitalist development in a post-colonial state. In the first place, it permits an emerging class to increase the rate at which it can appropriate elements of the social surplus – again through the state apparatus rather than through production – at the expense of other classes, especially workers and peasants. Second, more unusually, it is also a device through which certain fractions of capital which have lost control of the state, can defend themselves against attempts by indigenous petit bourgeois elements to use the state to supplant them. Graft can be used to offset state regulations designed to curb settler capital and even multinationals.

Numerous instances of misuse of public office could be cited but my emphasis here will be on cases which have been fully described in official reports, the courts and the press. There are, of course, problems with such a strategy. The press tends to be more responsive to considerations of power than of truth; commissions and court evidence tend to be structured in terms of the political considerations which initiated them. In addition, to have received such public attention, the cases in question need to have represented particularly pernicious examples of the problem, incapable of being contained within administrative procedures. They are, therefore, by definition exceptional rather than typical of the process. Indeed, since graft does not lend itself to quantification, one always risks finding the atypical. Nevertheless, there are also some important advantages to choosing to use cases on public record. In the first place, the data are less subject to dispute. Second, their very exceptional character indicates their importance for the political process and the problems attending the state's efforts at political control. In this respect, they embody important problems for legitimation of the system. Third, in the cases considered below, it was impossible for the state to manage or control information about the events described because the revelations were part of a struggle between contending factions. These factions had an interest in exposing the perfidy perceived in their opponents and used every available avenue to do so. Finally, while the instances are exceptional, the features of the process which they demonstrate do not seem in any great degree to differ from that perceived in numerous other, undocumented instances which were discovered.

The 1968 Lusaka City Council Inquiry

In 1968 a commission of inquiry headed by the Chief Justice of Zambia presented a report of its investigations into the conduct of the affairs of the Lusaka City Council. This document constitutes the only systematic consideration of the conduct of public office since Independence in 1964 and is therefore worth considering at some length. Because it deals with a transitional period in the Council's history when the senior officers were still white expatriates and because expatriate civil service officers provided expert research and reports for the commission, the Report provides an assessment of the conduct of local government affairs in terms of the inherited norms and values of the colonial administration and in contrast to the pressures on many politicians to make political pay-offs to supporters and ensure individual advancement through the state. Thus the Report is itself an indicator of the degree of divergence between officially sanctioned rules of conduct and the practicalities of the spoils system.

The Commission found little evidence of actual illegality and some evidence that it had been resisted by members of the Council. Nevertheless, the Report comprises a chronicle of official impropriety made all the more impressive by the fact that the investigators did not attempt an exhaustive account of such behaviour. Two major categories of such impropriety can be identified, indicating both a wide range of forms and their interrelationship with patronage practices.

The first category comprises a number of activities through which individuals used public office or access to officials to advance personal wealth or position. One such instance was found in irregularities surrounding the allocation of Council housing and the collection of rents. The rapid growth of Lusaka's population after 1964 made housing extremely scarce and expensive and placed great pressure on inadequate Council resources. The Commission accepted that many of the problems surrounding housing were the result of inefficiency and lack of capacity, but it also was clear that other irregularities arose from the use of influence: an unusual number of houses went to prominent people for reasons which could not be explained to the Commission.

A much greater degree of irregularity was found in the allocation of trading stands and food-stall sites. Fifteen per cent of such properties allocated over the 1965-7 period went to Councillors (in one case to the wife of a Councillor) and another plot went to a person who later became a Councillor. Given that there were a total of 592 applications for 45 allocations, this represented an extremely high success rate by Councillors. It transpired that the procedure adopted was for a Councillor in committee to propose the name of a suitable applicant on the list and for this proposal then to be seconded; there were no records of debate or of counter-proposals.

This idiosyncratic behaviour appears, however, to have reached its zenith with the reservation of 103 residential plots for possible purchase by the Mayor in 1967 before any of them had been advertised for sale. For some ten weeks, prospective buyers were put off or refused these plots. Thereafter, following public queries the properties were released for public purchase but later ten of them (including two already allocated to the Bank of Zambia) were again reserved for the Mayor for a further 30 days. The Commission considered that the Mayor had 'brought undue pressure to bear upon members of Council staff'. It was also held that the Mayor had obtained advantage from the Council with respect to two other properties: in one case he had obtained a waiver of policy in order to obtain permission to sell liquor on land on which he had built a bar; and in another he was able to transfer his interest in one site to an interest in another (without the second being advertised) as a result of a special resolution by an appropriate committee. The property acquisition was, in any case, carried out improperly.

Council powers appear also to have been abused in order to attack members of the opposition ANC. In one case an application for permission to extend business premises owned by an ANC member was delayed for some 16 months because the applicant had been denounced by local UNIP officials and because one Councillor had urged that the applicant be evicted from the property (on what grounds, if any, is not clear). 'We entertain no doubt that the improper deferment of Mr M's application was due to political considerations', says the Report. In another case a decision to allocate a plot to a former Councillor who was an ANC member was reversed and his application to erect business premises was refused. The chairman of the Town Planning Committee noted that the applicant was 'not popular in the district'. And in the allocation and control of Lusaka's markets, the Report held that ANC marketeers had been discriminated against – presumably enhancing the patronage UNIP could dispense.

Abuse of Office

In 1977 President Kaunda dismissed the Minister responsible for Lands for what he called activities 'tantamount to abuse of office'. A Land Act had been passed in August 1975 with the intention of curbing land speculation and, by regulating the property market, providing an opportunity for Zambians to acquire valuable land previously monopolised by expatriates and the most wealthy Zambians. To these ends, the Act required government approval for transfers of state land (as opposed to land held under customary, communal tenure) and gave the Minister wide discretionary powers to approve both individual transfers and the price at which such transfers occurred. This implicitly gave officials the power to override even agreements between the contracting parties. And, not surprisingly, there soon followed allegations that attempts were being made to circumvent the intention of the Act. One MP, for instance, alleged that political leaders and top officials were acquiring many of these properties for themselves.

There were also rumours of improper influence at the Ministry, prompting the Minister to defend the leasing of state land to a Greek national by saying:

> He did not bribe me and he did not corrupt me in any way because I am not corrupt ... Allocation of this land was done as it should be and there is nothing scandalous about it.

The Minister's comment also included criticism of certain 'lawyers of fortune' who bent the law for their own benefit, which, in turn, brought a reaction from the Law Association. The Minister responded by criticising what he called 'a capitalist clique' seeking to restore freehold tenure and speculative prices. And the controversy escalated further when the Law Association's chairman, a prominent Zambian lawyer, questioned the Minister's exercise of his discretion. He alleged that the Minister had personally intervened in one transaction to lower the agreed price and to direct the vendor's lawyers to sell to a specified individual and to no other. He also claimed that in one case where consent had actually been given, an official intervened to halve the price agreed. In other cases, he stated, different prices had been assigned to identical housing units, a builder had been ordered to sell a house below cost, and in one housing area consent to alienate had been given for some new houses and refused for others. He concluded by claiming that 'this appears to be a prima facie case of abuse of power'. In the event the Minister was suspended pending an investigation; subsequently, as noted, he was dismissed.

Graft & Factionalism

The cases discussed clearly indicate the close connection between graft and patronage. Most demonstrate the interweaving of activities designed to ensure self-advancement and those seeking to promote friends and political comrades. This is hardly surprising since they are part of the matrix of a clientelist political system. In the context of electoral politics, access to public office requires the mobilisation of support and the need to make pay-offs to supporters in general and to political lieutenants and brokers in particular. In the Zambian case, this mobilisation typically involves the construction of political networks from a local and regional base so that political factions are generally regionally, provincially, linguistically or ethnically defined – although the lines of demarcation fluctuate over time and across issues. Political factionalism thus has a provincial flavour and is referred to by Zambian politicians as being 'tribal' or as 'tribalism'.

It is not surprising, therefore, that the accumulation of spoils should take a factional form and replicate or reproduce factional lines of cleavage. And the evidence would indicate that this in turn has tended to promote and reinforce 'tribalism'. In Zambia the allocation of senior party and government positions has reflected the need to balance the claims of contending factions. The Cabinet, for instance, has been characterised by a (shifting) balance of posts between provinces. When shifts in influence within UNIP have led to adjustments in this balance, tensions have surfaced in the party. And when factional conflict has threatened to alter the balance drastically, the party and government have been plunged into political crises.

The SPAFIF affair particularly illuminates this factional influence in the spoils system. The loan beneficiaries were drawn, essentially, from four provinces – Eastern, Western, Southern and Central. By 1968, these were part of a larger coalition seeking to offset gains made in the UNIP power structure by Northern Province Bemba. Two of the loan recipients, indeed, were among the most important political figures in the country. Dingiswayo Banda had strong support in Eastern Province and in the urban areas and Sipalo had been one of the main leaders of the independence struggle. The loan practices were, apparently, first reported by a Bemba District Governor and, when the President accepted the DPP report and reinstated those suspended, criticism alleging widespread irregularity and discrimination was voiced in the press by two leading Bemba politicians (one a member of the Cabinet). These claims resulted in the creation of the Doyle Commission which essentially upheld the DPP. In 1972 elements of the Bemba faction left UNIP in substantial numbers to form a new party, the UPP. All three members of this group involved in the SPAFIF controversy were prominent in the new organisation. The UPP drew significant support from Northern and Copperbelt Provinces and its challenge was sufficient to provoke the creation of a one-party state in 1972. The SPAFIF scandal thus reflected the growing factional strains within UNIP; but it also exacerbated them and produced grievances which set in train events of profound importance.

The case studies indicate also that the operation of patronage and corruption can redirect official policy in anticipated directions. The SPAFIF and Land Act cases, in particular, show that policy designed to broaden the social base of that public enjoying access to state resources can be hijacked in the interests of private accumulation. In the SPAFIF case this process is revealed most starkly. Funds contributed by, and intended for the benefit of, peasant farmers were appropriated, albeit not illegally, by high level officials for the purchase of private farms on state land.

The Land Act was passed in order to check pervasive land speculation and to give Zambians the opportunity to obtain state land in prime areas after President Kaunda had denounced price inflation in transfers of undeveloped land. The Act sought to check such speculation by suspending the land market and giving the state the power to approve all transfers. In the event, as we have seen, such powers were also used to direct sales to particular individuals and at particular price levels. In other words, the Act, instead of making land available to a broad public, increased the pool of resources available to those with access to public office. Indeed, one MP even claimed that property expropriated from absentee landowners (one of the provisions of the legis-lation) by the state was being purchased by political leaders and government officials.

Instead, what seems to have occurred is that spoils exacerbate the disillusion felt by many with the inability of the state to meet the overwhelming demands and hopes directed at it. Particular advantage is often bought, as has been seen, at the expense of inefficiency and the failure of development projects. Graft, in the context of scarce resources, implies that people are able to 'jump the queue'. Thus the fact that some previously excluded elements gain access to the spoils of office simply means that others are excluded from that access. In such circumstances, the consequences for the legitimacy of the state are likely to be negative. Widely held notions that the 'government is corrupt', even where not true, are likely to produce low levels of commitment to the political system.

Class Formation & Class Struggle

The case studies indicate a fundamental relationship between state resources and the capitalist class, one that is part of the most significant structural change in Zambian society since independence – the formation of an indigenous propertied class. It has already been noted that the spoils system provides access to resources, position and wealth only by excluding others from that access; it is a form of 'queue jumping' as we have mentioned. Graft is therefore not an egalitarian instrument of social mobility. Those who obtain resources are often able to set up in farming or business (or to use their gains for greater consumption) and so to enter into the bourgeoisie from which Africans were excluded before independence. As Cohen has observed:

> The major activity of the ruling groups is an attempt to use the benefits of political power in an attempt to redress the insecure position they find themselves in. This can be seen in more general terms as an 'embourgeoisement' of the ruling elite.... Mutual back-scratching exercises are inaugurated ... governmental contracts are appropriated or supplied to supporters.... Wealth acquired from the holding of political office is used to acquire land, houses or small service industries.... The behaviour and activities of the ruling groups in office show their overt indebtedness to the political process as a means of developing class crystallization and solidarity.

The case studies considered have clearly exemplified this process. The Land Act controversy was most obviously one surrounding the acquisition of immovable property and of some valuable businesses. The Lusaka City Council, less obviously, involved not only the first generation of Zambian politicians and officials in local government, but also a cross-section of Lusaka's bourgeoisie and petty bourgeoisie. The Mayor was a successful businessman owning a construction company and the bar mentioned. Another Councillor was also a prosperous businessman and, indeed, later joined the board of at least one multinational corporation. And other Councillors were small traders, including one who was chairman of the UNIP co-operative society which ran four of Lusaka's markets. Access to public office thus either constituted an asset by which entry into the bourgeoisie could be obtained or an attraction by which capital already accumulated might be enlarged. The link between political office, with all its insecurities, and private property which might be obtained by preferential access was most clearly expressed in the SPAFIF case, however. In this instance loans were taken from the funds for the specific purpose of buying farm land for the private use of public officials. Public office, in itself, was not always adequate as a former minister indicated in court when explaining why he had taken a loan:

> Round about October (1968) I was aware of the consequences of the general elections so I was looking for property for myself. I was aware that we were going to lose the elections in the Western Province and also that I was going to lose my job (as Minister).

Yet it is not adequate simply to regard the spoils system as one in which advantaged individuals obtain preferred access to public goods and so are able to acquire the capital stake essential for entry into the petit bourgeoisie or the bourgeoisie proper. The resources to which such access is enjoyed represent taxes and levies drawn from the public at large. The appropriation of such resources therefore constitutes a net transfer of wealth from society at large to some privileged sections of it. The state, therefore comes to serve as an apparatus through which parts of the social product can be redistributed to incumbents of office and their supporters. In the SPAFIF case, the class character of this transfer is starkly demonstrated: there was, in that instance, an expropriation of surplus from the peasantry to the emerging bourgeoisie through the apparatus of the state by means of the spoils system. This relationship was even understood, to some extent, by the Doyle Commission. Noting that it was 'discreditable' for people in public office 'to descend like locusts on a fund to which none of them had contributed and from which morally they should plainly have been excluded', the Report observed that:

it is plain that all the persons concerned were favoured in getting loans because of their position. The ordinary African peasant farmer for whom loans under the Ordinance were really intended and whose contributions formed the funds was completely disregarded indeed left in the dark – in favour of a horde of privileged persons in public positions.

It is suggested that this observable link between spoils appropriation and class formation underlines the argument advanced here that graft, as a concept, has limited utility in explaining political practice and individual appropriation of public resources. But it is of great value when understood as part (perhaps a symptom) of a larger process of social change with important implications for political practice and class relations.

Bibliographic Notes

This paper is derived from my 'Corruption and the Spoils System in Zambia', presented to the conference on corruption, University of Birmingham, 4–6 June 1982. The original will appear in a collection to be edited by Michael Clarke.

On graft as a concept, see:
Heidenheimer, Arnold J. (ed.) (1970), *Political Corruption: Readings in Comparative Analysis,* New York: Holt, Rinehart & Winston.
Riordan, William L. (1963), *Plunkitt of Tammany Hall: A Series of Very Plain Talks on Very Practical Politics*, New York: Dutton.
Scott, James (1972), *Comparative Political Corruption*, Englewood Cliffs, N.J: Prentice-Hall.

On the emergence of a Zambian property owning class, see:
Baylies, Carolyn L. 'The emergence of indigenous capitalist agriculture: the case of Southern Province, Zambia', *Rural Africana* 4–5 (Spring–Fall 1979); and Baylies, 'Zambia's economic reforms and their aftermath', *Journal of Commonwealth and Comparative Politics*, 20 (3), 1982.
Baylies, Carolyn L. and Morris Szeftel, 'The rise of a Zambian capitalist class in the 1970s', *Journal of Southern African Studies,* 8 (2), 1982.

A fuller discussion of the patterns of Zambian development in the post-colonial period is found in:
Szeftel, M. 'Conflict, Spoils and Class Formation in Zambia'. Ph.D. thesis, Manchester University, 1978.

On factionalism and the spoils system, see:
Szeftel, M. 'The political process in post-colonial Zambia: the structural bases of factional conflict', in *The Evolving Structure of Zambian Society*, Proceedings of a conference at the Centre for African Studies, University of Edinburgh, May 1980.

Reports and commissions referred to in the text, include:
Report of the commission of inquiry into the affairs of the Lusaka City Council, November 1968 (Lusaka 1969); Report of the commission of inquiry into the allegations made by Mr Justin Chimba and Mr John Chisata (Lusaka, May 1971) (The Doyle Commission); Report of the commission of inquiry into the affairs of Zambia Railways (Lusaka, March 1978); Report of the commission of inquiry into the salaries, salary structures and conditions of service of the Zambia public and teaching services, Volume I. The Public Services and the Parastatal Sector (Lusaka, 1975) (The Mwanakatwe Report). All Republic of Zambia commissions.

The Annual Reports of the Auditor-General (Lusaka) have been extensively consulted; instances mentioned here are from the reports of 1970 (First Report) and 1972. President Kaunda's criticisms of the use of public resources and land speculation are in The 'Watershed' Speech, Address to the UNIP National Council, Lusaka, 1975.

References to the press are specified, point by point, in Szeftel (1978). Here they are necessarily more general. See *Africa*, 69, May 1977 and *The Times of Zambia*, October 1975, and *The Zambia Daily Mail* during January, June and August 1976, for details of the controversy over the Land Act. Selling off plots by party officials: *TZ,* 25 February 1976 and 5 June 1976; *ZDM*, 10 May 1976. The sale of citizenship case was described in *TZ* in November and December 1972 and in *ZDM* in May, November and December 1972, January through March 1973 and on 9 April 1976. References to prosecutions and dismissals of officials are from *TZ* and *ZDM* for March 1973 and February 1976 and April 1982. The SPAFIF case was documented in *TZ* and *ZDM* from December 1970 though March 1971, in April 1972 and March 1973. Debts in 1979 owed to SPAFIF are recorded in *ZDM* 9 April 1979.

9 JOSHUA B. FORREST
The Contemporary African State:
A 'Ruling Class'? [1987]

A number of analysts claim that, by adopting an economically exploitative and politically aggressive posture towards rural society, the state in post-independence Africa in fact is acting as a type of ruling class. In this contribution I briefly review the arguments of the principal proponents of this view, after which I present a critique of these arguments, in which I challenge the conceptual basis of the 'state as class' analytic school.

The Proponents

Henry Bernstein finds that the contemporary African state ' ... comes to be consolidated and reproduced as a class through its aggrandisement vis-à-vis civil society'. The notions of 'organisational bourgeoisie' and 'public sector bourgeoisie' were devised, respectively, by Markovitz and Hill, who view the state as consisting of managers in control of the overarching systems of political and economic power, personally benefiting from their pivotal positions and collectively acting as a class in pursuit of interests that are in conflict with those of other social classes. Their conceptualisations may in fact be viewed as advanced versions of Fanon's 'administrative bourgeoisie'. Stein extends this line of argument in particular regard to Tanzania, asserting that the means of organisation constitute the actual means of production, as the monopolisation over information and technical knowledge gives rise to a fourth great 'bureaucratic' class intent on reproducing the state by assuring that agricultural surplus is appropriated by and allocated in its interests, resulting in the organisation of economic activity under a 'bureaucratic mode of production'. Stein's analysis is largely consistent with von Freyhold's characterisation of a local governing class of 'Nizers', although it differs from Samoff's depiction of a more socially fluid and internationally influenced 'bureaucratic class'. Brett's presentation of a 'bureaucratic mode of production' in Uganda, where, he claims, the state directly and independently controls the means of production, also parallels Stein's view, although Brett understands the state to act not so much as a class in itself as in the interests of the local capitalist class. More closely sharing Stein's perspective is Thomas Callaghy, who shows that in Zaire as well – and even more so in Kenya (here relying on Swainson, Leys, Kitching, Beckman and Langdon) – a 'political ruling class (develops) out of the patrimonial administrative state and creates an economic base for itself' by entering the sphere of production and ensuring that domestically generated capital accumulation is appropriated by and serves those who comprise the state.

Several critics find that the nature of the African state as a class can best be understood within the context of its economic ties to international capitalism. Amin offers a particularly determinant view of a 'state bourgeoisie' either dominated by the local business sector and together with it forming a comprador class, or asserting its economic control over the domestic economy, but in both cases dependent on and acting as a transmission belt for the industrialised world-centre of international capitalism. Shivji finds that the 'bureaucratic bourgeoisie' comprises the upper stratum of the petty bourgeoisie which, now in a position of state power, seeks to consolidate that power against the commercial, working class and peasant sectors but objectively acts in the interests of the international bourgeoisie. While Saul similarly views the post-independence African state as commanding a hegemonic economic position over society and acting to consolidate internationally backed capitalism, he breaks with Shivji by focusing on the significance of political struggles within the bureaucratic sector, which he interprets as reflecting a variety of political and ideological positions among competing wings of the bureaucratic elite. For this reason Saul finds that, despite its connections to international capital, the class alliances formed by the state are not structurally predetermined, as they depend on which political tendency has the upper hand at a given historical moment. A more fully developed argument along this line of reasoning is suggested by Currie and Ray, who perceive the state as an arena of fractional class conflict, attempting to serve as a bonapartist arbiter of domestic antagonisms despite being limited in its hegemonic effort by societally based class interests. This emphasis on internal struggles is appreciated somewhat differently by Leys, who argues that the state reflects the particular contours of the class struggle within society, so that the political position of the state expresses the relative strengths of competing class segments. Therefore, the state is not necessarily beholden to or serving the interests of any one class, nor does the state in and of itself represent a ruling class. Nonetheless, Leys does stress that this apparent state autonomy is objectively deceptive, as the state does ultimately serve the interests of international capital, which remains the strongest economic element in post-colonial African society. In his 1978 article, Leys in fact came closer to accepting the notion of the relative autonomy of the state vis-à-vis international capitalism.

In an earlier, well-known analysis that set the stage for the dependency framework even though it rejected the class basis of the state, Meillassoux noted that, while the state bureaucracy does gain control of the economic infrastructure and attempts to use that control as a means of exploitation, it does not control the means of production and remains economically dependent on Western interests. As a result, while the bureaucracy does represent a 'new social group' that holds key political and economic power, its dependence on external forces and the fact that it was essentially created by the ex-colonial power rather than arising from a fully formed social class precludes consideration of the state bureaucracy in domestic class terms.

Sklar and Schatzberg offer the reverse perspective, de-emphasising the dependency relationship while offering an especially adaptive interpretation of the state-class connection. Sklar proposes the concept of a 'managerial bourgeoisie' that reflects the 'class consolidation' of a 'newly developing private sector' and a 'preponderant yet protective public sector' devoted to the management and distribution of wealth rather than to its creation. Schatzberg writes of a crosslinked 'political-commercial bourgeoisie' that dominates a pyramidal power structure in state and society, with the state playing the critical role because of its 'access to and control over the resources' of society, even though it does not control the means of production. The fluidity of class boundaries not only allows individuals to shift in and out of the state sector and to hold multiple class allegiances, but makes possible a 'perpetual structuration and destructuration' of classes themselves. Thus, while the state holds political power and the political-commercial elite jointly control the economic resources of the country, the class basis of the state is constantly changing and depends on the specific power configurations among the personnel within the higher levels of the state and the commercial sector. This 'contextual and processual' approach is employed in expanded form by Young and Turner, who see the state as

> a congealed representation of class relations, provided that no exclusive determinism is attributed to this factor, and that the on-going flux and change produced by processes of social conflict remain within the analytical field of vision.

Kasfir has recently lent theoretical depth to this approach, arguing that a Weberian state-centred and marxian class-focused framework can be 'conjoined' to better account for the mutually supportive interconnections that typically bolster the power of both the state and the capitalist class in present-day African countries.

Finally, a particularly dynamic approach to the state-class question is assumed by Bayart, who asserts that it is wrong to argue that the high functionaries of the state constitute a dominant class precisely because they do not enjoy real control over the means of production. Rather, the Cameroonian state both: 1) makes possible the privileged positions of dominance held by the ruling elite and 2) serves as a matrix of micro-conflicts within this elite among those whose positions of dominance are based on a) class (born to the pre-colonial aristocracy or made newly rich in the colonial or post-colonial period), b) power (administrative or party officials) or c) strategic positions of economic enrichment (in agriculture, real estate, commerce, transport, industry).

The Critique

With the exception of Bayart and Meillassoux, all of these analysts regard the African state as comprising, linked to or part of the dominant class, but there are several major conceptual and analytic difficulties underlying these various approaches which render problematic their utility in understanding the nature of the state and state-society relations in post-independence Africa. The first is expressed by Sklar (and adopted by many of the above analysts), who bluntly declares that 'class relations, at bottom, are determined by relations of power, not production'. This is a statement that in my view obfuscates and defuses the structural and dialectical significance of the notion of class, yet it serves as an underlying theoretical basis of the analyses of Sklar, Callaghy, Markovitz, Schatzberg and Young and Turner. These critics all explicitly recognise that the basis of the economic power of the state is political, resting in the control of the organisational superstructure of society and to some extent of key trading and marketing sectors. However, I do not find that this justifies conceiving of the state or its ruling members as a class: the fact that a group holds political and economic power does not *ipso facto* make it a 'class', much less a 'ruling' class, and certainly not any kind of 'bourgeoisie'.

The strength of a given class, as Meillassoux, Brett and Bayart have pointed out, in fact depends on its relationship to the means of production, which in turn determines its relative *power* vis-à-vis other classes. If a class does not *control* the means of production, then it is not a *ruling* class. The bourgeoisie (capitalist class) possesses private property, is able to expropriate the product of production, controls the means of production (wage labour and privatised land), and appropriates capital through profits and rent gained from private investments. The state in Africa does not act as a bourgeoisie in any of these senses,[1] and because it does not exercise substantive control over the means of production (land, labour and tools) cannot act as a ruling class. The people who make up the state do hold power at the national level, and they do seek to carry out their interests as political leaders and administrators, but they do not form a class or a bourgeoisie.

I, therefore, oppose the notion of 'organisational', 'public sector' or 'bureaucratic' bourgeoisie, of 'managerial class' and of 'ruling political class'. As Perry Anderson demonstrates in his study of feudalism, the state may well play a key role in assuring economic exploitation and may even appropriate unto itself much peasant wealth through, for example, extractive interference in marketing or via taxation, but this does not indicate that the state itself constitutes a social class. While it is arguable that contemporary Eastern European states may be seen in class terms, this is in light of their truly extensive control of the production processes – a situation which, as Bayart and Meillassoux have noted, African states are not close to attaining, despite the arguments of Stein, Callaghy and Hill.

A second and related difficulty is that the efforts by Sklar and Schatzberg to alter the marxian concept of class, which they do in an attempt to clarify the empirical situations they describe, in fact renders the theoretical notion of class less meaningful. Schatzberg, for example, adeptly depicts the social fluidity within the Zairian state structure and the ways in which state, socio-economic status, ethnicity, lineage and organisational affiliations combine differently depending on the particular context. However, the theoretical discussion concerning the 'contextual' changeability of class serves only to detract from his otherwise instructive analysis and to overturn the significance of class as a socio-historically specific, and therefore meaningful, social grouping.

Similarly, Saul's interpretation of competing *ideological* positions among the Tanzanian state elite as representing 'class struggle' is an unconvincing reification of intra-elite debate, obscuring actual class struggle that may be occurring in Tanzanian *society*. Saul's view is partially shared by Leys and Shivji and reflects an unfortunate tendency among some Africanists to impose a modified marxian framework on a social context in which classes are in fact quite difficult to locate. I am not claiming that class analysis is not relevant to a number of African social formations, but rather that, as Bayart and Schatzberg show, the extensive social fluidity within African societies renders clear identification of classes particularly difficult. This does not necessarily mean that we ought to dispense with the marxian concept of class so much as to employ it with the analytic care that is necessary to retain its materialistic meaning as a social grouping with a particular relationship to the means of production (a relationship which must be defined) in a specific mode of production (which also must be defined). Without specifying the class means-of-production relationship and without defining the role of a particular class in an identified mode of production, the notion of class loses its heuristic utility, its analytic meaning, its historicity and its power of explanation regarding both political conflict and economic change. The failure of most of the above analysts to do this has weakened the conceptual strength of their paradigms, as 'class' is transformed into no more epistemologically significant a term than 'group', 'caste', 'clique', 'status', 'name', 'identity', or 'affiliation'.

Finally, the emphasis placed by Amin, Shivji, Saul, Leys and Meillassoux on the connection of the post-independence state to international capitalism in Africa does indicate that domestic bourgeoisies and class conflict have not arisen in a fully developed manner despite the continuing penetration of the capitalist market economy.

Nonetheless, in appraising the contexts of their analyses it appears that dependency theory over-emphasises the political role of international capital and substantially underplays the significance of domestic political factors. In particular, the unwillingness to view the state as attempting to exploit society *for itself* instead of for a Western-based bourgeoisie – constitutes a delusive analytic limitation. Collusion between Western capital and the African state is not a one-way relationship, and the claim that the state is 'objectively' or 'ultimately' dependent on or subservient to the international bourgeoisie masks both the benefits in economic power gained by the state through such collusion and the exploitative role of the state – *qua* state, not as dependent 'class' – in domestic society.

Thus, the state in post-independence Africa is not a ruling class or a bourgeoisie, nor is it singularly beholden to the forces of international capitalism. It is, rather, an institutional composite of elites who hold national political power within a given territorial framework and who wield that power in order to advance their self-defined organisational, political and economic interests. While class analysis remains essential for understanding social change and political conflict in contemporary African societies, it is a conceptual error to assume, as most of the above-discussed analysts do, that the African state may itself be viewed as comprising, or as part of, a social class.

Endnote

1 While the state does pay the salaries of a relatively large number of public servants, its role as wage employer is too limited to embrace more than a fraction of the total working population, the overwhelming majority of whom are in the peasant sector.

Bibliography

Amin, Samir (1974), *Unequal Development, An Essay on the Social Formations of Peripheral Capitalism* and *Accumulation on a World Scale,* New York: Monthly Review Press.
Anderson, Perry (1974), *Lineages of the Absolutist State,* London: NLB.
Bayart, Jean-François (1979), *L'Etat au Cameroun,* Paris: Presses de la Fondation Nationale des Sciences Politiques.
Beckman, Björn (1980), 'Imperialism and Capitalist Transformation: Critique of a Kenya Debate', *ROAPE* 19, pp. 48-62.
Bernstein, Henry (1981), 'Notes on State and Peasantry,' *ROAPE* 21, pp. 44-62.
Brett, E. A. (1978), 'Relations of Production, the State and the Ugandan Crisis', *West African Journal of Sociology and Political Science*, 1, 3, pp. 249-84.
Callaghy, Thomas M. (1984), *The State-Society Struggle: Zaire in Comparative Perspective,* New York: Columbia University Press.
Currie, Kate & Ray, Larry (1984), 'State and Class in Kenya – Notes on the Cohesion of the Ruling Class', *Journal of Modern African Studies*, 22, 4, pp. 559-93.
Hill, Frances (1977), 'Experiments with a Public Sector Peasantry: Agricultural Schemes and Class Formation in Africa', *African Studies Review*, 20, 3, pp. 25-41.
Kasfir, Nelson (1984), 'Relating Class to State in Africa', in Kasfir (ed.), *State and Class in Africa*, London: Frank Cass, pp. 1-20.
Kitching, Gavin (1980), *Class and Economic Change in Kenya: The Making of an African Bourgeoisie,* New Haven, CT: Yale University Press.
Langdon, Steven (1977), 'The State and Capitalism in Kenya', *ROAPE* 8, pp. 90-98.
Leys, Colin (1975), *Underdevelopment in Kenya: The Political Economy of Neo-colonialism,* London: Heinemann; (1976), 'The "Overdeveloped" Post-Colonial State: A Re-evaluation', *ROAPE* 5, pp. 39-48; see also 'Capital Accumulation, Class Formation and Dependency', in Ralph Miliband & John Saville (eds) (1978), *The Socialist Register,* pp. 241-66.
Markovitz, Irving Leonard (1977), *Power and Class in Africa,* Englewood Cliffs, NJ: Prentice-Hall.

Meillassoux, Claude (1970), 'A Class Analysis of the Bureaucratic Process in Mali', *The Journal of Development Studies*, 6, 2, pp. 97-110.

Samoff, Joel (1983), 'Bureaucrats, Politicians and Power in Tanzania: the institutional context of class struggle, *Journal of African Studies*, 10,3, pp. 84-96; (1979), 'The Bureaucracy and the Bourgeoisie: decentralization and class structure in Tanzania', *Comparative Studies in Society and History*, 21, 1, pp. 30-62.

Saul, John S. (1979), 'The State in Postcolonial Societies', in his *The State and Revolution in Eastern Africa* New York: Monthly Review Press; London:Heinemann, pp. 167-99.

Schatzberg, Michael G. (1980), *Politics and Class in Zaire*, New York: African Publishing Company.

Shivji, Issa G. (1976), *Class Struggles in Tanzania*, New York: Monthly Review Press.

Sklar, Richard L. (1979), 'The Nature of Class Domination in Africa', *The Journal of Modern African Studies*, 17. 4, pp. 551-2.

Stein, Howard (1985), 'Theories of the State in Tanzania: A Critical Assessment', *Journal of Modern African Studies*, 23,1, pp. 44-62.

Swainson, Nicola (1978), *The Development of Corporate Capitalism in Kenya 1918–1977,* Berkeley: University of California Press.

von Freyhold, Michaela (1977), 'The Post-Colonial State and its Tanzanian Version', *ROAPE*, pp. 75-89;

Young, Crawford & Turner, Thomas (1985), *The Rise and Decline of the Zairian State,* Madison, WI: University of Wisconsin Press.

Young, Crawford (1982), 'Patterns of Social Conflict: State, Class and Ethnicity', *Daedalus*, 3.2, pp. 71-98.

10 EIICHI SHINDO
Hunger & Weapons:
the Entropy of Militarization   [1985]

The Hungry Third World

When delivering an appeal for the abolition of nuclear weapons to a United Nations university symposium in Cambridge, the Japanese representative was somewhat taken aback by the response from Third World delegates that the anti-nuclear movement was a movement of the First World, and that what was important to the Third World was a solution to the problem of hunger. Our common sense about the causes of hunger inclines us to the view of nuclear weapons and hunger as the separate phenomena of separate worlds, in which hunger is a phenomenon unique to the Third World. According to this common sense view, hunger is caused exclusively by the vagaries of a cruel nature, in particular by the drought which affected the Third World, especially Africa, continuously during the 1970s. Attention should, however, be directed to the fact that human factors not only are involved in that hunger but also constitute a structural cause of it, that cause being intimately linked to the behaviour of the advanced world.

Another Myth

Quite apart from looking to the 'outside' for the human causes of the hunger of the developing countries, it is also possible to look for them in the 'inner' elements of the countries themselves, especially in the special character of their political-economic systems. The classic example is the view which sees the socialist system as being the main cause of hunger. According to this view, the inefficiencies peculiar to socialism cause hunger in that people who have their land taken away from them by the state when the land is nationalized under socialism lose the will to produce. Famine in Tanzania and Mozambique is ascribed to the same cause. And in general this is correct. In both Ethiopia and Mozambique, productivity and harvest are greater in 'household farms' than in 'state farms', and the central governments fall into the evils of 'socialist' bureaucracy and become unable to take into consideration the voice of farmers on the spot.

Two Common Factors

The affinity between famine in Africa and the socialist system stems from at least two common factors, apart from the 'inefficiency' of the nationalized 'Animal Farm'. First, most of the new states which established their independence from colonial rule oriented themselves towards the socialist system. Secondly, these new states which oriented themselves towards the socialist system became to a greater or lesser extent enmeshed in war and changed into 'heavily armed' states.

May we not then see the famine which engulfs the newly emerging 'socialist' states of Africa as due not so much to the 'inefficiency' inherent in the socialist system as to the large number of refugees produced by war, and to economic crisis deriving from insufficiency of national capital being directed to production for the civilian sector as a result of the transition to the 'heavily armed' state?

The simple statement of the Mozambique farmers – 'Life was fine for two or three years after independence, but became hard here about three years ago' – should perhaps be understood as indicating this process by which the newly emerging 'socialist' state is transformed into an 'armed state', rather than a systematic weakness inherent in socialism. Only then will we grasp the significance of on-the-spot reports that what the farmers of the hunger-stricken newly emerging 'socialist' countries of Africa lack is not so much the will to work as the means to work – ploughs and hoes.

The Conditions of Independence

Many new emerging countries, after casting off the yoke of colonialism or neo-colonialism, chose the socialist, rather than the Western capitalist system. Unfortunately for these newly emerging states, enormous difficulties had to be faced as a result of adopting the socialist system and trying to break free of the world capitalist system.

First, no sooner has independence been gained than the advanced Western countries, particularly the former sovereign power and the multinationals, try to intervene in the 'new authorities' of the newly emerging country with the aim of seizing their still remaining rights and interests. When this happens, the advanced Western states, in order to maintain the international political and economic order which favours the advanced countries, a polarized order, become a counter-revolutionary force, or a force for the frustration of the revolution, together with the supporters of the 'old regime' that still survive at a stage when the new authority is being formed. Witness the classic cases of the Russian and Chinese revolutions.

Second, the newly emerging states start off pregnant with peculiar elements of confusion inherited from the colonial system. In the case of the African countries, the element which has to be stressed among these is that the new governments start off with an inheritance of a variegated racial and tribal mosaic, and therefore these new 'socialist' states with their weak power bases find themselves caught up in a situation of fierce civil war.

On top of this, the rapid social change that stems from the choice of a socialist system produces fierce clashes with the traditional local value system and reduces to tatters the threadbare national mosaic. The Ethiopia-Somalia war is one example: a combination of the effects of the Eritrea and Ogaden-Somalia liberation struggles.

The third point to be made is that revolution and counter-revolution on the part of the African states extends beyond national frontiers. So far as Africa south of the Sahara is concerned, there is confrontation between the group of revolutionary states made up of Angola, Zambia, Tanzania, Zimbabwe and Mozambique, and the counter-revolutionary force centred in South Africa. For example, South Africa has given military assistance to two counter-revolutionary forces in Angola since that country's national independence – UNITA (Angolan National Union for Complete Independence), and FNLA (Angolan National Liberation Front), and has kept fanning the flames of counter-revolution, while it has provided military assistance to various anti-government struggles and continually cast from outside the coals of war and counter-revolution in Zimbabwe.

Thus, no sooner are the newly emerging states independent (or have their revolution) than, facing war internally and externally, they have to strengthen their military power in order to cope with war and to maintain their power. In other words, while being engulfed in war, the newly emerging states are for that reason led along the path to heavy armament – and famine. This is the heavy burden that must be borne by the new states just after they establish their power, or at an early stage when they possess only a weak power base.

Civil War & Heavy Arming

It could in fact be said of all the newly emerging African 'socialist' countries afflicted by famine that they are states ravaged by civil war, in all of which the degree of militarization is being intensified.

FAO (United Nations Food and Agriculture Organization) emergency food aid is concentrated on 24 countries south of the Sahara. If Guinea-Bissau, which is struggling with a food crisis of similar proportions, is added to these, 13 countries, or over half of the 25, are spending more than 15 per cent of their government expenditure on military items. If countries are counted in for whom the cost of weapons imports exceeds that of (ordinary) military expenditure, and which is often covered by loans, the number of 'heavily armed' states amounts to 24. Nearly all of these militarized states are, in one way or another, in a state of war.

For some years now, for example, military expenditure as a percentage of government expenditure has been running at about 30 per cent in Mozambique and Chad and 40 per cent in Ethiopia, while in Cape Verde, Somalia and Uganda, weapons imports amount to between 30 and 60 per cent of all imports and cost far more than the total (ordinary) military expenditure.

Opportunity Cost & Military Government

The logic of heavy weaponization leading to famine can be amplified in the following way.

First, in that increased military expenditure blocks expenditure on the civilian sector that is more urgently necessary than anything, it is accompanied by huge opportunity costs. In extreme cases, this takes the form of famine. Without any doubt it makes the allocation of resources to the civilian sector, increasing food productivity, irrigation works, and health and welfare more difficult; it prevents economic development and creates the basic conditions for famine.

Second, 'heavy weaponization' leads to the relative strengthening of military power. This in turn lends extra force to the process of ballooning military expenditure. Completely contrary to the argument of the modernizationist development economists who hold that, because the military is almost the sole coherent bureaucratic organization in developing countries, it functions as the proponent of modernization, so that the military triggers off the energizing of the developing country's economy, the opportunity costs of militarization are increased under the military regime. Actually, one-third of the famine countries of sub-Saharan Africa, and more than two-thirds of those of other 'famine powers', are under military regimes or heavy military influence.

Regimes from Brazil and Thailand to Ethiopia and Uganda which took power by military coup d'état thereafter without exception increased their military expenditure by between three and six times.

But it is not just that heavy militarization increases the opportunity costs of militarization or strengthens the power of the military. In accord with the established economic theory of heavy militarization itself, the economies of the developing countries are eroded and the man-made conditions for famine are generated from within. According to the classical theory, military expenditure and militarization are understood to function in both developing and advanced countries not as blocks to economic development but as stimuli. First, military expenditure, like other public investment, creates effective demand since it produces consumption and employment in the ordinary civilian sector. Secondly, investment in military technology stimulates technological innovation in the ordinary civilian sector, strengthens the technology base of the domestic economy, and contributes to economic development through a technological linkage effect. In fact, contrary to this hypothesis, the peculiar character of the contemporary armaments industry is such that it is bound to function always as a blocking factor, never making any contribution to the economy of the developing country. The militarization of the developing countries also distorts the development of healthy democratic politics and serves to reincorporate the post-independence developing country in the polarized hierarchical system of advanced country control.

Why is it that the militarization of the developing countries becomes a factor blocking their economies? And why do developing countries become militarized? And finally, why is it that when the developing countries invest a certain amount of their energies in military matters this serves to reinforce their dependence on the advanced countries?

The Rotting Economy: The Significance of the Deformed Weapons Economy

The point to be made at the outset is that the contemporary structure of militarization produces a dual distortion. First, militarization operates not just at the centre of world politics, as in the past, but extends to the periphery. This is especially evident in the dramatic escalation of Third World military expenditure. For example, although Third World military expenditure in the 1950s amounted to no more than 5 per cent of world military expenditure, it reached 19 per cent in the 1970s and 25 per cent in the 1980s. Now, while the average annual growth rate of military expenditure is only 1 per cent among the advanced countries, it is nearly 10 per cent in the Third World. The expansion of militarization to the periphery is sustained by the export of weapons from the centre. While weapons transfer to the periphery formerly accounted for only an extremely small proportion of weapons exports from the centre (20 per cent in the 1960s), now the opposite situation prevails and it constitutes the bulk of them, 80 per cent.

Second, within this change in the structure of militarization, the character of military power is changing from labour-intensive to technology- and capital-intensive. Because of this, the negative influences upon the civilian economy of developing countries which are oriented towards militarization, are bound to increase.

It produces a rapid escalation in the cost of weapons production, thereby making it necessary to divert vast resources to armaments. For example, the cost of a fighter-plane, at current prices, escalated by 15 times between the beginning of the 1960s and today. Government expenditure on a hitherto unprecedented scale is necessary today in order to reinforce military power. This substantially diminishes the opportunity of investment in the agricultural sector that is crucial to the 'survival' of developing countries.

Although about 50 per cent of GNP is produced by agriculture, between 10 and 50 per cent of government expenditure goes to the military, and government investment in the agricultural sector is only a fraction of what goes to the military. And, because of the shift towards technology-intensive military power, the increase in military spending is unable to help relieve the Third World's growing unemployment problem. To the extent that military power becomes technology-intensive, weapons are mechanized and a large force of soldiers becomes unnecessary. This is evident in the fact that, even in developing countries which possess considerable military power, the number of soldiers is relatively few, in many cases remaining at the level of less than 10 per 1,000. Even in the case of a developing country that has been able to build up its own weapons industry, it is only the final, weapons-assembly stage that is labour-intensive. Therefore, unable to generate significant employment, the tendency rather is to reinforce the conditions of unemployment and famine.

The transition to technology-intensive military power strengthens the tendency towards weapons systems, pushing the rest of the economy into deeper straits as a result. Nowadays, increasingly, weapons cannot function by themselves but only as part of a large-scale system. For the construction of such an infrastructure, investment which should be going to subsistence agriculture has to be diverted in large quantities to the military sector.

Besides, when a developing country undertakes the role of forward base for an advanced country by beginning to produce weapons, this involves a fattening of the 'base-type' or 'war-type' economy through an extraordinary expansion of the secondary industrial sector and explosive growth of the tertiary, base-oriented service sector. Either way, all that happens is that the distortions suffered in the rest of the economy are accentuated, the local agricultural base is destroyed, and the underlying conditions of famine are strengthened. The situation would perhaps not be so serious if the cost of weapons imports was made up only of the price of the weapons. Since contemporary weapons are technology-intensive and highly systematized, the import cost of a bomber or a tank does not exhaust the cost of the weapons system. Consequently, weapons imports become much more expensive than their actual 'price'. This puts pressure on the finances of poor developing countries, creates large deficits on trade account, and thus reinforces dependence on the advanced country.

Furthermore, the imported weapons and weapons systems, unlike ordinary machines for civilian use, make little contribution to expanding the productive capacity of the developing country and therefore the export capacity. Moreover, because excessive weapons imports put pressure on the government's finances, and investment in the agricultural sector is inadequate, the volume of food imports has to be increased. The import of weapons from the advanced countries is not just a matter of weapons; it also makes necessary accompanying imports of food.

Regression to Monoculture

How can developing countries solve the dilemma brought on by increased weapons imports? They tried to solve the dilemma by playing their last trump card, that of increasing their export strength by increasing the output of domestic raw materials such as oil or copper or increasing the production of cash crops such as coffee, pepper, cocoa and peanuts. It is the logic of increasing coffee production to buy weapons.

But the industrial structure of the developing country is bound to be distorted by the increased production and export of mineral resources and cash crops. The actual consequence is that the developing country society is made to regress to the structure of monoculture that prevailed under the colonial system. This undoubtedly undermines the economy of the developing country and leads to famine.

Fully Domestic Production to Export

Not all developing countries are confronted with such a predicament arising from weapons imports. Those states among them which are advanced in industrialization commonly adopt two strategies for resolving the dilemma.

One is the move towards domestic production of weapons, and beyond that to export of weapons. These may be described as the second and third phases of developing country militarization. These two stages are, in the industrialization of developing countries, the stages of development from import substitution to export promotion.

But, unfortunately for the developing countries, consistent progress in the direction of domestic weapons production does not necessarily help alleviate the conditions of Third World famine. This is because, as we have already stressed, contemporary military power is changing to a capital-intensive model. The domestic production of weapons has become something which consumes vast quantities of raw materials. In fact, to the extent that the domestic production of weapons involves devouring the developing country's scarce resources, the flow of capital is reduced to the subsistence sector which is crucial to staple food production, and that sector becomes weaker and is de-developed.

Furthermore, even if large amounts of raw materials are exploited and domestic production of weapons is successfully undertaken, the military technology which is developed does not have much multiplier effect on the ordinary civilian sector. Since military power is high-technology-intensive, it is quite remote from the indigenous technology of the traditional society of the Third World and cannot meet the requirements of local industry.

Yet many developing countries are today trying to develop a domestic weapons industry in order to reduce the economic and political costs of weapons imports. Those countries that succeed in doing this then move to adopt weapons export policies, in order to ameliorate the 'dis-economies of scale' associated with domestic production, i.e. inefficiency stemming from the narrowness of the domestic market. The weapons themselves have become high-technology-intensive, and the speed of technological innovation is extremely rapid; the developing countries with their weak technology base are unable to keep up with such rapidly advancing waves of technological development.

The fact that the design to become a weapons exporter leads rather to increased imports of weapons and technology is given further impetus by pressures from the armaments industries of advanced industrial countries like the United States and France. The armaments industry of the advanced countries promotes sub-contracting arrangements, or direct investment, in the developing countries, in order to take advantage of their cheap labour. Such sub-contracting arrangements are today particularly developed in the electronics sector. Many parts and semi-processed goods are assembled using the low wages of the relatively low 'country-risk' countries, including the developing countries known as NICs – South Korea, Taiwan, Singapore,

Hong Kong and Mexico – and then re-exported to the advanced countries.

Then there is the flow of direct investment, including a trend in the armaments industry towards production under so-called vertical joint production arrangements. Arms production itself, being closely tied up with state secrets, may not necessarily be easy to promote. The trend towards direct investment has recently developed very rapidly, both because it has become difficult to draw a clear distinction between military and civilian and because the level of dependence on advanced country technology for repair and maintenance has increased rapidly as a result of technological complexity.

Increase in Accumulated Debt

The move on the part of developing countries from domestic weapons production to weapons export reinforces their economic dependence on the arms industry of the advanced countries, and through such ties also reinforces their political dependence on the advanced countries. But this does not exhaust the negative effects of the move to domestic production and the export of weapons. The industrial structure of the developing country is distorted, substantial debts to the advanced countries are incurred, and these accumulated debts reinforce dependence on the advanced countries.

The conditions for a worsening of accumulated debt are aggravated in the case of the so-called 'middle developed countries' which are striving to 'catch up' with the advanced industrial countries by stepping up the pace of their industrialization. This is because the very act of 'catching up', like that of entering upon domestic weapons production, is bound to deepen economic dependence on the advanced countries which are overwhelmingly superior on the basis of their advanced technology and abundance of capital.

The following facts are known about the relationship between accumulated indebtedness and famine. First, many of the developing countries which are militarized and troubled by vast accumulated debt are either major famine countries with starving populations of over 10 million, like Indonesia, Brazil, Philippines and Pakistan, or if not yet major famine countries, are nevertheless states in economic depression with unemployment and inflation rates in double figures, like Egypt, Argentina, Algeria, Peru, or Morocco.

Second, while the new sub-Saharan 'socialist' countries in Africa, which have broken away from the Western capitalist system, are afflicted by famine, they are relatively free of the pressures of accumulated debt. Not only are these 'socialist' states still at a stage of pre-industrialization, but they are also influenced by the fact that loan conditions in the case of loans provided for weapons export by socialist countries including the Soviet Union are advantageous to the recipient country.

Third, the expansion of accumulated debt has been promoted by the positive credit provision policies mainly by the advanced Western countries. In this sense, the militarization of the developing countries is being encouraged and promoted in the interests of the governments, finance capital and the armaments industries of the advanced countries, and the underlying conditions of famine thereby aggravated. It becomes impossible to see the militarization of the advanced countries, concentrated around nuclear weapons, and the economic crisis of the developing countries symbolized by famine as the separate phenomena of two different worlds.

Bibliographic Notes

The data on military expenditure and armaments are taken from:
Kaldor, Mary and Eide, Asbjorn (eds) (1979). *World Military Order*, New York: Praeger.
Komatsu So (1983) 'Sengo shihonshugi no hatten kozo' (The development structure of post-war capitalism),
   Part 1, Keizaigaku Ronshu, March.
Neuman, S. G. (1984) 'Third World Military Industries', *International Organisation*, Winter.
Stockholm International Peace Research Institute (1984) *SIPRI Yearbook*.
UNICEF (1984), UNICEF Information No. 84102, April.
United Nations (1982), *The Relationships between Disarmament and Development*, New York: UN.
UN Information Centre (1984), *Dateline UN*, No. 81, February.
US Arms Control and Disarmament Agency, *World Military Expenditures and Arms Transfers, 1972–82*,
   Washington, DC.
Whynes, D. K. (1979), *The Economics of Third World Military Expenditure*, London: Macmillan.

On the relationship between armaments and employment:
Melman, Seymour (1970), *The Political Economy of Pentagon Capitalism*, New York: McGraw-Hill, while
   on the relationship between arms and the broader economy, see Kaldor, M. (1977), 'The Role of Arms in
   Capitalist Economies: the Process of Overdevelopment and Underdevelopment' in D. Cariton and C.
   Schaerf (eds), *Arms Control and Technological Innovation*, London: Croom Helm; on military produc-
   tion and technology, see for example, Tuomi, (1982) and R. Vaeyrynen (1983), *Militarisation and Arms
   Production,* London: Croom Helm, also Kaldor and Eide (eds). op. cit.

On militarization and third world debt, see *IMF Annual Reports,* and *Financial Statistics*, Washington, DC:
   IMF annually, and monthly respectively.

On arms transfers to the third world, see R. Vaeyrynen, 'Economic and Political Consequences of Arms
   Transfers to the Third World', *Alternatives*, VI (1980); Minoru Sekishita, 'America teikokushugi to buki
   yushutsu' (American imperialism and arms exports), and Ryusuke Takita, 'Dai san sekaiî he no buki
   yushutsu to ìshinshokuminchi-shugiî no tenkai' (Arms export to the 'Third World' and the new phase of
   'neo-colonialism'), *Keizai*, January 1979.
See, for example, Senghaas, D., 'Military Dynamics in the Context of Periphery Capitalism', *Bulletin of
   Peace Proposals*, 1977–78.

11 BJÖRN BECKMAN
The Military as Revolutionary Vanguard: A Critique [1987]

The Context of Debate

What is the likelihood that the military will play a leading role in the revolutionary transformation of Nigeria? What are the theoretical premises for such a possibility and what is the historical evidence that may offer support? It is only recently that the Nigerian left has started to ask such questions in a serious manner, as distinct from fits of messianism and indulgence in myth making. Messianism is the hope in the emergence of a powerful leader that will offer redemption. There is a distinct left military variety of this myth in Nigeria, from Major Nzeogwu (1966) to General Murtala (1975) and Major Umar (1985). However, the deepening economic crisis and the crisis of bourgeois state power have placed the left military option on the agenda of scholarly debate.

Tyoden's Revolutionary Vanguard

In addressing these concerns the most immediate point of departure, however, is a recent argument presented by Sonni Tyoden, a Jos political scientist, in a paper, 'The Military and the Prospect for Socialist Construction in the Third World' (1985). It can be seen as a response to another Jos scholar, Iyorchia Ayu's 'To Smash Imperialism in Africa: Militarism and the Crisis' (1985). Ayu takes a 'classical' marxist position: the military must be understood as the repressive apparatus of the state and the ruling class. Its role is therefore primarily counter-revolutionary. In the current African context this means, according to Ayu, that the military intervenes either to dislodge regimes that threaten to move to the left (e.g. Nkrumah, Modibo Keita) or to prop up dependent capitalism in crisis. Ayu is dismissive of certain currents on the left that 'either out of frustration with the lack of momentum of revolutionary ferment or for organisational inaction, believe, or seek consolation in militarist solutions'. He argues that such solutions 'can not substitute for an organised and ideologically disciplined revolutionary movement':

> For, inspite of the few African armies which have jumped on the revolutionary truck, the terrain is still populated heavily with counter-revolutionary militarism. And probabilistically speaking the promise is that future intervention will continue to follow the dominant pattern – taking the side of reaction. (Ayu, 1985:5)

According to Tyoden, on the other hand, there is nothing to prevent a socialist fraction within the Nigerian military from taking control of state power. Tyoden's position should be seriously examined. It is an attempt to develop a scientific argument rooted in the tradition of marxism. According to Tyoden, the deepening crisis of global capitalism, the peculiar form that this crisis takes in a neo-colonial society, and the type of 'critical social forces' which emerge in such a situation are all factors which contribute to raising the possibility of the military acting as 'a vanguard for the socialist transformation of Africa'. It is even a possibility 'that stares us in the face'. He agrees with Ayu that the military in Nigeria has so far 'been nothing but an extension of the bourgeoisie in uniform'. But things are changing:

> there is nothing in the present conjuncture to prevent the emergence of a socialist fraction in the Nigerian military in control of state power in Nigeria. With this emergence, the first steps towards the socialist transformation will be a reality. Until then however we shall continue to wallow in our bourgeois neo-colonial existence (Tyoden, 1985:7).

Not only is such a socialist take-over a possibility, according to Tyoden, but it is *the* way that socialist transformation will begin in this country. Not only that: it is *the* hope for deliverance from neo-colonial misery! Tyoden builds his own position on a critique of 'the dogmatic and unscientific intellectual tendency that dominates marxist discussions of the military in the politics of Third World states'. In the marxist theory of the capitalist state, the military, according to Tyoden, is seen as the repressive arm of the state apparatus. Yet, an inflexible application of this position to all societies in all times goes against the very spirit of marxism. Marx's own analysis referred to advanced capitalist societies with fully developed class forces. Marx warned against his own sketch of the rise of capitalism in Western Europe being taken as a theory of the 'general path every people is fated to thread, whatever the historical circumstances in which it finds itself' (Marx's rejoinder to Mikhailovsky as quoted by Tyoden). It is therefore necessary, according to Tyoden, to consider the forms and possibilities for socialist transformation that can be realised in a specific historical conjuncture with its specific constellation of class forces.

This sounds like an admirable methodological position. The problem, however, is that Tyoden fails to offer such an analysis of concrete conjunctures and social forces. He is therefore left with a theoretical non-position as his ultimate defence. It is wrong, he claims, to *exclude the possibility*. This is not good enough for a scientific argument which is supposed to offer support for political positions. There is a wide gap between Tyoden's theoretical and political positions. On the one hand, he wishes merely to 'expose us (even if only theoretically), to the possibility of the military being a vanguard of socialist transformation'. He argues that it is unscientific and un-marxist to exclude such a possibility. This theoretical modesty contrasts, on the other hand, with the extravagant conclusion that there is nothing that prevents this theoretical possibility from being realised in Nigeria right now. The first position merely suggests a theoretical possibility, however small; the latter suggests that the probability is high. There is no need to disagree with the first position. It is indeed wrong (theoretically) to exclude possibilities, even if they are unlikely. However, such a position does not offer much of a basis for political analysis. We are interested in probabilities, not theoretical possibilities. It does not mean that we are only interested in what is most probable. Also lesser probabilites are important as they may be affected by political struggles.

This is, by the way, a point where Ayu errs. He is wrong to be dismissive of the experience of left-wing military coups in Africa on the basis of right-wing ones being more probable. Even if this is so, we are still interested in the probability of left-wing coups, as long as it is not negligible, because they as well will have implications for political developments and left strategies (see the quote from Ayu above). But not just that. Ayu's own position becomes seriously undermined if he fails to also allow for the deviant cases. It is no good claiming that military coups are 'counter-revolutionary' if there are cases which do not fit this pattern. We need to understand the basis for the deviation and how it affects the theory.

Tyoden, however, has little to offer in support of the probability of a socialist military take-over in Nigeria, either theoretically or empirically. His argument is limited to passing references to the global capitalist crisis and its neo-colonial manifestation. There is no attempt to discuss what there is in a neo-colonial society in crisis that produces socialist forces within the military capable of taking over state power. Why, for instance, is it not more likely that the military is prompted by the crisis to intervene on behalf of the threatened bourgeoise, as suggested by Ayu? If both tendencies are there, what is the nature of the social and political forces, within the military and outside, that allows us to evaluate probabilities, high and low? Tyoden's military revolutionary vanguard remains elusive. Little scientific reasoning underlies the ideas about how the first steps towards the socialist transformation of Nigeria will become a reality. The idealism contrasts glaringly with the professed commitment to a materialist method in the 'spirit of marxism'.

Soviet Theory: the Army as Motive Force

Tyoden indicts marxism for its dogmatic views on the military. The indictment seems particularly unwarranted if we look at contemporary Soviet theories. In fact, we find here what is absent in Tyoden, an attempt to offer a theoretical and historical explanation of the revolutionary role of the military in the Third World. We find no 'inflexible attachment' to an 'anti-militarist view' (Tyoden, 1985:4).

> In the past the armies under the antagonistic system were as a rule, a dependable support for reaction and conservatism; today, on the contrary, patriotic tendencies in the army have become prevalent and are exerting a major impact on developments in a number of countries (Dolgopolov, 1981:5).

Dolgopolov does not speak of 'vanguard' as do Tyoden and Madunagu, but his choice of words is equally strong. He speaks of democratic and patriotic army sections as *motive force* and even the motive force of national liberation and democratic revolutions (p.6). The armies of the liberated countries, that is, the ex-colonies, differ radically, he says, from those of the imperialist states which are instruments of class oppression. They differ because they are born in the struggle for independence and therefore 'largely anti-imperialist in nature'. They set themselves national tasks and 'serve as the mainstay for a national resurgence and social progress' (p.40). This is the *general tendency*, although great variations exist between socialist-oriented regimes at one end and right-wing ones, at the other. Part of the explanation of the revolutionary potential lies in the social origin of the officers. In the (advanced) capitalist armies, the upper echelons have close class, business, family and other ties with big business (p.58). In many armies of Asia and Africa, on the other hand, officers come mostly from the petty bourgeoisie:

> Their ties with the bourgeois-landlord circles are generally weak and they are close to the people. They not only, therefore, oppose imperialist and feudal oppression; they also, under certain conditions and to certain extent, oppose capitalist relations, too (Dolgopolov, 1981: 45).

This difference in social composition is in turn related to differences in levels of development. In tropical Africa, for instance, 'the classes of modern society have only just begun to take shape' (p.44). Lower levels of class development also mean lower levels of class antagonism. This is reflected in a greater 'community of interest of officers and men, and the overwhelming majority of the nation in their fight to free themselves from foreign oppression' (p.22).

The opposition to imperialist domination leads to the politicisation of the army: the struggle over the choice of development course takes place also within its ranks. It opens up the possibility of a broad democratic front in the fight for economic independence and the eradication of backwardness and poverty (p.39). In Africa, the leading role of the army becomes particularly important because 'the class structure is amorphous and the political parties, if any, are not strong enough'. In this situation the army is 'the most organised social force' (p.39).

The Soviet argument centres on two related aspects: the low development of class forces, on the one hand, and the primacy of imperialist domination in shaping contradictions in society, on the other. How far does the theory help us to explain developments in individual cases of non-capitalist or socialist orientation?

Dolgopolov refers primarily to Afghanistan, Ethiopia, Yemen (PDR), Congo, Angola, Mozambique, Benin and Madagascar. He notes that they represent a diversity of conditions but that in all of them 'revolutionary-democratic representatives of the armed forces lead the implementation of the progressive changes that are bringing about socialist orientation' (pp.55–6). He does not attempt to show how the movement in the direction of socialist orientation in each case can be explained with the help of the theory.

How far do these cases support a theory of the military as revolutionary vanguard? The problem is not so much the varying fit of the individual cases. The theory can be interpreted so as to be wide enough to accommodate them. The problem is rather that it is so wide that it ends up explaining very little. Third World societies, virtually by definition, exhibit a relatively low level of development of class forces. Also by definition, most of them are dominated by imperialism. Yet, antagonistic class relations have developed almost everywhere. So what will be more decisive in influencing the military? To what point will the 'unity of the army and the people' on an anti-imperialist platform prevail?

In particular, how do we take account of the dominant pattern of right-wing military regimes in the third world, e.g. Indonesia, Pakistan, Bangladesh, Thailand, South Korea, Taiwan, Turkey, Argentina, Brazil, Chile, Nigeria, Egypt, Zaire, Sudan, only to mention some of the major ones during recent times? We must be able to relate different tendencies of military involvement in third world politics to one theoretical framework that is capable of explaining the differences.

In what sense could we be justified in talking of a general tendency? We could do so even if the right-wing cases are numerically dominant, as long as the theory makes it plausible that the left-wing ones are on the increase. It seems, however, as if the basic assumption about the low development of class forces suggests the opposite: that it is a theory with a declining territory as these forces continue to develop and solidify. The theory seems in fact to highlight an essentially transitional political conjuncture in the passage from colonialism to independence. It does not address itself to the regrouping and formation of capitalist-oriented class forces, internal and external, that take place in the neo-colonial situation.

How Does Nigeria Fit?

The Soviet theory speaks of a general tendency towards progressive army involvement, but it also recognises countries where the armed forces have developed features 'typical of bourgeois armies' (Dolgopolov, 1981:40). So which one is Nigeria?

It is difficult to see Nigeria as a society where antagonistic social relations and classes have not developed or where class contradictions have not affected the armed forces. The anti-imperialist tendencies within the petty bourgeoisie, including the army, may well be there. But there are also strong links between the officer corps and the propertied classes that benefit from the present social order. It is difficult to imagine Dolgopolov's 'community of interest' and unity within the armed forces on a national platform. The nationalism of the dominant classes differs from that of the dominated ones. The army itself has served as a powerful vehicle of bourgeois class formation, with a growing number of senior officers establishing themselves in business, either alongside their army careers or on early retirement. Many serve as managers in state enterprises or as members of boards of directors, both in the private and public sectors. Defence contracts have created avenues for dealing profitably with transnational companies, not just in arms but in communication technology and in the more mundane requirements of the armed forces, such as cement for army barracks. The petty-bourgeois origins of perhaps a majority of these officers is of little consequence for their distinctly bourgeois class careers.

Whatever opening there may be for socialist-oriented elements within the Nigerian armed forces, it seems closer at hand to see it as a function of the intensification of antagonistic relations in Nigerian society, rather than, as the Soviet theory suggests, in their absence or low level of development.

As Tyoden acknowledges, 'we have to situate the military concretely, within the interstices of ongoing socio-political processes and the context of class struggle in society'. Unfortunately, Tyoden fails to do so himself. Dolgopolov also suggests that the class composition of the army reflects the nature of the state and is therefore in the final count 'determined by the class relations existing in the country' (p. 8). He does not, however, make use of this theoretical insight in his analysis. Instead, we meet, just as in Tyoden's case, a strong element of idealism.

Idealism, Class Suicide & Relative Autonomy

By idealism in this case, I refer to the tendency to stop at the level of people's preferences (ideologies, etc.) when explaining why they act (for instance, make revolutions). This is in contrast to the attempt to identify determinants of people's choices and the range of options open to them at a material level, that is, in relation to the configuration of power in society as determined ultimately at the level of production and manifested in class formation, class struggles, and political organisation.

Tyoden speaks of the possibility of the military fraction of the bourgeoisie committing 'class suicide', that is, abandoning its class interests in favour of the oppressed classes. We meet similar suggestions in Dolgopolov's work: patriotic and democratically minded officers are expected to 'renounce the role of an instrument of the exploitative upper crust' (p.112). There is a tendency to see the struggles within the army as one between different ideological orientations ('opposite social trends'). It obscures the extent to which social forces impress themselves on the class orientation of different segments of the armed forces.

This is linked to a theory of petty-bourgeois politics that emphasises ideological vacillation and lack of class determination (cf. Williams, 1976). In explaining, for instance, the abandonment of the non-capitalist road in Egypt, Dolgopolov speaks of 'some petty bourgeois sections shifting to pro-capitalist positions and taking up conservative and reactionary views' (p.47). This does not explain anything. What was it that made such sections shift to the right? What was the underlying balance of class forces in society that gave direction to petty-bourgeois vacillation? It is also suggested that Nasser failed to remove offsprings of rich bourgeois families from military command posts which 'largely predetermined the victory of the pro-capitalist trends in the country' (p.58). Was this failure an oversight? Should it not be seen as reflecting the actual character (and limitations) of Nasser's revolution, as well as the very real strength of the bourgeoisie?

Instead of social forces with materially determined class orientations, we meet ideological class categories, left-wing and right-wing groups, competing for power. Armies, we are told, develop features typical of bourgeois armies 'where power has been captured by the right-wing' (Dolgopolov, p.40). As an explanation this is circular. The army is spoken of as an 'arena' for contestation between different tendencies. It obscures the fact that the arena itself is materially determined, and so are the rules of the game under which such contestation takes place. The 'relative independence' attributed to army politics in Soviet theory (p.42) is part of a view of the class character of the state that informs the theory of non-capitalist development: a low level of class determination, due to the lack of strong bourgeois or proletarian class forces, which creates an opening for ideological struggles within the petty bourgeoisie that holds positions of state (military) power. There are strong similarities with theories of the 'relative autonomy' of the post-colonial state, at least in the manner in which these have been applied to Africa (see Goulbourne, 1979). Here the state apparatus is inherited from colonialism, rather than emerging from the development of classes within the social formation itself. This is supposed to enhance the relative autonomy of the state vis-à-vis local classes.

It is only in the African context that this 'relative autonomy' argument has been linked to the 'freedom' of the petty bourgeoisie to choose between socialism and capitalism. In its original formulation by Hamza Alavi (1972) in relation to Pakistan, there was no doubt about the bourgeois class character of the state.

The concept of relative autonomy, whether applied to state or the army, is unhelpful in so far as it offers exemption from a substantive analysis of the social determinants of political options. Once it is realised that the range of options is itself materially determined, the usefulness of the concepts becomes limited.

Imperialism & the Ruling Class

Central to the Soviet argument as well as to much of the left analysis in Nigeria is the notion of a dominant national contradiction between the people and imperialism. It is this that is expected to give an anti-imperialist and thus potentially socialist orientation to alternative regimes despite the absence of a politically significant working class. It is the basis of the broad national unity that is expected to sustain the left forces within the military when embarking on their road to socialist transformation.

The problem with such identification of contradictions is that it underestimates the extent to which imperialist domination is incorporated in the social formation. The advancement of local bourgeois class forces, for instance, is closely linked to world market relations as mediated by foreign firms. While there is competition in business opportunities, the contradiction between foreign and domestic capital is not antagonistic (Beckman, 1981, 1982, 1985). Even in situations where the domestic bourgeoisie is still weak (which is not the case in Nigeria), a broad range of bourgeois-oriented commercial classes, including importers-exporters, distributors, contractors, cash-crop producing farmers, etc., are critically dependent on and anxious to maintain the imperial link. They are certain to resist any drastic policy of de-linking. They can not be reduced to a compradorial element that can be easily isolated and eliminated. They occupy a critical role in the social formation, mediating relations between imperialism and all social classes in the circulation of commodities.

These strong commercial links also penetrate the state apparatus including the armed forces. Public institutions are central in circulation and accumulation. Any attempt to challenge the imperialist domination of the society is therefore likely to lead to confrontation with these broad and politically important commercial strata.

Far from being a source of national unity, imperialist domination is the hub of bourgeois class formation and the development of antagonistic social relations. Imperialist domination has a decisive influence on the class orientation of state power but in a rather different way than suggested by the theories discussed here. While it may give rise to anti-imperialist tendencies in society, the primary function of imperialist domination is to reinforce pro-imperialist state power. It is not the absence or low development of capitalist class contradictions, therefore, which will generate a basis for anti-imperialist politics, it is the intensification of such contradictions.

Furthermore, the theories underestimate the extent to which imperialist domination is translated into external support for faltering capitalist-oriented regimes as well as the obstruction of pro-socialist break-away attempts. The successful break-aways are few and their survival is threatened by imperialist-sponsored destabilisation and counter-revolution. Even when such threats can be contained with support from the socialist countries, they subject the revolutionary process to extreme strains that undermine both its material achievements and its democratic foundations. The external threat under-scores the critical role of firmly rooted democratic organisations capable of sustaining the process and protecting its democratic content.

Underestimating imperialism also means underestimating the ruling class. This is why Tyoden sees nothing that prevents a socialist military take-over in Nigeria. It borders on a world view without ruling classes where power is a question of a free-for-all struggle between ideological tendencies, left, right and centre. In Dolgopolov's study the nature of ruling class power is obscured by expressions such as the exploitative or reactionary 'upper crust', 'upper echelons' or 'upper stratum' (pp.6,22,66,112). Such metaphors help to separate ruling class power from the general structure of power relations in society, including its imperialist backbone. As a consequence, the political effort necessary to achieve a broad unity, behind a national revolutionary programme and the removal of such 'upper crust', is underestimated.

The ease by which regimes are toppled in Africa has given the erroneous impression of a 'power vacuum', only waiting to be filled by determined left forces. Such ideas draw support from arguments which point to the failure of bourgeois regimes to establish hegemonic power. This makes them unstable and prone to be overthrown by the military (Falola and Ihonvbere, 1985:258–9). Their inability to achieve hegemony is in turn explained by their dependence on imperialism which obstructs the development of capitalism (ibid., p.261). Acheampong's overthrow of Busia and Rawlings' overthrow of Limann met with very little resistance, despite the fact that both regimes could claim a recent parliamentary mandate. In Nigeria, many have therefore seen revolutionary openings in the present deepening crisis of the bourgeoisie, as evidenced by both the collapse of the Shagari regime and subsequent fractional manoeuvring within the armed forces.

But crisis at the level of political regimes cannot be equated with a crisis of ruling class power. Lack of consolidation, fractionalism, failure to solve questions of succession by constitutional methods, etc. do not necessarily threaten ruling class power. That power is entrenched both in the economy and in the state apparatus, irrespective of the coming and going of regimes. Moreover, the weakness or strength of the ruling class can only be assessed in relation to non-ruling class forces. The weakness of the former only creates revolutionary openings if the latter are strong enough to sustain alternative state power. The 'power vacuum' that seems to be created by political crisis may therefore be deceptive.

Political Implications: Adventurism & Democracy

Despite protestations to the contrary (for instance Tyoden, p.7), military vanguardism is an invitation to adventurism. By this I mean a tendency to commit political forces in support of left-military bids for power in situations where the prospects of succeeding are small. It is a gamble with high stakes. While such bids may succeed in temporarily installing a left-wing regime, its ability to contribute meaningfully to social trans-formation is obstructed by the weakness of its organised political base and the resilience of ruling class forces entrenched in production and the state apparatus.

The attempt to rally left forces around such a project exposes them to the prospects of right-wing repression when the project collapses. It may shatter existing organisa-tional efforts and eliminate scarce cadres. But repression may also come from the left-military regime itself. Precisely because of its weak organised democratic base and its susceptibility to 'counter-revolutionary' subversion, such a regime will tend to be highly insecure and intolerant with opposition also within its own camp. The experience of existing socialist-oriented military regimes in this respect points to this danger.

Left-wing organisations may also seriously discredit themselves in the eyes of the people if they rally behind regimes whose misjudgment of the balance of social forces makes them end up administering ruling class policies. The militarist tendency encourages the neglect of political organisation. The military is made to substitute for the missing political vanguard. In discussing the role of the military in Third World revolutions, however, the primacy of political organisation has been forgotten. There is a conspicuous absence of references to the relationship between the military and the rest of society except in general formulas such as the 'unity of the army and the people' and the necessity of 'the participation of the broad population' (p.7) We are left ignorant about who is to direct the revolutionary process and ensure its democratic content.

We have seen how military vanguardists take the organisational weakness of the left as an alibi for military substitutionism. A more relevant response to this weakness would be to give highest priority to organisation including the struggle against state repression, the strengthening of internal democracy, and struggles in defence of popular interests so as to earn the confidence of the people.

In Nigeria, we may only look at the difficulties faced by the trade unions, the weakness of their democratic structure, the low level of effective unionisation (partly concealed by the check-off system), their vulnerability to state repression, and their powerlessness in face of the crisis policies imposed by the state. In such a context, the military vanguardist project is diversionary.

The neglect of democratic organisation by the military vanguardists throws some doubts on the class nature of their revolutionary project. For what revolutionary forces is the military supposed to provide the vanguard? The emphasis on the national unity on an anti-imperialist platform and low levels of class antagonism suggest a revolution that is more national than democratic. This impression is reinforced by the way in which the revolutionary regime is seen as substituting for a missing 'national bourgeoisie' in the task of emancipating the nation. There is a common view within the Nigerian left, that the first stage of any national democratic revolution must seek the broadest possible alliance of forces on a national, anti-imperialist platform. This does not mean that the class content of the national democratic project can be left to a later stage. What will ensure that the benefits of the national revolution reach the people?

The national democratic movement therefore needs to be firmly committed to democracy: to the establishment of the most favourable conditions possible for the development of democratic organisations. The experience of Afro-Asian countries is one more confirmation of Lenin's thesis that the proletariat and all the working people must pass through the hard school of struggle for democracy as the essential condition of successful struggle for the socialist transformation of society (Ulyanovsky, 1980: 144).

Military vanguardists are perturbed by what they consider as the excessive emphasis placed by 'vulgar anti-militarists' on the political form of regimes, 'pushing the main thing – its class essence and social goals – into the background' (Dolgopolov, p.69). Tyoden has a similar formulation. According to him, the dogmatic anti-militarists refuse to see that *type* of regimes does not matter. The importance is whether they address themselves 'to the needs and aspirations of the mass of the people' (p.4). This obscures the basic relationship between political form and political content. The popular democratic content of a regime (whether military or civilian) will reflect the strength of popular democratic forces in society and their ability to impress themselves on the administration of State Power. The organised democratic basis of a regime is a central aspect of its political form. As this tends to be neglected by the military vanguardists, the democratic content itself is endangered.

How to Relate to the Military Left

The rejection of military vanguardism is not to deny the vital role of patriotic and democratic elements within the armed forces. What is criticised is 'substitutionism', the tendency to assign the military a leading role, in the absence of organised democratic forces. The positions of a national democratic front would have to be energetically pursued also within the armed forces. There is no case for vulgar anti-militarism. The strong anti-democratic traditions within the armed forces, their self-appointed role as arbiters in politics, and the authoritarianism of the military command system make it the more necessary that a democratic orientation should be developed within the ranks. Democratic and patriotic officers and soldiers could then increasingly come to define their role as part of the national democratic movement and be responsive to democratic leadership and direction. Nor does the rejection of military vanguardism preclude relating constructively to left military intervention in politics if and when it happens.

Bibliography

Alavi, Hamza (1972) 'The State in Post-Colonial Societies: Pakistan & Bangladesh', *New Left Review*, 74.

Ayu, Iorchia D. (1985) 'To Adjust or to Smash Imperialism in Africa: Military and Crisis', paper presented to CODESRIA/CSER Conference on the Economic Crisis, Zaria.

Beckman, B. 'Imperialism and the National Bourgeoise', in this volume.

Beckman, B. 'Whose State? State and Capitalist Development in Nigeria' in this volume.

Beckman, B. (1985) 'Neo-colonialism, Capitalism & the State in Nigeria' in Bernstein, H. & Campbell, B. (eds), *Contradictions of Accumulation in Africa*, Beverly Hills, CA: Sage.

Dolgopolov, Yevgeny (1981) *The Army and the Revolutionary Transformation of Society*, Moscow: Progress.

Falola, T. and Ihonvbere, J. (1985) *The Rise and Fall of Nigeria's Second Republic: 1979–83*, London: Zed Books.

Fatonga, D. (1986) 'The Army in Politics', *New Horizon*, Lagos, 6, pp. 1–2.

Fatunde, T. (1985) *No Food No Country*, Benin City: Adena Publications.

Goulbourne, H. (ed.). (1979) *Politics and State in the Third World*, London: Macmillan.

Graham, Y. (1984) 'Ghana, the Politics of Crisis: Class Struggle and Organisation, 1976–1983'. Paper presented at ROAPE Conference, Keele; also abbreviated in *ROAPE*, 34, 1985.

Madunagu, E. (1986) 'The Army as a Political Party', *The Guardian*, Lagos, 9 & 16 January.

Nigerian Political Science Association (1984) *State and Society in Nigeria: Selected Proceedings of the Annual Conference.* Benin City.

Palmberg, M. (ed.) (1978) *Problems of Socialist Orientation*, Uppsala: Scandinavian Institute of African Studies.

Tyoden, S. G. (1985) 'The Military and the Prospect for Socialist Construction in the Third World'. Paper presented at the Seminar on Nigerian Economy and Society since the Berlin Conference, Zaria.

Ulyanovsky, R. (1980) *Present Day Problems in Asia and Africa*, Moscow: Progress.

Williams, G. (1976) 'There is no Theory of Petit-Bourgeois Politics', *ROAPE* 6.

12 JOHN MARKAKIS
The Military State
& Ethiopia's Path to 'Socialism'
[1981]

In black Africa in recent years, socialism has appeared in military uniform and it is quite likely this will become the fashion in the continent. Unlike the routine intervention of the military in politics designed to shore up the sagging post-colonial system, the radical military coup is aimed against that system. As a result it inspires visions of a badly needed social transformation and attracts, initially at least, significant popular support. When the soldier-politicians make bold to invoke marxism and use the rhetoric of the class struggle, then the vision becomes that of a socialist revolution regardless of the objective conditions in their society. Such invocations generate sympathy in progressive circles abroad among those who, having despaired of popular initiative in Africa, are inclined to disregard the contradictions inherent in attempts to impose socialism from the top. Sooner or later these contradictions manifest themselves, forcing a reappraisal accompanied with a sense of betrayal.

Both the initial elation and the subsequent let down have been greater in the case of Ethiopia, where the intervention of the military has proved more radical, violent and controversial than elsewhere in Africa. While there is no doubt that the revolution of 1974 in that country was the outcome of class conflict and that it set off a process of social transformation, the direction this process has taken under military rule is a matter of continuing bloody dispute. The discussion in this article traces and interprets the course of events since 1974, following what might be termed Ethiopia's path to 'garrison socialism'.

The Ancien Regime

The collapse of the *ancien regime* was caused by a juncture of elemental forces arising out of national and class conflicts. The old regime's favourite appellation, 'Ethiopian Empire', was not a misnomer. The Empire had been created during the last quarter of the 19th century by the Christian feudal society of the northern highlands, the Abyssinians of old, through the conquest of the southern half of the present state. The Northerners took most of the good land in the south as the spoils of victory, and reduced the Muslim and pagan inhabitants of the region to the status of vassals. Class and ethnic divisions – the lines separating Abyssinian and others, lord and peasant, Christian and non-Christian – coincided ominously within the empire. Little changed in that equation during this century. In 1974, most of the large landowners in southern Ethiopia were Christians of northern origin, while their tenants comprised the majority of the indigenous population. It was the landless peasantry in this region that joined the revolution spontaneously and was to gain most from the land reform enacted subsequently.

Because the Abyssinian system of feudal rule could not be transplanted easily in the midst of an alien and hostile peasantry in the south, it became necessary to reform the state by reinforcing and renovating its central structure under the throne. A process of centralization-cum-modernization was promoted during the first half of this century. The functions of government were institutionalized in a bureaucratic form. Standing army and police forces were established. A system of modern education was founded· also to produce the required manpower for the state's new apparatus. Interrupted by the Italian occupation from 1936 to 1941, the process of centralization was resumed in the post-war period and raised the power of the throne to its absolutist zenith, in the familiar final phase of feudalism. Haile Selassie's remarkable reign spans the entire period.

In the post-war period the renovation of the imperial state was substantially assisted by the involvement of western powers in the internal affairs of Ethiopia. The emergence of the Middle East as an arena of great power competition greatly enhanced Ethiopia's strategic importance in the region. In the early 1950s, the United States replaced Britain as the patron of the imperial regime, providing military aid, economic assistance, capital investment and trade links. Nourished with American aid, the Ethiopian army became the largest force in sub-Saharan Africa in the mid-1960s. In the course of two decades (1950s and 1960s) Ethiopia received more military aid from the United States than the rest of the states in Africa combined. In return, the United States acquired a pliable ally in that volatile region, and was allowed to establish a huge, self-contained air base at Samara devoted to communication and intelligence functions.

The expansion of the state's repressive apparatus was required to meet an assortment of increasingly serious challenges to the integrity of the empire and the position of its ruling class. The latter was a hybrid group comprising a stratum of imperial retainers with modern education groomed to manage the newly-established administrative and military apparatus at the centre, and the feudal aristocracy which, though it had relinquished most of its traditional ruling functions and some of its power, retained intact its provincial authority and held on to its massive landholdings. The army and police were continually engaged against nationalist movements and peasant uprisings, while more recently they were also used against workers and the radical student movement which harassed the regime during its last decade.

Dissident nationalism posed the first and gravest challenge. The struggle of the Ogaden Somali against the imperial regime spanned the entire post-war period. Inevitably, it turned to irredentism when the Somali Republic attained independence in 1960, and the conflict kept Ethiopia and Somalia on the brink of war for several years. In the early 1960s it spread into the adjacent Bale province, where the Muslim Oromo population made common cause with their Somali coreligionists.

The nationalist struggle in Eritrea began in 1961. The area had come under Italian colonial rule late in the 19th century, at the time of the Ethiopian expansion southwards. The expulsion of the Italians in 1941 brought Eritrea under British rule and launched a struggle concerning the region's future. The desire for independence, particularly strong among Muslims, who comprise one-half of the population, was countered by a claim for unification with Ethiopia, forcefully promoted by the imperial regime. A compromise worked out by the great powers and sponsored by the United Nations in 1951 gave Eritrea self-government within a federal union with Ethiopia. Eritrea's model constitution and open political system made it an unsettling contrast to the feudal domain of Haile Selassie, and offered no guarantee against the growth of dissident nationalism. No sooner had it been agreed upon than the regime in Addis

Ababa set about undermining the arrangement. Ten years later it succeeded in incorporating Eritrea into the imperial state as a simple province. Immediately thereafter, the Eritrean liberation movement began an armed struggle for independence which continues to this day, having earned already the unenviable title of 'Africa's longest war'.

The development of the urban sector during the post-war years and the appearance of new social groups produced additional sources of conflict. Welcomed by an obliging Ethiopian government which offered every possible inducement and also itself invested heavily in the development of infrastructure, foreign capital was attracted into manufacturing for import substitution during the 1950s and 1960s. With only minimal participation from private domestic capital, Ethiopia acquired a modest, modern economic sector which was mostly foreign-owned. By the end of the 1960s, three-quarters of the private paid-up share capital in manufacturing was in foreign hands, as was the management of nearly all member concerns of the Federation of Employers of Ethiopia. Foreign firms also controlled import and export trade, while expatriate communities settled in the country dominated the intermediate trade sector. Confined to local and retail trade, the Ethiopian trader community, which was predominantly Muslim, nursed a double grievance against the imperial regime which championed Christianity and protected foreign merchant capital. Thus instead of fostering the growth of an Ethiopian middle class with a base in the modern economic sector, nascent capitalism actually inhibited the development of such a class, thereby precluding a bourgeois succession to the *ancien regime*.

Nevertheless, capital created its counterpart, wage labour. The Ethiopian working class grew to a very modest size by the mid-1960s. Thereafter it ceased to grow, as preference for capital-intensive production methods reduced the capacity for labour absorption in industry to nil. Employment in manufacturing never rose much above 50,000, out of an estimated total of 400,000 in urban productive employment; at the close of the 1960s the population of Ethiopia was estimated at about 25 million. In order to maintain a cheap, docile labour force as an incentive for foreign investment, the imperial regime forbade labour organization until 1962, when its absence became an embarrassment. Thereafter, it closely regimented the nascent trade union movement, which proved unable to defend its members against the crude exploitation characteristic of infant capitalism. Wages of unskilled workers remained the same for more than 15 years, despite the inflationary trend in prices during the last years of the regime. Young and raw though it was, the Ethiopian proletariat could not fail to perceive the linkage between the imperial state and foreign capital. Frequent, forceful intervention of the first on behalf of the second during industrial disputes provided a constant demonstration of this fact, and helped develop the political consciousness of the workers.

The intelligentsia, yet another social group spawned by the *ancien regime*, comprised the administrative and technical salariat in the public and private sectors. Its size was small; according to one estimate, the number of university and secondary school graduates in 1967 did not exceed 40,000. Until then, while the public and private sectors expanded steadily and offered secure employment, educated Ethiopians enjoyed an enviable standard of life and rising social status. Despite growing intellectual alienation and political frustration, they appeared a submissive group. This was not to last, because the long-term prospects for this group were unpromising. The *ancien regime* had relegated it to a permanently subordinate position in the social structure. The intelligentsia could not aspire to the role of a national bourgeoisie, since foreign capital and management had largely pre-empted this role. Nor could many educated Ethiopians hope to rise to the higher levels of bureaucratic officialdom, because promotion to that level, always limited by the presence of the imperial retainer clique, proved increasingly difficult as the public sector became crowded with relatively young people.

The complete alienation and political radicalization of the intelligentsia in the late 1960s coincided with the onset of unemployment and inflation. The closure of the Suez Canal in 1967 caused a sharp decline in trade and contracted the main source of state revenue. A parallel decline in the price of coffee, Ethiopia's main export, further diminished state revenue. As a result, the expansion of the state sector was halted, and the educated stratum was deprived of its main source of employment. This coincided with the stagnation in the employment capacity of the private sector, and produced an employment crisis that remained unresolved until the demise of the regime. Unemployment hit the educated group for the first time and even university graduates had to scramble for positions. Furthermore, world inflationary pressures were manifested locally by 1969 in rising import prices, and were reinforced by the impact of domestic drought which drove food prices upward in the early 1970s.

The 'February Revolution'

The popular upheaval that became known as the February Revolution erupted in the middle of that month in 1974. It began with a strike of taxi drivers in Addis Ababa provoked by an increase of 50 per cent in the price of petrol. During the months that followed, a mounting wave of strikes, boycotts and demonstrations hit the urban sector with cumulative force, loosening the eroded foundation of the regime. The movement involved all the alienated social groups in the urban sector, including students, teachers, workers, civil servants, traders, Muslims; even a section of the Christian clergy joined it. The teeming crowds of the urban unemployed participated enthusiastically. At the same time, scattered peasant attacks in the southern provinces put landlords and officials to flight and paralysed the provincial government in that region. Soon the people's demands became explicitly political, ranging from the dismissal and punishment of corrupt officials to a call for constitutional government. Class alliances were forged in action, as workers and the intelligentsia joined forces in a direct attack on imperial officialdom and foreign capitalism. Both these groups championed the cause of the landless peasant and attacked the landlords. In the midst of it all, Ethiopians were stunned by revelations about the lethal progress of a major famine in the northeastern region, which had begun a year earlier and was to claim ultimately an estimated 200,000 lives. Though forewarned, the imperial government had taken no action to prevent the catastrophe. It had exerted some effort only for the purpose of suppressing public mention of it. To that end, it rejected all offers for assistance from abroad, and involved the international aid agencies in a conspiracy of silence through which it sought to smother the calamity. When the truth became known, it was skilfully used by the opposition to dissolve the remnants of imperial mystique still clinging to the minds of the common people.

The class struggle that was tearing the fabric of Ethiopian society was faithfully reflected within the ranks of the military, producing a series of mutinies that shattered the regime's main instrument of repression. The initial mutinies were provoked by the harsh conditions of continuous service in remote areas of Eritrea, Bale and the Ogaden, while fighting inconclusive wars against nationalist guerrilla forces. The inadequacy of salaries and allowances were additional grievances, exacerbated by contrast with the perquisites with which Haile Selassie sought to buy the loyalty of the higher officer corps. The initiative in these affairs was taken by non-commissioned officers and ordinary soldiers who arrested all officers and took command of their units. This element in the military represented the peasant class from which it was recruited.

The majority of the junior officers shared the social background and aspirations of the intelligentsia. Founded in 1957, the Military Academy at Harar drew its students from among the better secondary school graduates, while another training school at Holeta put capable non-commissioned officers through an abbreviated officer training course. By 1974, the oldest graduates of the Harar academy had reached the rank of major. The junior officers proved highly sympathetic to the mutinous mood of the soldiery, and were able to participate from the outset in the military rebellion. Eventually they assumed a guiding role, and emerged ultimately as the dominant element in the Co-ordinating Committee of the Armed Forces which took command of the military establishment in June 1974.

The Dergue ('Committee'), as it became known, was partly elected and partly co-opted to represent the various branches and units of the military establishment and, later, the police and territorial army. Initially it was composed of 120 persons, ranging in rank from plain soldier to major. Subsequently the Dergue rejected demands to renew its membership through election, and to fill the vacancies created by the purging of over one-half of its original members. Shortly after its formation, the Dergue decapitated the military hierarchy by decimating the higher officer corps through execution, arrest and dismissal. A series of arrests during the summer months netted also most of the high officialdom of the *ancien regime*, and isolated the octogenarian Haile Selassie, who made no serious effort to stem the encroachment into the imperial prerogative by what foreign journalists dubbed the 'creeping coup'.

While the Dergue felt its way cautiously towards a coup d'état, a powerful ideological current flowed through the popular movement. Its source was a group of radical intellectuals who had espoused marxism in the 1960s. They formed the core of two generations of university and secondary school students who had mounted a militant opposition to the imperial regime during its last decade. Now the radicals aimed to raise the class consciousness of the masses and to guide the popular movement towards a social revolution. They defined the nature of the struggle as anti-feudal, anti-capitalist and anti-imperialist. They urged the soldiers to acknowledge the class character of the conflict, and demanded the overthrow of the imperial regime as a prerequisite to fundamental change. While urging the military in that direction, they also warned against a military takeover of the state. Pointing out that a social revolution could not be achieved without popular participation, they called for the formation of a Peoples' Government. The radical message was formulated in clear and concise form, had a widespread circulation through a regular underground press, and gained immense influence among the urban population. It had a catalytic effect by providing a common ideological focus for the aspirations of the various social groups swept into the revolutionary current that was battering the regime. Though barely familiar with ideological notions, the disadvantaged classes instinctively responded to the radical initiative, thus making it the dominant orientation of the uprising against the *ancien regime*. In the course of the year, all organized groups, such as workers, teachers and students adopted resolutions which reflected vividly the influence of the radical left.

Military Rule & Class Conflict

At the outset, the Dergue appeared ideologically innocent and without any programme. Its motto 'Ethiopia First' seemed a typical nationalist clarion call. The Dergue's initial list of objectives, issued in July 1974, was a familiar catchall. It proclaimed the 'dignity of labour', but made no mention of the class struggle, nor did it betray any ideological affinity. The soldiers' conception of social transformation at the time appeared to encompass simply the elimination of corruption, nepotism and tax evasion, as well as the promotion of literacy, hygiene and other instrumental notions of development. When the Dergue removed one prime minister in July, it replaced him with another member of the high aristocracy. The Dergue seriously considered retaining Haile Selassie on the throne as a constitutional monarch and when, after months of hesitation, it deposed him (on 12 September 1974), the soldiers named his son as his successor. At the same time, the Dergue renamed itself the Provisional Military Advisory Council (PMAC) and assumed the powers of the state.

The new regime could hardly afford to ignore the social forces that had enabled it to seize power. In fact, it proved keen to accommodate them and gain their support. The soldiers themselves were quite receptive to the radical formulation that had captured the popular mood. In fairly short order, they sought to make up for their ideological naivete and lack of programme by adopting the radical orientation of the marxist intellectuals and by appropriating most of their programmatic suggestions as well. This alignment seemed natural enough, given the congruence of class between the popular and the military movements. It was also an expedient one, for it was calculated to win popular support and provide a legitimising ideology for the new regime.

Once in power, the PMAC came under great pressure to establish its revolutionary credentials by dismantling the socio-economic foundations of the old regime. The radicals advanced their own motto – 'The Broad Masses of Ethiopia First' – and subjected the inexperienced soldier rulers to withering criticism of their every move or failure to move. Specific policy proposals came from youthful radicals who gained rapid promotion in the civil service under the new regime, and from a coterie of radical intellectuals who acted as advisers to leading members of the Dergue. Under this pressure, the PMAC began the nationalization of the means of production at the beginning of 1975.

In March of the same year, a sweeping land reform decree was proclaimed, which went further than most Ethiopians had anticipated. All agricultural land was nationalized, possession was limited to a maximum of ten hectares, and the sale or rent of land was prohibited. Thus both landlordism and tenancy were eliminated at one stroke. Peasant associations were formed to implement the provisions of the reform, which included the redistribution of available land into equal shares within each association. In July 1975, urban land and extra housing were also nationalized, ownership being limited to one housing unit per family. Rents were substantially reduced for the cheaper housing, benefiting the lowest income group.

The reforms were enthusiastically received, and popular organizations associated with their implementation sprang into life overnight. The emancipated southern peasants rose to the occasion by their eager participation in the peasant associations, which showed promise of becoming instruments of genuine local self-government. Despite the 'provisional' tag in its title, the PMAC was quick to formulate an appropriate rationalization for prolonging its rule indefinitely. The 'men in uniform' had become the vanguard of the revolution by historical necessity. The insistent call of the radical left for a peoples' government was rejected as untimely, and its proponents were dealt with increasing severity. To ensure its monopoly of power, the PMAC set about dismantling the few existing organizations that could possibly serve as vehicles for political opposition.

The first victim was the Confederation of Ethiopian Labour Unions (CELU) which claimed about 50,000 members at the time. CELU had come into its own as the workers' representative in March 1974, when it staged an unprecedented general strike, and succeeded in forcing the resignation of the imperial cabinet, another event without precedent in Ethiopia. During the hectic months of 1974, this formerly docile labour organization staked increasingly radical positions under pressure from the rank and file and the goading of radical intellectuals who infiltrated its inner councils. Barely a week after the military takeover, CELU called a general strike in support of the demand for a peoples' government. Premature and ill-prepared, the action failed and brought CELU under heavy pressure from the new regime, which determined to turn the labour organization into an instrument of its own rule. A year of harassment followed, during which CELU's leadership languished in prison, while the regime manoeuvred unsuccessfully to place its own agents in control. Throughout 1975, the labour movement lay dormant. Pending the appearance of a new labour code, all labour activities were banned, all collective agreements were suspended, and new ones could not be negotiated, nor could the trade union movement organize workers in areas from which it had been excluded by the previous regime. A promise to form worker councils in the workplace was never implemented. A wage freeze lowered real wages in a time of continuous inflation, and unemployment rose substantially as many foreign-owned enterprizes shut down. Force was readily used to suppress spontaneous worker protests and several shooting incidents occurred.

Repression failed to cow CELU, whose last congress, held in September 1975, passed a series of resolutions defying the PMAC. The latter responded in December of the same year with the proclamation of a new labour code, which abolished CELU and replaced it with a new organization called the All-Ethiopia Trade Union (AETU). This was a pyramidal structure, in which authority was centralized and hierarchical, a bureaucratic monolith designed to regiment labour and render it pliable to state control. The new labour code proved to be a conventional document. Although 'socialist principles' are mentioned, the word 'class' does not appear in it. Worker rights and conditions of labour are defined according to conventional bourgeois standards. Apart from a vague reference to the promotion of collaboration between workers and their 'allies', the stated objectives of the labour movement are strictly productionist in nature, and the provisions concerning industrial dispute settlement are designed to eliminate strikes. Neither a minimum wage nor any social security provisions – both basic labour demands – were included in the new code.

The predicament of organized labour under the new regime stemmed from a cause more basic than the overt political challenge posed by CELU. In fact, the nationalization of the means of production in the urban sector had dissolved the ephemeral conjunction of interests that had brought the intelligentsia and the proletariat together in the uprising against the *ancien regime*. The incorporation of production into the state domain expanded the bureaucratic sector considerably. Elements of the intelligentsia that chose to collaborate with, or simply acquiesce in, the rule of the military – and that included practically all those who neither fled the country nor joined the active opposition – assumed the role of management and the inevitable concern with labour productivity, costs and discipline. The new management proved no less attached than the old one was to the existing relations of production predicated on the centralized, hierarchical and authoritarian organization of the work process. In order to assert its authority, increase productivity and fulfil its development goals, the bureaucracy had to ward off the challenge posed by the rise of working class consciousness and the militancy of the labour movement.

The outcome of this and similar confrontations, which pitted the expanding bureaucratic sector against popular organizations formed or invigorated by the initial surge of the revolution, was decided by the forceful intervention of the military regime. Ultimately, the reassertion of bureaucratic control over labour was accomplished fairly easily, because the new regime chose to anchor itself in the existing and familiar state structure, rather than risk being carried away by the strong populist current in an unknown direction. The state apparatus of the *ancien regime* survived the revolution essentially intact. The military regime not only preserved this structure and enlarged it considerably through the expansion of the economic role of the state, it also strove to complete the process of centralization begun by the old regime, and strongly reinforced its authoritarian character by investing it with unlimited ('revolutionary') authority backed by the concentrated force of the military establishment. This was hardly surprising, since the military itself had been a key part of the old structure. Despite the purging of the senior officer corps and the radicalization of the soldiery, the Ethiopian military remained a conventional institution. It could hope to rule the country only through the mediation of state institutions that corresponded with it, that is, they were of the same vintage as itself. Consequently, it had to defend the bureaucracy against the populist aspirations of the mass organizations spawned by the revolution. These were to become pawns in a violent contest between the PMAC and the radical marxist opposition.

The PMAC's conversion to socialism and the proclamation of the reforms split the ranks of the radical intelligentsia into two uneven factions. The majority remained strongly opposed to military rule, regarding it as the major obstacle to a genuine social revolution. Fundamental change, they argued, could not be achieved by fiat from above in the imperial manner. A social revolution could not be carried out when the masses were limited to the role of an audience. The dominant presence of the junior officer group in the Dergue, it was feared, pointed to a military dictatorship with petty-bourgeois aspirations. The majority of the radicals maintained that the formation of a peoples' government is the indispensable prerequisite in the transition to socialism. By obstructing the advance of the revolution in that direction, the military regime was performing a counter-revolutionary role, and the radicals who grouped themselves in the Ethiopian Peoples' Revolutionary Party (EPRP) in 1975 prepared to make war on it.

On the other hand, a minority of the radical intelligentsia believed there was no realistic alternative to military rule at the time. Convinced that the Dergue itself was ideologically divided, they proposed to manipulate it through its 'left wing' and to steer the regime in the desired direction. This faction proposed to give the PMAC 'tactical support', that is, to support or oppose it according to the merits of its actions. Leading members of this group functioned as advisers to the emerging strongman of the regime, Major Mengistu Haile Mariam, whom they regarded as the leader of the Dergue's left wing. They also formed a political organization in 1975, the All-Ethiopia Socialist Movement (MEISON) which, like the EPRP, aspired to become the vanguard of the socialist revolution. The radical intellectuals who led MEISON became the ideological mentors of the military regime, and their followers spearheaded the campaign of repression against the EPRP. A Provisional Office for Mass Organization Affairs (POMOA) was set up to mobilize support for the regime.

Buoyed by the enthusiastic support of the students who returned to the towns when the campaign for rural development ended in the summer of 1976, and heedless of its limitations, the EPRP began an armed struggle in the form of urban guerrilla warfare in the autumn of 1976. The regime's response was to enlist the popular organizations, controlled and guided by MEISON and POMOA, in the battle against the EPRP. Previously, the PMAC had resisted pressure from the left to extend the jurisdiction of the associations so that they could function as instruments of popular local self-government, and had refused to allow the formation of armed units in the associations to combat counter-revolutionary activities in the rural areas. When the challenge of the

EPRP was forcibly manifested, and the associations had come under POMOA control, this attitude changed. The urban associations formed militia units recruited from the lumpen element in the cities. Directed by POMOA cadres, these were thrown into the internecine struggle against the EPRP. The peasant associations were also allowed to form defence squads. During 1977, under the pressure of the Eritrean and Somali offensives, a peasant militia numbering hundreds of thousands was raised and thrown into battle. Thus, while the military regime was fighting for survival against a multitude of foes, the popular organs attained considerable importance and largely supplanted the traditional agents of the state at the local level. The militia of the associations replaced the police, most of whose members were sent to the war front. The judicial tribunals of the associations supplanted the judiciary, and tax collection in the rural areas was taken over by the peasant associations.

While the EPRP struck selectively at prominent targets, the reaction it provoked was massive, savage and indiscriminate. It took a heavy toll, particularly among the youthful supporters of the EPRP who defied the regime openly. They were exterminated methodically, sometimes in groups of hundreds, and without regard to age. The officially proclaimed 'Red Terror' gave the regime's henchmen authority to apply 'instant revolutionary measures' – execution – against known or suspected opponents. The Red Terror raged throughout 1977. In the middle of that year, it engulfed those who had inspired it, the MEISON group. The PMAC had become wary of its radical associates, who constantly strove to weave a mass political base through linkages to the popular organizations, the functions and powers of which they sought to augment at the expense of the bureaucracy. When the Soviet Union and its allies threw their massive weight behind the regime, radical support was no longer indispensable for the PMAC. MEISON overreached itself when it tried to gain control of the peasant militia, a potential counterweight to the military itself, arguing that it ought to be placed under revolutionary control. Alarmed, the regime turned on its radical mentors, and MEISON was suppressed in a bloody purge in mid-1977. POMOA was rendered inactive and was finally abolished in 1979. MEISON influence in the official labour organization was eliminated through two successive purges of the Executive Committee of the AETU.

The EPRP struggled a while longer until its forces were decimated, and the remnants split over the wisdom of continuing the struggle in the cities. Thousands of young Ethiopians were forced to flee their country. A small number joined their comrades in the mountains of the north, where an armed unit called the Ethiopian Peoples' Revolutionary Army had maintained a precarious existence for some time. This belated attempt to establish a rural base failed, and the EPRA disbanded in 1980. Several coteries of radical intellectuals were allowed to lead a semi-clandestine existence in Addis Ababa and to hope that they would form the core of a 'proletarian party'. Their presence served to lend credence to the regime's oft-repeated and much-discussed promise to create such a party. These hopes were dashed in 1979, when it was announced that the party would be formed by the recruitment of 'individual communists', not the merger of existing factions. The remaining radical factions were suppressed at that time. Thus, within five years, the radical left, the conscience of the revolution, was eliminated from the political scene in Ethiopia.

Military Rule & National Conflict

The organic link between the military establishment and the structure of the imperial state determined the new regime's attitude to the national conflict within Ethiopia. As indicated by a succession of mottoes it adopted –'Ethiopia First', 'Unity or Death', 'All for the Motherland' – the PMAC regarded as its primary task the preservation of the structure and authority of the state it had taken over. This was hardly surprising, for this had been the task of the Ethiopian army since its creation this century. It is worth noting again that, despite purging and radicalization, this army has remained a conventional institution, with rigidly centralized and highly authoritarian internal processes: features that have become characteristic also of the state under military rule. It was to be expected that the PMAC should resist violently the loosening of centralized state authority, an essential prerequisite to any possible solution of Ethiopia's manifold nationality conflict. Precisely the maintenance of this system of state authority remains the raison d'être for the existence of the military in its present form. Any rearrangement forced by dissident nationalism would be bound to have a serious impact on the military establishment; it might be required to vacate regions, integrate nationalist guerrilla elements into its ranks, tolerate militia units under local control, etc. Any compromise in this area would also undermine the regime's rationale for military rule: that it guarantees the integrity of the state.

The military in Ethiopia were not insensitive to the festering conflict provoked by the exploitation and chauvinism of the imperial regime. Many of the soldiers and numerous officers were recruited from the subject nationalities of the empire. The army had long been engaged in a fruitless effort to subdue dissident nationalism. The affinity of the soldiers' rebellion to the popular movement reinforced military sensibility of this problem. Confronted with the challenge of Eritrean nationalism, and following a lengthy and agonising soul-searching in the late 1960s, the radical left in Ethiopia had resolved to support the right of national self-determination up to and including independence. The EPRP demanded an immediate end to the protracted effort to subdue the Eritrean nationalist movement by force. Consequently, the national issue was at the top of the political agenda when the soldiers seized power.

The PMAC did not attempt to ignore the issue. National conflict, it was stated, arose under the *ancien regime* due to the oppression of the feudal ruling class. Since the overthrow of this class had liberated all the peoples of Ethiopia, there was no longer any justification for the demand of national liberation. Cultural differences among the many nationalities in Ethiopia could be accommodated on the basis of equality and within the framework of local self-government. National liberation movements were termed 'secessionist' and 'counter-revolutionary', because objectively they sided with international reaction against socialist Ethiopia. The slogan 'Ethiopian Unity or Death' was hoisted to the mast of the revolution.

Relegating the national conflict to the realm of cultural diversity, the military regime denied its political nature and *precluded any negotiated* solution to it. It was on this basis that the PMAC made an initial approach to the Eritreans in the autumn of 1974 and was rebuffed. The offer of regional self-government had a hollow ring, particularly for the Eritreans, who had learned from bitter experience earlier that regional autonomy is incompatible with a state whose central government claims absolute power. Subsequently, the war in Eritrea intensified greatly.

The embattled Ethiopian regime was faced at this time with a grave shortage of war material, due to the increasing reluctance of the United States to provide an avowedly marxist regime with the means required for its survival. The Soviet Union, until this moment Somalia's patron, now offered to underwrite the PMAC as well, apparently thinking it would be possible to reconcile the two neighbours. The Ethiopian alliance with the Soviet Union was sealed on 1 May 1977, and soon afterwards the delivery of weapons and advisers to Ethiopia began. The Somalis decided to attack before the

Ethiopians had time to assimilate Soviet military technology. Their forces launched a full scale invasion of the Ogaden in September of the same year. Rolling back the Ethiopian troops before them, Somali units laid siege to the town of Harar, where the battleline was drawn for the next five months.

During the winter months of 1977-1978, the Soviet Union staged a massive supply operation via sea and air to Ethiopia. Its Eastern European allies helped train Ethiopian soldiers in the use of Soviet weapons, and Cuba sent its own soldiers to the battle. Planned and directed by Soviet officers and spearheaded by Cuban combat units, the counter-offensive against the Somali was launched in February 1978. Within two months it had forced the invader to abandon the Ogaden. This victory, of course, did not resolve the issue. The Somali liberation movement did not renounce the struggle, and before long it had resumed guerrilla activity in the Ogaden and Bale regions. Cuban troops were permanently stationed in the area to bolster the Ethiopian defence. The people of the region suffered grievously. Nearly a million of them were forced to seek safety in refugee camps in the Somali Republic by 1980. During the summer of 1978, the Ethiopians mounted a major offensive against the Eritrean nationalist forces. Confronted with a vastly superior enemy enjoying Soviet logistical support, the Eritreans were forced to abandon all the towns they had captured, save their one stronghold at Nacfa. Undaunted by this setback, the nationalists reverted to guerrilla tactics, and the struggle in that war-torn province continued without hope of early resolution. Hundreds of thousands fled from the area to refugee camps in the Sudan.

Garrison Socialism

By the end of the 1970s, thanks to the forceful intervention of the Soviet Union and its allies, the PMAC had managed to dispose of all rivals for power and to regain the initiative in the battle against the various dissident nationalist movements. During that time, it had also purged itself of rival factions within the Dergue, which was now under the undisputed leadership of Lieutenant Colonel Mengistu Haile Mariam. It was now possible to devote some attention to the economic situation of the country, which had deteriorated steadily during the preceding years of bloody strife. The most obvious sign of this was what Colonel Mengistu himself described in September 1978 as 'a frightening situation in urban areas regarding the shortages of food'. The shortages were caused partly by the disruption of production and distribution due to the armed conflict throughout the country, also by the requisition of foodstuffs for the military: that is, causes that could be deemed temporary. Another factor was the scarcity of manufactured goods for which peasants trade their produce; to remedy this situation would take some time. Most significantly, the shortages reflected increased peasant consumption from what was previously the landowner's share, and unwillingness to sell at state-imposed prices that stood at one-half to one-third of those obtained on the black market. In other words, the regime faced the problem of extracting the agricultural surplus from the peasantry through extra-economic means.

The method chosen, with the blessing of Soviet advisers, was collectivization. 'We have to appreciate more than ever the value of collective farming' declared Col. Mengistu proclaiming the National Revolutionary Economic and Cultural Campaign on the fourth anniversary of the revolution in September 1978. The Campaign was the PMAC's first venture in the field of economic reconstruction since the nationalization proclamations of 1975. Its main target was the peasantry, whose individualism and petty bourgeois inclinations were denounced by the Chairman of the PMAC, for they 'could lead us not towards socialism, but towards capitalism'. To guide the peasantry in the proper direction the regime produced a new breed of functionary, untainted with radical left notions and presumably more reliable. Possessed of limited educational qualifications, the so-called Production and Political Cadres were put through short training courses at a military school, and then were attached to all enterprizes, associations and mass organizations to spur production and political education. According to Colonel Mengistu, 'since attitudes cannot change overnight, the role of the political cadres is paramount ... Without this new breed, socialism can only be dreamt of, not realised.'

In the rural sector, their task would be 'to agitate the peasantry to abandon individual cultivation and get organized into co-operatives'. It seemed that the state bureaucratic apparatus was being reinforced for the looming confrontation with the peasants.

By this time, the peasants had already had some experience with the regime's penchant for using their associations for its own ends, and the heavy-handed reaction of its agents when those ends were ill-served. Recruitment for the peasant militia used as cannon fodder in Eritrea and the Ogaden was one such instance. After repeated levies and the failure of many recruits to return to their villages, the associations balked at new demands. The regime then resorted to forced recruitment, often snatching unsuspecting peasants visiting the market towns. The expansion of the state farm sector often forced associations to surrender land and people to leave their homes. Collectivization was promoted by discrimination, in taxation for example, in favour of what are called production co-operatives. On the other hand, general taxes for rural producers, initially set quite low, were subsequently tripled. Resistance to these impositions brought the wrath of the regime down on the heads of the elected association officials, many of whom were arbitrarily removed through the simple device of ordering the peasants to elect new leaders. Not a few lost more than their office.

By the end of the decade, the PMAC had attained a degree of internal coherence that enabled it to commence erecting a political facade for military rule. This coherence was achieved at the cost of successive, bloody purges, in the course of which the first two chairmen, one vice-chairman, most of the prominent members of the early years, and over half of its original membership of 120, perished. Each purge cleared another step for the ascent of Colonel Mengistu. Since his assumption of the PMAC chairmanship in February 1978, most of the surviving members of the Dergue have been dispersed through appointment to various posts in the state apparatus. A large number of other military personnel, mainly officers, have been appointed to state posts. The provincial administration became the exclusive preserve of the military and officers were increasingly appointed to the formerly civilian Council of Ministers. This might be seen as a way of reinforcing military control over the state apparatus. It also served to facilitate promotion within the military establishment of men loyal to the Chairman of the PMAC. Colonel Mengistu's titles proliferated rapidly; he was also Chairman of the Council of Ministers, Chairman of the Supreme Economic Council, Commander in Chief of the Revolutionary Armed Forces, and Chairman of the Commission for Organising the Party of the Working Peoples of Ethiopia (COPWE).

Bibliography

ANCIEN REGIME
Clapham, Christopher (1969), *Haile Selassie's Government,* New York: Praeger.
Gilkes, Patrick (1975), *The Dying Lion: Feudalism and Modernisation in Ethiopia,* New York: St Martin's Press.

Greenfield, Richard (1965), *Ethiopia: A New Political History,* London: Pall Mall.
Hoben, Allan (1973), *Land Tenure Among the Amhara of Ethiopia,* Chicago: University of Chicago Press.
Markakis, John (1974), *Ethiopia: Anatomy of a Traditional Polity,* Oxford: Clarendon Press.
Perham, Margery (1969), *The Government of Ethiopia,* Evanston, IL: Northwestern University Press.
Shepherd, Jack (1975), *The Politics of Starvation,* New York: Carnegie Endowment for International Peace.

REVOLUTION

Hiwet, Addis (1975), *Ethiopia: From Autocracy to Revolution,* London: Merlin Press for the *Review of African Political Economy.*
Markakis, John & Nega Ayele (1978), *Class and Revolution in Ethiopia,* Nottingham: Spokesman for the *Review of African Political Economy.*
Ottaway, Marina & David (1978), *Ethiopia: Empire in Revolution,* New York: Holmes & Meier.
Raul Valdes Vivo, a Cuban official, supplemented the socialist camp's offerings in English with an embarrassingly naive eulogy of the military regime in Ethiopia: *The Unknown Revolution,* New York: International Publishers, 1978.
The Hungarian ambassador to Ethiopia in the mid-1970s, Zoltan Gyenge, produced a preliminary impressionistic account of *Ethiopia on the Road to Non-Capitalist Development,* Budapest: Hungarian Academy of Sciences, 1976.

NATIONAL CONFLICT

Davidson, Basil, Lionel Cliffe and Bereket Habte Selassie (eds.) (1980), *Behind the War in Eritrea*, Nottingham: Spokesman.
Farer, Tom (1976), *War Clouds on the Horn of Africa: A Crisis for Detente,* New York: Carnegie Endowment for International Peace.
Lewis, Ioan (1980), *A Modern History of Somaliland,* London: Longman (4th edition, 2002, *A Modern History of the Somali,* Oxford: James Currey).
Richard Sherman (1980), *Eritrea: The Unfinished Revolution,* New York: Praeger.
Selassie, Bereket Habte (1980), *Conflict and Intervention in the Horn of Africa,* London: Monthly Review Press.
Spencer, John (1977), *Ethiopia, the Horn of Africa and United States Policy,* Cambridge, MA: Institute of Foreign Policy Analysis.
Trevaskis, G. K. N. (1960), *Eritrea: A Colony in Transition,* London: Oxford University Press.
Vanderlinden, Jacques (1977), *L'Ethiopie et ses populations,* Brussels: Editions Complexe.

13 JAMES F. PETRAS & MORRIS H. MORLEY
The Ethiopian Military State
& Soviet–US Involvement in the Horn of Africa   [1984]

State & Class in Mengistu's Ethiopia

Soviet, Cuban and Western defenders of the Ethiopian regime cite the growth of the state sector – the nationalisation of property – as the key issue in defining its 'revolutionary' character. But notwithstanding the fact that the old feudal landlords, the new urban-based entrepreneurial class (an August 1974 decree nationalised all urban lands and houses not owner-occupied), the Church and the absolutist monarchy have been replaced, the fundamental question is by whom and for what? We cannot assume that what is not landlord is peasant; what is not capitalist is worker; what is not absolutist rule is popular-democratic government. The nationalisations established a new bureaucratic military class power that is neither feudal nor social revolutionary. It destroyed one set of hierarchical exploitative relations and raised another.

For example, the peasants, in return for benefiting from the land reform, were pressed into the military as cannon fodder to sustain the imperial pretensions of the regime. The peasant march on Eritrea organised by the Dergue in early 1976, for example, involved perhaps as many as 40,000 peasants. With few weapons, almost no training, and inept leadership, they were no match for the Eritrean guerrillas who routed them in two separate engagements, forcing the Dergue to abandon the march in mid-June. Forced conscription and what can only realistically be described as death marches are in their own fashion as exploitative of the peasants as the rent-gouging carried out by landlords under the Haile Selassie feudal monarchy. The location of peasant sacrifice is different, the rhetoric is certainly novel, but the result is the same: peasant life and labour are sacrificed for alien ends. The overall balance sheet of military agrarianism or, better still, reformism harnessed to military conquest clearly demonstrates that from the perspective of the peasant, life has not improved: landlord-induced insecurities are replaced by new state-inflicted concerns.

The question that proponents of the notion that Ethiopia has experienced a social revolution must answer is whether there can be a revolutionary class in the modern world that is neither peasant nor worker and that also acts in a systematic and violent fashion to exploit and destroy the independent organisations of urban and rural labour. If so, they must demonstrate how and where this new revolutionary class emerges and they must specify the substance and nature of the society that this 'revolution' produces. But the fundamental reality any such analysis must confront regarding post-1974 Ethiopia is that it is the political institutionalisation of bureaucratic-military rulers (the Dergue), not workers' councils, that defines the class nature of the state: a highly centralised and authoritarian state-capitalist regime.

Soviet Policy & the Dergue: Regaining a 'Sphere of Influence' in the Horn of Africa

The growth and deepening of Soviet ties to the Ethiopian military dictatorship is not a result of its so-called radical social reforms or its anti-imperialist foreign policy. Neither is it a reflection of growing Soviet 'social imperialism'. Rather, it is the result of the Soviet Union's declining position in the Horn of Africa and its relative weakness vis-à-vis the United States and conservative Arab states in the region. A brief examination of the context of Moscow's involvement with the Dergue will bring these issues into focus.

Up to 1977, Soviet policy in the Horn paid limited attention to nationalisation and land reform in Ethiopia, preferring to focus its efforts and resources on maintenance of existing alliances with regimes in Somalia and the Sudan providing large-scale military and economic assistance in return for access to military facilities and construction of new bases. During this period, Egypt, which had ousted the Soviets in 1973 and harshly repressed its domestic supporters, and Saudi Arabia, with its formidable oil-based financial resources, both sought actively to weaken Soviet and increase US influence in the region. In 1971, bolstered by a Saudi guarantee of sufficient financial assistance to purchase military equipment from the West, the Numeiry government in the Sudan had jailed and assassinated pro-Moscow Communist Party members as a prelude to the expulsion of Soviet military and embassy officials from the country. This setback was further compounded later, in 1977, when the Somali government abrogated its 1974 treaty with Moscow, ordered the Soviet military mission to leave and moved to establish closer ties with Riyadh and Washington. President Carter immediately directed his senior foreign policy officials 'to move in every possible way to get Somalia to be our friend' (*Washington Post*, 5 March 1978).

The massive Soviet military commitment to Ethiopia was made in the aftermath of these major political defeats and amidst growing diplomatic isolation in the Horn – and then only after the Mengistu dictatorship had demonstrated a capacity to consolidate its rule, weakened its ties with Israel and agreed to effect a decisive break with the United States. It was also made subsequent to most of the internal socio-economic changes instituted by the Dergue. If it were not for the behaviour of existing regional allies in expelling the Soviets and establishing new ties with Washington, it is doubtful whether Moscow would have made its move to bolster the sagging Mengistu regime in order to regain some of its prior influence in the area (especially access to military facilities on Ethiopia's Red Sea coastline to replace air and naval bases lost at the port of Berbera in Somalia), at least not on the scale and scope that it did. In the four-year period 1978 to 1981, Soviet military assistance to Addis Ababa totalled approximately $2 billion (*Washington Post*, 25 November 1980 and 31 December 1981). Above all, Soviet policy during this period was conditioned by the shifts in state-to-state relations and the importance attached to regaining political and military leverage in the Horn.

On a more basic level, the Soviet Union's ties to Third World regimes such as Mengistu's are 'extensive' at the state-to-state level but do not penetrate into the society and are not linked to any revolutionary class forces. Ethiopia's economic relations with the outside world, for instance, have been largely unaffected by the shift in Soviet policy. The country still remains firmly integrated within the capitalist world economy. In 1978, the US and the European Economic Community accounted for over 50 per cent of Ethiopia's total trade compared with approximately 2 per cent conducted with the Soviet Union and Eastern Europe (Ottaway, 1981:64-5). American buyers also represented the principal market for its coffee exports which account for approximately 80 per cent of Ethiopia's foreign-exchange earnings. Meanwhile, individual capitalist governments and Western financial institutions continue to provide not insignificant sources of external financing to the military regime. Between 1976 and 1982, the multilateral development bank loans and credits to Ethiopia totalled more than $300 million, according to USAID. And it should finally be noted that in early 1983 the Dergue enacted a law to re-open most sectors of the economy to private foreign investment, and permit the transfer of shares and the repatriation of capital – creating the potential for a deepening of Ethiopia's existing economic ties to the capitalist world.

Capitalist and pre-capitalist relations of production operate as a sea around the islands of nationalised enterprises in state-capitalist regimes such as Ethiopia's. While the Soviet emphasis on state-to-state ties at the apex of Third World societies is designed to gain outposts of political influence and strategic advantages (military base, naval port, etc.) they are, at the same time, highly vulnerable to reversal in the event of shifts within the governing clique. Massive Soviet support has not changed Mengistu into a Soviet-style communist of the Eastern European variety. On the contrary, there is a high probability of the Soviets being ousted as they were in Somalia and the Sudan (and earlier in Egypt), if and when the bureaucratic state dictatorship deems it to be in its interest.

What the Soviet state has sought to obtain in Ethiopia and elsewhere in the Third World is political and military influence at the level of the state. Intervention is based on obtaining 'spheres of influence', not promoting social revolution. While pursuing strategic locations, bases, ports and diplomatic support, however, Soviet civil and military missions do not develop deep ties with important collaborator classes in countries like Ethiopia. It is precisely for this reason that what many writers describe as Soviet 'client states', 'surrogates', etc., are able to dislodge the Soviets with such ease. Unlike Western imperialism which develops long-standing, deeply rooted structural relations with local landowners, capitalist industrialists, etc., the Soviets have repeatedly failed to develop organised ties with old oppressors or new exploiting classes.

Soviet policy supports regimes which weaken US imperialism but do not threaten Soviet-style socialism by raising the issue of democratic control. Moscow's reliance on military-political influence at the level of the state is designed to avoid involvement in revolutionary mobilisation that might break out of the boundaries of bureaucratic-statist regime-states. These types of capitalist regimes are viewed as being more compatible with Moscow's internal class and ideological interests as well as its foreign policy objectives. This combination of internal and external reasons explains why Soviet policy-makers continually reiterate their support for 'non-capitalist regimes' despite the frequency with which they turn against the Soviet Union.

The US & the Horn of Africa: Declining Hegemony & Confrontation on a Global Scale

The decline of the US imperial state and the upsurge of anti-imperialist struggles are indicative of the fact that no substitute imperial state can play Washington's formerly dominant role. The proliferation of regional power centres and the growth of intra-Third World wars are symptoms of the new fragmentation of power. They reflect attempts by Third World regimes to resolve the crisis of legitimacy through external conquest. The rise and demise of bourgeois nationalism in Ethiopia stands as a clear example: the Mengistu regime simultaneously promoted 'national liberation' and national oppression. While the contradiction between its economic backwardness and political hegemonic aspirations was temporarily resolved through massive external dependence (on the Soviet Union), the military rulers lacked an underlying strategic predominance to carry off their dual goal: the country's low level of material life undercut any appeals its leadership might make to the Eritrean masses. Put another way, Ethiopia's high rates of illiteracy, technical backwardness, general low level of economic development and dictatorial form of government did not provide for a kind of 'Napoleonic liberation' from above and outside. Without Soviet intervention, the strategic historical advantage was clearly with Eritrea, a more developed society with higher skills and the motivation of an invaded country.

The most salient feature of the revival of the Cold War has been a massive military build-up directed at strengthening US global military interventionary capacity, bolstering Third World clients, and bludgeoning European and Japanese allies into sharing the military costs commensurate with the benefits that they derive from the imperial system. Operationally, this effort by the Reaganites has involved the development of new weapons systems and their location in positions designed to intimidate nationalist and anti-capitalist Third World regimes, the search for new military bases and the strengthening of old military alliances, and the consummation of new military-strategic alliances with such countries as Israel and South Africa which can serve as 'regional policemen' sharing in the destabilisation of zones of revolutionary mobilisation. Arms sales and 'strategic agreements' have been hammered out with many regimes. The military bases and joint military activities within these regions have directly involved the US armed forces in the role of defending incumbent dictatorial regimes against popular movements within their own borders.

The capacity for US intervention is thus built on a two-fold basis: initially, direct military support of established dictatorial regimes and, ultimately, the effort to construct a regionally based police force that can provide for the collective security of any particular regime threatened by domestic upheaval. The impact and consequences of US policy under Reagan for the Third World are profound: the decline of diplomacy and political negotiations as instruments of policy in favour of a new arms build-up and the ascendancy of a policy of military confrontation. This does not mean that all negotiations have been eschewed, especially in the light of constant pressure on the part of Washington's senior alliance partners. What it does mean, however, is that negotiations and summit meetings with socialist and revolutionary regimes have become ritualistic affairs – propaganda forums for the Reagan White House to 'demonstrate' the ineffectiveness of such regimes and reinforce the commitment to policies of confrontation.

The Reagan effort to reconstruct the world in the image of the 1950s posits a number of fundamental changes in the capitalist and socialist world (for example, 'military supremacy' over the Soviet Union, US dominance over Europe's economic and foreign policy), most of which are beyond the realm of possibility. The foremost strategic task in pursuit of the larger goal has been, and remains, the containment of revolutions in the Third World. Beyond the revival of preventive interventionism is the serious planning, and even implementation, of policies to reverse revolutionary regimes. The image of revolutionary societies that the Reaganites project is revealing: they are crisis-wracked systems devoid of popular support and depend on outside power to sustain them. The response has been to adopt a confrontationist strategy that at one and the same time neutralises the Soviet's role (through a new military build-up) and creates the basis for 'regionally centred' military interventions in Central America, the Horn of Africa and elsewhere in the Third World.

The Horn of Africa is of particular importance to Washington because of the adjoining regions of which it forms an integral part: namely, the countries facing the Red Sea and giving access to the Indian Ocean. Thus, while the Horn in itself does not have great economic interest, it does have 'strategic significance'. Influence in the region provides major powers with leverage in shaping policies in countries where economic interests are paramount – in particular, the oil-rich Middle East countries.

The formulation of US policy toward the regimes in the Horn of Africa is therefore shaped by how these area governments interact with Washington's overall regional policy. This core concern with projecting American power in the Middle East radiated outward to the adjoining region, including the Horn of Africa. US policy toward such countries as Somalia and the Sudan was in large part dictated by their relationship toward Egypt and its participation in the Camp David framework. Washington's attitude toward the Horn countries was also shaped by the nature of their relations with the Soviet Union and their disposition to negotiate agreements providing for US military bases and naval facilities facing the Indian Ocean.

Washington's major military (and economic) commitment to the Sudan, Somalia and Kenya is partly premised on these countries' hostility toward Moscow and their willingness to provide air and naval facilities for American forces in the Indian Ocean area. 'Somalia and Kenya', in the words of Chester Crocker, 'are critical to our logistical supply systems in the event of a security crisis in the Gulf or Middle East and Sudan plays a key role in containing Libyan aggression in East and Central Africa.'

American Policy Toward Ethiopia

Prior to its overthrow in February 1974, the Haile Selassie monarchy in Ethiopia was Washington's most important post-war ally in the Horn of Africa. In December 1974, the Ford administration undertook a major reassessment of its policy toward Ethiopia. Despite expressions of unease over the Dergue's domestic policies and its treatment of political opponents, the White House decided to maintain economic and military assistance and adopt a 'wait and see' approach. Although Washington responded tardily to a February 1975 Dergue request for $29 million in emergency military assistance following a series of battlefield defeats in the war in Eritrea and a major challenge for control of the provincial capital of Asmara, total US military aid (grants, credits and cash sales) increased from $28.5 million in 1974 to $57.5 million in 1975, and reached its highest level ever in 1976 when cash sales alone amounted to more than $100 million (M. Ottaway, 1982). Secretary of State Kissinger reportedly played a central role in formulating this aid policy which was shaped by largely strategic considerations: retaining continued access to the Kagnew Station and opposing the Soviet presence in the Horn (especially in Somalia). In August 1976, an American official characterised the Ethiopian regime as 'inconsistent' rather than 'basically anti-United States' (quoted by M. Ottaway, 1982). By year's end, however, the White House had begun to view the Dergue's internal reforms, its footdragging on compensation for expropriated American properties, its human rights record and its developing military relationship with the Soviet Union through a more hostile lens. One of President Ford's last acts before leaving office was to terminate all military grant aid to Ethiopia, confining future military assistance only to credit sales.

In February 1977, a bloody struggle for power occurred within the Dergue. The outcome was a victory for the most 'radical' faction under the leadership of Mengistu Haile-Mariam. Later that same month, the new Carter administration announced that

US military assistance to Ethiopia would be reduced because of human rights violations. In April, all arms supplies were suspended and the White House also decided to reduce its Military Assistance Advisory Group (MAAG) personnel in the country substantially and close the Kagnew Communications Station later in the year. Mengistu's immediate response was to shut down the Kagnew Station, expel all MAAG personnel from Ethiopia, terminate US Information Agency operations in Addis Ababa, and dramatically expand Ethiopia's ties with the Soviet Union.

The growing Soviet (and Cuban) military presence in Ethiopia prompted a major policy review within the Carter White House leading to a renewed emphasis on East–West confrontation and a downgrading of the earlier administration focus on African nationalism, economic development and opposition to white minority rule on the continent. In May 1978, Secretary of State Vance told a closed congressional hearing that 'strenuous efforts' were under way to counter Soviet and Cuban activities in Africa, including increased military assistance to friendly regional governments and public and private diplomatic initiatives. Despite this policy shift, the military spigots to Ethiopia were not completely turned off. In early 1978, Washington fulfilled Mengistu's request for jeeps and American-made fighter plane spare parts (originally part of a May 1977 weapons order) and cluster bombs that were intended for use in a large-scale offensive against the Eritrean liberation movement.

Carter-Brzezinski hostility to Mengistu's alliance with the Soviet Union, the presence of Cuban troops in Ethiopia, and the lack of 'significant progress' towards satisfying the approximately $22 million in compensation claims by nationalised American investors did not, however, induce the White House to cease any consideration of a future negotiated settlement with the Dergue.

At the inception of the Reagan presidency, the points of conflict between the US and Ethiopia revolved around three issues: the Mengistu government's alliance with the Soviet Union; its failure to compensate expropriated American corporate interests; and its foreign policy which was highly critical of the US role in South Africa, Puerto Rico, and elsewhere, but refused to condemn such Soviet actions as the Afghanistan intervention. At the same time, there was no disposition on the part of the new administration to totally eschew the negotiating option and normalised relations with the Dergue. For the transition from Carter to Reagan was not accompanied by any lessened belief among Washington policy-makers as to the superficial nature of Ethiopian military Marxism, the willingness of the Mengistu regime to manoeuvre and, most of all, the fact that Soviet involvement had not basically affected the country's traditional ties to the capitalist world market.

Although there has been no major shift in the nature of US-Ethiopian relations since Reagan took office, the question of an improvement in ties has remained a White House agenda item. Given the class nature of the Ethiopian state, it would be no great surprise to see it switch sides in the Cold War, shifting its primary source of economic and military assistance from Moscow to Washington. The economic basis exists for the Ethiopian regime to make a shift in its international policy once it has exhausted its strategic needs from the Soviet Union and decides to tap into Western financial institutions and public state agencies again. The relatively small American investment stake in Ethiopia has limited the impact of the compensation issue on the outward-oriented US capitalist class as a whole and has translated into minimal pressures from within the class to get imperial state officials to pursue a hard line on this issue with Addis Ababa. Ultimately, the key is Washington's ability to replace Soviet influence and retake strategic military positions and what the Reagan White House can offer the Mengistu regime in exchange.

Conclusion

In the final analysis the Ethiopian experience demonstrates that no progressive social reform can be sustained internally while an imperial war is being pursued abroad. This is true from a practical point of view, expenditure, and from an ideological perspective – military brutalisation abroad reverberates at home and vice versa. The initial responsiveness of the military regime to mass demands was eroded by the constant pressures generated by the external military commitments. Economic stagnation, food shortages, limited social expenditures and declining foreign-exchange reserves are all directly related to the growth of military expenditures.

While some leftist interpretations of the Ethiopian experience under the Dergue have emphasised the international realignments and internal changes carried out by the regime, in doing so they have blithely overlooked the state and class context within which those changes have taken place. The harnessing of peasants and workers to an expansionist chauvinist state together with an alliance with the Soviet Union for the prime reason of securing arms to maintain a colonial relationship does not denote a revolutionary regime but describes a colonial version of state capitalism – one in profound crisis and without the internal flexibility to alter its course.

The political consequences of the struggle between the state-capitalist regime in Addis Ababa and the Eritrean people are clear. The continuance of the war against Eritrea drains the national resources of the Ethiopian nation, thus preparing the way for the return of imperial dependence which, in the long run, can only compromise the initial anti-imperialist impulse. In denying the national independence of the Eritreans, the Mengistu regime will ultimately lose its own national identity. The fate of the Ethiopian national liberation movement depends on ending the war of conquest in Eritrea. The continuance of the war can only heighten imperial influence and further erode Ethiopian nationalism.

Bibliographic Note

The basic works on the region referred to in the text are:
David, Stephen (1979) 'Realignment in the Horn: The Soviet Advantage', *International Security*, Vol. 4, No. 2, Fall.
Halliday, Fred and Maxine Molyneux (1981), *The Ethiopian Revolution*, London:Verso Editions/New Left Books.
Ottaway, David (1981), *Afrocommunism*, New York: Africana Publishing Company.
Ottaway, Marina (1982), *Soviet and American Influence in the Horn of Africa*, New York: Praeger Publishers.
Ottaway, Marina and David (1978), *Ethiopia: Empire in Revolution*, New York: Africana Publishing Company.
Selassie, Bereket Habte (1980), *Conflict and Intervention in the Horn of Africa*, New York: Monthly Review Press.

For a fuller treatment of 'state capitalism', see Petras, J. F. (1981), *Class, State & Power in the Third World*, London: Zed Books.

14 JACKLYN COCK
Keeping the Fires Burning: Militarization
& the Politics of Gender in South Africa   [1989]

The linkages between women and the process of militarization are generally obscured. They are mystified by two opposing perspectives – those of sexism and feminism. Both exclude women from war on the grounds that they are bearers of 'special qualities'. Sexism excludes women from the ranks of the military on the grounds of their physical inferiority and unsuitability for combat roles. One variant of feminism similarly excludes women on opposite grounds – that of their innate nurturing qualities, their creativity and pacificism. The outcome of both positions is that war is understood as a totally male affair. This chapter adopts a different approach. It focuses on the connection between women and war in South African society. It argues that women contribute to the militarization of society in both material and ideological terms.

Militarization as a Contested Concept

> Our whole social organism is riddled by the disease of militarism (Bahro, 1982:89).

An understanding of militarization hinges on a clear distinction being drawn between three social phenomena: 1) the military as a social institution: a set of social relationships organized around war, taking the shape of an armed force; 2) militarism as an ideology which values war and legitimates state violence as the solution to conflict; 3) militarism as a social process that involves mobilization for war through the penetration of the military, its power and influence, into more and more social arenas, until the military have a primacy in state and society. In the literature there is a good deal of slippage between these three phenomena.

The military is frequently conceptualized as a discrete institutional entity. While Enloe refers to 'the military institution', others have expanded the notion to depict a 'military-industrial complex' or even 'the military-industrial-technological-bureaucratic complex' (Eide and Thee, 1980). This is sometimes identified with the state. For example, Williams (1985:224) refers to an organized grouping of arms production, military, research and state-security interests which has, in effect, moved beyond the control of civil society and is the true contemporary form of the state itself.

This insight is tethered to what E. P. Thompson has termed 'exterminism': a deadly system, first of weapons and then of institutions and ideas which has slowly assumed a total and ultimately destructive control. He has criticized the use of concepts which attempt to delimit the problem.

We speak of the 'military-industrial complex' or of 'the military sector' or 'interest' of the arms lobby. This suggests that the evil is confined in a known and limited place: it may threaten to push forward, but it can be restrained: contamination does not extend through the whole societal body (Thompson, 1982:21).

Contamination is the crucial insight in his analysis; 'the USA and the USSR do not have military-industrial complexes: they are such complexes' (ibid:22).

Clearly different societies have experienced different levels of militarization. However one measures the level of militarization through empirical indicators, South Africa is a highly militarized society (Frankel, 1984; Grundy, 1983, 1986; Frederikse, 1980):

> virtually every member of the white and black populations is immersed in the militarization of (South Africa) society, either as wielders of coercive and restrictive power or as objects or respondents to that power (Grundy, 1983:10).

Women & Militarization in South Africa

> Shooting comes as naturally as baking in the kitchen ('Ouma' Marina Hogenboezen, *Paratus*, 28 (2), February 1987:12).

White women are incorporated into the militarization of South African society in a variety of ways (Huston,1982). These points of incorporation will be discussed in two main sections, direct and indirect incorporation. Direct incorporation is clear in the increasing use of white women within the South African Defence Force (SADF) in a variety of roles from nursing through to cartography. Indirect incorporation is also extensive as women provide a considerable degree of support (both ideological and material) to the SADF.

The distinction between these direct and indirect linkages cannot be drawn in clear terms. One of the defining features of South Africa as a militarized society, a society engaged in a 'civil war' (as viewed by the black majority) or in defending itself against the 'total onslaught' (the view of the state and the vast majority of whites) is that the battlefield is the entire society. A clear demarcation of the battlefield is the fulcrum of the connection between militarization and the politics of gender. If the military are viewed as a bastion of male identity, then

> it must categorize women as peripheral, as serving safely at the 'rear', on the 'home front'. Women as women must be denied access to 'the front', to 'combat' ... the military has to constantly define 'the front' and 'combat' as wherever 'women' are not (Enloe, 1984:15).

In a civil war or struggle such as that being waged in contemporary South Africa, the landscape of combat is redrawn as the experience of war is dispersed among the general population. In this process an important breach in the ideological constructions of gender is threatened and considerable efforts are made to avoid this breach and elaborate a traditional but expanded notion of femininity for women within the SADF.

Indirect Linkages: Material & Ideological

The most remote connection between women and militarization lies in the 'mother-providing-cannon-fodder' role. In South Africa, as in Nazi Germany, the state attaches a particular importance to family, domesticity and child bearing in the white community. This implies a celebration of women's domestic role as mothers and wives; an equation of femininity with domesticity. Women's role is 'to keep the home fires burning', to stay at home, produce babies and support 'our boys on the border'.

At the indirect material level, there are three linkages between women and war, or three ways in which white women contribute materially to the militarization of South African society: first, they are active in support organizations such as the Southern Cross Fund which provides food parcels and recreational services for 'the boys on the border', and Operation Ride Safe which used to organize lifts for national servicemen; second, they are active in Civil Defence and Commando units; and third, they are engaged in armaments production for Armscor.

The Southern Cross Fund is an important agency through which white South African women provide material support for the SADF. The Southern Cross Fund works for both the SADF and the SAP (South African Police) and its motto is 'they are our security'. It has 250 branches throughout the Republic and raises money for the security forces on a full-time basis. Since its inception in 1968 it has raised over R14 million (*The Citizen*, 31 May 1986). The money is used to provide aid and comfort to soldiers in the operational area. They also visit hospitalized soldiers at No.1 Military Hospital near Pretoria regularly. According to Frankel (1984:98)

> the actual effect of Southern Cross activity is to market militarisation in a way which encourages public identification.

White women are also active in commando units and civil defence organizations. Civil Defence involves people in various aspects of work such as traffic control, fire fighting, first aid, drill, fieldcraft, crowd control, explosive identification, weapon training, road-block routines, anti-riot procedures and lectures on internal security.

The Civil Defence Programme attempts to mobilize the civilian population for the military defence of the apartheid state. While white women are increasingly active in Civil Defence organizations operating within urban areas, their involvement in Commando Units involved in counter-insurgency in rural areas is also intensifying.

> My men cannot be everywhere at once but by training farmers *and their wives* [my emphasis] in the use of weapons and communication systems we have an answer to terrorism in the area (Colonel Swanepoel, *Paratus*, 38 (2) February 1987).

In this process of incorporation traditional notions of femininity are restructured and expanded. For example, in the Soutpansberg Military Area commando members gathered recently for an evaluation. In the past two years the Soutpansberg Military Area Unit has concentrated on taking counter-insurgency skills to the farming folk in the area, turning *Oumas* and housewives into trained auxiliaries of the Defence Force (ibid.).

It is important to stress that traditional notions of femininity are not abandoned in this restructuring. For example, on one occasion the day's programme included a fashion show.

At the indirect material level, the final linkage between women and militarization in South Africa is the involvement of white women in armaments production for Armscor where they perform only a fraction of the work that promotes militarization, but a growing fraction nonetheless. Armscor has twelve nationalized subsidiaries whose activities are controlled by the corporation. It distributes work to over 1,200 private industry contractors and subcontractors. It is difficult to gain detailed information on the workforce in this sector. However, Ratcliffe has identified a clear pattern in which women appear to be the predominant grouping of the Armscor workforce (Ratcliffe, 1983:77). He suggests this is because women are one of the weakest sections of the workforce. Women are perceived to be less militant than men and are thought to have greater dexterity for intricate assembly line production (ibid:85).

The second indirect linkage or point at which white women are incorporated into the militarization of South African society, is that they provide a crucial source of ideological support. The importance of this ideological support has been articulated by many SADF leaders on numerous occasions. Its function in maintaining soldiers' morale was expressed by General C.L. Viljoen, the chief of the SADF at the time:

> I would especially like to thank those who stayed at home to keep the fires burning while the men were at the P.W. Botha Training Area. Without the support of their loved ones at home the men on the ground would not have been as successful as they were. The support from their loved ones is an important factor for the morale of the men who took part (*Paratus*, 35, October 1984).

Colonel L.J. Holtzhausen, Officer Commanding the Seventh Division's Mobilization Unit, believes women to be 'the mightiest weapon against the current threat'. However, gender roles must remain intact:

> Remember the woman must remain a woman and keep on allowing her man to feel like a man because the men are fighting throughout our country not for material things but for their women, children and loved ones (*Paratus*, 35 (2) February 1984).

The wife of the Officer Commanding a parachute battalion in Blomfontein explained the rationale:

> We want to reach the woman and try through her to work on the man. A mother has influence over her son and a girlfriend over her boyfriend (*Paratus*, 34 (9) September 1983).

The importance of 'working on the man' is that it 'is never easy for the armed forces to acquire the manpower they claim they need' (Enloe, 1983:75). In South Africa, manpower is acquired directly by the conscription of white males into the SADF, and indirectly through an ideological conscription into militarism. It is in this latter respect that white women are crucial. They elaborate an ideology of gender roles which link masculinity to militarism. In this process they are a vital source of emotional support and incentives to men to 'act like men' both in battle and during their national service.

The significance of this connection between masculinity and militarism should not be underestimated. It is a connection by women; they socialize men into a particular definition of masculinity that is violent. Mothers do so from an early age through the provision of war toys and the censure of emotional expression. The army then carries this process to the extreme.

However, it is as wives that women are the most important source of ideological legitimation and emotional support. Wives of serving members of the SADF automatically belong to the Defence Force Ladies Association. This Association strives to promote 'sympathetic understanding and active support for the husband's duty as defender of the Republic of South Africa' (White Paper on Defence, 1982:51 cited by Ratcliffe, 1983:70).

The central concept here is a definition of 'loyalty' which includes the following components: a knowledge of communism, meticulous grooming, self-knowledge, optimism, shared values, regular correspondence, responsibility, and commitment. These interpretations of loyalty as the key quality of the soldier's wife emphasize an ideology of domesticity. Furthermore they suggest a notion of an 'incorporated wife' who is entirely submerged in her soldier-husband's role, lacking autonomous identity. The extent to which the wife is incorporated in her soldier-husband's role is best illustrated by the Johannesburg City Council's 1986 decision to restrict paid maternity leave to women employees whose husbands were presently doing or had done military service. Those to be excluded were 'specifically the wives of religious objectors' as well as all blacks, coloured, Indians and single women (*Weekly Mail*, 24 January 1986).

Another related role is that of entertainer. Much of the content of this entertainment reinforces an ideology of domesticity in which women and 'loved ones' provide a rationale for the soldier's privations. The message is conveyed through radio and television programmes and tours of the 'operational areas' on the part of female entertainers, media personalities and beauty queens. This 'centrefold' type use of women is a further component in the linkage between the politics of gender and militarism. A sexist abuse of female sexuality is evident in at least two different ways: the indirect visual abuse of women as sex objects in 'pin-up' illustrations, and the direct physical abuse of women in the case of rape. As regards the former it is interesting that *Paratus* used to have a monthly 'pin-up' page. A photograph of a woman, either fully clothed or in a bathing costume filled the final page of every issue until mid-1977 (Fine and Getz, 1986:30). This clearly reinforced a splintered and contradictory image of women – an image fractured between the extremes of moralism and sexuality, 'Damned whores and God's police', sources of moral authority and dangerous sexuality (Summers, 1975).

The Direct Linkage: the Increasing Incorporation of White Women in the SADF

In global terms women are increasingly used as a military resource. This may be related to a number of factors such as manpower constraints stemming from falling birth rates, a general militarization of many different societies, and the rise of equal rights feminism.

Armed forces everywhere are distinctively patriarchal institutions. 'The military, even more than other patriarchal institutions, is a male preserve, run by men and for men according to masculine ideas and relying solely on manpower' (Enloe, 1983:7). The patriarchal nature of many societies smoothes or facilitates the connections between the armed forces and other institutions. For example, Enloe writes of the military-industrial complex as a patriarchal set of relations thoroughly imbued with masculine-defined militarist values. The network 'depends on male bonding, male privilege, and military derived notions of masculinity' (ibid, 1983:193). 'Maleness' in this ideology of gender is a relational concept – it implies a dichotomous relation between opposing sets of qualities which constructs 'femaleness'. Militarism is structured upon this dichotomy. It is this dichotomy which explains women's exclusion from combat roles. However, this exclusion may be eroded under the pressure of 'manpower' constraints and shortages. When this occurs there are usually attempts to keep the ideology of gender roles intact.

In South Africa there are frequent injunctions to women not to allow their role in the SADF to contaminate their femininity. Physical appearance must be carefully cultivated (*Paratus*, 30 (5), 1979). The important point is that, despite the increasing direct incorporation of white women into military structures in South Africa, the ideology of gender roles is not seriously breached. It is largely maintained by a sexual division of labour within the SADF whereby the vast majority of women are mainly employed in back-up jobs such as secretarial work or catering, with very few in the top levels of policy and decision-making. This sexual division of labour is reinforced by the elaborate cultivation of a superwoman image whereby these women are encouraged to combine non-traditional jobs with their domestic responsibilities as wives and mothers. Both mechanisms are clearly apparent in the SADF.

* According to the most recent estimates available there are now about 1000 white women in the Permanent Force. In other words, women constitute a significant proportion of its 18,000 members (*Financial Mail*, July 1987). This proportion has increased steadily in recent years. Women's exclusion from combat roles is legitimated on a number of different grounds.
* Women are instinctively unable to kill: 'It's the task of women to give life and to preserve it … generally, the female has no place on the battle front' (Colonel Hilda Botha, Senior Staff Officer 'Women', *Rand Daily Mail*, 18 March 1980).
* Women's socialization is inappropriate: 'Women encounter nothing like the extreme physical discomfort and danger of combat in their everyday life so they're not taught to cope with this sort of thing' (Alma Hannon, *Rand Daily Mail*, 18 March 1980).
* Women are incapacitated through physiological functions such as menstruation: 'Some women suffer from premenstrual tension and, at this time, they may be less mentally agile and well coordinated than at other times. A percentage are also more accident prone during this time' (Senior Consultant in Gynaecology at the Johannesburg Hospital, *Rand Daily Mail*, 18 March 1980).
* Male chivalry: 'It would be very difficult to use women in an operational task. The physical implications like toilet and sleeping facilities would create endless difficulties. Men would find it difficult to prevent themselves saying things like 'after you' or 'I'll take that, it's too heavy for you' (Commander Jurie Bosch, Commanding Officer of the South African Irish Regiment, *Rand Daily Mail*, 18 March 1980).

This exclusion from combat roles is essential to maintain the ideological structure of patriarchy because the notion of experiencing military 'combat' is central to the social construction of masculinity. Although white women in the SADF are not used in combat they are no longer relegated to the traditional female roles of medical and welfare work, and are involved in telecommunications and signals, logistics and finance, military police and instructional activity. The emphasis is on those who can present the image of women in uniform positively (*Paratus*, 35 (9), September 1984). The crucial theme is that there is no contradiction between femininity and serving in the SADF. Thus the ideology of gender roles is preserved.

The increasing incorporation of women as a minority of the armed forces has not seriously breached the ideology of gender roles or the sexual division of labour. The most common functions women fulfil in militaries are clerical, administrative and servicing. These are jobs similar to those held by women in the wider labour market. They do not contaminate the ideology of femininity which reinforces the sexual division of labour. It is therefore difficult to see how this increasing use of white women as a military resource can be considered as advancing equality between the sexes: 'women's participation in the military has failed to challenge traditional and very basic sexist ideologies. It reinforces a sexual division of labour sharper and more rigid in the armed forces than in civilian life' (Stiehm, 1982:391).

Contradictions

The linkages between women and war, the incorporation of white women both directly and indirectly, materially and ideologically into the militarization of South African society, are not smooth, uniform processes. The linkages are complex and straddle contradictions which are embedded deep in the peculiar social conditions of South

Africa. While white women are contributing to the process of militarization, white women are more active than white men in the extra-parliamentary struggle against the apartheid regime which militarization defends. Of course the relatively higher level of white women's participation in such groups has to be set against the high degree of passive acceptance and support for the apartheid regime among white South Africans generally. However, women's participation is shaped by the politics of gender in contradictory ways. This will be illustrated by pointing to white women in the African National Congress.

Among the small number of whites convicted in South African courts for furthering the aims of the banned ANC, white women form a significant proportion. There have been a number of famous cases: Barbara Hogan, Helene Pastoors, Jansie Lourens, Trish Hanekom and Marion Sparg. The latter is a twenty-nine-year-old former journalist who, in 1986, was sentenced to twenty-five years imprisonment on charges of high treason and arson. She is the first white South African woman known to have served as a member of the ANC's military wing, Umkhonto we Sizwe. Pleading guilty to all the charges against her, Sparg admitted planting the limpet mines which exploded in Johannesburg's police headquarters and an East London police station in 1986. She said she knew it was possible policemen or civilians would die in the blasts, 'but my motive was not to injure or kill people. It was one of a soldier in Umkhonto we Sizwe, a military army. I followed orders just like any other soldier' (*Weekly Mail*, 7 November 1986).

The politics of gender were used to deny and trivialize the validity of such choice and commitment. Shortly after her arrest in March 1986 several South African newspapers depicted Sparg as a failed woman, as a lonely, overweight, unattractive female who had turned to revolutionary politics not out of commitment but out of a desire to belong and win acceptance. She was depicted as a failed woman rather than a revolutionary. Paradoxically she was still a woman and so *ipso facto* could not have acted independently. As a woman, she had to be manipulated by a man of special persuasive powers. Sparg was described as acting under the influence of one such man whom Williamson of the South African Security Police described as 'a sort of Charles Manson figure' (*Observer*, 31 March 1987).

The revolutionary commitment of these women is denigrated by the suggestion that, as women, they could not have been acting autonomously. However, their status as white women also provides a degree of camouflage. It has been suggested that white women attract less attention than men, and under the guise of their femininity are able to travel more freely around the country fulfilling vital roles in the underground war, a role which is likely to expand in the near future (ibid).

Editors' Note: This article is an abbreviated version of a paper prepared for a volume on militarization in South Africa. We are grateful to the author for permission to publish it in shortened form. A longer version is published as 'Manpower and militarization: women and the SADF' in J. Cock and L. Nathan (eds) (1989), *War and Society: The Militarisation of South Africa*, Cape Town: David Phillip, which is reviewed in this issue.

Bibliographic Notes

Bahro, Rudolf (1982), *Socialism and Survival*, London: Heretic Books.

Brownmiller, Susan (1976), *Against Our Will: Men, Women and Rape*, Harmondsworth: Penguin.

Eide, A. & M. Thee (eds.) (1980), *Problems of Contemporary Militarism*, London: Croom Helm.

Eisenhart, R. Wayne (1975), 'You Can't Hack it Little Girl: A Discussion of the Covert Psychological Agenda of Modern Combat Training', *Journal of Social Issues*, 31, 4.

Enloe, Cynthia (1983), *Does Khaki Become You? The Militarisation of Women's Lives*, Boston, MA: South End Press.

Feinstein, Andrew et al. (1986), 'Some attitudes towards conscription in South Africa', *Psychology in Society*, 5, pp. 66–80.

Fine, P. and Andy Getz (1986), 'The Examination of the Role of Women in the Militarisation of South African Society', Industrial Sociology Project, University of the Witwatersrand.

Frankel, Phillip (1984), *Pretoria's Praetorians: Civil-military Relations in South Africa*, Cambridge: Cambridge University Press.

Frederikse, Julie (1986), *South Africa: A Different Kind of War*, Johannesburg, Ravan Press; London: James Currey.

Grundy, Kenneth (1983), *Soldiers without Politics: Blacks in the South African Armed Forces*, Berkeley, University of California Press.

Grundy, Kenneth (1986), *The Militarisation of South African Politics*, Cambridge: CUP.

Human Awareness Programme (HAP) (1986), *Militarisation Dossier*, Durban.

Huston, Nancy (1982), 'Tales of War and Tears of Women', Women's Studies International Forum, 5, 3/4.

Mason, Tim (1976), 'Women in Germany, 1925–1940', *History Workshop*, Vol.1.

McLean, Scilla (1982), 'Report on UNESCO's Report: The Role of Women in Peace Movements', *Women's Studies International Forum*, 5, 3/4.

Orr, Rachel (1983), *Women, Militarism and Non-violence*, London: Peace Pledge Union.

Ratcliffe, Simon (1983), 'Forced Relations: The State, Crisis and the Rise of Militarism in South Africa', Honours Thesis, University of the Witwatersrand.

Roberts, Barbara (1984), 'The Death of Machothink: Feminist Research and the Transformation of Peace Studies', *Women's Studies International Forum*, 7,4.

San-Juan, Diane (1982), 'Feminism and the National Liberation Struggle in the Philippines', *Women's Studies International Forum*, 5, 3/4.

Stiehm, Judith (ed.) (1983), *Women and Women's Wars*, Oxford: Pergamon Press.

Summers, Anne (1975), *Damned Whores and God's Police: The Colonisation of Women in Australia*, Victoria, Australia: Penguin Books.

Thompson, Edward (1982), 'Notes on Exterminism, the Last State of Civilisation', *New Left Review*.

Thompson, Edward (ed.) (1982) *Exterminism and Cold War*, London: Verso.

Williams, Raymond (1985), *Towards 2000*, Harmondsworth: Penguin.

15 ROGER CHARLTON & ROY MAY
Warlords & Militarism
in Chad   [1989]

After considering the inadequacies of the prevailing concern in African studies
with violence and the collapse of the postcolonial state, the authors argue that the
uses made of concepts of 'militarism' and 'militarisation' are equally confused and
inadequate, particularly in explaining recent Chad history. They suggest an alternative approach, the elaboration of the warlord model used to discuss Chinese
history between 1916 and 1928. They argue that there are striking parallels between
the China of that time and Chad from the late 1970s in the form of the collapse of
central control, the rise of regional centres of power based on personalised rule
and military force, and the consequent prevalence of a politics of conflict and
war.

The capacity of Chad and Chadians to spring surprises on Africanists appears to be
inexhaustible. No sooner had the country been written off as a permanently 'broken-
backed' state (Tinker, 1964) than it, apparently, rose from the dead and reconstituted
itself – with American and French assistance – as a viable political and military, if not
yet economic, entity under Hissene Habre. It then proceeded to expel the Libyans, first
from occupied Chadian territory, then, albeit temporarily, from much of the disputed
Aouzou strip. Briefly, it even took the war of state reconstitution into Libya itself. An
OAU-inspired cease-fire was announced on 11 September 1987, followed by a
statement from Colonel Quaddafi on 17 September that henceforth Chad would be left
to the Chadians. Since then (from October 1988) diplomatic ties between Chad and
Libya have been reopened, in turn helping to precipitate an attempted military coup in
April 1989. This failed coup, paradoxically, underlined Habre's personal ascendancy
and, at the same time, left him (as the magazine *West Africa* neatly put it) an
increasingly 'lonely warlord'. Thus, a not inappropriate point has been reached to begin
conceptualising or, perhaps better, re-conceptualising more than two decades of always
eventful and mainly turbulent independence.

However, this exercise is not undertaken in the expectation that Chadian politics is
necessarily entering a new era, or even a new chapter of its troubled history. On the
contrary, it seems clear that so deep-seated is the factionalism that is at the centre of the
Chadian political process, that any notion of the ending of an era is at best premature
and, at worst, naive and misplaced. Indeed, it is the almost permanent instability of
Chadian politics that makes that state's political processes fascinating and, in most
respects, unpredictable even with the benefit of hindsight. It also leads to Africanists
generally finding it more prudent to describe seemingly kaleidoscopic developments
than to attempt to step back and understand or explain them theoretically.

In part at least this tendency to theoretical abdication is a fault of the conceptual models commonly used by Africanists. These tend to the unilinear and, therefore, can only be uncomfortably applied to a state whose fortunes oscillate with such incredible rapidity. The problem many Africanists have of separating the wood from the trees is, however, one common to area studies. Equally to blame is the inadequate development of theories of armed forces and society capable of dealing with highly complex cases of militarism such as that exhibited in the erratic trajectory of the Chadian state (and its successive regimes).

In the case of Chad it is interesting (and personally comforting) to note that analytical inadequacies and consequent failure of prediction are not confined to academics alone. French policy, too, has been characterised by vacillation and inconsistency such that almost every contestant for power since independence has, at some time or other, received French backing – including both President Habre and his chief rival, Goukouni Oueddi. Moreover, as Lemarchand has stressed, every significant faction in Chad politics has also received, at some time or another, support from Libya as well – although the latter is presently paying the price of picking weak (and therefore hypothetically more manipulable) clients. Since it is the US State Department's contention that 'you can no longer buy an African state, you can only rent one by the day', it is ironic that the implications of this claim as far as it applies to Chad are better understood (having been painfully learned) in Paris and Tripoli than in Washington. To date, the US, uniquely among Chad's contending foreign patrons, has been consistent in its policy aims – described by Helen Kitchen as 'bashing Libya's Quaddafi' – and in its support for its own instrument – Hissene Habre. Yet the Bush regime is likely to have to face a crucial policy choice avoided by its predecessor: what to do when Habre (assuming his survival) finally establishes a working relationship with Libya, as he must if he is to stabilise his regime in the long term.

This article therefore, after dealing briefly with Chad from the perspectives of African studies and of the wider literature of militarisation and militarism, seeks both to justify and to develop a theoretical perspective which, while remaining open-ended as to future prospects, takes advantage of hindsight to focus specifically on the key features of the Chadian situation. It is our contention that a 'warlord' perspective – to date utilised in a widespread but rather loose and casual manner by Chad specialists – provides this desired focus and, in particular, while situating the Chadian case within a developing theoretical and empirical literature, also raises important questions to guide future research.

Chad & African Studies

In evaluating the post-independence performance of the continent's fifty-odd states it can hardly be argued that Africanists have adopted particularly exacting standards of judgement. 'A generation after independence', Christopher Clapham argues, 'the survival of African states is their main achievement'. In some cases, and notably that of Chad – Africa's 'basket case' to borrow René Lemarchand's evocative phrase – it has sometimes appeared as if formal state survival was the **only** achievement.

Moreover, following Jackson and Rosberg's arguments, many Africanists have come to accept that it is the operation of the international or inter-state system which provides the key as to 'why Africa's weak states persist' (*World Politics*, 35, 1, 1982). From this perspective African states are juridical expressions rather than empirical entities, surviving to date simply because the international system has 'successfully outlawed force as a method of producing new states in Africa. This is perceived as especially apt in the case of Chad where, as Rothchild & Foley put it, 'internationally accorded "statehood" stands in for the last vestiges of "stateness"' (1983:313). Most of the continent has therefore been confined to a limbo between the heaven of stable statehood and the hell of dismemberment, with international recognition bringing only the continued assurance that no African secessionist or irredentist movement is likely to achieve its ultimate aims – even if, as Donald Horowitz said of Chad from 1979, 'everyone has seceded'.

Given the concentration, even fixation, of African studies on the question of state weakness and collapse, it is not surprising that Chad specialists in particular were unprepared to cope theoretically with the upward trajectory of the Chadian state after 1979. Concentration on the ease with which state deconstitution occurred perhaps blinded them to the rapidity with which such trends could be reversed and reconstitution could occur. In short, Africanists moved too rapidly and too completely from observations of empirical unilinearity to assumptions of theoretical unilinearity.

The unilinear inadequacies of contemporary African studies' theorising become particularly obvious when the assumptions underlying theories of state weakness and marginality are considered. For, underpinning these perspectives, is the view that the most pressing current threats to state integrity and coherence stem directly or indirectly from rising tides of intra- and inter-state violence – a view exemplified by the widespread assumption of the growing 'militarisation' of African political processes. The empirical basis for this view, in turn, is to be found in the perception of a growing propensity to resort to force as a first rather than as a last resort. Thus, as Robin Luckham puts it, 'force has become a critical component of the post-colonial settlement'.

In this respect Jackson & Rosberg's most recent listing of the 'empirical conditions' currently facing Africa's states is most instructive: it covers refugees, genocide, ethnic massacres, strife and discrimination, coups, coup attempts and plots, civil wars and other internal armed conflicts, and dictatorships both malign and more benign. Only after these violence-related dimensions have been listed are 'generally poor' economic performance and endemic corruption mentioned.

Thus violence, frequently viewed by theorists of the development of the modern European state as historically functional, indeed essential, for effective state building, is perceived by Africanists as automatically and inherently dysfunctional for contemporary state building. Yet if, as Charles Tilly, among many others, contends, 'European states took shape through external war and internal coercion', why should Africanists not appreciate that contemporary violence might have comparable effects?

To some extent, of course, the answer to the above question lies in the very recent nature of independence and the inevitable inadequacy of intellectual perspectives generated in response to a series of what may well be short-term, but are certainly very serious, crises of statehood, exacerbated by global recession and Cold War resurgence in a regional context of climatic disasters, ecological collapse and burgeoning population. Indeed, it would require a rather considerable leap of the intellectual imagination to conclude that effective state building is occurring in those African states afflicted by crisis since independence and, perhaps in particular, in those states such as Uganda and Chad itself, in which over much of this period, violence has become both more prevalent and increasingly severe at the same time as the state's ability to counteract or even to cope with such violence frequently appears to have declined.

Nevertheless, it is impossible not to conclude that the fixation of Africanists on the issue of state collapse, and their equally firm assumptions concerning the causal connection between collapse and rising violence (May & Charlton, 1986) has led African studies into its current intellectual cul-de-sac, whereby significant state building almost appears to be impossible by definition, except in some rather exceptional cases (Botswana, Kenya, Ivory Coast) where mineral resources and/or external linkages coincide with stable regimes. Accordingly, our suggestion, to be pursued below in the context of Chad, is that the assumption that African violence is related to attempts by the state to accumulate power be retained, but without its attendant assumption that rising violence is necessarily totally dysfunctional for state formation, thereby leaving the question of positive or negative relationships open to empirical investigation. Quite simply, more detailed and more discriminating conceptions and measures of both the levels and types of violence that are currently practised in Africa are required in order to fully evaluate the nature of the potential and actual relationships between violence (in all its forms and degrees), 'statehood' and 'stateness'.

Militarisation & Militarism

Unfortunately, in developing such typologies of violence and its impacts we cannot turn to any developed or satisfactory body of theory within either the broad context of global analyses of war and society or even in the more focused literature on civil-military relations. Theorists of armed forces and society currently operate with confusing and confused concepts, notably 'militarisation' and 'militarism', which have no generally accepted definition and are therefore used idiosyncratically and often indiscriminately. 'The very terms "militarism" and "militarisation"', argues Marek Thee, 'need more elucidation, and need to be given a meaningful contemporary currency. These terms are often used with different connotations in east and west, north and south, and are too often applied in the political debate without precise definition' (1980:15). Unsurprisingly perhaps, Thee's own definitions of the two terms illustrate rather than remove the definitional nightmare and, in particular, the tendency to conflate the two concepts. 'We' do indeed, as Thee enjoins, 'need more research and more informed discussion on problems of militarism and militarisation'.

Equally unsurprisingly, this definitional and conceptual disaster area has been replicated in the still burgeoning literature on African militarism and militarisation. For example, Simon Baynham in a recent and judicious survey of the literature notes 'repeated charges that the continent is being rapidly militarised and that a new arms race has been unleashed in Africa'. Over the last decade or so, the focus of this militarisation literature has changed very markedly: militarisation is now no longer primarily perceived in terms of a threat to the remaining civilian regimes of the region but instead redefined in terms of a perception of an increasingly hostile continental and global environment and ultimately seen as a potential threat to world peace, liable to turn 'seemingly parochial African disputes into occasions for superpower competition' (Foltz, 1985:171). However, the key concepts, militarisation and militarism, are still utilised loosely, frequently without any serious attempt at definitional precision (to refer to any military-related developments in the region): in this sense the literature is characterised by continuity rather than change.

Moreover, where definitions are given they are, inevitably, idiosyncratic and too broad to adequately discriminate between the experiences of the different states in the region. For example, Robin Luckham's depiction of 'the militarisation of Africa' involves a wide-ranging 'process that includes not only the acquisition of weapons, but also an expansion in the size of professional military establishments, the prevalence of authoritarian regimes relying on force as an instrument of government, and an increase in both external and internal war' (1980:179). With such a definition, even broad distinctions, such as that between civilian and military, or between different African states and regimes, disappear and all African states can be perceived as militarised.

Such a perspective fails to allow for the numerous paradoxes and contradictions that any detailed analysis of the African experience immediately highlights. In particular, how does one account for the apparent paradox of the exceptionally high levels of intra-state violence which have frequently pertained in states such as Chad and Uganda, states which have relatively small armed forces and comparatively small military budgets?

In this context our initial argument is relatively straightforward. A more discriminating and theoretically coherent account of intra- and inter-state violence in African states can most simply be gained by distinguishing between militarisation and militarism rather than conflating the two. Such a distinction, commonly made in everyday speech, separates the increase or spread of things military (militarisation) from the rise of military ethos or spirit (militarism).

Thus, militarisation, following Eide and Thee, is manifested in any 'increase in armaments, advances in the destructive capacity of weapons, growing numbers of people under arms, and ... increases in military expenditure' (1980:9-10), as well as in any consequent rise in the political role and impact of the military, whether or not that impact manifests itself in the form of a military regime. Militarism, on the other hand, is manifested in the attitudes and behaviour both of states and of significant groups within states, insofar as they rely on force as a normal political tactic.

Clearly, further and more detailed analyses of both militarisation and militarism in Africa are now required along with enquiries which explicitly seek to examine the empirical relationships between these two analytically separable processes. Most importantly, the impacts of militarisation and of militarism may in practice vary at least somewhat independently of each other in any individual state; it is possible that relatively high levels of militarisation may be accompanied by relatively low levels of militarism and vice versa. The assumption that underpins the militarisation literature (that militaristic attitudes accompany the process of militarisation) needs to be tested in each case. Furthermore, we also suggest that militarism and the use of force, conventionally viewed as an independent variable, could profitably be designated as the dependent variable in future studies.

The Relevance of a 'Warlord' Model

Our own research has led us to identify Chad as one particularly promising case for such an analysis. For Chad is an almost classical example of a state in which force has become the norm rather than the exception in the political process: a state riven by factional fighting and suffering from apparently incurable political decay. Indeed, it has seriously been contended that the very concept of a Chadian state is itself almost a contradiction in terms. Michalon, for example, bluntly talks of *un Etat Fictif*. Two decades of internal schism, compounded by the involvement of external powers in Chadian politics, have often made that country the very epitome of juridical rather than empirical statehood – a state which persists sometimes in name alone. It is true that a number of other African states have also suffered violent regional or factional challenges to the authority of their central governments, and some have even appeared to suffer fates similar or comparable to that of Chad, in the sense that central governmental control over significant areas of territory has sometimes been lost for significant periods of time – Angola, Ethiopia, Mozambique, Nigeria, Uganda and Zaire immediately spring to mind. Yet, in none of these examples, save possibly that of contemporary Uganda, has the breakdown of authority and the prevalence of force and arms as political resources been so complete as in the Chadian example.

In this context it may well be illuminating to seek to compare Chadian militarism – the propensity of its factions to resort to force as a first rather than a last resort – to other extreme examples of internal militarism not only in other contemporary African states, but also in other regions. Indeed the great advantage of such an eclectic approach is that it may provide – given sufficient empirical similarities – theoretical and explanatory insights which more limited comparisons may fail to reveal. For example, two related processes are apparent in the historical development of Chadian internal militarism. First, it involves a process of de-institutionalisation and organisational decay at the level of the central government. Second, it involves a concomitant and progressive growth of regionalism, ultimately emerging as a regionalisation of the whole political process. Both of these processes, in both sequence and substance, seem, at least superficially, strikingly similar to events which occurred in China between 1916 and 1928, the classically 'confused and destructive' period of 'warlord politics' which followed the collapse of the Imperial system and the inauguration of a Republic.

In a pattern which appears to have been replicated in Chad, the breakdown of central authority in Republican China was accompanied by both an increasing reliance on force of arms to settle political disputes and to determine policy, and a regionalisation of the political process. Both developments came together in the rise of the 'warlords': those regional leaders who exercised or sought to exercise power in such a system. Like the competing Chadian factional leaders, the Chinese 'warlords' relied upon their personal politico-military skills to establish, first, their control over a regional power-base and second, drawing upon the economic resources of their fiefdoms, to expand, by force if necessary, their domain of effective power. However, as in Chad, the expansionist ambitions of any one 'warlord' immediately impinged on the sphere of influence of neighbouring 'warlords', leading to periods of often intense but ultimately indeterminate fighting, leaving the whole system suspended in a state of competitive disequilibrium, aptly described in the Chinese case as 'internal anarchy'. In China, of course, this particular form of anarchy was to a large extent ameliorated, if not entirely ended, by the growing military predominance of what had originally been one 'warlord' faction, the *Kuomintang*. Such an outcome appeared (at least until very recently) unlikely in contemporary Chad where direct foreign interventions encouraged the perpetuation of a situation of internal stalemate. Nevertheless the parallels between post-colonial Chadian history and events in China between the Revolution in 1911 and 1928 – the year which saw the successful conclusion of the 'Northern Expedition' by the Kuomintang and effectively ended the classical era of Republican 'warlordism' – are sufficiently striking to suggest that further, more detailed comparative study is warranted.

Indeed, it may now even be prudent to extend such comparisons beyond 1928, given recent developments in Chad. For Hissene Habre's remarkable resurrection of a united (however loosely) and unified (however temporarily) Chadian state at least raises the possibility that he may be that state's Chiang, though it is somewhat improbable that he might be Chad's Mao! In particular, the recent recrudescence of Chadian factionalism, even before the euphoria over apparent reunification has begun to wane, is at least superficially similar to developments post-1928 in China. In that case, if the classical era of 'warlordism' was effectively ended in 1928, 'militarism' certainly was not. As Ch'I points out, 'militarism remained a dominant feature of Chinese politics for a long time after', crucially continuing 'as an important aspect of the Nationalist Government between 1928 and 1949', although taking a rather different form under the altered politico-military conditions pertaining under Nationalist rule (1976:237-9). Crucially, some warlords survived and continued to operate, leading to one depiction of the overall situation as 'residual warlordism' (Sheridan, 1966:15). Significantly, this situation was almost precisely replicated in Chad, where two important warlords loomed large over Habre's Third Republic, namely Goukouni Oueddei (the former President) and Acheik Ibn Oumar. Currently only the former remains (outside Chad) a focus for opposition forces. The latter, after rallying to the government in November 1988, was appointed Foreign Minister in March 1989, an event that contributed to the coup attempt in April.

Chadian Politics: Warlord Perspectives

A major part of the potential utility of a developed 'warlord' perspective, particularly as it is being currently developed by sinologists, is its flexibility and, specifically, its salience in dealing with highly complex and apparently mutually contradictory developments in which incipient and often hidden state building occurs alongside apparent state collapse and/or in which state weakness and collapse is imminent in apparent state formation. A 'warlord' model can generate useful hypotheses and raise significant new questions about both the progressive or, better perhaps, regressive, collapse of the Chadian state after Independence and/or its present seeming resurgence under Hissene Habre. Most important, it can link these apparently divergent developments in a single analytical framework.

Equally significantly, a warlord model is also perfectly compatible with both of the currently dominant theoretical perspectives offered by Chad specialists to 'explain' post-colonial political developments and processes: Lemarchand's factionalism model and Decalo's centre-periphery approach. Indeed a major strength of the warlord perspective is that it can be used to combine and synthesise these two existing models into a single and, hopefully, more coherent whole, based on the central ideas of armed factionalism, militarised regional autonomy and central state collapse, defined in terms of loss of physical control over significant portions of both national territory and population.

At the same time it is vital to underline that there is no single conceptualisation of Chinese developments which could be defined as 'the' warlord model and applied *in toto* to the Chadian case. In practice it is more appropriate perhaps to refer to Chinese 'warlord studies' and resultant 'warlord perspectives', involving a whole series of wide-ranging and very diverse historical and conceptual studies from which a series of theoretical models are emerging with widely differing foci and implications. Currently these models coexist alongside each other, each one illustrating different facets and dimensions of military, political and socio-economic reality as well as regional and temporal variations within an astonishingly diverse and incredibly complex period of Chinese history, during which, in only 16 years from 1912 to 1928, more than 1300 warlords fought more than 140 separable wars (Ch'en, 1968:563).

In short, for both states but clearly much more particularly so for Chad, the idea of the 'warlord model' refers to work in progress rather than a finished product. In particular, Chad specialists have only just begun to tap the explanatory strengths of the warlord analogy. To date the concept of warlord and of warlord politics has been rather casually and loosely applied to Chadian factional/regional/personal schisms and armed conflicts. In fact Chadian warlord studies are currently roughly at the state identified two decades ago by Jerome Ch'en for its sinological counterpart. Then, in an important review article inspired by the publication of James Sheridan's path-breaking *Chinese Warlord*, Ch'en noted the existence 'of various projects on Chinese warlords. It is hoped', he continued, 'that they will eventually take this subject from the state of "gossip columns" to that of proper history' (ibid). In the intervening years Ch'en's wish has been amply fulfilled and the body of relevant studies continues to grow rather rapidly with 'a considerable number of scholars' tapping, as Diana Lary underlines in an important recent review essay, 'vast, rich and sometimes overwhelming arrays of source materials'. In the Chadian case source materials are never 'overwhelming', always patchy and generally considerably more difficult to obtain, while work on the ground can reasonably be termed difficult, sometimes hazardous and often impossible, leading to more constrained research possibilities. Nevertheless, there remains, as in the Chinese case, much untapped material, particularly if research 'on the ground' outside N'Djamena becomes possible. Moreover, much useful work can be done in the Chadian case by simply reworking and reinterpreting, with the benefit of hindsight, already familiar material. For example, in an earlier (1985) formulation we predicted that a Chadian equivalent of the Chinese reunification under the Kuomintang was 'an outcome which appears somewhat unlikely' due to the fact that 'direct foreign intervention currently ensures the perpetuation of the present situation of internal stalemate'. Such an interpretation was, in turn, consistent with conventional interpretations which underlined the likely determinative effect of intervention by non-African powers. What we failed to see then, but cannot fail to see today, was that the equilibrium or stalemate that existed between apparently evenly matched coalitions of external and internal actors was much more precarious than it appeared. In retrospect, there were two rather obvious reasons for this.

In the first place, our analysis underestimated the extent to which the Libyans, as an occupying power, would undermine their own credibility and acceptability in the eyes of the Chad population and would do so particularly in the occupied territories, rapidly negating any original appeals based on ethno-religious commonality. Jean-Claude Pomonti, writing in *Le Monde* as early as 1982, illustrates this point amply, underlining 'the unpopularity of the occupation by the Libyans, who pillaged the country without furnishing it the least economic aid'. Libyan behaviour, in turn, engendered radical second thoughts among some members of the pro-Libyan warlord coalition as they perceived 'what began as a Libyan-sponsored rescue operation' turning 'into a full-scale annexation' (Lemarchand, 1984).

In the second place, our earlier analysis also underestimated both Habre's politico-military abilities and the extent to which he was perceived by the mass of Chadians and external backers to be a leader with a programme coherent enough to offer hope for the future and determined enough to make his prophecies of a reunited Chad come true, despite his previously chequered politico-military career and his often troubled relations with France.

Developing a Warlord Model

In both cases, Libyan occupation and Habre's trajectory, Chinese analogies – a Japanese invasion and occupation and Chiang Kai-shek and the Kuomintang respectively – would have pointed rather clearly to the present outcome. Accordingly, in the remainder of this article, we will first outline the warlord model as it has been applied, both explicitly and implicitly, to the Chadian case to date and, second, highlight some dimensions of the wider warlord literature and of the Chinese situation which might prove to be either conceptually illuminating or analogically useful in the Chadian context.

Chad, all commentators now appear to agree, has warlords with an equal amount of consistency in identifying their key features. As in the parent model, 'two basic characteristics of a warlord' are posited; namely, 'a private army and an area under his control'. Jerome Ch'en's formulation for China is paralleled by the stress of Chad specialists on both these features, in the form of the personalisation of politico-military leadership and its regionalisation. Accordingly, James Sheridan's early definition neatly summarises key features of both the Chinese and Chadian cases. 'A warlord', he argues, 'exercised effective governmental control over a fairly well-defined region by means of a military organisation that obeyed no higher authority than himself' (1966:1). David Yost makes a very similar point. 'Faction leaders in Chad', he claims, 'are equivalent to warlords. Several have exercised (and disputed) effective autonomous control over different territories within Chad.' Moreover, Chad specialists also conceptualised the rules of the political game in terms much more than superficially reminiscent of the Chinese case. For example, Chiang Kai-shek's formulation of the five essential characteristics of warlord behaviour (lack of a political principle, occupation of an area, an insatiable need for money and property, love of his own skin, and dependence on imperialist support) is rather precisely replicated in numerous depictions of the behaviour of Chadian politico-military factional leaders. As David Yost, for example, puts it, Chadian warlord loyalties 'have shifted frequently' and he underlines this point by quoting René Lemarchand's graphic description of the mainsprings of factionalism: characterised by 'short-term calculations' in their dealings with fellow Chadians and their outside backers alike, involving 'opportunism, bribery, revenge and assassination' and utilising whatever resources come to hand 'from cattle and cash to guns and ammunition'.

Implicitly at least, Chad's specialists also agree that the state suffered from the structural and functional equivalent of 'the warlord period' in Chinese history: defined by Wang Gungwu in terms of the 'disintegration of political authority' and, therefore, analytically separable from all the many earlier periods of schism, division and instability in Chinese history which were, as Diana Lary stresses, contextually different in that they were merely 'breakdowns of central administration'. In the Chadian case, as in the Chinese, much argument is likely to continue as to exactly when the respective warlord periods began, as well, no doubt, in the future as to when it could be defined as ending. For Chad, following the arguments presented by Roy May in the most detailed application of a warlord perspective to date, we have suggested 1978 as the most appropriate date of origin (1985).

However, to Africanists generally, the main analytical utility of the above definition of a 'warlord period' may well be less to aid periodisations of Chad's history – a state in which it is universally agreed there was a 'disintegration of political authority' at the centre from at least the late 1970s – than to situate the Chadian example of state collapse in a more satisfactory comparative perspective. In particular, the Chadian example of disintegration is often lumped together with other cases of regionally focused instability, notably those in Angola, Ethiopia, Nigeria, Sudan, Uganda, Zaire and, most recently Mozambique. Collectively these are defined as cases in which the respective 'central governments lost control of important areas in their jurisdiction during struggles with rival political organisations' (Jackson & Rosberg, 1985).

However, what a warlord perspective would suggest – at least on the basis of the Chinese example – is that, with the possible exception of Uganda, all the other above-mentioned African examples can more properly be defined as closer to temporary 'breakdowns of central administration' than to the type of degree of state collapse achieved in either China or Chad in their warlord periods. At the same time it must be stressed that the concept of warlord is analytically separable from the idea of a warlord period and if the latter concept (fortunately) has but a relatively restricted relevance to contemporary Africa, the former is, sadly, quite widely applicable.

Probably the clearest point of difference that emerges from a comparison of the two literatures, Chinese and Chadian, is the omnipresence of non-Chadian actors, notably French, Libyan and US as well as numerous regional participants. Interestingly, despite Chiang Kai-shek's stress on the dependence of warlords on 'imperialists' for support, the Chinese literature focuses relatively little on the impact of external forces in either inaugurating or sustaining the warlord era. In this respect, the contrast in the style of presentation and the focus of analyses internally focused for China and stressing the political room for manoeuvre open to the warlords, externally focused for Chad and stressing political constraints, is striking. It caused Roy May to question the applicability of the whole Chinese model because, despite the existence of external intervention and support in the Chinese case 'it did not have the central significance that the external influences appear to have in Chad' (1985).

Interestingly, however, May was, even then, torn between the possibility of a 'lack of "fit" in the applicability of the Chinese model to the case of Chad' and the alternative possibility that 'external' support was important but not crucial to the survival of major Chadian leaders and, most importantly, that even without such support 'they would have survived anyway'. In retrospect, we feel that the second possibility is worth further consideration but that, more significantly, this earlier formulation expresses the conceptual alternatives too starkly. Our current suggestion is that – as underlined by the Habre trajectory – the determining influence of competing external actors in maintaining Chad in a state of constant disequilibrium was perhaps exaggerated in earlier accounts.

In this respect we feel that sinologists – noting, as Ch'en points out, that while 'some prominent warlords did obtain foreign support ... many especially small ones ... did not' – are right in generally not following Chiang by including external support as part of the definition of a warlord. As Diana Lary forcefully points out, any 'notion that warlords were simply the running dogs of imperialism has never been specifically proven, and ... has in some cases been explicitly debunked'. Yet as with Chad, any political room for manoeuvre available to China's warlords occurred within the severe economic constraints exerted by substantial external controls over both sources of armaments and of funds: controls which were probably, overall, little less severe in the Chinese than in the Chadian case. Moreover, in both cases, warlord predominance discouraged further direct economic penetration by removing any possibilities for productive investment to occur, whilst, at the same time, producing the conditions of state collapse and weakness that encouraged a single predatory foreign power – Japan and Libya respectively – to exploit the situation militarily and invade.

Thus, we feel, Chad specialists could profitably take a leaf out of the sinologists' book and look more closely at the internal bases and outcomes of warlordism. In particular, much work needs to be done on the internal socio-economic underpinnings of warlordism in Chad and, in particular, on its fiscal and financial workings and the attendant administrative arrangements it engendered. In the Chinese case much fascinating work is under way involving analyses of the economic and social relationships between the 'gentry' and warlords at the local and regional levels (Ch'en, 1979). In Chad, with a miniscule middle class at independence, did the warlord era encourage class development and the emergence of a comparable 'gentry' to manage the process of extraction and provide the rudiments of a local bureaucracy? Alternatively, how much of warlord behaviour in Chad was simply uncontrolled predation: what, in China, would have been termed 'banditry'? Only detailed fieldwork on the ground, outside N'Djamena, will answer such questions.

Certainly, the formulation of states better able to extract than control seems apt for much of contemporary Africa, even where state control has not been threatened to the degree it has in Chad. However, in cases such as that of Chad, studies have concentrated almost exclusively on the problems of loss of control, ignoring the issue of state extraction almost entirely. Could they, therefore, have also ignored some incipient state-building beneath apparent chaos?

Clearly, in the case of Chad at least, this question must remain an open one for some time to come. The crucial tests will come in the aftermath of the actual, as opposed to formal, ending of hostilities with Libya. In terms of our own formulation Chadian politics has suffered from an excessive dose of militarism, but not (at least on most conventional indicators) from a correspondingly serious case of militarisation. In this context, the parallels with Uganda are, at least superficially, both rather obvious and rather discouraging since, in the latter case, levels of violence appear not to have fallen and life, even in Kampala, remains precarious.

Indeed, in Chad itself the apparent resilience of the politics of elite factionalism is already clear and there are no signs that this particular dimension of the political process has been in any sense transformed by recent developments. Indeed, if Chinese parallels have any relevance, it is as well to remember, in this context, the corresponding resilience of militarism under the Kuomintang. Thus, it is tempting to end this article on the same note that we adopted in 1985: 'If the suggested parallels between Chinese history and contemporary African politics are valid the prognosis for ... those African states, such as Chad and Uganda, already heavily affected by rising tides of militarism, is indeed grim.'

Yet, albeit tentatively and cautiously, we would now wish to add a slightly more optimistic note, at least for Chad. Even given that a recent past of militarism and the predominance of force may well prove very hard to transcend in a determinedly factionalised polity, it seems to us that there is at least one significant difference between Yoweri Museveni of Uganda and Hissene Habre of Chad.

The latter's trajectory, although surprising, was much less sudden and unexpected than the former's and may have allowed him to build a more than transient socio-economic basis of support within an incipient Chadian entrepreneurial middle class; a Chadian version of a military-gentry coalition. This, in turn, with continued outside support may be sufficient to allow him both to remain as the warlord of Chad, and to move from a successful politics of extraction to a more effective politics of control. Habre's own political agenda, as outlined in *Le Monde* in 1983, is uncompromising: 'There will be no more warlords, no more factions, no more private armies.' Moving from rhetoric to reality will not, however, be easy. Even within his own coalition turning warlord commanders into a conventional military bureaucracy and synthesising them within a civilianised administration poses a number of weighty problems, problems amply illustrated by the participation of three of Habre's closest associates in the April 1989 coup attempt.

Bibliographic Notes

Earlier versions of this papers were presented at the Biennial Conference of the Inter-University Seminar on Armed Forces and Society, Chicago, Illinois, 8-10 October 1987 and at the 30th annual meeting of the African Studies Association (US), Denver, Colorado, 19-23 November 1987. The authors are grateful for the criticism and comments made there.

On the background to the conflict in Chad, see: Hugh Tinker, 'Broken-backed states', *New Society* 30 January 1964; S. Decalo, *Historical Dictionary of Chad* (Scarecrow Press, 1977); Decalo, 'Chad: the roots of centre-periphery strife', *African Affairs* 79 (1980); Decalo, 'Regionalism, political decay and civil strife in Chad', JMAS 18(1) 1980; R Buijtenhuis, *Le Frolinat et les Révoltes Populaires du Tchad 1965–76* (Mouton, 1978); R. Lemarchand, 'Chad: the roots of chaos', *Current History*, December 1981; B. Lanne, *Tchad–Libya: La Querelle des Frontières* (Karthala, 1982); special issue on Chad, *Politique Africaine* 16 (1984); M.P. Kelley, *A State in Disarray. Condition of Chad's Survival* (Westview, 1986); V. Thompson & R. Adloff, *Conflict in Chad* (Hurst, 1981).

On the state of African Studies: C. Clapham, 'Comparing African states' *Political Studies* 34 (4) 1986; R. Lemarchand, 'The crisis in Chad' in G. Bender, J. Coleman & R. Sklar, eds, *African Crisis Areas and US Foreign Policy* (U. of California, 1985); Donald Horowitz, *Ethnic Groups in Conflict* (U. of California, 1985); Robin Luckham, 'Armaments, underdevelopment and demilitarisation in Africa', *Alternatives* 6 (2) 1980; D. Rothchild & M. Foley, 'The implications of scarcity for governance in Africa', *International Political Science Review* 4 (3) 1983; R. Jackson & C. Rosberg, 'The marginality of African states' in G. Carter & P. O'Meara, eds, *African Independence* (Indiana UP, 1985); C. Tilly, 'War and the power of warmakers in Western Europe and elsewhere 1600–1980' in P. Wallenstein, J. Galtung & C. Portales, eds, *Global Militarisation* (Westview, 1985); R. May & R. Charlton, 'State weakness in Africa: a critique' *Politics* 6 (2) 1986.

On militarism and militarisation: M .Thee, 'Militarism and militarisation in contemporary international relations' in A. Eide & M. Thee, eds, *Problems of Contemporary Militarism* (Croom Helm, 1980); S. Baynham, 'Introduction: Armed Forces in Africa' in S. Baynham, ed, *Military Power and Politics in Black Africa* (Croom Helm, 1986); R. Charlton & R. May, 'Militarisation and militarism in Africa: a research note' *Culture et Développement* 16 (3–4) 1985; W.J. Foltz, 'The militarisation of Africa: trends and policy problems' in W.J. Foltz & H.S. Bienen, eds, *Arms and the Africans* (Yale UP, 1985).

On Chad and warlordism: T. Michalon, 'L'Impuissonce d'un etat fictif' *Le Monde Diplomatique* September 1983; Roy May, 'Political authority in Chad: the relevance of the warlord model', African Studies Association of UK, Symposium, University of Birmingham, May 1985; R. May, 'The state of Chad: political factions and political decay', *Civilisations* 33 (2) 1983; H's Ch'l, *Warlord Politics in China 1916–1928* (Stanford, 1976); J. Sheridan, *Chinese Warlord* (Stanford, 1966); Diana Lary, 'Warlord studies', *Modern China* 6 (4) 1980; J. Ch'en, 'Defining Chinese warlords and their factions', *Bulletin of the SOAS* 31 (3) 1968; J.C. Pomonti, *Le Monde* (5 February 1982) quoted in D. Yost, 'French policy in Chad and the Libyan challenge', *Orbis* 26 (4) 1983; R. Lemarchand, 'Putting the pieces back together again', *Africa Report* (November–December 1984); J. Ch'en, *The Military-Gentry Coalition* (Toronto, JCMEA, 1979); L. Pye, *Warlord Politics* (Praeger, 1971); P. Duara, 'State involution: a study of local finances in north China 1911–1935', *Comparative Studies in Society and History* 21 (1) 1987.

Recent work on Chad's prospects includes: 'Chad: the factions return', *Africa Confidential* 28 (15) 22 July 1987; R. Buijtenhuis, 'Chad 1965–87: the narrow escape of an African state', and S.C. Nolutshungu, 'The radiance of the state: politics and the state in Chad since about 1975', both presented at the SOAS Conference on West African States since 1976, London 25–27 June 1987; R. Buijtenhuis, *Le Frolinat et les guerres civiles du Tchad 1977–84* (Paris, Karthala, 1987); R. Lemarchand, 'Chad: the misadventure of the north–south dialectic', *African Studies Review* 29 (3) 1986; R. Lemarchand, *The Green and the Black* (Indiana UP, 1988); R. May & R. Charlton, 'Chad: France's "fortuitous success"' *Modern and Contemporary France* 37 (1989); R. May, 'Internal dimensions of warfare in Chad' (Cambridge, Centre of African Studies, May 1989).

16

HUSSAINA ABDULLAH
'Transition Politics'
& the Challenge of Gender in Nigeria   [1993]

This article will examine the situation of women in the transition to civilian government in Nigeria from 1985, when General Babangida took power in a palace coup, until 1992. This has been the first Nigerian government which has officially addressed the 'woman question' and placed it explicitly on its political agenda. It is timely therefore to analyze the significance of these organizations for Nigerian women. The analysis will focus on the objectives and activities of government and non-governmental organizations explicitly concerned with gender issues. At the governmental level, the Better Life Programme for rural dwellers (BLP), the National Commission for Women (NCW) and the manifestos of the two political parties will be discussed. At the non-governmental level, the roles of the National Council of Women's Societies (NCWS) and the Nigerian Association of University Women (NAUW) will be discussed as these organizations have been the most significant in alerting women to their roles in the Third Republic.

We shall conclude that, despite an apparent acknowledgement of women's issues, the genuine liberation of women in Nigeria cannot be achieved through state-instituted reforms as envisaged by the BLP, NCW, NCWS and NAUW because the agenda of the Nigerian state is to keep women in their stereotyped role as 'mothers' and secondary wage earners (Eisenstein, 1981:248). What is needed is a women's organization that can tackle the issues of gender and class within the democratic movements, trade unions, the political parties and the family.

Women in the Politics of Transition

Government Organizations

The palace coup which brought General Babangida to power in August 1985 overthrew the military government of Major-General Buhari. In 1986, General Babangida set up a political bureau with the responsibility of undertaking a comprehensive study of the Nigerian socio-economic and political system. In the course of its deliberations, selected social groups and organizations were invited to make submissions to the bureau. From the various submissions to the bureau on women in Nigeria it was agreed that women as a group are marginalized in the socio-political life of Nigeria. The reasons identified as causing this marginalization of women were religious and cultural beliefs, patriarchal attitudes, the capitalist relations of production and the influence of colonialism (Directorate for Social Mobilisation, 1989:157). The political bureau made recommendations to put an end to the disadvantaged position of women. These included:

The full involvement of women in politics is one method of defending women's interests in society. They can participate fully if they are members of the legislative and executive arms of government. For this reason, we recommend the allocation of five per cent of the legislative seats to women in all three tiers of government. This five per cent seats allocated to women is to be filled by nominations through the political parties ... and the formulation of a national policy on women and development (*ibid*.:159).

The bureau's recommendation on seat allocation was rejected by the government. In its White Paper on the political bureau's report:

Government notes the reasons for the Bureau's recommendation on the representation of women ... But does not accept the implications of reverse discrimination embedded in that recommendation. Government believes in equality of sexes, individuals and groups (Government White Paper on the Political Bureau Report, 1987:24).

Although the Government rejected the bureau's recommendation on legislative seat allocation and is yet to formulate a national policy on women, it established the BLP and the NCW at federal and state levels, created women and development departments in the state ministries of culture and social welfare to enhance the integration of women in the development process, and appointed women to top administrative and political positions. What is the role of these governmental organizations in the mobilization of women for the transition to civilian government?

The BLP was launched in September 1987 after a conference hosted by the Directorate of Food, Roads and Rural Infrastructure (DFRRI). The theme of the conference was 'Better Life for the Rural Woman'. Its purpose was to work out effective strategies for mobilizing rural women for development and to exchange ideas on how best to maximize the productivity and effective contribution of rural women to the development of their respective communities in general and their individual lot in particular (Better Life Programme, 1988:9).

At the launch of the BLP, the co-ordinators presented the 'elevation of womanhood and the promotion of rural development' as their primary concern (Better Life Programme for the Rural Women, 1990:9). The aims and objectives of the BLP included raising the consciousness of women about their rights and responsibilities, bringing women together for better understanding and resolving to mobilize women for concrete activities towards achieving specific objectives, including seeking leadership roles in all spheres of national life. In 1990 the programme was broadened to include all rural dwellers, ostensibly to ensure that women received the support of their husbands in their quest for equitable development in rural areas.

Since its inception, the BLP has pursued various income-generating projects for women. The BLP has also concerned itself with adult literacy and vocational education, political enlightenment campaigns, social welfare and health programmes for women (BLP:27-28). The impact of the programme is described by its national co-ordinator:

The BLPI has made rural women more confident and take pride in their work ... The political awareness created in women is manifested in increased interest and participation in the transition to civil rule programme especially the massive turn-out during election (Babangida, 1991).

In furtherance of its stated policy of integrating women into the development process, the Federal Military Government established the National Commission for Women by Decree No. 30 of 1989. In his speech inaugurating the Commission, General Babangida outlined the following as the aims and objectives of the Commission:

to integrate women as participants and beneficiaries in the development process, promote healthy and responsible motherhood, enhance women's civic, political and socio-economic education ... eliminate socio-cultural practices that dehumanize and discriminate against women (NCW, 1991:6).

Within the political arena, the NCW embarked on a political awareness campaign from July to August 1991, prior to the 1991 primaries for state gubernatorial positions. The Commission also took out electronic and print media advertisements and its officials made visits to the National Electoral Commission (NEC) with a view to stating the case for women's greater participation in the politics of the transition to the Third Republic. The campaigns also had the aim of sensitising women to their political role in society as well as encouraging them to vote for women candidates. But, in spite of this campaign, the results of the elections in terms of numbers of women candidates elected were dismal.

Conversely the manifestos of the two government political parties proclaimed no commitment to the ending of gender subordination in Nigeria. There is no difference of substance between the 'little to the right' National Republican Convention (NRC) and the 'little to the left' Social Democratic Party (SDP). This is not surprising as the constitutions and manifestos of both parties were written by the Federal Military Government, and reflected the view of the FMG that the women question would be resolved within the framework of existing government policy and organizational structure.

Non-governmental Organizations

At the non-governmental level, the NCWS and the NAUW have been most closely associated with the mobilization and conscientization of women in Nigeria under the present government. The NCWS, formed in 1959, is the officially recognized non-governmental women's organization. It is an umbrella organization to which every non-governmental women's organization is expected to be affiliated in order to be accorded state recognition. The organization also receives an annual subvention from the Federal Government (Shettima, 1991; Mba, 1982:189). NCWS is a federation of non-political women's organizations which seeks to create an awareness of 'good citizenship' amongst its members; to promote the welfare and progress of women, especially in education, and to ensure that women are given every opportunity to play an important role in social and community affairs. The NAUW, established in 1964, is an affiliate of the NAWS and the International Federation of University Women (IFUW). As its name suggests, the NAUW is an organization of professional middle-class women. Membership is open only to women who have spent at least two years studying in a 'recognized' university, either on a certificate, diploma or degree course in any discipline. Among the objectives of the organization is the promotion of women's education at all levels and the involvement of women in every aspect of 'nation building' (NAUW, 1988:69). Both the NAUW and the NCWS are welfare-oriented and seek to promote the interests of their members and a concern for 'under-privileged' members of society.

In relation to the democratic process, both the NCWS and the NAUW have organized various seminars and workshops on women's participation in politics. Even though the NAUW is an affiliate of the NCWS, it has organized its seminars independently. The NAUW seminars have concentrated on encouraging women towards full participation in the democratic process and government with the aim of stimulating women to attain leading positions in policy-making in the Third Republic (Ademola, 1991:4). To this end they have organized voter education workshops for rural women, a seminar on political participation and accountability for women and another on women and leadership, and also a workshop for prospective female legislators. Although the NCWS's seminars have the same objectives as the NAUW, one issue common to both is how to resolve the crisis of power-sharing between privileged women and men.

An Assessment of Women's Organizations

From the discussion outlined so far of the roles played by government and non-governmental organizations in the mobilization and conscientization of women in transition politics, it is clear that the issues of gender subordination in society have not addressed issues such as the sexual division of labour and women's subordination to men at home and in the workplace which are at the heart of feminist discourse. Why has this been so? First, it is not possible for a regime which is implementing the structural adjustment programme (SAP) of the IMF and the World Bank to mobilize or politicize women for genuine liberation and development. Such an objective would contradict the government's economic restructuring agenda. The SAP in Nigeria has had extremely adverse effects on the population, especially low income earners in cities and the rural poor, of which women are the majority. The drastic cuts in state welfare services, the introduction of user charges for health services, the decline in real incomes, the reduction in education facilities, the fall in the fuel subsidy, the retrenchment of employment, have all led to a massive deterioration in the living standards of the poor. This has created an additional burden for women as 'managers' of the domestic unit. For example, it is women who have had to cope with sharply diminished household budgets, and with having to walk long distances searching for cheap food, cultivating vegetable plots and repairing clothing.

Second, the formation of the Better Life Programme can be more clearly understood as an extension of the government's structural adjustment programme. Part of the rationale for the SAP is to facilitate the opening up of the rural areas by providing 'incentives' to (male) farmers to increase their productivity and generate higher money incomes. By introducing the BLP, the Nigerian Government has brought rural women directly into the arena of capitalist exploitation. And by explicitly refusing to implement the affirmative action programme recommended by the political bureau, the Federal Government has thrown doubt on the assumption that the creation of the BLP, the NCW, and all the other governmental bodies relating to the advancement of women, was based on a conviction or commitment to the elimination of gender oppression in Nigerian society. This lack of commitment to positive action on behalf of women is notable given the fact that such policies are allowed for in the Nigerian Constitution and have been used on 'ethnic' grounds as a criterion for employment in the public and private sectors and to provide the basis for admission to schools, polytechnics and universities. Third, military regimes are by their nature repressive and undemocratic and cannot therefore undertake responsibility for the liberation of any sector or group in society.

Apart from being creators of military dictatorship implementing a SAP policy without a popular mandate, the BLP and NCW and their non-governmental counterparts are unable to become organizations which will effect the emancipation of women in Nigeria because they conceptualize the continued oppression of women in Nigeria as being solely the result of the lack of equal opportunities between men and women, and the continued existence of discriminatory laws against women. Their strategy for change has been based on the Women in Development (WID) approach to the gender question which rests on the principle of 'integrating women into the development process', and on the assumption that women's 'backwardness' will end once women are absorbed into the mainstream of industry, commerce, education and politics. For this to be achieved, measures have to be introduced to encourage the establishment of co-operatives and income-generating projects and adult literacy classes for women as well as by electing women into political office and by implementing affirmative action programmes (Boserup, 1970; Rogers, 1980).

Furthermore, these organizations cannot be expected to work for the elimination of gender subordination because their structure, objectives and constitutions negate the need for the mobilization of the majority of women in Nigeria. These organizations are made up of upper and middle class women whose concerns are with improving the provision of services rather than changing the consciousness of women (Heyzer, 1986:126). In addition, they are hierarchical and have not developed a clear understanding of gender subordination or its relationship to other forms of social and economic oppression (Sen and Grown, 1986:90). Sometimes they appear to have been created to provide a useful and appropriate occupation for the wives of important state officials. For example, Mrs Babangida, the wife of the Head of State, is the National Co-ordinator of the BLP with the wives of the Vice-President and senior military officers and a group of upper and middle class women known as the 'M Team' to assist her at the national level, while, at the state level, the wives of governors are the co-ordinators of the BLP.

The BLP, the NCW, the NCWS and NAUW, have taken their role to be the mobilization of women in support of the transition programme and the SAP. They have even 'come out' at various times to openly espouse anti-feminist positions stating that they do not wish to antagonize men or to claim equal rights and to denounce women for demonstrating against government policies that affect them. The pro-government position of the NCWS in matters of national importance has earned it the nickname 'AGIP' meaning 'Any Government in Power' (Shettima, 1991). In justification for taking up an anti-feminist position, the then Director-General of the NCW, Mrs Ifene, said:

> The NCW does not endorse for Nigeria, the western stand on women's liberation, what we are after is emancipation which means release from constraints wherein people (both males and females) can participate fully in the development of this country, irrespective of their sex (*Daily Times of Nigeria*, 16 March 1992).

It is evident from the role that these governmental and non-governmental organizations have played in the political transition process in Nigeria that they do not represent the interests of poor women nor do they raise feminist issues in their campaigns which are primarily intended to incorporate women into the objectives of government policy in an 'acceptable' way.

Bibliography

Abdullah, H. J. (1991), 'Women in Development: A Study of Female Wage Labour in Kano's Manufacturing Sector, 1945–1990', Ph.D Thesis, University of Hull.

Ademola, K. (1991), 'Mobilising Women for National development' in O. Jegede, C. Osinulu & J. Ogonna (eds.) *Women and Leadership*, Lagos: Nigerian Association of University Women.

Ananaba, W. (1969), *The Trade Union Movement in Nigeria*, London: C Hurst and Company.

Andrae, G. (1990), 'Gender and Unions in African Textile Industry: The Case of Nigeria in a Comparative Perspective', research proposal.

Babangida, M. (1991), Text of a speech at the 1991 Africa Prize for Leadership for the Sustainable End of Hunger, reproduced in *New Nigerian*, 13 October 1991.

Bandarage, A. (1984), 'Women in Development: Liberalism Marxism and Marxist Feminism', *Development and Change*, 15(3) pp. 495–516.

Better Life Programme (1988), 'Better Life Fair for Rural Dwellers', Alimbar Tribune Lagos.

Better Life Programme (1990), 'Better Life Rural Programme for the Rural Women', Lagos.

Boserup, E. (1970), *Women's Role in Economic Development*, London: Allen & Unwin.

Bujra, J. (1986), 'Gender Class and Capitalist Transformation' in C. Robertson and I. Berger (eds.), *Women and Class in Africa*, London: African Publishing Company.

Dennis, C. (1987), 'Women and the State in Nigeria: the Case of the Federal Military Government, 1984–5' in H. Afshar (ed.), *Women, State and Ideology*, London: Macmillan.

Directorate for Social Mobilization (1989), *Report of the Political Bureau*, Abuja: Mamser.

Eisenstein, Z. (1981), *The Radical Future of Liberal Feminism*, New York: Longman.

Elson, D. & R. Pearson (1981), 'The Subordination of Women and the Internationalization of Factory Production in K Young, C Wolkowitz and R. McCullagh (eds.), *Of Marriage and the Market: Women's Subordination Internationally and its Lessons*, London: Routledge and Kegan Paul.

Federal Ministry of Information (1986), Press Release No. 888, Lagos.

Federal Republic of Nigeria (1987), *Government Views and Comments on the Finding and Recommendations of the Political Bureau*, Lagos: Federal Government Printer.

Feldman, R. (1984), 'Women's groups and Women's subordination: An Analysis of Politics Towards Rural Women in Kenya', ROAPE No. 27/28.

Heyzer, N. (1986), *Working Women in South East Asia*, Milton Keynes: Open University Press.

Jacquette, J. (1982), 'Women and Modernization Theory: A decade of feminist criticism', *World Politics*, 34(2), pp. 261–84.

Jaggar, A. M. (1983), *Feminist Politics and Human Nature*, Brighton: Harvester.

Mba, N. (1982), *Nigerian Women Mobilized*, Berkeley: University of California Press.

Mba, N, (1989), 'Kaba and Khaki: Women and the Militarized State in Nigeria' in J. L. Parpart and A. K. Staudt (eds), *Women and the State in Africa*, Boulder, CO: Lynne Rienner Publishers.

National Commission for Women (1991), *Annual Report*, Abuja.

Nigerian Association of University Women (1989), *Voter Education for Rural Women*, Lagos: NAUW.

Nigeria Labour Congress (1981), *Workers' Charter of Demands*, Lagos.

Otobo, D. (1981), 'The Nigerian General Strike of 1981', *ROAPE* 22, October–December, pp. 65–81.

Pittin, R. (1984), 'Gender and Class in Nigeria', *ROAPE* 31, December, pp. 71–81.

Rogers, B. (1980), *The Domestication of Women: Discrimination in Developing Societies*, New York: Tavistock.

Sen, G. & C. Grown (1986), *Development Crisis and Alternative Visions*, London: Earthscan.

Shettima, A. (1991), 'Engendering Nigeria's Third Republic', Mimeo. .

Women in Nigeria Editorial Committee (1985), *The WIN Document: Conditions of Women in Nigeria to the Year 2000*, Zaria: Ahmadu Bello University.

Newspapers: *Daily Times of Nigeria, The Guardian, New Nigeria, The Punch Business Times.*

17

JEAN COPANS
No Shortcuts to Democracy
The Long March towards Modernity
[1991]

Introduction

We should surely be able to assess the theoretical and practical issues raised by a commitment to 'democracy' at this time and identify the intellectual prerequisites for any realistic democratic programmes. My major concern here is to contribute to the development of a genuine African political theory of social change capable of recognizing the relationship between knowledge and democracy. I see three major areas for initial consideration: the relationship between the making of history and modernity in Africa; the possibility of an anthropological approach to the conception of democracy; and the present and future role of African intellectuals.

History, Modernity & Development

African Studies are clearly dominated today by History. This contributes very positively to our understanding of the present, of the ways in which this present was produced, and of the methods by which it could be modified and changed. Increasingly, history is seen as a dialectical process involving the more or less conscious creation of social and cultural history by social actors and by professional historians alike. Let me quote, at some length, from a few of the professional historians who have contributed to this new conception of history. The first quotation reveals the extent to which the historian has to incorporate the histories constructed by the social actors themselves:

> Here, we are primarily intrigued by the way in which these subjects are discussed, turned over, and debated among the Luo. We sense that this dynamic edge of discourse is, first, older than the twentieth century, second, more than a product of modern schooling, and third, other than simply a response to the depictions of outside observers. After all for the Luo, more than for the outside observers of the Luo, what constitutes culture, what is correct behaviour, what is history, are questions that are heavily fought over. And, crucially, these struggles constitute essential pieces of the past and of the present of Luo society and culture; they are intellectual debates that power the process and shape the structure of Luo culture and society ... we attempt a perspective both removed and intimate: removed so that one can gain control of the sociology and intellectual history of the ethnographic literature itself; yet intimate so that one can come to terms with the ways in which people – in ordinary, commonplace activities – have produced society and culture not only through social practice but also through the formation of histories and anthropologies. (Cohen & Atieno-Odhiambo, 1989)

But the interaction between the people and the scholars is best illuminated in the work of Lonsdale:

> My initial assumptions, from which all else follows, are that free political argument is essential to the formulation of alternative societal futures and that without such argument there is no sure means of mobilising active consent to present authority. But political argument demands self-awareness in its protagonists, a public acceptance of the moral autonomy of political actors and, perhaps above all, a usable political language. By that I mean a commonly understood set of symbols which sum up, by allegory, myth and metaphor, the core values which ought to (but seldom do) govern the always disputable relationships between individuals and any society in their provision for the future, which is implicit in the way they reproduce the present out of the past. A political language unites people over what to argue about, it provides the images on which they can base their ideologies. Ideologies mobilize political support around social division and can be used in attempts to suppress debate, but they can neither enlarge understanding nor fire enthusiasm unless they accentuate, recreate, or manipulate the common symbols of the language. Agreement on symbolic values is thus a necessary precondition for constructive debate about the distribution of their societal costs and benefits. Unless they share a political language, people can pursue their conflicting interests only by coercion or evasion – both denials of the possibility of a shared and productive, if still disputed, future. A common political language and its inventive usage by the divided members of a political community can be produced in only one way – by historical process. Historical awareness is the only form of self-knowledge. (Lonsdale, 1989:27-8)

My hypothesis is therefore the following: the production and reproduction of a society and the elaboration of knowledge concerning this same society, intended for its own usage, are related in a specific way. The process of the making of modernity is the result of a certain type of formalization of this relationship. In fact it is a double formalization: legal and ideological on the one hand, and intellectual and scientific on the other. This formalization then allows for a political synthesis. The autonomy of political thinking becomes the essence of modernity. The numerous theoretical, cultural and practical inventions of democracy since the French Revolution constitute ample historical proof of this phenomenon.

In Africa, modernity has taken the form of mere modernization, of an imposed acquisition of various disorganized and disembodied traits of modernity. It is not a *sui generis* process. Of course one could imagine modernization without modernity; but it is a fact that in the western world the two phenomena were concomitant from the 18th century onwards. In Africa today, however, it is quite the contrary: the two are totally separated and until now modernity remains more an imitation than anything else. Modernization has preceded modernity; and this is a trap, because modernization is a permanent process to abort modernity. The process is even an intentional one: in contemporary Africa, the dominant and so-called hegemonic groups act very vigorously to crush any action or especially any thinking which might promote the double process that constitutes modernity.

We are not suggesting that Africa is still in a kind of mediaeval or renaissance phase. The logic of domination and power in Africa does not need, it seems, a formalization of the social and scientific domains; this is still to some extent the realm of the west. African power-holders have been dispossessed (and have accepted this dispossession) of their own thinking about development, about *their own* development. This stems from the fact that development is not a mere economic and sociological transition: it is a procedure for maintaining the status quo on an international scale and it is the *means* (and no longer the end) of development that is the true objective of political power.

Most intellectuals are integrated into the state bureaucracy. They have generally failed to develop any kind of 'autonomous' thinking. My conclusions are quite straightforward: the long and slow path of African history, the predominance of extra-African mechanisms for the production of social theoretical thought, and the absence of any kind of positive and dialectical relation between the groups in power and the 'modern' producers of such thinking have together impeded the making of modernity, as we have defined it. This is in no way a pseudo-evolutionist or racist appreciation of contemporary African social history. The situation is not a crisis, although it might become one if the actual form of development is not put into question. To conduct such an enquiry one should try and define an analytical method to help map out the building blocks and the concepts for the development of democratic demands.

An Anthropological Method for Thinking Democracy

We must begin with the process whereby the various political communities are formed. Anthropo-logics, as George Balandier would put it, are the substance of all political messages and actions. 'Natural communities' do not exist any more; political communities are always historically constituted.

Age and gender are significant in all contemporary communities. And it is true that youth and women can be organized as such. Youth could become a political danger and maybe a political asset but it is yet far from clear that it can experience a common identification as such. Though Parpart (1988) has elaborated on this topic, I am not sure one could come to the same conclusions with regard to women. There is a contradiction between these global anthropological conditions and the very localized and conjunctural form they are able to take as political forces. Associations, informal committees, and neighbourhood groupings do exist and are all very active for some precise purpose. But their overall scope is quite limited. Of course official and national groups or institutions are made up of patronage and clientele relations but these have in no way been able to condense the diffuse energy of age and gender.

The third social and cultural form, and the most problematic of all, is the ethnic group. Recent research in history and anthropology has generated new understandings and analyses in this respect. Ethnicity is a process, a basic political one, and not a form of false consciousness. The xenophobic nature of ethnic strife, the political condemnation of tribalism, are concrete realities which prove that the ethnic reference does have some capacity for mobilization and political appeal and that we cannot do without it. We should be careful because Lonsdale goes even further in this line of thought:

> The new historiography of 'tribe' could provide a language, not for the avoidance of cultural issues but for the celebration of the central cultural issue, the universal problem at the heart of all our particularities, which is the relationship between the individual and society. Far from being the creature of civic irresponsibility, 'tribe' has been one of Africa's central metaphors of civic virtue. But without doubt, too, they are also among the few historically resonant sources available for the construction of a language of debate about the future, if only the interior perplexities of 'tribe' were to assume the same degree of importance in the textbooks as their external cultural pluralism. The familiar problems which people argue about are more important than the strange tongues in which they speak. The history of African political thought which would permit this transcendence of ethnic particularity by human universality has yet to be written, and the delicate statesmanship would still be needed lest it could be eloquent with a locally-constructed political language rather than tongue-tied by the studious avoidance of one. (1989:137–8)

Ranger, Lonsdale and other Africanists (see also Bayart and Mbembe, for example) mention yet another political community: that of religious organizations and institutions such as churches, brotherhoods and sects. It is as if a conscious cultural form of ethnicity was spread out all over Africa. In fact we have here a new broker between the people and the state. Both the Muslim brotherhoods in Senegal and Christian churches in Kenya help maintain social cohesion. Of course for a long time churches were direct instruments of the state, voices of authority and to some extent they still are. Mbembe questions the possible radical content of Christianity today; no model for a theology of liberation is in the making, unfortunately.

One last community or rather non-community should be mentioned: that of refugees. Over five million people are considered refugees in Africa. Statistically this is just one per cent of Africa's population, but almost half of all the world's refugees. Refugees are both a negation of nationalism and a prey to international domination and control. Refugees prove again that internal conflict and external intervention cannot be separated. Transnational *bantustans* are being established 'on a temporary basis'. What a paradox if this takes place just as the more permanent ones of South Africa may be about to disappear!

Let us now turn to the making of democracy itself. I shall distinguish three different processes: those of formation, those of realization and those of political modernity. It seems impossible for me to think about democracy without referring to the written word. Oral traditions, and even more so modern 'oral traditions' (through radio and TV), are continually reinterpreted and transmitted. Cultural and political traditions are such that equality in the accumulation and distribution of information and knowledge seems impossible. Liberty of thought, of opinion and of expression can be experienced at an oral level but the true learning and sharing of political experience can only be discussed and valued objectively through the written form. Unfortunately many, many African languages are not being taught and read. The breaking down of the educational system, of academic research and teaching, is also a severe hindrance to democratic experience. Senegal is one of the very rare countries where a real plural and professional press (mainly weeklies and monthlies) can be found. But one should remember that it took years for this press to get rid of its very ideological tone and to promote a genuine political debate.

It is the very process of political representation and accountability that is thereby put into question. The experience of contradictory programmes or the report of a political mandate, the semantics of politics (what 'national' language, what conceptual and practical terms?) have never been the object of public scrutiny and debate. Even if other equivalent processes should be invented, the importance of an open relationship between political communities and their means of thinking and expression has to be acknowledged. But one must remember, at the same time, that we are thinking in terms of citizenship and not just of academic political actors. Our hypotheses have to be put into practice and into question through the daily creation of African political life.

Finally one comes to the concept of political modernity and to the process of formalization I mentioned earlier. Here, it is impossible to suppress the influence of the west. Whatever the tragic outcome of Stalinism, whatever the melancholy reality of (western) democracy (see Bruckner, 1990), those models were never applied in practice. But one has to know if some of its symbolic content can be used to facilitate the adoption of 'democratic' principles. Political symbols of western origin are volatile – both at the same time hypocritical ideologies when related to genuine and ordinary day-to-day values and practical efficient means of power, whether involving 'nationalist' rhetoric or repression and political silence. This explains why political modernity is being now defined through the symbol of human rights.

Human rights must be related in some ways to social reality; the current atmosphere of denunciation and witch-hunting, of ideological conformism, is more disturbing than simply the fate of political prisoners. In Kenya, for example, the 'Big Brother' perception of politics is a human rights problem; the scale and extent of domestic and civil violence is truly very depressing. But to speak of human rights is to raise also the question of the supervision and control of those rights by the State itself. Recent African history does not allow us to have confidence in the State for any legal, ideological or political matter. Multi-partism can always be reinvested by astute heads of State (like Bongo or Mobutu); and it is always possible to change semantics and symbols. But how can we propose new programmes, or rather new methods if 'the experts' do not carry out their job? (especially if they are also part of the problem, and therefore of the solution!). In my understanding 'the experts' are the African creators of culture and of ideas: writers, academics and intellectual brokers of all persuasions.

Conclusion

A social history, a social anthropology of knowledge seems therefore possible and might provide an efficient preface to a more direct political rethinking on the matter of modernity. We cannot by-pass this experiment because it enables us to cope with the demands of the day. First and foremost, abstract ideologies such as Pan-Africanism, ethno-authenticity or nationalism should be discarded. Genuine African thinking is not just a matter of semantics and self-congratulations. It can be original on all counts and develop in unprecedented fashion.

The question is: how should we understand Africa's social cultural, political, reality and how can we share it, discuss it, transmit it in local vernacular 'languages' as well as in a conceptual and international form? Cultural and intellectual productions may be related in various ways and come to constitute a complex web of interacting components. But in Africa this is not yet the case. Popular novels, the concerns of the modernized elite and academic works are like isolated islands and reciprocal influences are few. There is a *de facto* parochialism which is both consolidated and undermined, in a negative perspective, by international co-optation and the brain drain.

There is a need to create a more dynamic interaction. This exists to some extent in Nigeria or Senegal. In some countries those isolated islands can be very popular or powerful but the division of labour and of social functions inhibits, through social stratification, intimate experiences and contacts. What is necessary is the creation of a new category of intellectual and cultural brokers and synthesizers. The popular intelligentsia, whether from 'traditional', rural backgrounds or from local level civil servants (teachers, health workers and extension agents), should be given more respect and status. The elite fraction of the intelligentsia should begin to acknowledge its existence and try to produce and diffuse popularized forms of knowledge and information in collaboration. I would even go so far as to say that literacy in maternal and vernacular languages should be openly tackled so that reciprocal dissemination of cultural and intellectual artefacts can be made possible.

The project to which I refer needs pragmatic and empirical instruments of enquiry. Lenin told the revolutionary activist in *What is to be done?* to go and work in all classes of society. The idea is a good one if we relinquish the clandestine and subversive model of the Bolshevik party. Because this is the other side of the coin: we are in dire need of political theorizing. This idea has to be put into practice, for political theorizing is a fundamental and historical task. Since there is no Pan-African, national or ethnic solution it must involve many people. That is why a transitional period of social and cultural experimentation has to be accepted. Social movements, political groupings and intellectuals must all change their way of thinking. It is a truly surgical job. I am not reverting to Amilcar Cabral's theory of social suicide of the petty bourgeoisie. I am just saying: to produce modernity and therefore a transition towards a more 'democratic' form of society (not a purely political and institutional democracy), one has to acknowledge the role of intellectuals. But a new social definition has to be suggested and a new type of practice, both more down to earth and populist on the one hand, and more theoretical on the other, has to be invented and elaborated.

Intellectuals should share their knowledge and find material ways to do so. But how will these changes come about? Massive demands do exist, at the educational level and in the information sector. The potentialities of the popular intelligentsia are tremendous. But how is it that academics seem to be removed from that very concrete world? I suggest because the theories, even the radical ones, and the western models they associate with, have educated them not to do so! Is it not possible to invent languages and semantics, images and ideas, which can be grasped and shared throughout each society? The prophetic solitude of the intellectual has to disappear. This is the true paradox of African modernity: it has to begin again at the beginning! A beginning which has nothing to do with the European experience; a beginning that has surmounted the disastrous effects of imitating an aged and too ethnocentric model.

We western Africanists should collaborate as well because we too know all too well that the old approach is also an antiquated one, even for us.

Bibliographic Note

For a further elaboration of my own ideas, see J. Copans, 'The Marxist Conception of Class: Political and Theoretical Elaboration in the African and Africanist Context', *Review of African Political Economy*, 32, 1985; 'Mode de production, formation sociale ou ethnie? Les leçons d'un long silence de l'Anthropologie marxiste française', *Canadian Journal of African Studies*, 20, 1, 1986; 'No shortcuts to democracy: the making of democracy in black Africa', Paper presented to the ROAPE Conference, Warwick, September, 1989; *La longue marche de la modernité africaine – Savoirs, Intellectuels, Démocratie*, Karthala, 1990; 1998. 'L'Afrique autrement', *Politique Africaine*, 39, 1990.

Bayart, J.F. (1986), 'Civil society in Africa', in P. Chabal (ed.), *Political domination in Africa*, Cambridge: Cambridge University Press.
—— (1985) 'L'énonciation du politique', *Revue Française de Science Politique*, 35, 3.
—— (1989) *L'Etat en Afrique*, Paris: Fayard.
Bruckner, P. (1990) *La mélancolie democratique*, Le Seuil.
Cohen, D.W. & E.S. Atieno-Odhiambo (1989) *Siaya*, London: James Currey.
Jewsiewicki, B. (1989), 'African historical studies – Academic knowledge as 'usable past' and radical scholarship', *The African Studies Review*, 32, 3.
Lonsdale, J. (1981), 'States and social processes in Africa: a historiographical survey', *The African Studies Review*, 24, 2–3.
—— (1989) 'African pasts in Africa's future', *Canadian Journal of African Studies*, 23, 1.
Mandaza, Ibbo (1986), 'Introduction: the political economy of transition' in I. Mandaza, (ed), *Zimbabwe: the Political Economy of Transition, 1980–1986*, CODESRIA Book Series.
Mbembe, A. (1985), *Les jeunes et l'ordre politique en Afrique Noire*, Paris: L'Harmattan.
—— (1988) *Afriques indociles: Christianisme, pouvoir et Etat en societe postcoloniale*, Paris: Karthala.
Ngugi wa Thiong'o (1989), 'Interview', *Third World Quarterly*, 11, 4.
Omotoso, K. (1988), 'Fiction rebuked by reality – and the future of the novel in Africa', in *African Futures*, Edinburgh: Centre of African Studies.
Parpart, Jane (1988), 'Women and the state in Africa', in *African Futures*, Edinburgh: Centre of African Studies.

Ranger, Terence (1986), 'Religious movements and politics in Sub-Saharan Africa', *The African Studies Review*, 29, 2.

—— (1989), 'Refugees in Africa – the dynamics of displacement and repatriation', *The African Studies Review*, 32, 1.

Shivji, Issa G. (1989), *The Concept of Human Rights in Africa*, CODESRIA Book Series.

Southern Africa Political and Economic Monthly (SAPEM), 1987–1989.

Vail, Leroy (ed.) (1989), *The Creation of Tribalism in Southern Africa*, London: James Currey.

18 LARS RUDEBECK
The Effects of Structural Adjustment in Kandjadja, Guinea-Bissau [1990]

On 14 November 1980 a military coup d'état apparently put an end to the first phase of independence in Guinea-Bissau. The coup was triggered by mounting structural contradictions in post-colonial society. Standards of living were not improving, the anti-colonial alliance between a 'petty bourgeois' leadership and popular forces had begun to fall apart, industrialization efforts through import substitution and high technology investment in groundnut processing had failed, the gap between state and peasantry widened and the democratic momentum of the liberation movement appeared to be grinding to a halt. The coup did not bring substantial changes, as virtually the same people continued to occupy the top posts in the state hierarchy and the objective structural conditions of development continued.

I have analyzed elsewhere this transition to state power from anti-colonial liberation movement (Rudebeck, 1982, 1983, 1988, 1989), concluding provisionally that although these anti-colonial liberation movements contained strong democratic impulses and aroused demands and expectations for radical development policies, there were no guarantees of success. People's development, democracy and people's power do not fall from the sky. They appear, if at all, in certain historical conjunctures as tendencies rather than as fully-fledged givens. Since independence, however, the balance of forces in Guinea-Bissau has been shifting away from radical democratic tendencies. In 1982, as a result of the worsening economic situation, a programme of structural adjustment was worked out with the IMF and World Bank.

Structural Adjustment in Kandjadja

Since early 1976 I have followed the socio-economic and political developments in the village of Kandjadja in northern Guinea-Bissau through recurrent visits. My article in ROAPE 41 (1988) summarizes the situation up to early 1986. In December 1988 I returned again, at the height of the structural adjustment. The policies were officially intended to release the latent energy of the rural people, contributing both to rural welfare and national development, but how were the people of the village reacting? Had the new policies reached Kandjadja at all?

No village is, of course, statistically representative of anything other than itself. Kandjadja does, however, share many characteristics with hundreds and thousands of other Guinean and African villages subsisting on the outskirts of the world market, while still being integrated into it, living under the jurisdiction of a state with declining legitimacy in the eyes of the villagers.

Kandjadja, a forest village of perhaps 1,200 inhabitants, is located near the river Farim, in the sector of Mansaba, in Oio region of northern Guinea-Bissau. It is the central village of a political-administrative area containing 13 smaller villages. The people slash and burn the green forest to grow their crops. Their cattle graze quietly in the bush, not far from the village houses, grouped along a road with cross-cutting lanes. The distance on foot to the highway connecting Farim, the regional capital, with Bissau, the national capital, is about 20 kilometres northeast, mostly along a track originally built with forced colonial labour but under reconstruction in 1988-89 through a programme of integrated rural development, run by the government with Swedish assistance. The distance to Bissau is about 100 kilometres on the highway once the twelve kilometres of bad eastbound track road through the forest have been covered. Thirty kilometres to the north is the international border with Senegal's Casamance region, which appears incidental from the point of view of the villagers.

This ancient West African land is where Mandinga (Malinke) people of Moslem faith lived as farmers and traders long before Portuguese sailors first set foot on the Guinean coast in the middle of the 15th century. From around the thirteenth century, these areas were included in the great Mali empire, encompassing the Kaabu state structure, which survived the decline of Mali at the end of the 14th century. For several centuries, Kaabu provided the dominant state structure of the region stretching from the Atlantic Ocean to the Futa Jallon highlands of present-day Guinea-Conakry and bordered to the north by the river Gambia. It was not decisively broken up through civil wars and superseded by colonial state structures until the end of the 19th century (see, on Kaabu, Bowman Hawkins, 1980:52-106; *Ethiopiques*, 1981).

Structural Adjustment: Political & Socio-cultural Implications

After visiting Kandjadja in early 1986, I wrote about the political disappointment noticeable after eleven years of independence. According to the villagers' own analysis, I noted that the people's strength alone, although essential, is not sufficient for development in the sense of increasing material security and human dignity. Some support from more broadly based authority, a 'state', is also necessary:

> The village/s do not get the 'support' they deem necessary because they do not influence, let alone control, state power – or for that matter any other power outside their own community. The Bissau policy-makers, on the other hand, do not reach the villagers with their plans and wishes because the social basis of their power is elsewhere. Thus they do not formulate their plans and actions in concrete and democratic cooperation with the villagers. (Rudebeck, 1988: 26, 27)

Political Life
The most recent research confirmed this trend. The people of Kandjadja exercise no political power beyond the local level, although they clearly have an interest in what the state does: as tax-payers, as potential beneficiaries of educational and social policies, as producers and consumers, and via the influence, in various ways, of long-range macro-economic measures.

At the local level the people are nevertheless politically organized, as in the rest of Guinea-Bissau. The central village has its locally elected 'base committee' of five members of which at least two are women. Kaba Turé, the chief of the village of Kandjadja, is the president of the 14-village section with the same name. He is also a committee member of the 38-village 'administrative section' of Olossato of which

Kandjadja is part. Also, he was one of the 75 regional councillors of the Region of Oio until the election of 1989. What does all this imply in practical terms, of the functioning of the structural adjustment policies?

The base committee, of which there are between three and four thousand in the country, is in official theory a hybrid state/party organ. In reality it is the most local-level organ of the country's administrative and representative system. Formally, Kaba Turé is not a member of the Kandjadja village committee, as he is the president of the whole section of 14 villages. But in reality, nothing is done by the committee without Kaba being involved. *Vis-à-vis* the other 13 committees, all within at most four kilometres from the central village, he has the position of consultant and co-ordinator.

Seen from a local viewpoint, this political set-up is new, post-colonial, or 'modern' only in a partial or partially superficial sense. Kaba Turé was a PAIGC militant during the liberation war. He still keeps Amilcar Cabral's picture on the wall inside his home. He sees himself as a modernizer, a carrier of the message of *national* liberation and construction. But most of his authority in Kandjadja is locally rooted in the cultural traditions and power structure of the Mandinga community. It is derived from the local standing of the Turé family – members of which hold posts both on the Kandjadja committee, on the committees of two other villages, the sectional court of justice, and the sectional committee of the youth organization, Juventude Africana Amilcar Cabral (JAAC) – rather than from the PAIGC and the state of Guinea-Bissau. Thus, in reality, Kaba functions as a mediator between the 'modernizing' state and the daily realities of societal reproduction and production in the villages of the section. The less the state fulfils its developmental promises, the more dependent Kaba becomes upon his locally derived authority, and consequently the less able he is to mobilize the local people for activities they do not spontaneously embrace – such as paying taxes or sending their children to the state school rather than the Koranic school.

Even the very process of Kaba Turé's attainment of his present position, in the late 1970s, mirrors this gradual undermining of the original developmental legitimacy of the PAIGC party/state. As mentioned in earlier articles (Rudebeck, 1982; 1989), the original party/state representative in post-colonial Kandjadja was not Kaba Turé but a man called Malam Sana, originating from Olossato and sent to Kandjadja by the PAIGC in 1975 to be the political commissar of the section. There are four or perhaps five 'important' families in Kandjadja; one is the Turé family, the others are Sisse, Seidi, Camara, and Dabu. All except Dabu are represented on the village base committee, and Sisse by two family members. Malam Sana is said to have had the support of the Sisse family, which still has two members on the village committee. But basically he was imposed upon Kandjadja by the party, and was always considered somewhat of a 'stranger'.

During the early years of post-colonial political fervour, Malam Sana was still able to function politically as the commissar of the Kandjadja section. But in the late 1970s he was 'asked to return' by the villagers to his native town of Olossato 'to take a rest'. In December 1988 he worked in Olossato as the employee of a private retail store, while retaining a political/administrative position as member of the committee of the administrative section of Olossato (together with Kaba Turé, among others).

After Malam Sana had been forced out, Kaba Turé was called in by the local people to take over, with the consent of the party/state. Although he himself is a PAIGC member in personal sympathy with the radical and modernizing goals of the liberation movement, the circumstances of his coming into office and the basis of his political authority are illustrative of the growing gap between state and rural society in post-colonial Guinea approaching the end of the 1980s. Very little of Kaba Turé's political authority in Kandjadja seemed to derive from party and state.

Cultural Multiplicity

Like most African countries, Guinea-Bissau is multi-cultural, arbitrarily carved out of its wider historical context through the process of colonization and decolonization. It is thus made up of several peoples and ethnic groups, not necessarily ready, spontaneously, to be 'nationally integrated' under the authority of the existing state – at least not without seeing any chances of fulfilment of some of their most essential developmental aspirations. Kandjadja reflects this multiplicity with its potential for both integration and disintegration.

We have already noted that culturally the dominant people of the area are the Mandinga. But other peoples and other cultures are present too, notably the Fula and the Balanta.

Amilcar Cabral discussed the distinction between societies where power is organized along vertical and horizontal lines (Cabral, 1964 and 1966; also Lopes, 1982 and 1987). This distinction opposes the traditional vertical and hierarchical power structures of the Fula and Mandinga peoples (with about twelve and ten per cent, respectively, of the Guinean population) to the more horizontal structure of the Balanta people (about 30 per cent, predominantly but not exclusively found in the south, and thus the largest ethnic group in the country).

As opposed to the strongly hierarchical societies of the Fula and the Mandinga, where the religion of Islam predominates, the traditionally animist Balanta society is often described as 'stateless' and more egalitarian. The Balanta have no central authority, but rather a horizontally recruited council of the elders representing the extended families of the community. The position of women is considered to be relatively free both socially and economically, as opposed to the situations of both Fula and Mandinga women. Juridically, though, even according to Balanta customary law, the women are subject to male authority in the public realm (see Handem, 1986).

Returning to Kandjadja, it is striking that the central village is sometimes called *Kandjadja-Mandinga* (Topsoe-Jensen, 1988). This is to distinguish it from *Kandjadja-Fula*, at about three kilometres distance, and even closer, a little over one kilometre from Kandjadja-Balanta, a village of several hundred inhabitants with a completely different culture, language, religion, eating and drinking habits (pork and alcoholic beverages are consumed in the Balanta village).

The central village of Kandjadja is orderly and quiet, with yards and roads well swept, houses in rows, cattle kept at some distance from the dwelling houses and no pigs anywhere because of Islam. Kandjadja-Balanta, in contrast, offers a less orderly image, is less clean, less quiet, palm wine is drunk, cows and pigs are close to or even inside the houses, and the dwellings are irregularly grouped. The language spoken by the people of Kandjadja-Balanta is at least as different from Mandinga as, for instance, Russian is from English. Balanta belongs to the West-Atlantic group of African languages and Mandinga to the Mande group (Roug, 1988:10). Nor is there any trace of Islam in the basically animist religion of the Balanta people.

The social structure and religion of the people of Kandjadja-Mandinga are much more similar to the people of Kandjadja-Fula than to those of Kandjadja-Balanta. The Fula people of Kandjadja, in contrast to their Mandinga neighbours, do not cultivate groundnuts but concentrate on rice, millet, beans, cassava, and cotton. Historically the Fula and the Mandinga people are rivals in the area, as the Fula did not penetrate into the territory of present-day Guinea-Bissau in any great numbers until the 18th century, pushing the Mandinga westward toward the sea. The Mandinga and Fula languages, too, are as different from each other as are Mandinga and Balanta. Fula, like Balanta, belongs to the large

West Atlantic group of languages, although it is in a different sub-group (Roug, 1988:10).

Thus three of the four largest peoples of Guinea-Bissau (the fourth being the Manjaco people with about 17 per cent of the population) are represented by communities within the territorial confines of the section of Kandjadja. It is not possible, on the basis of my present knowledge, to say anything specific about the effects on inter-ethnic relations of the structural adjustment policies, by way of simple cause and effect propositions. It nevertheless seems probable that the present tendencies of increasing Mandinga self-consciousness will not facilitate political organization across ethnic boundaries. Both Kandjadja-Fula and Kandjadja-Balanta maintain their own ways of life. In the case of the Balanta village, this is more strikingly conspicuous than in the Fula case, as Kandjadja-Balanta is so close to the central village, and as the cultural differences are so outwardly visible. Still, people from the two non-Mandinga villages maintain regular relations with the central village for commercial and other reasons, for instance participation in a vaccination campaign. Kaba Turé, too, exercises his administrative and political functions in these two villages as actively as in the other eleven.

The Balanta community of Kandjadja is probably too small in the face of Mandinga dominance to carry any political weight in the section. But at the national level, their role is crucial. They are the largest ethnic group of the country, and were the most active in the liberation struggle. Since independence, however, Balanta cultural and political self-consciousness has tended to be interpreted officially in terms of 'tribalism' and was thus resented.

Around 1984, a revivalist movement arose, first in the south, among the Balanta people, critical of ignorance, corruption, elders' despotism, witchcraft, and many other things. It is called the *Yanque-Yanque* movement, initiated by a prophetess and mobilizing mostly young people, both women and men. *Yanque* (or *Yang*) is the name taken by the founder-prophetess, meaning in Balanta 'shadow' and indicating, according to one interpretation, that nobody is able to touch or catch her (Rocha, 1989:28). Although the movement's criticism is directed mainly at Balanta society itself, it has been viewed with great suspicion by the government and even accused officially of being connected with an attempted coup d'état implicating the vice president Paulo Correia, himself of Balanta origin, who was convicted of treason and executed in 1986. The existence of such a connection is doubtful (ibid.:30), as well as many aspects of the alleged coup attempt.

Because of Mandinga dominance in Kandjadja and surrounding areas, the *Yanque-Yanque* movement is not actively present as such in the section, although it is very much present in the minds of the state officials at the level of the administrative section of Olossato. When visiting Kandjadja, officials warn against the 'backward practices' of the *Yanque-Yanque*. The important point here is that even at the national level the *Yanque-Yanque* movement, which is perceived as dangerous by the state and has been much more openly critical and structured than any other tendency in Kandjadja, still remains largely within an ethnic framework. After some years of fervour, the movement appeared by the late 1980s to have lost its political impetus and was now being directed more exclusively against 'witchcraft' (Rocha, 1989:31).

Education provides us with more concrete evidence of the political role of cultural/ethnic sentiments today compared with earlier years, particularly the disintegration of the official school system.

The School as an Example

In 1976, when I first visited Kandjadja, the school was probably the most revolutionary institution in the village, in an ideological sense. Three young and highly motivated teachers, two of whom had lived with the guerrillas since their childhood, taught a little over 200 students. The training was a combination of conventional education and political teaching on the history and significance of the struggle for national liberation.

Even then, it seemed that the modernistic and ideological message of the school was somewhat out of tune with the cultural aspiration of the community and with the transformation that the local society was undergoing (Rudebeck, 1988:20). There was also a different type of school, the Koranic one, run on a completely voluntary basis. The teacher was a young man of around 20, the same age as his colleagues in the state school, and enrolled at the same time as a student in the second year of their school. The people of Kandjadja call the state school 'the school of the Europeans' or 'the whites', because that is where 'modern' or 'European' things are taught. The Koranic school, which in 1976 gathered every evening at sunset some ten boys to study the holy texts, is often called 'the school of the marabu' (local saint or holy man). Subsequently, there has been a constant decline in the activities and level of authority of the official school in the community.

There is general agreement among observers that the official school system of Guinea-Bissau has been in a serious and worsening situation of crisis throughout the 1980s, unable to meet either the expectations of the people or the developmental needs of the country. The crisis is social, economic, political, pedagogical, as well as financial (Carr-Hill & Rosengart, 1982; Lepri, 1984; Djalo, 1987; Sanha, 1988; Lepri, 1988).

The situation in Kandjadja corresponds with the national condition. In December 1988, the Kandjadja village school was reduced to a tiny straw house where the teacher received no more than 16 students: five in first grade, seven in second, and four in third. There was not one girl among the students. Ten were from Kandjadja-Fula, one from Kandjadja-Balanta, and only five from the central village, where the school is located. The teacher is a Balanta from the south, sent to Kandjadja in 1985 as part of a national policy to transcend tribal divisions and strengthen 'national' sentiment (Rudebeck, 1988:25). In 1988 he had adapted to his difficult situation, but still had an increasingly hard time convincing the Mandinga parents of Kandjadja to send their children to his school, not because of any dislike of the teacher, but because 'the lack of support' for the school from the state led people to conclude that they had to fall back upon their Mandinga identity and traditions in order to manage their lives. Thus the growing distrust among the population for 'the school of the whites', and the parallel growth in support for the local Koranic schools. Compared with the official goals, the Kandjadja school is in a disastrous state. The teacher even proposed to the regional educational authorities that it be closed down for lack of community support. He received an answer that such matters were outside of his competence, and that even with only five students he should continue. In 1989 the school was finally closed.

The teacher saw no immediate way out of the school's crisis. Kaba Turé, in principle, supported his efforts. But the village leader was under strong pressure from the elders of Kandjadja who have long ago given up whatever confidence they once had in the new school. In reality, Kaba Turé is quite powerless regarding the school. However, it is not what is sometimes called an 'Arab school', where Islam is taught in an analytical way, but the ordinary elementary Koranic school of memorization and chanting. In 1976, in spite of the political commissar's reserved attitude, it drew perhaps ten students daily, while the official school had a couple of hundred. By 1988, the situation was reversed. Every evening except Wednesday and Thursday, the Koranic teachers gathered large groups of up to 70 children within the village. The children sit in circles around fires, singing and reciting the Koran. The atmosphere is lively and intense, the feeling of community support strong, in stark contrast to the official school.

The dissolution of the official school and the traditional Koranic school riding on a wave of popular Mandinga support can be linked to the structural adjustment policies in at least two ways. First, the utter material poverty of the state school has became worse in recent years. The teacher's salary was far below a reasonable minimum. Before it was closed, the school lacked all essentials, including notebooks, pencils, teaching materials and crayons. With inflation it has become even more difficult than before for the parents to provide their children with any of the basic necessities for school work. Secondly, in a political sense, the failure of the state to fulfil its educational developmental promises is throwing the people back on their own resources and old identities, undermining in the process many of the positive values gained with independence, by concepts such as 'nation', 'party' and 'state', which had also been underpinned by some material gains in the zones controlled by the liberation movement during the war. This growth of distrust *vis-à-vis* the state began before the policies of economic stabilization and structural adjustment hit Kandjadja, but the process has accelerated during the 1980s, rather than the reverse as intended by the government.

It is significant that political alienation thus far expresses itself in the crisis of the school rather than through any type of autonomous political organization transcending ethnic lines of division. The only 'national' framework is the official one, which is far from democratic enough to respond constructively to popular aspirations and frustrations as these are lived and experienced at the local levels.

Editors' note: An extended version of this article can be found in 'At the cross-roads: political alliances and structural adjustment', report from an AKUT seminar in Uppsala, May 1989, by K. Hermele and L. Rudebeck; 'Actes du Colloque international sur les traditions oracles du Gabu', Dakar, 19–24 May 1980 in special issue of *Ethiopiques* (Dakar), 28 October 1981.

Bibliography

Bowman Hawkins, Joye (1980), 'Conflict, interaction and change in Guinea-Bissau: Fulbe expansion and its impact, 1850–1900' (doctoral dissertation), University of California, Los Angeles.
Cabral, Amilcar (1978), 'Breve analyse de estrutura social da Guine "portuguesa" 1964', in Mario de Andrade (ed.), *A arma de teoria. Unidade e luta*, vol. 1, 2nd edition, Lisbon, pp. 101-7.
―― (1966) 'Fundamentos e objectives da libertacao nacional em relacao com a estrutura social', in Mario de Andrade (ed.), *A arma da teoria*.
―― (1978), *Unidade e luta*, vol. 1, pp. 199-213.
Carr-Hill, Roy & Gunilla Rosengart (1982), *Education in Guinea-Bissau 1978-81. The Impact of Swedish Assistance*, Education Division Documents 5, Stockholm: SIDA, September.
Djalo, Ibrahima (1987), 'Contribuição para uma reflexão-educação: multilinguismo e undade nacional', *Soronda*, Bissau: INEP, 3, pp. 101-112.
Ethiopiques (Dakar), 28 October 1981.
Handem, Diana (1986), *Nature et fonctionnement du pouvoir chez les Balanta Brassa*, Collection 'Kacu Martel' 1, Bissau: Instituto Nacional de Estudos e Pesquisa (INEP).
―― (1988), 'A Guine-Bissau: o no do ajustamento', *Boletim de Informacdo Socio-Economica*, Bissau: INEP, 2, pp. 53-76.
―― (1980), *Introdução a geografia economica da Guine-B'ssau*, Bissau: State Commissariat of Economic Coordination and Planning.
Lepri, Jean-Pierre (1984), *La Guinee-Bissau en question(s). Essaid'analyse sociale, economique et sociologique*, Bissau: Ministry of National Education, UNESCO Project 702/GBS/10, April.
―― (1988), 'Formaçao de professores, locals, materias escolares e insucesso escolar na Guine-Bissau',

Soronda, Bissau: INEP, 5, pp. 83–102.

Lopes, Carlos (1982), *Ethnie, état et rapports de pouvoir en Guinea-Bissau, Itinéraires, Actes et travaux*, 22, Geneva: University Institute of Development Studies.

—— (1982), *A transicao historica na Guine-Bissau. Do movimento de libertacao nacional ao estado*, Thèses en études du développement,16, Geneva: University Institute of Development Studies.

—— (1987), *Guinea-Bissau. From Liberation Struggle to Independent Statehood*, Boulder, CO/ London:Westview Press/Zed Books.

Rocha, Ana Maria (1989), 'Höggudar och häxeri – mot en ny afrikansk varldsbild?', *Sociologisk forskning* (Lund), 1, pp. 24–35.

Roug, Jean-Louis (1988), *Petit dictionnare etymologique du Kriol de Guinea-Bissau et Casamance*, Collection 'Kacu Martel' 5, Bissau: INEP.

Rudebeck, Lars (1982), *Problémes de pouvoir populaire et de développement. Transition difficile en Guinea-Bissau*, Research Report 63, Uppsala: Scandinavian Institute of African Studies.

—— (1983), 'On the class basis of the national liberation movement of Guinea-Bissau', Department of Afro-American and African Studies, University of Minnesota, Minneapolis, May (mimeo).

—— (1988), 'Kandjadja, Guinea-Bissau, 1976–1986: Observations on the political economy of an African village', *ROAPE*, 41, pp. 17–29.

—— (1989), 'Observations sur la base sociale de la mobilisation anticoloniale en Guinée-Bissau coloniale', Bissau: INEP.

Sanha, Iusuf (1988), 'Guine-Bissau: programa de ajustamento estructural', *Boletim de Informacao Socio-Económica*, 2, pp. 37–52.

—— (1988), *Sociedade e Escola: O caso de Bunau*, Bissau: INDE.DEPOL, Ministry of Education, Culture and Sport, October.

Topsoe-Jensen, Bente (1988), *Sector de Mansaba. Inquérito socio-económico*, Bula: Programa de Desenvolvimento Rural Integrado (PDRI)/Zona 1, September.

19

CRAIG CHARNEY
Political Power & Social Class
in the Neo-Colonial African State   [1987]

It would be useful to reflect on the possible application of the concepts of Althusser and Poulantzas to the reality of the neo-colonial state. (Jean Copans)

Even experienced practitioners acknowledge that it will hardly do for a Marxist political analysis simply to ship Professor Poulantzas out to West Africa and set him promptly to work in the environment as best he may. (John Dunn)

Neo-colonialism in Africa has been much discussed, but rarely defined and even less often theorised. When definitions of the phenomenon have been proposed, they have generally been descriptive rather than analytic. They refer to the absence of fundamental social change since the end of the colonial era without specifying the factors which account for the continuities, or those which distinguish neo-colonial societies from other types of capitalist social formations. Despite the vague definitions offered, the notion of neo-colonialism clearly refers to something real. Contrary to the hopes of some and the fears of others, in Africa the position of the dominated classes, the power of foreign capital and the international division of labour have changed little since independence. These continuities are all the more striking in view of the frequency of changes of government in many African countries, and given the social tensions and political struggles even in the states which have remained relatively stable. The issue raised by these phenomena is the nature, form and function of the neo-colonial African state.

The premise of this paper is that the neo-colonial state is a type of capitalist state associated with a particular stage of capitalist development in Africa, and produced by a given set of class struggles. It can be analysed in terms of the same criteria as other capitalist states, while taking into account the particular characteristics of African societies.

This analysis is based upon concepts drawn from the work of Gramsci, Althusser and Poulantzas. In their perspective, class domination is produced by a combination of force and hegemony. Force, by its nature, means acts of repression which inspire fear. Hegemony, in contrast, is politico-ideological leadership, which pervades the entire social formation (including the dominated classes). In developed capitalist societies, Poulantzas defines it as

the specific characteristics of the dominant capitalist ideology by means of which one class or fraction succeeds in presenting itself as the incarnation of the general interest of the people-nation, and in so doing conditioning a specific political acceptance of its domination on the part of the dominated classes. (1968:239)

The ways hegemony is exercised in neo-colonial states differ somewhat from those in the developed capitalist countries, but the notion of hegemony remains both applicable and essential for their analysis. In my view, it represents the unifying concept permitting the comprehension of the functioning of African states, including many aspects considered paradoxical by political scientists or economists.

I propose to define the neo-colonial state as a formally independent state, in which transnational capital is the hegemonic class and the indigenous petty bourgeoisie the reigning class, whose economy remains extroverted and subordinated to the world market, and which diffuses commodity relations within precapitalist modes of production. My argument is that in the neo-colonial state, foreign capital retains its hegemony through a contradictory alliance with local dominant classes, a strategy rendered possible by the interpenetration of capitalist and domestic modes of production. The evolution of this articulation permits class hegemony and state legitimation to be maintained via lineage-type discourses rationalising an increasingly capitalist reality. Clientelist networks justified through this discourse enable African dominant classes actually to lead the subordinate classes and to contain opposition to the ruling alliance. In these circumstances, merely spreading ideas of resistance is difficult, and acting upon them dangerous; the safest strategy open to the dominated classes is to play the game of their patrons.

The Different Basis for Hegemony in Peripheral States

One of the major tasks of the authoritarian neo-colonial state, inseparable from the emergence of a dominant class, concerns the formation of a civil society which guarantees the functioning of the capitalist mode of production. (Bayart, 1978:26)

Bayart's assertion poses the question of how the hegemony of the dominant classes is maintained in the neo-colonial state. In a sense, it is a restatement of the classic question of Pashukanis: 'Why does class domination not appear for what it is, that is, the subjection of one part of the population to another?' However, it cannot receive the same response that he and other marxist theorists formulated for developed capitalist societies.

The hegemony enjoyed by capital in the centre presupposes the generalisation of commodity relations into production and reproduction, as well as exchange. Under these conditions, commodity fetishism (the notion that the wage received for labour represents an equal exchange between possessors of two types of commodities) hides the fact that the capital relation is a social relation of inequality and unequal exchange. Social inequality is justified on the grounds of competition among individuals who are theoretically equal. The separation of the worker from the means of production corresponds to the separation of the economic and the political spheres under capitalist conditions of production, where the capital-labour relation no longer involves personal dependence or political constraint. (Poulantzas terms the separation of the economic and the political under capitalism the 'isolation effect'.)

The capitalist state thus need not appear as a class state. It is legitimated rather as impersonal, neutral and above-the-fray. It treats each citizen as a subject, not an object, legally free, independent and equal. Just as citizens are equal before the law, they are equally free to sell their labour power, and have an equal right to vote for the government, which is presented as the incarnation of the national will. Class is formally absent from the institutions of the state; it is a 'national-popular' class state. Thanks to the isolation effect, political and economic struggles are perceived as separate, often in atomised or individualistic terms, rather than in class terms. This ideology is reinforced by the action of various ideological state (or class) apparatuses: schools, the mass media, etc.

In Africa, however, bourgeois hegemony and state legitimacy cannot be founded exclusively on exchange relations, as commodity production is far from universal. A large proportion of reproduction takes place within domestic or lineage relations, rather than through commodity sales. Furthermore, much of production is organized around personal relations of direct dependence between peasant or worker and chief, merchant, marabout or bureaucrat, rather than through an impersonal market. In these circumstances, the isolation effect cannot operate, since from the viewpoint of the subaltern classes, the economic and political orders are one and the same.

Legal and political equality are likewise sharply circumscribed. Independent African states inherited bourgeois legal systems, but their writ does not run in many respects. 'Traditional' or religious authorities often have considerable power, while the law is simply ignored in a large part of the economy (the informal sector). As to formal democratic rights, in most African states these are limited or absent altogether. The role of the state in the reproduction of the labour force is also much more limited than in the developed countries; thus apparatuses such as the schools or the press have much less influence.

The Role of 'Lineage' Ideologies

In the neo-colonial state, the dominant classes maintain their hegemony and the capitalist state its legitimacy by reproducing relations of dependence organised on the basis of lineage-type discourse. The non-universality of commodity relations in these states stems from the interpenetration of capitalist and domestic modes of production (Meillassoux, 1975; Wolpe, 1971). This interpenetration, produced by capitalism's evolution in Africa, permits the dominant classes to profit from the ideologies of legitimation and state structures characteristic of the different modes of production in which they originated. As Poulantzas wrote:

> Just as the structures of the state in a concrete formation present, under the domination of one type of state, structures which come from other types, these structures often participate, under the domination of one type of legitimation, in other types of legitimation; specifically, in previous dominant ideologies, corresponding to classes which are no longer the politically dominant classes ... The gap between a type of state and the dominant legitimacy in a form – corresponding to different political forms – is particularly striking in the case of developing or decolonizing countries, in Africa for example, where the establishment of 'modern' states is constantly dominated by traditional ideologies. (1968: 242)

However, these ideologies are not mere illusions. They explain the codes of access to the means of production and reproduction in neo-colonial societies.

The domination of capitalism in Africa (and elsewhere) was originally imposed upon societies organised in lineage or kinship communities based upon domestic modes of production. The process began with the monetarisation of prestige goods and armaments, which set communities to procuring slaves and producing exportable products. From this time on, the heads of lineage communities were acting as agents for capital. Through the conquest of Africa, the colonial state expanded the *économie de traite* over the whole of the continent, extracting labour power on capital's behalf indirectly (taxes stimulating commodity production and proletarianisation) and directly (forced labour). This phase of initiation was almost everywhere finished by the 1940s, when capitalism could count on the enlarged reproduction of commodity relations through the operation of the market, thanks to the partial monetarisation of individual and social reproduction: food, clothing, tools, school fees, dowries, etc. Forced labour was abolished and taxes became less important, as 'free' labour at least partly separated from the means of production flowed towards the towns. Nevertheless, domestic modes of production and reproduction remained intact, even though capitalism was sucking more and more labour power out of them.

Despite great variety in levels of productive forces and details of social organisation, societies in which domestically-based modes of production are prevalent share certain common features. Production, distribution of product and reproduction occur largely within the domestic household (extended or nuclear family). The economic and political instances are not separated; an individual's place in one determines his place in the other. Authority rests in the hands of chiefs (elder males); women and younger men (the 'social cadets') are powerless. Social organisation of units larger than one household is centred around lineage segments, with real or fictitious common ancestors (Meillassoux, Sahlins).

The ideological instance is also closely linked to the economic and political spheres in lineage formations. At lower levels of productive forces it is identical with them. The dominant class reinforces the power it enjoys via reproduction through a monopoly on sacred knowledge. This is manifest in the spiritual powers of elders, chiefs and kings, ancestor worship, etc. At higher levels (feudalism), ideology is a separate instance, operating as a hegemonic apparatus justifying exploitation (church or mosque). As P. Anderson put it, 'The super-structures of kinship, religion, laws or the state necessarily enter into the constitutive structure of the mode of production in precapitalist social formations' (Anderson, 1974:403).

There are two characteristic aspects of the ideologies of the dominant within domestically-based modes of production:

1) *Hierarchy*: relations of domination are ascribed to real or fictitious relations of blood or seniority; relations between different lineage communities to an order of precedence. Less developed forms base these ties on common ancestry; more highly articulate versions elaborate notions of social ranks, castes, or a 'great chain of being';

2) *Reciprocity*: the submission of dominated groups and the offer of their labour power or surplus, in return for redistribution of other goods and protection on the part of the dominators. Thus youths and women must efface themselves before older men, serfs and vassals before their lords, talibes before marabouts.

In neo-colonial societies, the beneficiaries of systems of legitimation based upon domestic or lineage-type ideology are often different from those of pre-colonial times. The local dominant classes need not necessarily be descendants of the pre-colonial aristocracy, where one existed (though they often are). Other dominant classes or fractions may also control apparatuses of dependency based upon lineage units and discourse: bureaucrats, religious leaders, the petty bourgeoisie, landowners (Copans, 1978:145).

Though the dominant groups may vary, however, at the bottom of the neo-colonial system are regularly found the exploited of both capitalist and domestic societies: peasants, workers, youths, women and disfavoured lineages. This is the product of the interpenetration of the two modes as capitalism develops. Younger sons, women and members of subordinate lineages tend to have the least access to land and other resources, and most often become workers. While the opportunities for social mobility open to individual members of the dominated groups vary, the general effect of political and economic organisation on the basis of lineage-type ideology is to keep them 'in their place' (Bayart, 1979).

Clientelism

Lineage-type discourse enables the capitalist-dominated power bloc and neo-colonial state to achieve legitimation through the clientelist practice of power. Clientelism is a personalised relationship between two individuals or groups belonging to different classes or class fractions, based upon reciprocal exchange of goods and services. These relations entail the extraction of labour power, surplus and political loyalty, in return for economic, political, military and religious services. When classes form and exploitation appears in social formations, domestic or lineage relations become clientelist relations. Clientelist strategies mask exploitative exchange behind lineage-type discourse stressing hierarchy and reciprocity. Clientelist relations are rationalised in terms of kinship or pseudo-kinship ties, mutual obligation, redistribution and solidarity.

The fluid and ever-changing structure of group relations within African states is the product of clientelist relations, which have permitted the subordination of domestic units in various kinds of collectivities. As Lemarchand has noted, clients may take on their patron's tribal identity, broaden the focus of their own identity or become one of many lineage-defined groups in a wider political system, depending upon the scope and discourse of the relationships. The phenomenon can be viewed as the pyramiding of patron-client ties, as surplus and services are exchanged at a variety of levels (Foltz, 1962). Domestic units could thus be hooked into clan or, where they existed, pre-colonial states, by appropriate pseudo-lineage ideologies (such as the invention of mythical common ancestors). The establishment of the colonial state enabled state legitimation and primitive accumulation to take advantage of lineage ideology as well, a function that continued even as capitalism transformed the bases of production and reproduction. Domestic units were hooked into the state and capitalist production via clientelist structures of indirect rule (chiefdoms, tribes, factions, etc.), irrespective of whether the metropole's policy for the petty bourgeoisie was 'assimilation' or 'separate development'.

This clientelist practice has been carried over and extended within the neo-colonial state. Continued adherence to lineage-type strategies fulfils political and ideological functions for the dominant classes, not merely the economic function (reproduction of the labour force) highlighted by economic anthropology. They offer a way to legitimate state and class power even in societies penetrated by capitalism to the point where the reproductive function of the lineage mode has declined drastically. They also remain important in maintaining the ideological conditions for the subjection of the dominated classes even where the ideological instance has been partially separated from the political-economic by the organisation of churches or mosques. (Often in fact lineage-type religious practices exist side-by-side with Christian or Muslim practice, reflecting the continuing ideological efficacy of the dominant elements within lineage groupings.) This type of discourse has a popular resonance in part because it draws upon shared symbols and history, but particularly because the dominant class patrons 'deliver the goods' through clientelist mechanisms. The lineage-type discourse shows how conformity must be expressed in order to obtain satisfaction, while clientelist practices make the independent organisation of the dominated classes very difficult.

Changing Forms of the State

While the discourse and shell of lineage formations have been kept, their interpenetration with capitalism and the development of the state have transformed the material bases of clientelism which existed in pre-colonial Africa. The productive and reproductive vitality of domestic organisations has been steadily eroded by capitalism. In consequence, clientelist ties increasingly regulate access to capitalist means of production and reproduction, often via the state, according to lineage-type ideologies. The very process through which state and capital undermined the economic foundations of pre-capitalist structures created the new resources and lines of authority channelled through them. In the simple domestic mode of production, the bases of power lay in the processes of reproduction: control of surplus and women. Colonial capitalism intensified the contradictions within it, often to breaking point, while establishing new means of domination. In turn, the domestic modes gave rise to individual and collective strategies of lineage-based access to resources within the capitalist sphere.

To understand the development of class dominance on the basis of clientelist strategies, one must consider them in relation to the evolution of productive and reproductive relations, and the form of state or place of the state within them. In Poulantzas' terms, the state form changes with phases of the capitalist mode of production (initiation and enlarged reproduction), capital seeking different types of state intervention in the economy in each. Following Marx, he says the absolutist state corresponded to the 'initiation' phase in Europe, and the liberal state to that of enlarged reproduction. While African states can be periodised on the same basis, the characteristics and peripheral position of African societies produced rather different state forms. The initiation phase involved a 'peripheral absolutist' state: an authoritarian, foreign-controlled administration which forcibly extracted labour power and extended commodity relations on the basis of pre-existing forms of production. After World War II, the phase of enlarged reproduction permitted the establishment of a 'developmentalist' state form, symbolised by the Colonial Development and Welfare Act and the *Fonds d'Investissement pour le Développement Economique et Social*. This state intervened actively to intensify agricultural production needed by the metropole and to promote limited industrial development, on the basis of 'free' labour and a more liberal political order. It remains in existence today, despite changes of regime at or since independence.

During the initial phase, state coercion tightened the grip of pre-colonial forms of exploitation while slotting new resources into them. Forced labour and taxation intensified demands for labour time and encouraged dependence on marketed food and tools by the dominated classes. In addition, the monetarisation of dowries and other goods opened possibilities of accumulation (particularly of wives), leading elders to increase labour demands and reduce redistribution. Producers unable to meet taxes and ever-rising expenditure needs fell into debt and deeper dependence on patron creditors. Some migrated to become clients elsewhere in the countryside; others went with groups seeking work in the towns. Both trends broadened the scope of lineage clientelist ties. Thus, within the early colonial order, local dominant classes acquired a variety of powerful new means of patronage: money, access to land, jobs, and means of production, the delegated power of the colonial state to arbitrarily tax or punish.

In the phase of enlarged reproduction, expanded state intervention afforded larger quantities and additional kinds of patronage resources. State aid provided farm implements, infrastructure and credit to rural patrons and a fortunate few among their clients. Paradoxically, however, indebtedness grew: those unable to accede to crop-boosting new technology were bound ever tighter to their patrons by the loans they needed to survive. For those who joined the exodus to the towns, a search for new patrons lay ahead. The total amount of labour power for sale was determined by the push-pull of rural impoverishment and urban development, but individual access to jobs was regulated less by the 'free' market than upon the basis of lineage-type relations. The gradual expansion of franchise rights and of the local dominant classes' role in the administration permitted the crystallisation of a party system corresponding to the clientelist politico-economic order. Participation in the factional political struggles of patrons represented for members of subaltern classes a form of struggle for essential reproductive or productive goods (which explains the intensity and violence of electoral struggles despite the absence of challenges to the fundamentals of the system).

Though independence did not change the form of the state, it brought deepened class dependence. Peasants rely ever more on rural notables for land, seeds, cattle and tools, as well as credit until harvest, commercialisation and access to state services. The myriad of 'agricultural development' and foreign 'aid' programmes only increased the resources at the disposal of dominant class patrons and the reliance of the dominated classes upon the market. The accelerating collapse of rural subsistence systems unleashed an unprecedented wave of migration towards African (and overseas) cities.

In the towns, similar relations of dependence exist on fairly similar bases, African cities recalling what Gramsci (1971:91) labelled 'medieval-type cities'. In the informal sector of the economy, where half or more of the workforce is employed, commodity production is based upon domestic rather than exchange relations. Regulation takes place through lineage or pseudo-lineage ties which ignore the capitalist legal order – and are usually ignored by it. Workers tend to share family, tribal or caste links to the proprietor. They often go unpaid or receive only pocket money, and enjoy no protection under contracts, labour laws or state insurance schemes (Salama and Mathias, 1984: 61–79). In the formal sector, where employee and employer no longer share domestic ties, clientelist networks have nonetheless been reproduced on the basis of access to jobs and state power. Present local dominant classes either grew up within the bureaucracies, or took them over. In any case, they need to control urban workers and maintain good relations with the dominant rural classes. This has produced the tribalisation of access to posts and subsidies, where pseudo-lineage ideology ties the urban petty bourgeoisie to sectors of the workforce and its rural peers. To some extent exchange relations also permit the 'isolation effect' to play a legitimating role: even when workers have achieved class unity at the economic level through trade unions, their political consciousness remains tribal. As far as reproduction is concerned, town dwellers are far less self-sufficient than rural residents. In many cities, workers in both the formal and informal sector for housing are beholden to 'chiefs' or landlords who can allocate plots. In other cases, state services for reproduction are particularly important: public housing, site and service schemes, school and health facilities, road and sanitation services and pensions. These resources constitute the substance of the patronage dispensed by the dominant classes through tribal political machines, the typical form of clientelism in African cities.

Thus, the ever-deepening penetration of capitalist relations and state structures in African social formations has created networks of control with a hold on members of dominated classes in town and country alike. The benefits for capitalism from such lineage-type clientelism were succinctly stated by Lemarchand (1972:148) 'Traditional clientelism regulates political mobilisation along traditional patron-client lines and maintains a measure of cohesion among ethnic segments, meanwhile permitting the accumulation of political and economic capital at the centre.'

The Working of Clientelism in the Neo-Colonial State

The lineage or pseudo-lineage clientele networks owe their efficacy as hegemonic organisations to their capacity to mystify class conflicts and channel them so that they reinforce rather than challenge the status quo. They determine the strategic options open to members of the dominated classes. Because the patron-client tie is personal, individual members of the dominated classes must confront dominant class patrons alone. Organisation is vertical: those at the base have no possibility of communication or solidarity with other members of their class. Conformity is but logical, since a challenge to the patron can cost dear – loss of access to vital means of production and reproduction – and individual action is almost surely futile. Moreover, the pervasiveness of lineage-type ideologies and clientelist relations helps ensure that members of the dominated classes will rarely be exposed to other ideas, or come to accept them through a consciousness-raising process of independent political participation. If a client does protest or voice a demand, he must express it in the terms and forms which the dominant classes expect – as a loyal tribal subordinate, caste brother, *talibe*, etc., beseeching his better. If his request is granted, the likely result is merely to reinforce his sense of belonging to the clientelist group, provoking feelings of gratitude and reciprocity. Not for nothing did Pitt-Rivers call the clientelist bond a 'lopsided friendship': inequality and ideology are both present (quoted in Powell, 1970).

The same processes – mystification and channelling – occur in relations between patrons and groups of clients in the subaltern classes. Clientelist blocs exist to compete for productive and reproductive resources; the underdevelopment of African societies intensifies the struggles. This competition is described in terms of lineage-type discourse: 'I am a Baoule, a Zulu, a partisan of M'Backe', and so on. Clients from the subordinate classes accept the leadership of 'their' dominant-class patron, as designated by the dominant ideology, and the obligations of reciprocity which follow. Unlike the state in developed capitalist countries, which presents itself as 'national' and 'popular', the neo-colonial state is 'popular' but particularist (tribal or sub-national).

The neo-colonial state is stronger than the colonial state, because the patrons at every level are themselves Africans. Clients in the dominated classes can identify with them as part of a racial or lineage-type community, and they respond as such. They have no interest in racially discriminatory legislation or limitations upon the professional advancement or accumulation of fellow Africans; contrary to what was the case under colonial regimes. their appropriations of land do not take the form of compact, racially-reserved zones, highly visible and resented. Most important, vastly more patronage is available to them with the enormous expansion of state activity and receipts, both in local exactions and foreign aid, which has occurred since their accession to political power. All these factors render them capable of exercising a form of popular leadership quite impossible under the colonial state. These factors of course help explain why anti-colonial revolution took place essentially in white-ruled colonies.

The mass organisations of African neo-colonial regimes (ruling parties, youth and women's movements, trade unions, etc.) serve to channel demands from subordinate groups and classes within the clientelist system. They replicate and encapsulate the contradictions between dominant and dominated in the society as a whole. While they may afford terrains of struggle to members of the subaltern classes, the practice of the patron classes generally ensures that such struggles are waged in terms of the system's own lineage-type ideology. One-party states and unitary mass organisations represent efforts to preclude the development of alternative foci of organisation and communication to the official system. Put more crudely, they permit the banning of organised opposition without sacrificing the forms of democratic representation. However, multi-party states function in much the same manner as one-party states with regard to the dispensing of patronage. Usually, a single party is dominant, at least regionally, and feels its clientelist organisation strong enough to face down a legal opposition. The dominant classes also practise patronage politics in no-party states, but directly via the state rather than mediated by political party organisations.

When insubordination does present itself, clientelism also helps the dominant classes to neutralise it. At the individual level, discontented members of the subaltern classes may respond in a variety of ways: refuse to plant export crops, join the exodus to the towns, change job or region, use alcohol or drugs, engage in crime or practise sorcery. The common element in all these responses is that they change the position of the individual without changing the system of dependency itself. Indeed, after practising many of them, the individual needs a new patron. Even collective resistance to the system often takes place on its own terms. They tend to struggle to replace chiefs or patrons, rather than attacking the institutions of class society themselves. The ideological effects of lineage-type discourse may also help shape the form of messianic cults, where magical beliefs mix with political ideology, potentially co-optable in lineage clientelist terms.

Editors' Note: The original article was very long and we have only included the first section. The second part discussed the development of relations among the dominant classes, while the final section considered the conditions in which the neo-colonial alignment might break down.

Bibliography

Althusser, L. (1971), 'Idéologie et appareils idéologiques d'Etat', *Positions,* Paris: Maspéro.
Anderson, P. (1974), *Lineages of the Absolutist State,* London: New Left Books.
Bayart, J-F. (1978), 'Régime du parti unique et systèmes d'inégalité et de domination au Cameroun: esquisse', *Cahiers d'Etudes Africaines,* 78
—— (1979), *L'Etat au Cameroun,* Paris: Presses de la Fondation Nationale des Sciences Politiques.
Copans, J. (1978), 'Paysannerie et politique au Sénégal', *Cahiers d'Etudes Africaines,* . 81.
Coquery-Vidrovitch, C. (1984), *L'Afrique Noire de 1800 à Nos Jours,* Paris: Presses Universitaires de France.
Coulon, C. (1981), *Le marabout et le prince,* Paris: Editions Pedone.
Flynn, P. (1974), 'Class, clientelism, and coercion: some mechanisms of internal dependency and control', *Journal of Commonwealth and Comparative Politics,* 12.
Foltz, W. (1962). *Social Structure and Political Behaviour of Senegalese Elites*, Occasional Paper Series. New Haven, CT: Yale University Press.
Freund, W. (1984), *The Making of Contemporary Africa,* Princeton, NJ: Princeton University Press.
Gramsci, A. (1971), *Selections from the Prison Notebooks,* New York: International Publishers.
Lemarchand, R. (1972), 'Political clientelism and ethnicity in tropical Africa: competing solidarities in nation-building', *American Political Science Review,* 66.
Leys, C. (1975), *Underdevelopment in Kenya: the political economy of neocolonialism,* London: Heinemann & James Currey.
Meillassoux, C. (1975), *Femmes, Greniers et Capitaux,* Paris: Maspéro; English edition (1978), *Maidens, Meal and Money: Capitalism and the Domestic Community,* Cambridge: CUP.
Pashukanis, E. (1970, *La théorie générale du droit et du marxisme,* Paris; English edition (1978), *Law and Marxism: A General Theory,* London: Ink Links.
Poulantzas, N. (1968), *Pouvoir politique et classes sociales,* Paris: Maspéro; English edition (1973), *Political Power and Social Class,* London: New Left Books.
Powell, J. (1970), 'Peasant society and clientelist politics', *American Political Science Review,* vol. 64.
Rev, P -P. (1971), *Colonialisme, néocolonialisme, et transition au capitalisme,* Paris: Maspéro.
—— (1973), *Les alliances de classes,* Paris: Maspéro.

Sahlins, M. (1974), *Stone Age Economics,* London: Tavistock.

Salama, P. and G. Mathias (1984), *L'Etat surdéveloppé: des metropoles au Tiers-Monde,* Paris, La Découverte.

Salama, P. & P. Tissier (1982), *L'industrialisation dans le sous-développement,* Paris: Maspéro.

Saul, J. (1979), *The State and Revolution in Eastern Africa,* New York: Monthly Review Press.

Scott, J. (1972), 'The breakdown of patron-client bonds and social change in rural Southeast Asia', *Journal of Asian Studies,* 32.

Sûret-Canale, J. (1972), *French Colonialism in Tropical Africa,* New York: Pica Press.

Wolpe, H. (1971), 'Capitalism and cheap labour power in South Africa: from segregation to apartheid', *Economy and Society,* 1.

20

BASIL DAVIDSON & BARRY MUNSLOW
The Crisis of
the Nation-State in Africa   [1990]

This discussion is an edited transcript of a conversation recorded at Basil Davidson's home in Somerset in 1990. At the time he was writing *The Black Man's Burden: Africa and the Curse of the Nation-state* (1992, James Currey). The book draws the historical parallels between Central and Eastern Europe on the one hand, and Africa on the other. Although the following discussion concentrates on the situation in Africa, the still relevant comparative experience of Central and Eastern Europe is interwoven throughout.

Davidson: People ask me why it is that such a good beginning, as it seemed to be in the 1950s and 1960s with the independence of many African countries, should have ended in this really immeasurable disaster? Is it that the nationalist movements were unable to produce competent and honest cadres? Is it that they were cut off from their historical base by becoming nationalists and therefore find themselves in opposition to the so-called traditional forces, in that they settled in the towns and did not give any thought to what happened to the people in the countryside? Is it that the North-South relationship is of such a nature that Africa can't prosper, no matter how competent Africans might be? These are the kinds of questions that people throw at me. Of course I don't know the answers and I don't wish to suggest that I do. But the book that I am now thinking of is going to try and produce at least a prospectus or summary of what the answers might possibly turn out to be.

The reason that I am writing it is, I think, because, whether it is published or not, people of my generation owe an obligation to meet the question – as to why things have turned out so badly – because we did try to enthuse our audiences with the notion that decolonization was not only a good thing in itself, but also would lead to the progress and expansion of the African peoples. How far were our judgements wrong?

The book I am writing will consider comparisons with what happened in Italy in the 19th century and in the Balkans in the early 20th, getting rid of the old Bourbon and Austro-Hungarian Empires. You find that much the same thing happens there as in Africa.

Consider what happened in the states released from the Austro-Hungarian empire. Almost all of them fell at once into military dictatorship, corruption, fascism, a mess. It can't be just an accident, it seems to happen everywhere. What, then, can be the answer?

We are stuck with the nation-state, there is no doubt about that. People think of themselves as nations, and nation-states exist. It's no good telling the Bulgarians that they shouldn't have a nation-state, because they won't listen to you! It's no good telling the Angolans they are quite wrong to build a nation-state, they won't listen to you either.

But if the nation-state, as it has come down to us from the European examples, always ends in a mess – and so far it always has ended in a mess – what can be the future for the African examples?

I think the answer has to be in the consistent decentralization of power from the stiffly centralized bureaucratic kinds of state which have been created in Africa. Decentralizing down to local government, whilst on a larger scale moving towards regional constellations and confederations of power – extending ECOWAS (Economic Community of West African States) or SADCC (Southern African Development Coordination Conference) into something real. That is what the Africans themselves see now. They begin to see the nation-state as a curse, whereas before it was seen as an act of liberation, which initially of course it was.

This is what more and more African thinkers are saying and some African countries are beginning to try to achieve. To the point, you have a situation in Nigeria where something like 400 local governments have been created and developed into 21 states. Of course they find it extremely difficult to make these work against the habits of bureaucracy, with bureaucracy behaving as though it was the boss. Local government, therefore, is not taking over as it should.

That's where I found the Cape Verdian experience extremely instructive. It's not that it is exemplary, it can't be exemplary given that Cape Verde is a very small country. But without making great claims, they have been trying to find a way in which the habits of top-down bureaucratic centralism, which was at the heart of the Portuguese empire, are turned around so that local people do actually begin to take charge of their own local affairs more and more widely. This is what they have been trying to do in Cape Verde. Obviously they are at an early stage, and in that sense a *luta continua*, because there is naturally great opposition to it. The petty bourgeoisie and bureaucracy do not like it, the Americans don't like it. Tremendous pressure against 'participation thinking' is being applied. The struggle is on, and the right side is winning at the moment. But the question is still open as to who will win in the end.

But if you do take this perspective, then the way out of the nation-state collapse is going to be through increasing decentralizations of power and increasing regionalizations of power. They are beginning to say that even in Senegal, in Ghana, in Nigeria, all over the place.

Munslow: How can the move towards democratic participation be related to the broader political and economic institutions of the nation state? How can we avoid the fragmentation that we see for example in Yugoslavia? Here there was an effort towards decentralization and self-management. But the continuation of the viability of the national economy has now been in jeopardy for some time.

Davidson: As far as Yugoslavia is concerned, of course one is very interested. And I get some feedback in a schematic and occasional way. What I would say is that the decentralizations introduced in the 1945-55 period in the wake of the war, were extremely positive and have been a great success. Federal Yugoslavia is not a joke. It has worked extremely well, with one exception, Kosovo. But it has almost totally fallen down now. Yugoslavia today is a mockery of what it should have been and even of what it was. The reason for that, largely, is the one party, bureaucratic, Leninist concept. There is no doubt that this is what has gone wrong. The party took over power no matter what camouflage it adopted. The real power was not handed down. When it was handed down, it was handed in such a way that people did not feel responsible for the wider issues. Hence self-management would be good in a factory, but the workers would immediately carve up the proceeds and not give a damn about other factories. So the one-party state has been a disaster because the party has been utterly identified with the state. The power of the state has been the power of the party and vice versa. This is what has dragged them down.

The Soviet Union's not a state which works at any level at all. Now we know this. It's no longer even controversial to say it. So it is high time that this was read into other situations. It is high time that the Africans themselves, those who still think they are marxist-leninist, should take this on board.

In Cape Verde, to come back to the case which has been at the front of my mind, they have said from the very beginning that the power of the party is not to be fused or confused with the power of the state. The two are separate. The party has no executive power at all except at the very top. Down the line none.

Coming back to your earlier point of how do we cause these two problematics to approach, democratization at the base and international cooperation: how do you put this together with the concept of devolution of power? I do not know the answer, but I think that life is going to give us the answer. You have in West Africa this maze of frontiers across which every night and every day people and goods are passing illegally. People who are otherwise law-abiding citizens completely disregarding the law. So all of the major economic 'indicators' are quite unreliable. The only way to solve this problem is to accept that people have voted with their feet. They don't want the frontiers. ECOWAS, for example, should now move rapidly towards the stated aims of abolishing or seriously reducing frontier controls. But then you arrive at the centralized bureaucracy. This says 'Hey! You are taking away our power.' They haven't faced this yet and until they do face it there will be no solution to the problems.

Munslow: I don't know how it is possible to break through the problem of the maintenance of the national frontiers as the unity of the nation-state is completely tied up with the welfare of the ruling elite of the nation-state. All efforts at federation, such as that between Senegal and the Gambia, seem to founder on the fact that it would mean giving up the exclusive right to pillage and plunder. At the same time, we see that the struggle between contending elites tends to be the dominant feature of politics in Africa. Between those who have and those who would like to have, but are excluded from having, control of the right to plunder. How can this problem be overcome?

Davidson: Yes, that's the central question, isn't it? No answer to it yet, and so Africa sinks ever deeper into the mire. We need an agenda for the reconstruction of a post-colonial Africa: not a mere 'neo-colonial' Africa but one that's built on post-colonial assumptions and objectives and possibilities. I don't think that any of the contending parties have accepted the structurally indispensable requirements of that kind of agenda – but maybe it's on the way. Nothing less can do the job that's got to be done if Africa is going to climb out of the mess instead of sinking more deeply into it.

Munslow: So this means there has to be a return to the kind of visionary leadership we had with Nkrumah and Cabral in the past, albeit with new policies adapted to fit a very different set of circumstances. The problem remains of where this leadership will come from.

Davidson: This I don't know, of course. But I'm sure this is necessary. We need the agenda, and we need a return to the Pan Africanism which is no longer as unrealistic, utopian and romantic as it used to be. It must be based on the very real factors which you can read, for instance, in the conclusion of debates in SADCC and its realm, or even in ECOWAS. If you read the ECOWAS papers they have got it all there, but nothing happens for the reason that you have given. The central state bureaucracies each want to hang onto their little bit of power.

Munslow: The multilateral donor institutions are providing a stimulus to regional cooperation. Some international institutions and bilateral donors find it easier to deal with larger groupings of African states. This is frequently driven by administrative expediency, to reduce the cost of the administration of aid dispersal.

The problem is, that perhaps this positive aspect, driving regional cooperation forward in Africa, may at the same time be undermining the potentiality for the smaller-scale local participation and control of the development process to take place. It is only really with the NGOs that we have an ability to deliver at a scale of operations that is actually controllable by village and district communities.

Davidson: This is true and I think that this is another central issue. There is evidently a great danger in this situation because the whole push towards regionalization, backed by the various international authorities, is on the face of it going to undermine this grass roots, patient, detailed, 'small' approach which goes on in villages to allow committees to be elected, to decide on building small roads and so on.

Unless the contradiction is resolved, the ultimate aims of SADCC and ECOWAS will never be achieved. Therefore, the agenda that we are considering has to say that salvation begins at the base. The base is peasant society and peri-urban society. The rest has to emerge from this.

We then come onto the next point that I want to discuss: that nationalism went wrong because the nationalists turned their backs on what they said was traditional Africa.

They said 'we have to come out of the savage backwoods into the open where nations are made' (a quote from Attoh Ahuma's book, published in 1911). They turned their backs on everything that African history had so far achieved, in terms of internal self-development. In some respects one understood that very well. I thought they were right, because there you had those backward old monarchs like the King of Ashante – what's that got to do with the modern world? The structures by which they had self-developed Africa were structures where power began at the base. I am not suggesting that one can go back to tradition. Of course not. But somehow or other there has to be taken into account that Africa self-developed itself, with remarkable success, over many centuries up to the 18th and 19th centuries. Here we had a continent with a steady increase of population and a steady increase of the means to support that population.

Traditionally in Africa there had not been any great periods of crisis and famine. The crisis of today is the first of its kind. Somehow, therefore, there has to be a revision of attitudes. Not in order to get back to traditional structures, which would mean that Africa would have to be divided into 500 units instead of 50 or so. But a revision of attitudes, of policies, of priorities.

I also see a positive lever for the future, driving community participation forward, which is that it can actually be successful in development. In a continent with so much economic failure, if things work and a surplus is produced, then there is every incentive, not least amongst those ruling at the top, to encourage those initiatives because the surplus they produce gives the wherewithal for the state and the bureaucracy to exist. However, it also poses a threat, because that level of self-organization can also mean that there is a more vocal series of demands placed upon the centre for the distribution of such central resources as exist.

More and more we are looking for a change in the relationship between the base and the centre. The old idea which has proved so disastrous, is that the state will be 'doing' development, controlling and managing this process. In the African context the state's role can be better formulated as a facilitating role. How to change around the government cadre from a 'doer' and 'dictator', to facilitating others to do, requires a fundamental change of attitude. How is it that this change of attitude can be installed?

As things stand at the present the only way this will be possible is to build upon the successes that have been scored. One of the things that should be done now is to make an assessment of the successes. We all know about the maize miracle in Zimbabwe and the reasons for this. But there are other things that can be done, down to ecological factors such as those discussed by Paul Richards in his book (*Indigenous Agricultural Revolution*, Hutchinson, 1985). The peasants after all do understand what intercropping means. It isn't new to them. It does work. You only have to see any tropical farm to understand that. It would be well worth doing to raise a little fund to go around and inspect what's being done in this perspective: what succeeds, and how, or why it is caused to fail when it does fail. That would be unquestionably useful.

I'm in favour at this stage of events of making an unofficial and no doubt unpopular assessment of successes and failures at the local level. For if we are right in saying that salvation comes from the base, unless it is just rhetoric, then let us prove why we are right or why we are wrong. This can only be done by looking at a large number of cases where local initiative has succeeded or has failed.

We need a view of what unofficial Africa is actually doing. I increasingly doubt anything that is said at the official level. They simply don't take account of the parallel economies.

Munslow: This means that the role of planning as an alternative to the free market economy has to be radically rethought.

Davidson: It may have a value in terms of the central administrative bureaucratic budget. It has small general value in the 'real' economy. If you look at the history of it, you see two major sources of bad advice since the 1950s. The first lot comes in from the West, simply following on the old colonial pattern of thought. 'We know best, planning is needed, you have no administration, you have no bureaucrats, no statistics etc, it must be planned in this way.' Then you have the other one, even more destructive, coming in from Moscow and Berlin, with little voices from Sofia and Budapest chirping in every now and then, coming in with their even more pernicious nonsense. 'You must industrialize, until you do this you will not be able to advance and therefore you must milk the peasants. If the peasants don't like it, send in the troops.' That is broadly speaking what was done in Europe.

Planning of course has a value, because that is how you construct your programme. But the notion that you are going to solve it by national plans ... all national plans should be abolished and nearly all aid advisers should be pensioned off and sent to the Seychelles where they can't do much harm.

Instead, there should be funds available to assist local initiatives. The local initiatives will have to ask for it and show that it is a realistic request. It is not you, it is them. They are making the request and if you think it is useful, give it to them. It's different from the planning concept which says, there should be this, therefore the peasants should have it, they may not want it!

Munslow: How does one build up from the local initiatives into a national and regional economic framework. What does this mean? Free trade between the local units? How does one create the cohesion of a national and international economy?

Davidson: This is where the problem actually resides. At the present moment, nobody can handle this process, because nobody is taking on board what actually is happening. I think constantly of SADCC in relation to Mozambique and its neighbours. There you have northern Mozambique, consisting of four or five ethnic groups, all of whom are also living in countries across the frontier. Clearly this makes no sense at all. How do you get from there to abolishing the frontier, is a question which has to be posed.

Let me tell you a story. In 1979 I was in Mozambique. Samora (Machel) said let's have an evening of discussion and we'll ask impossible questions. We had a meeting with Marcelino dos Santos, Jorge Rebello, Oscar Monteiro, Mariano Matsinho, about eight in all, the eight who have essentially led Frelimo since 1968, sitting in a room with nobody else present. Samora said, Go on Basil raise the impossible questions. And I said, O.K. I'll raise the impossible questions, but be patient. You say that you in Frelimo have united the various ethnic groups, peoples, languages and cultures in a solid national front which has won independence.

Then I said, you have united the people of Mozambique within a front but the peoples of Mozambique live also in Malawi, Zimbabwe, Zambia, Tanzania and South Africa. Why then do you stop at the frontiers? If it is right to unite these various peoples within a colonial frontier imposed upon you, why is it wrong to say let us unite with these peoples outside of the frontiers?

So I don't think we can answer the question of the process that you have raised, how to get from a to b, because we are only dealing with one side of the question at the moment. We are dealing with what the state says happens, but not with what the people say happens.

Munslow: The model of grassroots participation in Africa is normally held up to be the experience in the liberated areas during the period of anti-colonial nationalist guerrilla warfare. Was this the aspiration more than the reality? Was it only confined to small pockets or did it become more generalized? One might have to talk specifics, according to movements and countries but I wonder generally how you feel about this. How much of genuine alternative activity actually took place?

Davidson: Perhaps I overstated it. I would be more cautions now in hindsight, but that is always the case. Yet I am sure that in Guinea Bissau it went very far indeed, with the exception of the economic field where they didn't have time and didn't do it. But political and social decision-making and co-operation went very far. I don't think it ever did in Angola. There was never much chance that it could. Even the little that I thought existed in 1970, I think probably didn't exist. Mozambique is a little harder to say. But it seems to me from the incomplete evidence that we have that it went quite far in Cabo Delgado, that it began in Niassa, but got nowhere else of course, because it didn't have time. If you read *The Fortunate Isles* you'll see the story of the 90 cadres who came out of the Guinea-Bissau struggle to build alternatives in Cape Verde. They felt they had got hold of the method to be applied. Whether it was sufficiently applied in time of war may be another question. But that's the method that they have been applying in Cape Verde now, with what success we shall of course see.

Munslow: You always seem to have given the priority of attention in your writing to the need for political organization, especially at the base, much more than the economic considerations. I wonder what is the relationship that you see between the two? At the moment we seem to have a series of epic struggles going on in China and the Soviet Union concerning the relationship between economic and political reform. How can this work out, and what is the interrelationship between the two elements?

Davidson: What you have just said is perfectly true. I paid far too little attention to the economic dimension. Partly because I don't think I understood it, and partly because you are up against these two great stereotypes. Is it going to be a capitalist form of development or is it going to be, in quotes, 'a socialist form'? Neither are real, mark you, it's Scilla and Charybdis. Here is this little boat of 'popular participation' trying to get between these two.

My view was and remains, that the great achievement of the liberation struggles was not of course in any form of economic reorganization. It was in raising questions and getting debate at the base, so that the peasants begin to think about the situation they are actually in. This was a cultural experience of enormous importance.

I feel that all the way down the line people have suffered from a deep belief that Africans have not been able to develop themselves, that African history is not a history of self-development, that whatever salvation comes, is going to come from outside. Until we turn our attention back to the process of self-development that went on in Africa before Europe got there, we shall not be able to see this other side of the process.

21 JOCELYN ALEXANDER
State, Peasantry & Resettlement in Zimbabwe
[1984]

The end of minority rule in Zimbabwe seemed to herald dramatic changes in agrarian and local government policies, as well as in official attitudes towards the rural areas more generally: the newly elected ZANU(PF) government promised a dramatic decentralisation and democratisation of government structures and a large-scale redistribution of land. After independence, the restrictions of the Lancaster House constitution as well as the government's decision to pursue a policy of 'moderation and reconciliation' left much of the Rhodesian state and economy intact. While important changes followed from the lifting of discriminatory legislation, democratisation, the extension of services in communal areas, and land redistribution, continuities were striking.

Decentralisation & Development Planning: Continuity & Change

Though the ZANU(PF) government promised increased popular participation in development planning through elected councils and committees, its policies were strongly shaped by those of the colonial era. In the early 1960s, both Edgar Whitehead's government and that of the Rhodesian Front endorsed the internationally fashionable policy of 'community development'. The policy called for a rollback in the coercive implementation of centrally formulated policies in favour of development driven by the 'felt needs' of 'natural' communities represented by councils and community boards. In practice, the policy was dominated by the need to re-assert state control in the face of intense resistance to the government's agrarian policies and the spread of nationalism. The policy stressed the role of chiefs and headmen in creating political stability: councils, boards and courts were based on 'communities' associated with officially recognised chiefs and headmen.

By the late 1970s, councils lay largely moribund while in areas where the war was closely contested chiefs had been forced to withdraw from their often ambivalent cooperation with government officials or face violent attack. The first step in re-establishing peacetime local government was symbolic of later reforms, in terms of its pre-independence genesis and its top-down implementation. New district councils, established in lieu of the smaller chieftaincy-based African Councils, were designed by the transitional government and adopted just before independence. To implement the measure, the thin veneer of ZANU(PF) officials at the national level relied on an uneasy combination of the former officials of the Ministry of Internal Affairs and village-level ZANU(PF) and ZAPU committees. Initially, party committees played a key role in distributing aid, reconstruction, and communication with central government officials. However, though rural party committees were instrumental in the creation of councils, they found themselves rapidly displaced by them, and by the re-establishment of government bureaucracies in rural areas. Senior ZANU(PF) officials were reluctant to empower rural party committees for a number of reasons: they did not represent all members of rural society as councils theoretically did; they acted with an autonomy from the ZANU(PF) leadership which reflected both the lack of middle-level party structures and the disparity between local demands and government policies; and, notably in Matabeleland and parts of Midlands and Mashonaland West, they were not loyal to ZANU(PF). In 1980 and 1981, the demands of rural party committees were routinely over-ridden by the central government, with the effect of 'demobilising' them.

Other reforms were instituted with the ostensible purposes of replacing chiefs and headmen with elected institutions and further decentralisation. In 1981, the Customary Law and Primary Courts Act replaced chiefs and headmen's courts with elected presiding officers and assessors; in 1982, the Communal Lands Act gave district councils authority over land allocation thus removing the Tribal Land Authorities' powers. Proposals for decentralisation below the level of district councils were mooted in the 1982 *Transitional Plan*: the Plan promised further attention to 'popular local organizations and participation in regard to regional and local development'; it included mention of 'peasant associations' and 'village committees' (GoZ, 1982a:55,18,98). However, it was not until 1984 that a Prime Minister's directive created village and ward development committees, referred to as 'vidcos' and 'wadcos' respectively. These new 'democratic institutions of popular participation' were to promote

> the advancement of development objectives set by Government, the Community and the People. They would ensure that opportunities are created for greater participation by the mass of the people in decision making processes which lead to the setting of development objectives. (MLGTP, 1985:1)

The directive also created district and provincial development committees, consisting of civil servants and chaired by administrators, and the office of Provincial Governor, a political appointee. The much delayed Rural District Councils Act of 1988 provided for the amalgamation of the new district councils with rural councils, the local authorities which represented formerly 'European' farming areas.

In theory, the government had established democratic, secular, and non-racist channels for popular participation in planning and policy-making from 'village' to provincial level and had taken steps to expand the resource base of local authorities in the former Tribal Trust Lands (TTLS) to include 'European' areas. Change was not, however, so dramatic. First, the implementation of the Rural District Councils Act did not get under way until June 1993 due to conflict over borders and resources. The extent to which the Act will redistribute resources is at any rate questionable (Helmsing et al. 1991). Moreover, farm workers remained disenfranchised. Second, despite the establishment of elected councils and courts in place of chiefs and headmen, the central government instituted or perpetuated a number of measures which retained chiefs' status if not, initially, their late-colonial powers. The reasons behind these measures were diverse, with roots in Rhodesian policies as well as the new government's political project.

In the first chaotic year of independence a key source of support for chiefs and headmen lay in the former officials of the Ministry of Internal Affairs. In Manicaland Province, for example, Rhodesian-era administrators who still held their posts responded to the idea of excluding chiefs from their previous roles with horror. With the support of the Provincial Commissioner, one District Commissioner complained that, 'To destroy or diminish that structure (chieftaincy) without a definite plan on how to fill the vacuum, could lead to confusion if not anarchy in the communally occupied areas' (MLGTP, Chimanimani District, correspondence files). In the end, the Ministry of Local Government required that chiefs sit as ex-officio members of the new councils, even if local communities objected. In addition, chiefs' and headmen's salaries were maintained, leaving them better off than either elected councillors, who received a fraction of chiefs' salaries, or party and vidco leaders who received no remuneration (Kriger, 1992:225).

Prominent ZANU(PF) leaders publicly defended the continued recognition given chiefs under the mutable rubric of reconciliation and through an Africanist appeal for the preservation of culture, custom and tradition. Though this rationale had roots in the uses of African culture in nationalist and guerrilla mobilisation, the ways in which the ZANU(PF) government sought to 'preserve and conserve' culture, and the version of culture which it privileged, had less to do with cultural nationalism than with Rhodesian traditionalism. In a vein similar to earlier white politicians' attempts to woo chiefs, Prime Minister Mugabe held a series of *indabas* with chiefs in 1980. The Ministry of Local Government acted to protect 'tradition and dignity' by retaining central government control over chiefly appointments (Kriger, 1992:225, 233–4). By keeping chiefs as salaried appointees of the state, the government sought to pre-empt any opposition they might offer and, increasingly, to use them to build a rural constituency, and to aid in policy implementation. Indeed, at yet another *indaba* before the 1985 elections, Mugabe promised chiefs the return of control over courts, thus undermining one of the democratic reforms of the independence era, as well as compromising other legislation, particularly that granting women new rights. Just prior to the 1990 elections Mugabe went a step further, promising chiefs involvement in the selection of people eligible for resettlement land (Alexander, 1993).

Other aspects of Rhodesian community development also persisted. A handbook produced by the Secretary of Local Government, L. V. Brown, explained the 1982 District Councils Act to civil servants in terms of a familiar dichotomy between 'traditional' and 'modern' institutions: the Act was to 'marry traditional methods of administration ... to a modern system of local government' according to the 'philosophy, principles and practices of community development'. As in the rhetoric of the 1960s, the councils' 'driving force' was to be the 'felt needs of the people'. Brown continued:

> Any spirit of self-help that once existed in a community may have been dissipated by too-easy solutions having been provided in the past.
>
> All too many communities are seriously deficient in public spirited persons with the will to serve others without substantial reward.
>
> Much of the initiative and drive will be found in the executive [the district administrator and other civil servants] who themselves are often stimulated by the ideas promoted by Central Government Officials.
>
> For a long time to come District Administrators will have to lend their authority and prestige to bolster the efforts of councils and to give them confidence in their powers. However, it is important that communities should feel that the results achieved are due to their own efforts and have not merely been imposed from above. (GoZ, 1982b)

While Brown conceded that councils were allowed to reach decisions contrary to the advice given them by civil servants, he cautioned, 'This approach must not be taken too far' (GoZ, 1982b). The handbook was indicative of more than simply the last breath of a soon to depart Rhodesian official. Statements by ZANU(PF) officials, including the

Minister of Local Government, also employed the 'felt needs' vocabulary and stressed the role of district councils as implementors of centrally formulated policies. At times central control over service delivery was used as a threat to induce cooperation; 'participation' came to mean assent and compliance. Moreover, the District Councils Act retained the right of the Minister to assign any or all of the powers of the council to an officer of the public service. District administrators, who sat as the chief executive officers on councils, exercised great sway over councils and remained answerable to the Ministry of Local Government hierarchy, not elected authorities.

The conditions which had made the rhetoric of 'democracy' and 'felt needs' so empty in the Rhodesian era were perpetuated in other respects. Councils and vidcos were largely dependent on centrally generated and controlled resources while vidcos were based on the arbitrary unit of 100 households, a unit which did not necessarily comprise a community with shared resources, interests, or a common identity. Vidcos were nonetheless mandated to produce land use plans (of which more later), a goal which again did not reflect local demands and which proved well nigh impossible to carry out without the modification of boundaries and membership.

The institutional structures established to carry out development planning further marginalised councils and vidcos. Theoretically, vidcos submitted annual plans to ward committees which were co-ordinated and passed on not to the district council but to the civil servant-run district development committees. Ministry representatives on the development committees were supposed to incorporate ward plans into a district plan which would then be 'approved' by the council and passed on to the provincial development committee, again dominated by civil servants. In practice, vidcos rarely came up with more than lists of 'needs', ward committees hardly functioned at all, and district councils were not in a position to challenge plans produced by ministry officials. Instead, largely on the basis of submissions from service and technical ministries, plans were produced by departments of the Ministry of Local Government. Even some committees of the district council, particularly those concerned with the highly politicised area of land use, were dominated by appointed technical officials. The formulation and implementation of by-laws regulating the use of natural resources were likewise the province of technical ministries, despite a nod to the participation of councils (Thomas, 1991). Local authorities were thus left with some of the principal weaknesses of Rhodesian community development: though they were free to articulate 'felt needs', they were not in a position to redress them; ministries regarded local authorities primarily as policy implementing, not formulating, agencies; planning remained the realm of 'experts' employed by the government.

Failures to decentralise power to elected local authorities were parallelled by failures to achieve the lesser goals of devolution within and co-ordination among ministries through development planning. Despite the creation of the Ministry of Economic Planning and Development, and the emphasis on national planning to direct the transition to socialism, the central government's planning capabilities remained weak. The pre-independence Ministry of Finance, through the annual budget, dominated the allocation of resources: 'economic management took an essentially short-run, fiscal and external balance stabilisation orientation' (Khadani, 1986:111). The Ministries of Finance and of Economic Planning and Development were amalgamated in 1985.

In practice, the planning and finance ministries were represented only at the national level. Below the national level, the Ministry of Local Government dominated planning and the co-ordination of policy implementation. Despite the time and resources the Ministry put into planning, provincial and district plans were almost totally ignored and held no legal status. The Provincial Administrator for Matabeleland South commented:

The planning process ... is not affected much by decentralisation. The planning process is affected by the fact that power still rests with central government. If you are going to plan and plans are going to be workable you also need to control the budget. Power still remains in Harare and they still think that money cannot be decentralized. Vidcos and Wadcos, PDCs and DDCs are planning and the money is controlled elsewhere. They end up with good plans which are not implemented. (interview, 23 August 1988)

To add insult to injury, the Ministry of Finance did not even allocate funds for the production of provincial and district plan documents. The competition and conflict among centralised and autonomous ministries and departments which characterised the Rhodesian era continued. Despite the fact that technical and service ministries were represented on, and were supposed to co-ordinate their actions through, provincial and district development committees, they operated within the hierarchical structures of their own ministries. Diverse problems emerged from the failure to decentralise budgets and to empower co-ordinating committees at lower levels. Ministries formulated the details of projects and plans after the Cabinet had approved the national plan: where Cabinet directives were vague, and they often were, the ministry concerned could impose its own interpretations. If budget allocations were curtailed or redirected, entire programmes could be cut, despite their nominal inclusion in the plan. If a policy required the co-ordination of several ministries, such as was the case with agrarian reform, contradictory or redundant steps at local levels often ensued. In independent Zimbabwe, the government's decentralising rhetoric, the greater legitimacy and sympathy for local concerns of black civil servants and the presence of MPs and Provincial Governors, did allow room for contesting the control of the central government and for patronage. Nonetheless, and as in many other countries in Africa, Zimbabwe's decentralisation policies disguised a desire to ease the implementation of centrally formulated policies and increase control. The processes through which post-independence agrarian policies were formulated and implemented reflected the failures of decentralisation: continuities in centralised control reinforced the powerful influence which Rhodesian policies and practices exerted over agrarian reform.

Bibliography

Agritex (1988), 'The Communal Area Reorganisation Programme: Agritex Approach', discussion paper, Harare.
Alexander, J. (1991), 'The Unsettled Land: The Politics of Land Redistribution in Matabeleland', *Journal of Southern African Studies* 17,4; (1993), 'The State, Agrarian Policy and Rural Politics in Zimbabwe: Case Studies of Insiza and Chimanirnani Districts, 1940-1990' (D.Phil: Oxford); (1986), Association of District Councils, Minutes of the Third Annual Congress, mimeo.
Bratton, M. (1987), 'The Comrades and the Countryside: The Politics of Agrarian Reform in Zimbabwe', *World Politics,* 39,2.
Bush, R. & L. Cliffe (1984), 'Agrarian Policy in Migrant Labour Societies: Reform or Transformation in Zimbabwe', *Review of African Political Economy,* 29.
Chavanduka Commission (1982), Government of Zimbabwe, *Report of the Commission of Inquiry into the Agricultural Industry,* Harare: Government Printer.
Cliffe, L. (1986), 'Policy Options for Agrarian Reform: A Technical Appraisal', report submitted by the FAO for the consideration of the Government of Zimbabwe.
Cousins, B. (1990), 'Property and Power in Zimbabwe's Communal Lands: Implications for Agrarian Reform in the 1990s', Land Policy in Zimbabwe After 'Lancaster' Conference, University of Zimbabwe.
Drinkwater, M. (1988), 'The State and Agrarian Change in Zimbabwe's Communal Areas: An Application of Critical Theory', Ph.D, University of East Anglia (now published by Macmillan, 1989), 'Technical Development and Peasant Impoverishment: Land Use Policy in Zimbabwe's Midlands Province', *Journal of Southern African Studies,* 15, 2.
Gasper, D. (1988), 'Rural Growth Points and Rural Industries in Zimbabwe: Ideologies and Policies',

Development and Change, 19; (1990), 'What Happened to the Land Question in Zimbabwe? Rural Reform in the 1980s', The Hague: Institute of Social Studies, paper presented to EADI General Conference, Oslo; (1991), 'Decentralization of Planning and Administration in Zimbabwe: International Perspectives and 1980s Experiences' in Helmsing et al.

Gonese, F. (1988), 'A Framework for Communal Land Reorganisation in Zimbabwe', Seminar on Communal Lands Reorganisation, Harare: DURUDE.

Government of Zimbabwe (1981), *Growth with Equity: An Economic Policy Statement,* Harare: Government Printer; (1982a), *Transitional National Development Plan: 1982/83–1984/85,* Harare: Amalgamated Press; (1982b), *District Council Handbook,* Vol. 1, Harare: Government Printer; (1986), *First Five Year National Development Plan, 1986–1990,* Vol. 1, Harare: Government Printer; (1988), *First Five Year National Development Plan, 1986–1990,* Vol. I, Harare: Government Printer.

Harare Agrarian Reform Seminar (1988), Department of Rural Development in Collaboration with the FAO, 'Summary Report of the Seminar on Agrarian Reform and Communal Area Reorganisation', Harare.

Helmsing, A. et al. (1991), *Limits to Decentralization,* The Hague: Institute of Social Studies.

Herbst, J. (1990), *State Politics in Zimbabwe,* Harare: University of Zimbabwe.

Khadani, X. (1986), 'The Economy: Issues, Problems and Prospects' in I. Mandaza (ed.), *Zimbabwe: The Political Economy of Transition,* Dakar: Codesria.

Kinsey, B. (1983), 'Emerging Policy Issues in Zimbabwe's Land Resettlement Programmes', *Development Policy Review,* 1.

Kriger, N. (1992), *Zimbabwe's Guerrilla War: Peasant Voices,* Cambridge: Cambridge University Press.

Ministry of Economic Planning and Development (1981), *Zimbabwe Conference on Reconstruction and Development (ZIMCORD): Report on Conference Proceedings,* Salisbury: Government Printer.

Ministry of Lands, Resettlement and Rural Development (1985), *Communal Lands Development Plan: A 15 Year Development Strategy,* Harare.

Ministry of Local Government and Town Planning (1985), *Delineation of Village and Ward Development Committee Areas in District Council Areas of Zimbabwe,* Harare: Government Printer.

Moyo, S. (1986), 'The Land Question' in I. Mandaza (ed), *Zimbabwe: The Political Economy of Transition 1980-1986,* Dakar: Codesria; (1990), 'The Zimbabweanisation of Southern Africa's Agrarian Question: Lessons or Domino Strategems?', Harare: Zimbabwe Institute of Development Studies; (1991), 'The Role of Agriculture in Zimbabwe: Some Initial Findings', Zimbabwe Institute of Development Studies Seminar on Zimbabwe's ESAP, Kadoma; (1989), 'Medium and Long Term Prospects for Economic Development and Employment in Zimbabwe: Agriculture', Harare: Zimbabwe Institute of Development Studies.

Moyo, S. & T. Skalnes (1990), *Zimbabwe's Land Reform and Development Strategy: State Autonomy, Class Bias and Economic Rationality,* Harare: Zimbabwe Institute of Development Studies.

Murapa, R. (1986), *Rural and District Administrative Reform in Zimbabwe,* Bordeaux: Centre D'Etude D'Afrique Noire.

Ncube, W. (1991), 'Constitutionalism, Democracy and Political Practices in Zimbabwe' in I. Mandaza and L. Sachikonye (eds), *The One Party State and Democracy: The Zimbabwe Debate,* Harare: SAPES.

Nyanga Symposium, Department of Rural Development in collaboration with the FAO, 1987, 'Report on the National Symposium on Agrarian Reform in Zimbabwe', Nyanga.

Palmer, R. (1990), 'Land Reform in Zimbabwe, 1980–1990', *African Affairs,* 98, 355.

Ranger, T. (1988), 'The Communal Areas of Zimbabwe', Symposium on Land Reform in African Agrarian Systems, Urbana: University of Illinois.

Reynolds, N. & P. Ivy (1984), 'Proposals for a National Land Use Programme', Harare: Agritex.

Riddell Commission (1981), Government of Zimbabwe, *Report of the Commission of Inquiry into Incomes, Prices and Conditions of Service,* Harare: Government Printer.

Scoones, I. & K. Wilson (1988), 'Households, Lineage Groups and Ecological Dynamics: Issues for Livestock Research and Development in Zimbabwe's Communal Areas' in B. Cousins et al. (eds), *Socio-Economic Dimensions of Livestock Production in the Communal Lands of Zimbabwe,* Harare: Centre for Applied Social Studies, University of Zimbabwe.

Stoneman, C. (1988), 'The Economy: Recognizing the Reality', in C. Stoneman (ed.), *Zimbabwe's Prospects: Issues of Race, Class, State and Capital in Southern Africa,* London: Macmillan.

Stoneman C. & L. Cliffe (1989), *Zimbabwe: Politics, Economics and Society,* New York: Pinter Publishers.

Thomas, S. (1991), 'The Legacy of Dualism and Decision-Making: The Prospects for Local Institutional Development in "Campfire"', Harare: Centre for Applied Social Sciences, University of Zimbabwe.

Weiner, D. (1988), 'Land and Agricultural Development' in C. Stoneman (ed.), *Zimbabwe's Prospects: Issues of Race, Class, State and Capital in Southern Africa,* London: Macmillan; (1989), 'Agricultural Restructuring in Zimbabwe and South Africa', *Development and Change,* 20, 3; (1985), 'Land Use and Agricultural Productivity in Zimbabwe', *Journal of Modern African Studies,* 23, 2.

Weitzer, R (1984), 'In Search of Regime Security: Zimbabwe Since Independence', *Journal of Modern African Studies,* 2, 4.

Werbner, R (1991), *Tears of the Dead: The Social Biography of an African Family,* London: Edinburgh University Press.

Whitsun Foundation (1983), 'Land Reform in Zimbabwe', Harare.

World Bank (1985), *Zimbabwe: Land Sector Study,* Report No. 5878ZIM; (1991), Zimbabwe: Agricultural Sector Memorandum, Vol. 11, Report No. 9429ZIM.

22 YUSUF BANGURA
Structural Adjustment
& the Political Question
[1987]

The call for a national debate on Nigeria's political future has so far generated a lukewarm response. However, several tendencies have appeared which have serious implications for the struggle for democracy. Coming in the wake of the debate about Nigeria's relations with the International Monetary Fund (IMF), one would have thought that the 'political debate' would have been informed by the specific problems the economy is experiencing and the concrete adjustment policies the state has persistently implemented since 1982. Even some of the radicals who ought to have drawn the correct lessons from the diversionary tactics of the state in the IMF debate have tended to proceed as if we are starting from a *tabula rasa*, without any concrete economic policies which inform the state's quest for a new political order. This partly explains the reason for the strange convergence which seems to be developing between some radicals and the bourgeoisie in the articulation of a new political formula.

The thrust of this paper is to discuss the link between the state's adjustment programme and the question of political power. We argue that the adjustment programme of contemporary monetarism, which reached its highest expression in the 1986 budget, throws up specific types of political regimes ranging from zero/one and controlled two-party systems to military rule, civil/military diarchy and corporate representation. Against the background of the specific character of capitalist accumulation, with its monopolistic, anti-democratic and corrupt practices, the monetarist strategy of crisis-management pushes the state towards more authoritarian policies. Many contributors to the political debate have not grasped this point. The appropriate response to authoritarian rule should, therefore, focus on the struggle for democracy and the strengthening of the working class movement for socialist power instead of the strategy of co-determination which seeks to resolve the conflicting interests in the society under a unitary power structure that will accommodate the representatives of popular organisations.

Theoretical Issues: Structural Adjustment & Political Power

In this section, we emphasise the dictum that specific adjustment policies throw up specific types of politics and institutional structures. Capitalism has historically been distinguished by the 'freedom' it offers the wage workers in contracting their labour power which can be transferred from one employer to another; other pre-capitalist extra-economic forms of coercion give way to the 'dull compulsion of the economic system'. The 'fair exchange' which the market exhibits provides a very powerful ideological prop by concealing the relations of exploitation between the workers and the employers, insisting that wages paid to the workers are equal to the total value produced by them, leaving profits as the legitimate earnings of the employers. The ideology of free exchange was historically buttressed by liberal democracy which guaranteed workers their right to earn a legitimate wage and improve upon their conditions of living through collective bargaining and the formation of independent trade unions and political parties. Bourgeois democracy protected the 'economic rights' of the workers as they were reproduced by the fundamentally lopsided capitalist system.

Gough has shown how, on the one hand, the working class in Western democracies has used these liberal institutions to extend the frontiers of democracy and working class power and, on the other, how these very institutions have checked the militancy of the working class in the struggle for socialist construction.

Liberal democracy has not made any major impact in the Less Developed Countries (LDCs) even though the capitalist mode remains dominant. Capitalism arrived in the LDCs at the monopoly stage of its development. 'The political superstructure of this new economy, of monopoly capitalism', Lenin observed, 'is the change from democracy to political reaction.' Force and superior monopoly power were used to impose authoritarian colonial rule. Initially, the emergent elites were strong advocates of liberal democracy, but their transformation into a segment of the ruling class has forced them to dispense with democratic practices since they now depend upon monopoly power and the misappropriation of public funds for their development. Such practices undoubtedly promote thuggery and authoritarian rule as the appropriate forms of political behaviour.

Unmistakeably, the underlying competitive and free contractual relations which characterised the classical capitalist system in the form of bourgeois democracy have not occurred in Nigeria and other LDCs. The bourgeois forces, local and foreign, are not primarily interested in democracy as it does not correspond with their current aspirations; and the opposing class forces are yet too weak to enforce it. The current global economic crisis has occurred within the context of this general authoritarian tendency in the developing countries.

Structural adjustment seeks to further weaken the limited strength of the working class and strengthen that of the bourgeoisie by its insistence on the market mechanism as the primary regulatory force for the allocation of resources. The current IMF-inspired monetarist package is an antidote to the earlier Keynesian structural adjustment strategy that followed the depression of the 1930s. The latter's major emphasis was on state intervention to regulate distortions and inequalities in the market. It was correctly assumed that the market mechanism, on its own, would not be able to create the proper equilibrium relationships to foster stability and growth. The current crisis, occurring in the midst of massive state intervention, has strengthened the hands of the monetarists who insist on a return to the classical free market philosophy. Overvalued third world currencies, inefficient state-run enterprises, disequilibria between income and expenditure, import controls and subsidies are all seen by the high priests of monetarism as obstacles to the market mechanism in correcting distortions in price and cost relationships and restoring a balance at the domestic and payments level.

The core of the strategy is to spend not more than the available national earnings, allow the currency to find its level and liberalise the economy. The logic is quite straightforward and simple. If a country suffers from a balance of payments deficit it means that country's currency (in reality its commodities) is less in demand compared to the foreign currencies with which the country trades. The country can, therefore, correct its payments deficit by allowing the currency, ideally, to float until it finds its correct level, or to be devalued sufficiently to eliminate the distortion. This should discourage imports, promote more exports, attract more foreign investment to generate more production in the medium to long run to offset the short-run inflation. The country does not need to impose any controls on imports and exports as the market mechanism should do the job perfectly well. Once this fundamental logic is accepted the other fiscal measures fall in line, such as regulating the money supply to control public expenditure, removing subsidies and privatising the inefficiently run public enterprises. The various social classes are then forced to return to the naked forces of the 'free market'.

Although the theory derives its strength from the supposedly free contractual relations between buyers and sellers at the factor and products market, it should be obvious that the aim is to weaken the organised power of the working class and strengthen that of the business class. Contemporary capitalism has demonstrated a strong tendency towards monopoly, assisted, by and large, by an interventionist state. Organised labour has responded by forming strong trade unions, enabling them to demand high wages, welfare, allowances and bonuses outside the parameters of the free market which has ceased to exist. The monetarist strategy wants to break this limited political power of the working class without destroying the monopolistic power of the bourgeoisie. In fact, it seeks to consolidate and expand the latter's power.

Even though the working people have benefited from the expansion of public expenditure, they have done so within a subordinate position, with the monopoly firms reaping greater benefits in the supply of the inputs and commodities and the misappropriation of some of the allocated funds. Privatisation will only further enrich the monopolies, widen the gap between the rich and the poor, and force the workers to pay the new monopoly price of the goods and services. Also, devaluation will help the monopoly firms who will pass on the import cost to the final consumer. There are so many rigidities in the world market that there is no guarantee that foreign investment will respond adequately enough to promote local production and offset the short-run inflation. The cost of production will increase which the firms can only offset by price increases. The monopolistic control of the primary products makes it difficult to realise any meaningful gains from devaluation. The market does not operate independently of primary products associations and transnational corporations. Even the non-primary products exports are not likely to take off the ground since they will, in the final analysis, depend upon the goodwill of the transnational firms and the highly protected markets of the Western governments.

No wonder this strategy has not been successful anywhere in tackling the problems of underdevelopment. All it has succeeded in doing is to depress the living conditions of the poor people by changing domestic incomes and prices and creating some balance in the domestic and external account at the expense of basic social services. It even requires a massive dose of the adjustment programme to get this far.

Such a programme has very serious implications for political relations. It requires authoritarian policies to check the inevitable popular opposition to the package.

Such policies have tended to vary from a zero/one/two-party civilian dictatorship (Acheampong's Unigov scheme, Nigeria under the National Party of Nigeria government, 1983, Zambia, Senegal) to a military dictatorship (Buhari, Zaire) or a civil-military diarchy, (Liberia under Doe, a prototype in Sierra Leone), to a corporate system that will involve the co-optation of some of the leading members of popular organisations that will serve as rationalisers of the adjustment package (Rawlings' Ghana). multiparty systems are considered to be inappropriate since they tend to allow for some level of democracy and opposition; except, of course, if these parties can be controlled in such a way that they do not threaten the adjustment programme.

In many cases civilian dictatorships fail to adequately respond to the issues at stake and compel the military to take over power. But the problems of developing a Bonapartist military state, alienating some sections of the bourgeoisie, necessitate some marriage between the civilians and the military (diarchy). In some cases the military is called in to head the government in a single party structure, with the civilians and some service chiefs serving as ministers and presidential advisers (currently in Liberia and Sierra Leone). But such authoritarian systems usually face unrelenting opposition from the generality of the people as the economic crisis deepens. The rulers are then forced to support another variant of authoritarianism, but one which claims to involve the people through their organisations. This is co-determination or corporate representation, involving the participation of trade union leaders, students' leaders, religious leaders, farmers' leaders, chairpersons of employers' organisations and other elite groups. This is what Rawlings has tried to implement in Ghana but it is currently facing very serious opposition from the working class and some of the corporate organisations themselves.

In a recession, the bourgeoisie is largely indifferent to a multiparty system, except if it can control it; it strongly supports a zero or one-party or a military dictatorship to shore up the capitalist economy against popular opposition; it may also support a two-party system if both parties are bourgeois-inclined, or a diarchy that will institutionalise civil/military authoritarian rule if civil bourgeois rule has failed. It, in fact, prefers a diarchy to outright military rule; it will support corporate representation, if only to contain the militancy of the workers and other radical political groups. The Nigerian case has exhibited these tendencies.

The Empirical Context: Structural Adjustment & Authoritarian Rule

The Presidential System & the Single Party Dominant Tendency

Shagari's administration inherited a constitutional system that was tailored along the presidential model. Against the background of the failure of military rule under Gowon and the upsurge of popular demand for democratic rule, the architects of presidential civil rule, Murtala/Obasanjo, had hoped to bequeath to the Nigerian people a more lasting democratic system. The choice of the presidential system itself reflected the difficulties encountered with the loose parliamentary system in the 1960s, which was believed to have contributed to the collapse of the First Republic. The growing strength and fractious character of the bourgeoisie demanded a much more centralised political system. Such a tendency towards centralisation had, in fact, already started in the late 1960s and the first half of the 1970s, with the creation of states, changes in revenue allocation in favour of the centre and the establishment of various federal parastatals.

However, presidential civil rule was anything but democratic. Indeed, the presidential system itself which was to usher in democracy had effectively disenfranchised organised labour by its insistence that trade unions cannot form or fund political parties. Even when proletarian parties emerged and sought registration, the state-controlled Federal Electoral Commission (FEDECO) refused to register them, and only conceded at the last minute to the registration of the Peoples' Redemption Party as a token concession to the Left.

Even before the economic crisis erupted, the political system demonstrated very strong authoritarian tendencies. Shortly after Shagari was sworn in, in 1979, the caucus of his party, the National Party of Nigeria, approached the Unity Party of Nigeria, the

Nigerian Peoples Party, the Great Nigerian Peoples' Party and the PRP to form a government of national unity. It was when this policy failed that the NPN entered into an alliance with the NPP to bulldoze the president's bills through the House of Representatives and Senate. The other political parties responded by forming ad hoc alliances such as the meetings of the 'Progressive Governors' which were aimed at checking federal power, particularly in the allocation of resources. The increasingly authoritarian rule of the NPN pushed these parties to form the Progressive Peoples' Alliance (PPA) and ultimately the Progressive Peoples Party (PPP), which comprised the NPP and factions of the PRP and GNPP. The NPN, acting through FEDECO, blocked the registration of the PPP, but instead registered the rather colourless and amorphous Nigerian Advanced Party (NAP) 'with the hope that it will be a serious nuisance to the UPN'(Ake Presidential Address NPSA).

Shagari's administration deepened the forces of import-substitution at the level of industry and agriculture, intensified corruption and squandered substantial resources. The economy was in crisis by 1981, requiring stringent adjustment measures and the consolidation of bourgeois political power. The April 1982 Economic Stabilisation Act was the logical outcome of the crisis. Among other things, it called for public expenditure cuts, a wage freeze, import controls and other demand management measures, using fiscal and monetary policies. The government also entered into negotiations with the IMF for a stabilisation loan of $2.56 billion and with the foreign creditors for debt rescheduling and the reopening of the credit lines.

Obviously, the programme was not on all fours with the classical monetarist package. It failed to remove subsidies from petroleum, fertilisers and rice, insisted on an over-valued naira and refused to liberalise the economy. The dominant business class, party stalwarts and sections of the elite had made fortunes out of the over-valued currency by transferring huge amounts of money abroad. Furthermore, some of the parastatals were a conduit pipe for siphoning public resources. These private forces also controlled the subsidies on rice, fertilisers and food. The Fund's package required a high level of bourgeois discipline which the regime could not provide. The deepening crisis, however, made it imperative for the government to push for far more authoritarian policies to retain control of the economy and impose its own solution on the crisis. The main obstacles were (a) the general popular opposition from the working class and its allies, as represented, in the main, by the Nigerian Labour Congress, the students movement and the academic unions; (b) the threats from the opposition political parties in the north, such as the PRP and GNPP, controlling large areas considered to be natural constituencies for the NPN; and (c) the fragmentation of the bourgeois forces themselves along regionalist lines.

The official plan which seemed to have been unfolding was to disorganise and control the working class opposition, narrow the base of popular participation by limiting the effective political parties to one or two, strengthen the repressive arm of the state and impose some unity on the bourgeoisie. The NPN itself was a coalition of various forces, representing, in the main, the surviving forces of the NPC oligarchy, the rising petit-bourgeois Kaduna Mafia which had played a role in the post-1966 period as the vanguard for the development of the northern bourgeoisie and a motley crowd of southern petit-bourgeois and bourgeois elements that were anxious to either protect their businesses at the federal level or felt the party offered them better opportunities to ward off local competitors.

The core of the Left forces remained fragmented, forming various splinter groups and parties that were mainly active at the level of labour relations. The state, under Obasanjo, had tried to arrest the Left's influence in the trade union movement by its major labour restructuring programme of 1975/78. In demanding a much more central-ised trade union congress and the purging of the more consistent radicals from trade union activity, the state had hoped it could create a more pliable trade union movement. The trade union decree 31, section 15 of 1973 had prevented unions from funding or forming political parties, and the 1978 trade union act that established the NLC had tried to promote an orientation of civil-service professionalism in the running of the unions themselves with the hope that this might steer the unions away from politics. The 1978 NLC elections, however, recorded a resounding defeat for the state and its preferred candidates and a confirmation of the Left's strength within the labour movement. A desperate attempt was made by Shagari's administration in the elections of 1981 in Kano to support the compromised candidacy of Ojeli, the president of the Civil Service Workers' Union. It was the failure of such attempts that led to the strenuous and intimi-dating moves by the NPN to repeal the trade union act of 1978 (which had called for a single central labour organisation), to allow for the proliferation of several labour organ-isations and weaken the militancy of the NLC. This was after the NLC had demonstrated its organisational and leadership ability to defend workers' interests in the national strike of 1981 that led to the N125 minimum wage. Similar problems were encountered with the students' movement and academic staff unions. The regime was, however, unable to impose its will on these organisations. Although the Left itself, acting through these bodies, checked some of the excesses of the federal and state governments, it was not strong enough to sustain the democratic programme and create a liberal atmosphere that would eliminate the various anti-labour decrees and authoritarian practices.

The administration made considerable headway with regard to the other two objectives, imposing bourgeois authoritarian unity and tackling the problems of the opposition in the north. The NPN cashed in on the contradictions of the PRP by encouraging splits within the party and siding with the more reactionary elements against the radicals, thereby arresting the militant potentials of the party. This was backed by a systematic campaign against the governorship of Balarabe Musa in Kaduna State and his ultimate impeachment. By the eve of the 1983 elections, the NPN had made considerable inroads into the PRP and GNPP by refusing to register the PPP, promoting and exploiting splits within the PRP and GNPP and converting the strong Mallam Aminu Kano faction in Kano, now under Bakin Zuwo, into an NPN satellite. What remained was the flushing out of the PRP from executive power in Kaduna, the GNPP from Gongola and Borno and the substantial penetration of the UPN and NPP strongholds in the West and East respectively. The results of the 1983 elections with the NPN 'winning' seven of the ten northern states and Bendel, Anambra, Oyo and Ondo apart from Rivers and Cross Rivers in the South confirmed the NPN's drive for com-plete hegemony. The judiciary, the police and FEDECO were heavily compromised. The death of 'democracy' was imminent. The structures for a de facto dominant one-party rule were being laid.

The regime did not, however, have any solutions to the crisis. The industrial scene remained very volatile as companies either closed down, resorted to compulsory leave or reduced the working days. Many workers, civil servants and teachers were owed large amounts of wages and salaries. This situation sparked off a series of strikes by the affected unions. There was also quite a lot of dissatisfaction from the companies with the import deposit scheme and the way in which import licences were allocated.

Military Dictatorship

The ineffectiveness and alienation of Shagari's administration forced a military coup on 31 December 1983. The scale of adjustment which would have the intended effect on the income, price and cost structure required a much more disciplined regime. Notwithstanding its general authoritarian orientation, Shagari's administration had shown a clear incapacity to provide political leadership to the bourgeoisie. Even members of its own northern constituency, the so-called Kaduna Mafia, made serious contacts with the UPN to ditch the NPN. The UPN was seen as a more disciplined and efficient party, given the fact that the core of its leadership and financiers were well connected with industry and commerce. Furthermore, the near de facto one-party rule did not silence the growing popular opposition. The military solution therefore became imperative to save the political system from mass riots, prolonged uncertainty and stagnation.

Indeed Buhari's regime demonstrated the type of discipline the adjustment strategy required. It was anxious to rationalise the domestic capitalist base, impose some discipline on Shagari's austerity measures and push the adjustment programme a step further to encompass more public expenditure cuts, the curtailment of external borrowings, the imposition of a ceiling on domestic loans and the introduction of a package of other economic measures aimed at controlling local demand. A massive purge of the public service was executed, a wage freeze and various types of levies were imposed and a campaign against indiscipline was instituted.

The structures of repression were consolidated and deepened. There were the special decrees 1, 2 and 4 banning political party activities, giving unlimited powers to the Chief of Staff to detain without trial anybody considered to be a security risk, and the control of the investigative role of the press making it possible to detain journalists who publish information that was likely to embarrass a public officer, irrespective of the veracity of the story. Specific decrees were also passed aimed at legalising the state onslaught on the economic and political power of workers, such as decrees 16 and 17 which prevented workers from seeking legal redress against retrenchment and discouraging automatic payment of all benefits when retrenched. There were also other obnoxious decrees carrying the death penalty or long prison terms for common crimes like cocaine trafficking. As the crisis deepened and the opposition intensified, the government took another major step of banning all forms of political debate.

There was no question about the determination of the regime to use authoritarian measures to solve the economic crisis. However, even though the adjustment programme was already causing a lot of hardship, it did not go far enough in meeting the IMF demands which were aimed not just at the use of the fiscal instrument to control public expenditure but also the comprehensive implementation of far-reaching measures that will completely eliminate distortions in domestic costs and prices. This required massive devaluation, removal of subsidies from petrol and fertilisers, privatisation and the liberalisation of the economy. A stalemate developed between the regime and the IMF. The principal creditors refused to open the credit lines, forcing the regime to experiment with counter-trade and to raise the debt service ratio to 44 per cent. The latter was mainly a carrot to the foreign bankers to open the credit lines and reschedule the debts.

Although the regime refused to swallow wholesale the IMF adjustment measures, it was more than prepared to defend the capitalist economy against local working class and radicalised petit bourgeois forces. The adjustment plan had put it on a course of confrontation with the students over fees and food subsidies in May 1984, the doctors in 1985 over conditions of work and resource allocation to the medical sector, and various other categories of workers whose standard of living had massively deteriorated, daily haunted by the spectre of retrenchment. The National Association of Nigerian Students, the Nigerian Medical Association, the National Association of Resident Doctors and the pilots' union were later banned for daring to challenge the government. Many workers, doctors, pilots, traders and road-side mechanics lost their jobs and a good number of students were expelled or rusticated from the universities. A climate of fear gripped the workers unions, particularly the NLC whose internal contradictions intensified, rendering it ineffective in responding to the mass retrenchment. The authoritarian tendency of the regime increased with every victory over the popular organisations. The NSO had a field day; innocent people were arrested and kept in cells, tortured without inhibitions. The judiciary, the last bastion of bourgeois justice, was rendered impotent. The stage was actually set for a fascist dictatorship.

The government was, however, seriously alienated from all sections of the populace. Popular struggles continued, some overt, like those of the students, others covert like the biting cartoons of the journalists and some of the work of sections of the Left in explaining the fascist tendencies of the regime to the general public. What compounded the problem, moreover, was the failure to arrive at an agreement with the Fund, making it difficult to open the credit lines, reschedule the debts and reduce the burden on industry and the domestic economy generally. The economic crisis deepened under Buhari. Elements of the bourgeoisie and sections of the military were also alienated. Many people of property had been disgraced, jailed and had some of their assets seized after public probes. The national composition of the Supreme Military Council had also come under serious attacks from the Southern politicians and conservative sections of the petit bourgeoisie, supported by calls for confederacy. Sections of the military within and outside the SMC were also alienated. Military dictatorship did not endear itself to most of the principal class combatants except, of course, the Kaduna Mafia which was accused of controlling the government. A new solution was needed. Buhari's regime had to go, and it did on 27 August 1985.

The Quest for Diarchy & Corporate Representation

When Buhari's regime fell, sections of the Western press were confident that this was the first IMF coup in Africa. They were convinced that Buhari's intransigence in implementing the full conditions of the IMF had necessitated a coup to end the stalemate and push the economy to the full rigours of the market mechanism. The decision to have a debate on the IMF beclouded the issues at the beginning. Some argued that the regime wanted to be guided by the advice of the public whilst others maintained that if the regime was actually anti-IMF it would not have called for a debate in the first place. In any case, the government had appointed a technical team of orthodox pro-IMF economists, Kalu and Okongwu, to head the Finance and Planning ministries respectively. Subsequently developments showed that the pronouncements of the Western media were not actually far off the mark.

Even though the public was unequivocal in its opposition to the IMF, the government's 1986 budget pushed the adjustment programme to its logical monetarist conclusion. For the first time in the history of the crisis, a regime now exists which is ready to reason along the lines of the IMF by insisting on the correlation between stringent fiscal measures and a comprehensive structural adjustment programme that will elevate the full forces of the 'free market' to a hegemonic position in the economy. The budget was unequivocal in its support for privatisation, removal of subsidies from petroleum, export promotion, an appropriate market level for the naira, cuts in salaries and wages and a commitment to future liberalisation. Although the government has not accepted the IMF loan, a very good relationship now exists between it and the creditors. There are plans to even involve the IMF at the higher surveillance level to facilitate the rescheduling of the debts.

Now that the adjustment programme has been pushed this far, the policymakers are seriously concerned about establishing an appropriate political system to support the economic programme. This, I believe, is the major reason for the 'political debate' and the decision of the government to include the political questions in the 1986 budget. As we have seen, the concentration of power under civil rule, gravitating towards a de facto one-party system, has been tried under Shagari and found wanting; military dictatorship which exhibited the appropriate type of discipline has also been tried under Buhari without success. The political system remains unstable. Authoritarianism seems, however, to be a constant factor. Such a massive assault on the purchasing power and standard of living of the toiling people is not likely to go unchallenged. This explains why the core of the repressive Decrees, 1, 2, 16 and 17 have not been repealed and why the government has sought extra powers to reduce the wages and salaries of workers without reference to the contractual agreements.

However, the regime seems to have learnt a few lessons from the failure of the Buhari/Idiagbon military dictatorship by espousing human rights, exposing the NSO, appealing to the people to debate controversial issues, repealing decree 4 and lifting the ban on popular organisations.[1] It has tried to cut the image of a populist government, making token concessions to an undefined rural mass by promising to provide feeder roads to the rural areas using the revenue accruing from the removal of subsidies, increasing the allocation of money to health and education, removing the tax on workers' gratuity and extending the pay cut to companies' and landlords' profits and rents. All of this is supposed to be happening within the context of the most class-conscious Nigerian budget since 1960. This image of populism has been extended to the level of politics where the regime has tried to involve popular leaders and organisations in various areas of decision-making, and checking the so-called mafia domination of the SMC in the Armed Forces Ruling Council by giving some leverage to minority and southern elements who were dissatisfied with the ethnic composition of the Buhari regime. It has also tried to appease some of the disgraced politicians and businessmen by having their cases re-examined and releasing some of them from detention and prison.

There are strong indications that the state is keen on experimenting with the third variant of authoritarian rule – the institutionalisation of the military in politics (diarchy) and corporate representation which will involve the participation of a cross-section of the leaders of popular organisations in government. The government's pronouncements and some of its policies point to this direction even though corporate representation is not yet an official policy. Developments like the involvement of the leadership of the NLC to advise on how to extend the burden of economic recovery to other sectors of the economy in October 1985 when the NLC attempted to resist pay cuts, the experimentation with the 'People's Parliament' in Rivers State which involves consultations with local leaders of thought and selected individuals, and the 'popular spread' of the Kuru conference held to chart a new foreign policy for the country and the resolution of that conference to form a 'broadbased' foreign relations council to monitor the administration of foreign policy, provide some indications about this tendency to evolve a political system based on diarchy and corporate representation. Its implementation will actually require some changes in the organisation of state power to accommodate these new forces.

Corporate representation aims to buy off some of the leading sections of the popular organisations to legitimise government policy. Its objective is to smooth over the antagonistic class relations and prevent a radical, independent mass-based attack on the adjustment programme.

The current debate is already throwing some light on the political options of the ruling class. Most of them have bought the president's aversion to foreign ideologies which they interpret as socialism and have been calling for indigenous political systems that will allow the country to fall back on traditional African political systems which are alleged to be humanitarian and classless. It is against this background that triarchy (rule by traditional rulers, the military and civilians), diarchy (military and civilians), zero and one party systems have been advocated; there has also been a strong call to re-impose the centralised presidential system. The bourgeois option will not go beyond these authoritarian parameters.

Petit-bourgeois Radical Nationalism & Corporate Representation

Corporate representation has been given unqualified support by the radical section of the petit-bourgeoisie. Attention has been drawn to the political orientation of key members of the political bureau whose political views are similar to those of the PRP and the Progressive Peoples Alliance/Progressive Peoples Party of the Second Republic. Their populist orientation has been buttressed in the Academic Staff Union of Universities-sponsored political debate in Kano by sections of the Progressive petit-bourgeoisie who have clear sympathies for the populism of the PRP in the Second Republic. Some of the contributions of the Left in the annual conference of the Nigerian Political Science Association on 'Alternative Political Futures' also exhibited this tendency. The thrust of the proposal is to preserve a percentage of seats and offices in all decision-making bodies for professional associations, workers' unions and farmers' organisations with the hope that this might check the predatory character of the ruling class and the manipulation of the popular electoral votes. Since the organisations of the common people are supposed to be in the majority, it is assumed that the Left will then be able to push for far more democratic policies as a first stage in the construction of socialism. But whereas some contributors maintain that this should be achieved within a one-party structure, others insist on a two-party or multiparty system. Undoubtedly, those who call for the implementation of corporate representation within a multiparty structure are actually trying to marry two irreconcilable party systems: the multiparty system of bourgeois democracy and the one-party systems of socialist democracy and capitalist corporate representation. Corporate representation, it should be emphasised, is only practicable in a *one-party system* since it involves the distribution of roles and responsibilities in a planned 'non-class' framework. In a capitalist system corporate representation seeks mainly to legitimise bourgeois rule, clip the wings of militants and blunt the fundamental class interests in the society. What is more, working class and petit-bourgeois corporate organisations usually exhibit tendencies ranging from radicalism to technical professionalism and conservatism. There is the actual danger of these organisations gravitating towards economism or becoming tools of the bourgeoisie if they fall into the hands of the latter two tendencies. This is why corporate organisations, on their own, cannot be relied upon to create socialism. They take the existing relations of exploitation for granted. In any case, the appropriate policy to adopt towards popular organisations in this period of intensified repression is to promote their democratic activities and defend their independence from governmental control.

The political strategy of corporatism is rooted in the economic programme of some of the Left groups, on the Nigerian economic crisis: nationalisation of foreign trade and key industrial and financial enterprises; national economic integration; workers' participation in the management and ownership of the factories, etc. In short, state capitalism. There is no doubt about the progressive character of these positions. State capitalism, as Lenin observed, is a step forward in the transition to socialism. Once state capitalism is established, the struggle shifts to a higher level between state capitalism and socialism on the one hand and private capitalism and small-scale proprietors (petit-bourgeoisie) on the other, with the petit-bourgeoisie becoming the principal enemy in the march towards socialism because of its petty but irritating profiteering, hoarding, stealing and other forms of economic sabotage. As the crisis pushes the bourgeoisie towards privatisation, it becomes imperative for socialists to defend state capitalism, within a 'revolutionary-democratic state' system. There is also the ideological need to combat the bogus free-wheeling capitalism which the monetarist adjustment package seeks to impose on the populace. Finally, state capitalism is an important stage in the struggle against the imperialist domination of the *national economy*.

The problem, however, arises in properly handling the class contradictions involved in the organisation of state capitalist power and mobilising the appropriate political forces in smashing bourgeois power and establishing the national revolutionary democratic state.

Some of these positions on the class basis of the state have been well articulated in the Poulantzas-Miliband-Laclau-Picciotto debate particularly as it relates to the role of individual representation and the structural imperatives of capitalist accumulation. At bottom, the class character of the state cannot be changed by simply swamping the state apparatus with the numerical strength of the working people. The capitalist state does not necessarily pursue popular policies by giving people of working class background even one hundred per cent representation in the state institutions. The issue goes beyond representation and involves the control of the major means of production and reconstituting the relations of production.

This tendency towards co-determination is also connected with the more backward aspects of underdevelopment and dependency theory which assumes that no development has taken place in the LDC economies, with the accumulation system geared towards the *absolute* transfer of the surplus or the wasting of the unremitted wealth locally. If all the assets are externally located it follows that the internal basis of bourgeois rule does not exist. Opposition to bourgeois rule does not, therefore, depend upon analysing the internal class structure and organising the working class and its class allies but in collaborating with an undefined classless mass which will simply outmatch the bourgeoisie by laying claims to honesty and patriotism. But the bourgeoisie is strong in Nigeria. The fact that it has a constitutional crisis should not be mistaken for the existence of a power vacuum. Furthermore, its foreign connections really put it in a very formidable position, however shaky its legitimacy.

The radical petit-bourgeoisie is desperate for political power. It is undoubtedly driven by patriotic instincts but lacks the proper organisational discipline and ideological clarity to relate with the working class movement. In its fits of desperation it can even go for the military vanguardist solution by lining up behind radical elements in the army to bring about a 'revolution' in the country. In such a case, it abandons its tenuous democratic line and pushes the nationalist position, further exposing the democratic and socialist forces to the commandist imperatives of the military.

Conclusion: An Alternative Political Future

The various strands of authoritarian rule and the monetarist adjustment package pose serious dangers to the struggle for democracy. Structural adjustment has reduced wages, allowances and bonuses and narrowed the employment opportunities, social services and purchasing power of the working class. It has eroded the seemingly democratic nature of the process of 'free exchange' embodied in classical bourgeois ideology. At the political level, various decrees and laws are in existence which affect the self-determination of the working people such as the legal prohibition of workers' appeals against retrenchment, non-payment of retrenchment benefits, the problems of forming workers' parties, free collective bargaining, right of workers in 'strategic' industries to strike, etc. There are also constraints on free political organisation and debate, the establishment of viable workers' newspapers, an 'independent' judiciary, the rule of law and free and fair elections. These are immediate short-term problems which seriously affect the development of the working class. The long-term problem is, of course, how to end wage-slavery which provides the motor for the sustenance of these undemocratic measures. This involves the struggle for socialism.

The struggle for socialism is linked with the struggle for democracy. Although 'the achievement of democracy is ... harder under imperialism there can be no talk of democracy being unachievable' (Lenin). The democratic struggle involves the destruction of the imperialist domination of the national economy. Finance capital prevents the rapid, all-round development of the productive forces and the national integration of the economy and politics. Some of these problems are already being tackled by the bourgeoisie because of the objective limitations of import-substitution industrialisation leading to the local sourcing of raw materials and the imperatives of rationalising national production and generating a culture of efficiency. But these cannot be fully achieved under capitalism since the objective class interests of even the local bourgeoisie are to expand and collaborate with foreign capital. In any case, bourgeois rationalisation is likely to experience serious stop-gaps, depending on the orientation of the state authorities and the character and discipline of the adjustment programme. For instance, the current export drive which is supported by an array of state subsidies is likely to kill the budding incentive for local sourcing of raw materials since the budget does not contain any penalties for export industries that rely on foreign raw materials. Instead, it is likely to reproduce the problems of dependence at a new and higher level where the gains (if any) that will be derived from exports will be offset by the costs of importing the inputs.

What is more, a bourgeois-led self-reliant economic restructuring programme holds great dangers for the working class in terms of employment and wages. Companies are likely to adopt new technology to save costs and will resort to compulsory leaves, reduced working days, forced savings and the curtailment of bonuses, allowances and other facilities which are now very common with many companies trying to remain afloat as the crisis deepens.

The struggle for democracy and economic self-reliance has to be seriously taken up by the working class and their unions in terms of preventing the cost of the rationalisation programmes from being passed on to the workers while at the same time insisting on more effective ways of sourcing local raw materials and establishing appropriate technology. Local sourcing and appropriate technology should form part of the workers' strategy of protecting jobs by insisting on the right to be informed about the total operations of the company and by being actively involved in determining the direction of the rationalisation programme.

The effective pursuit of these measures requires a concerted struggle for the dismantling of the stringent adjustment measures of the budget. Pay cuts, levies, privatisation, removal of subsidies, public expenditure cuts, devaluation and liberalisation should be halted. They seriously weaken the capacity of the workers to struggle for a more humane social transformation programme. Such struggles at the level of the economy will be difficult to sustain without an open, democratic climate. One-party rule, diarchy, corporate representation or military rule will not bring this about. They will only legitimise the authoritarian culture by branding those that operate outside of those structures as saboteurs. This is why the struggle for democracy is on the agenda.

In the current political debate the working class and its allies have the singular responsibility of advocating for a multiparty system to allow for a democratic culture to flower and the formation of a workers' party that will fight against the concentration of political power, defend the interests of the working people and lay the foundations for the struggle for socialism which is the only answer to mass poverty, continued retrenchment, inflation, debt-slavery, wage-cuts and authoritarian rule.

Note

1. M.Sc. Dissertation, Ahmed Bello University, 1984.

Bibliographical Notes

Gough, I., *The Political Economy of the Welfare State*, Macmillan, 1979; J. Petras, 'Neo-fascism: Capital Accumulation and Class Struggles in the Third World, *Journal of Contemporary Asia,* 10, 1, 1980; V. Osadchaya, *Keynesianism Today,* Progress Publishers, 1983; P. C. Assiodu, 'The Impact of the Oil Crisis on the Nigerian Economy', public lecture, Nigerian Economic Society, Kaduna, 20 April 1986.

Africa Development, Special Issue on Nigeria, IX, 3, 1984; J. Ibrahim, 'The Kaduna Mafia Syndrome and the New Nigerian' (mimeo), Zaria 1986; Y. Bangura, 'Nationalism, Accumulation and Labour Subordination (mimeo) Zaria 1985; S. Bako, 'The Peoples' Redemption Party and Class Struggles in Kano State' (M.Sc. dissertation, Ahmed Bello University, 1984).

West Africa, 7 April 1986, p. 711 (note that the NLC representatives later saw the futility of the tripartite consultative committee on pay cuts; Ismaila Mohammed, *Sunday Concord,* 27 April 1986; 'On the Political Alternatives Open to Nigeria in the Present Era: the night of the Working People to Political Self-Determination' presented by Z. A. Bonat to the ASUU Conference on the Political Debate, Bayero University, Kano, April 1986; A. Abba et al, *The Nigerian Economic Crisis: Causes and Solutions* (1985); Y. B. Usman, *Nigeria Against the IMF* (1986).

23 CAROLYN BAYLIES
'Political Conditionality' & Democratisation
[1995]

The use of aid to impose political conditions on recipient countries, to further democratic and government reforms or to punish non-compliance with earlier demands, is a relatively new feature of the international aid regime. This article evaluates the proliferating donor and academic literature emerging on the subject. At the heart of discussion of democracy/governance policies are debates about transformation of the state, its relationship to economic development and the decreasing extent to which considerations of sovereignty limit donor interventions. The author argues that, while political conditionalities may assist the development of democratic movements in Africa, there is an irony in that structural adjustment risks undermining the state reforms seen to be essential to them while, equally, democratisation may challenge the processes of economic restructuring being imposed.

The explicit use of aid to promote political change is a relatively recent development. It has tended to take two forms: first, the funding of governance and democratisation initiatives in countries undergoing political transition; and, second, the use of negative sanctions, either where progress is deemed to be unsatisfactory or in order to induce adoption of democratic procedures. To some extent it has involved the extension into the political realm of the conditionality which forms the basis of structural adjustment packages, representing thereby a substantial enlarging of the scope of donor involvement (and interference) in prescribing the agendas and institutional frameworks of recipient countries. The intrusion of political issues into the granting of aid is not without precedent, however. Politics has always 'mattered', with underlying political considerations having figured in attempts to instill or reinforce a recipient's political allegiance to a donor. In a less calculated fashion, antecedents can also be seen in threats to withdraw aid in the context of human rights violations. Yet the tying of aid to political performance, in so deliberate a fashion as at present, does represent a significant change from previous practice and it is not misplaced to characterise it as registering the emergence of a new aid regime. While differences exist between donors in the extent of their adherence to 'political conditionality', a considerable consensus about the validity of the project has emerged. It is significant in that it reflects a reconsideration by donors (and many developmentalists) of what is achievable through aid negotiations and what is regarded as legitimate in terms of breaching the sanctity of national sovereignty.

Some of the earliest expositions of the new aid regime characterised by political conditionality have appeared in documents produced by the donor agencies. An academic literature focusing directly on the subject has also begun to emerge. But broader considerations of the politics of economic reform or the nature of political transitions (and, more explicitly, of processes of democratisation) also bear on this issue. Literature on the state and economic reform as well as on democratic transitions in Africa must also be considered in any account of recent work relating to political conditionality and democratisation. All will be drawn on in the present review.

A number of questions have preoccupied commentators: 1) how and why did political conditionality arrive on donor agendas; 2) how far and in what way does this represent a departure from previous practice; 3) what is the extent of its current or potential effectiveness and what factors bear on its probable significance in influencing political change; 4) what response has been encountered from recipient populations and governments and 5) how should the change it represents in the relationship between donor and recipient countries be conceptualised. As well as reviewing the treatment of some of these in the literature, particular attention will also be given here to the way in which adoption of political conditionality is associated with a changed understanding of the role of the state in processes of economic reform.

Origins & Meanings

A number of accounts of political conditionality, or the deliberate use of aid to improve governance, include a section on 'origins' (Archer, 1994; Leftwich, 1994). Indeed the importance of the new aid regime is precisely the acknowledgement, by both its architects and its analysts, that it represents something distinct from those which preceded it. While seeds of change have been discerned as early as the mid-eighties, the issuing of policy statements in this area dates from 1989 and 1990, with policy implementation following shortly thereafter. Reference has also been made to the way the donors' emphasis on the political coincides with broader concerns or issues emerging in the late eighties (Robinson, 1995b; Carothers, 1995; Uvin, 1993), most notably the demise of single party systems in various parts of the world and the ending of the cold war. The emergence of political conditionality thus reflects a generalised reconsideration of bilateral and multilateral relations.

In order to explore the extent to which this is something 'new', the literature also reflects a concern to identify antecedents and to trace the emergence of new preoccupations. As already indicated, human rights have been on some donor agendas for a number of years, with abuses in this area having served as a basis for suspension or withdrawal of aid, even if in a somewhat inconsistent manner. Certain donors have also targeted civil society and have injected funds into local NGOs and intellectual fora over a considerable time. Both of these concerns have figured in the new donor agendas. But Gibbon (1993:52,53) suggests a two-pronged basis for governance and political conditionality, the primary constituents of these new agendas. He locates the origins of the concern with governance in the emergent sub-text of a broader discourse promoted by the World Bank from the mid-eighties which expressed the need for an enabling environment to facilitate prescribed economic reforms. Emphasis was placed by the bank on the need for decentralising institutional reforms as well as for encouraging non-governmental organisations. Political conditionality, he suggests, has a considerably longer tradition in the dealings of superpowers – and particularly the United States – with developing countries. But it has been reformulated around a concern to universalise pluralist politics and combined with an urgent call to improve governance capabilities.

Political conditionality as an 'aid regime principle' was formally adopted by the EC Council of Ministers in 1989 (ibid:53) and subsequently elaborated in the policy directives of a number of European bilateral donors. In the middle of 1990 President Mitterrand issued a statement to the summit of African heads of state that France would reduce its aid to those countries that did not demonstrate progress toward democratisation (Robinson, 1993a:93). A similar pronouncement was made by the German government. The intent to use British aid to promote 'good government' was also signalled by Douglas Hurd, as Foreign Secretary, in June 1990. The United States, whose embassies had been required to monitor human rights for a number of years, and whose Information Service had been involved in sending potentially prominent individuals to the US for a period of 'leadership training' for considerably longer, added a 'democracy initiative' under the auspices of USAID in the early nineties. The agency's document 'Democracy and Governance' (1991), made clear that the promotion and sustainability of democracy were among the central objectives of US foreign policy.

Different donors have adopted different emphases and in some cases use different terminology. While 'democracy' and 'governance' are terms preferred by the United States, for example, the UK tends to use the expression 'good government'. The notion of 'political conditionality', with its coercive edge and catchphrase quality, is one to which donors object, but it has frequently figured in the analytic literature because of its capacity to allude to elements both of continuity and of difference. But terminology remains an area of only loose consensus. Indeed accounts in the literature are often characterised by attempts to name and thereby capture the essence of this new orientation. A variety of terms has been put forward, some purporting to encompass the aid regime as a whole and others only certain of its dimensions. Among them have been: the new politics of aid (Gibbon, 1993), foreign political aid (Robinson, 1995), political conditionality (Sorensen, 1993b; Burnell, 1994; Uvin, 1993), governance and/or good government or the good government approach (Leftwich, 1994; Burnell, 1994; Archer, 1994), democracy assistance (Carothers, 1995) or, simply, the new donor agenda.

The variety of terms is suggestive of the difficulty of pinning down the subject matter, but also reflects the fact that accounts are not always concerned with precisely the same thing. While the term political conditionality sometimes stands in for the aid regime as a whole, its more specific application is to the threat to withhold aid, should certain conditions relating to political structure and process not be complied with within a timeframe set by donors. It is the aid package as a whole, or a designated portion of it, or that part intended to assist in balance-of-payments support, which is frequently the object of threats of withdrawal. But the new aid regime also has a positive side, providing inducements as well as penalties; funds are directed toward projects anticipated to further political reform – through strengthening civil society, political structures and procedures, promoting human rights, and the like. Various accounts consider either or both of these alternatively coercive or supportive dimensions.

Concern in the literature is also directed at assessing the coherence of concepts, through probing meaning and exploring the degree to which usage reflects consensus (Leftwich, 1994; Archer, 1994). This is a subject matter which is as much grounded in discourse and its analysis as in the examination of practice. Perhaps not surprisingly, inconsistency and lack of clarity are easily revealed. And yet what is at the same time interesting is the degree of consensus among both donors and observers confirming that a 'new aid regime' has indeed come into play. That there is also rough agreement on its substance is largely a function of the way this regime has emerged: as a consequence not just of independent donor traditions and preoccupations but also of 'collective structures' through which donors (with the insistent prodding of the World Bank) have sought to coordinate their aid efforts.

If relatively quickly effected, the underlying rationale for the new aid regime has been laid down and elaborated over a number of years and is grounded in a broad rethinking of the reasons, not just for sustained poverty and poor economic performance, but also for the failure of previous attempts at adjustment and reform. It has been complemented and reinforced by political changes in Eastern Europe, which encouraged the universalising of a 'democracy agenda'. It has also been promoted by the independent development of new democratic movements across Africa, to which it has often given succour. But it is the shift in perception of the role of the state underlying the new orientation which is of particular significance and which will be looked at more fully here.

Rethinking the Role of the State

Political conditionality in its broadest sense – with its concerns for human rights, pluralist politics and efficient government – focuses directly on the state in its relationship to society and, more importantly, in its relationship to the economy. It rests on an assumption that state capacity and legitimacy are crucial for the enactment of economic reforms and represents a response to a paradox inherent in previous orthodoxy, whereby structural adjustment programmes both relied on the state to institute reforms and undermined its capacity to do so.

The paradigm shift which this rethinking constitutes (Husain and Faruquee, 1994) can be located within a broader sweep of theorising about the role of the state. Evans (1992), for example, has described a shifting orthodoxy in terms of three waves of conceptualising the state's relationship to the process of development. The first, which gained credence during the fifties and sixties, depicted the state as central to the development project. Serving as the model for many newly independent states, it affirmed the role of the state as fostering structural change, assisting in the transformation of agriculture, ensuring the provision of infrastructure and taking an active and often interventionist role in industrialisation. The manifest failures of this statist strategy led critics of this model subsequently to proclaim the state to be the focus of economic problems, rather than a generator of solutions.

This notion of states as deficient or inadequate and responsible for economic difficulties is clearly evident in the second theoretical wave, which Evans defines as the neo-utilitarian view and which others (e.g. Archer, 1994) have labelled neo-liberalism. One variation on this theme is developed in a chapter on 'Rethinking the State' in the World Bank's *World Development Report* of 1991, which links what it refers to as a 'big state' to poor economic performance. A 'big state', characterised by the pervasiveness of state enterprise, high levels of state regulation and a civil service constituting a major source of employment, was identified as being a consequence of political instability. But this sort of state, together with the economic policy that supported and extended it, was also diagnosed as economically inefficient. Its pervasiveness across economic sectors was regarded as discouraging private investment. A large civil service which soaked up scarce resources and a tendency for the state to serve as a means of direct and indirect distribution through allocation of 'rents' were perceived to have been the cause of poor performance and increasing indebtedness. A new orthodoxy therefore emerged in theorising the state in respect of development (Evans, 1992). Neo-utilitarian theories depicted state action as essentially involving an exchange relationship between incumbents and constituents, favouring thereby the payment of rents to supporters through the restriction of market forces. They also advocated the desirability of the state being rolled back from as many arenas as possible, through privatisation of state enterprise, retrenchment of the civil service and reducing the degree of state intervention and control. 'Governments', it was suggested, 'need to do less in those areas where markets work, or can be made to work, reasonably well' (*World Development Report*, 1991). They should also abandon their protectionist policies, their excessive spending and their interventions in the market via subsidies or price controls. Withdrawing from such forms of market regulation or ownership activity, they should rather concentrate on a more minimalist package of 'defining and protecting property rights, providing effective legal, judicial, and regulatory systems, improving the efficiency of the civil service, and protecting the environment.' (ibid.) Significantly, and in contrast to previous orthodoxy with its more limited focus, this did not constitute a prescription for developing countries alone, but was regarded as having global application. Even so, its enforcement was most pronounced in policies of economic liberalisation promoted by the IMF and imposed in packages of conditionality. In this regard Evans describes (second wave) neo-utilitarian theories of the state as accompanying real shifts in the development agenda and – importantly – as sitting comfortably with orthodox economic prescriptions for the management of structural adjustment (1992:140).

Yet this minimalist model, conceptualised as a lubricant to structural adjustment, posed a dilemma recognised and increasingly elaborated upon by the end of the eighties (Evans, 1992; Callaghy, 1990; Sandbrook, 1993; Wade, 1990; Kahler, 1990): while the state was perceived to be a problem, it was also considered as crucial to the successful implementation of reform programmes. As Evans says:

> orthodox policy prescriptions, despite their disdain for the wisdom of politicians, contained the paradoxical expectation that the state (the root of the problem) would somehow be able to become the agent that initiated and implemented adjustment programs (became the solution) (1992: 141).

In similar vein Sandbrook (1993:19) argues that, while the World Bank prescribed a minimal liberal state, experience had shown economic development to be facilitated by a pro-active interventionist government.

Thus the instrument charged with ensuring adoption of economic reform was subject to weakening by reform measures. Moreover, those components of reform packages requiring retrenchment of civil servants and freezing of their salaries were deemed capable of undermining the morale of that very group expected to champion technocratic solutions and to secure their application (Husain and Faruqee, 1994:427). An appreciation of this dilemma implied that the state could not be ignored, nor treated as a pariah; reform could not be delivered without local capable hands bolstered by an efficient bureaucracy.

Thus a reconceptualisation of the state – representing the third wave in Evans' treatment – occurred, specifically characterised by a reassertion of the state's centrality. Not only was the ability of technocrats within the state seen as crucial; so too was an effective and durable structure (Evans, 1992:141). Attention then focused on how states could be made to function more effectively as facilitators of economic reform (Husain and Faruqee, 1994:427) with particular concern being directed toward African states. The World Bank's review of adjustment in Africa concludes with the 'striking finding' that 'the global wind of change that is redefining the role of the state has not yet swept these countries, at least by contemporary standards' (ibid:427). Thus not only did it stand accused of being a significant part of the cause of crisis in its 'old' form; the contemporary African state has also been declared deficient in its 'new' guise.

It was because of its presumed deficiency that explicit attention on the state – both in building its capacity and ensuring its legitimacy – was regarded as justified. The exposition contained in the publication, *Governance: the World Bank's Experience* (World Bank, 1993) thus moves from castigating 'big states' to listing a constellation of features of what it calls 'poor governance'. While continuing to see the state as an important factor in past unsatisfactory economic performance, the shift also marks an appreciation of the importance of the political realm to 'development'. The negative attributes identified include 'arbitrary policy making, unaccountable bureaucracies, unenforced or unjust legal systems, the abuse of executive power, a civil society unengaged in public life, and widespread corruption' (ibid). Hence it was not just size but capacity and quality of performance which came to be regarded as important. Features were identified as constituting poor governance, moreover, precisely by virtue of their negative impact on economic performance. The Bank has been explicit on this point. Its very definition of governance as 'the manner in which power is exercised in the management of a country's economic and social resources for development' (ibid:1) affirms a necessary link between state and economy. Indeed, that the Bank is concerned with governance at all is precisely to ensure that the programmes and projects it helps to finance are sustained to positive effect.

The Rhetoric of Governance

If elements of poor governance have had a negative impact on economic performance, then it is regarded as important to sweep them away and foster or support their opposites. For the Bank, good, as opposed to poor, governance necessarily involves effective management of resources, appropriate design of policy and efficient discharge of functions – all attuned to achieving positive economic performance. The Bank's understanding of good governance is thus 'epitomized by predictable, open and enlightened policy making, a bureaucracy imbued with a professional ethos acting in furtherance of the public good, the rule of law, transparent processes, and a strong civil society participating in public affairs' (1993). The good governance model implies states which are 'strong', but also 'sharply delimited' (ibid). Thus some condemnation of the 'big' state is sustained in this affirmation of the state's essential and decisive role in development.

The World Bank declares one of the three dimensions of governance which it identifies – the nature of political regime – to be outside its official mandate but asserts its legitimate involvement in the other two – the exercise of authority in management of social and economic resources and government's capacity to design and implement policy and to discharge its functions. Hence its own good governance project is confined to public sector management, transparency, accountability and establishing a legal framework for development (1993). This stance in advocating good government, and indeed contributing to the theorising of a new orthodoxy, while officially distancing itself from some elements of practice, has contributed to an ambiguous (even if officially delineated) division of labour with respect to the new aid regime. An important aspect of the move to political conditionality is therefore the relationship between bilaterals (individual donor countries) and the multilaterals (IFIs). On the one hand this has entailed the bilaterals taking responsibility for enactment of political conditionality, while on the other the World Bank has retained a close coordinating role.

There is an important trade-off at work here underlying what is a higher level of consensus and monitoring than has occurred previously. As Gibbon notes, donor country consultative meetings, which emerged in the early eighties as vehicles by which bilaterals could coordinate pledges of new aid, subsequently evolved into a means for 'semi-formalised review of recipients' progress with policy reforms' (1993:39). Whereas the World Bank's role was initially merely one of chairing these meetings, it gradually incorporated both dissemination of economic information (via its own country reports) and the proposing of future options. While this involved some subordination of the bilaterals to the World Bank's agenda, it also permitted their access to information which they previously lacked (ibid). Political conditionality in this respect has involved important elements of organisational consolidation, increased donor consensus and routinisation of (collective) monitoring. But if increased coordination has occurred, the division of labour between multilaterals and bilaterals – as well as differing bilateral traditions (inevitably related in part to their domestic politics) – have led to differences in their working definitions of the components of political conditionality and different points of emphasis both of justificatory principles and of practice. In particular different stress has been placed on governance as opposed to human rights or the strengthening of civil society. The specific understanding (and, indeed, even inclusion) of democracy has also varied. And while the joining of political to economic reform – or, more specifically, the linked advocacy of a market economy and political pluralism – is frequently a common feature, the specific emphasis placed on either as well as the nature of their linkage also varies.

At least in comparison to the World Bank, however, the rhetoric of governance adopted by the bilaterals tends to be more explicit in its pronouncements on the nature of the political regime which aid is intended to encourage. In 1990 the British ODA listed a range of elements as constituting good government, among which was political pluralism. Ideas have been progressively refined and a more recent document from the ODA (1993), for example, defines components of a good government agenda as accountability, legitimacy and competence, with democracy, albeit with a degree of equivocation, included under the rubric of legitimacy. While acknowledging that 'most participants in international discussions have stopped short of prescribing a precise political system as a universal model of good practice,' it is also suggested that multi-party democracy in principle offers the best way of ensuring legitimacy (ibid).

The position of the US is rather more straightforward, explicitly combining democracy with governance and declaring the promotion and sustaining of democracy to be central objectives of US foreign policy. USAID has embraced a 'democracy initiative' intended to strengthen democratic representation and to encourage demo-cratic values as well as to support respect for human rights and the rule of law (USAID, 1991). As Carothers notes, the strong emphasis placed on democracy by the Clinton administration, which has resulted in specific democracy/governance initiatives in a number of African countries, emerges from a trend in the early eighties, when Reagan 'explicitly reintroduced the theme of democracy promotion in US foreign policy out of a desire to base his strenuous anti-communist policies on a positive vision' (1995:62). But the promotion of democracy is central to the activities of a number of other donors, as exemplified by the OECD's Development Assistance Committee linking the World Bank's notion of governance to democratisation, human rights and the concept of participatory development (World Bank, 1993).

This enthusiasm for democracy is, of course, related to the end of the cold war and specific political changes in Eastern Europe. The US in particular perceives an important opportunity to 'strengthen and support the global trend toward more democratic societies' (USAID, 1993). To this extent some may view democracy positively and independently of any possible impact on economic factors. The fact that it is tied to the broader discourse on governance, however, implies that democracy is regarded by the donors as positively linked to economic performance.

Tying Rhetoric to Agency – Political Conditionality

Not only has a dominant discourse emerged around governance (including democracy) and economic performance (particularly economic reform) but 'theory' has developed in close association with practice. As noted above, the World Bank's diagnosis of poor governance is central to its account of why developing countries have experienced poor economic performance (and why its own past assistance has had less effect than it would have wished). Its prescription of good governance is intended to ensure that its injected funds will not go to waste in the future. Similarly various bilateral donors have elected to sponsor good governance through supportive initiatives, with some adding assistance under the heading of democracy as well. Their application of general principles and their emphasis on particular aspects of a good government/democracy package varies. The UK tends often to concentrate on government-to-government assistance and to focus on the strengthening of institutions. Direct assistance to the constituent elements of civil society – and particularly to indigenous NGOs – is often characteristic of Scandinavian donors, as well as of the United States. Several bilateral donors include good government and indeed democratic objectives among the general conditions under which their economic assistance is extended but are not involved in any specific governance or democracy projects. But then the definition of what constitutes governance or democracy project aid also varies considerably from one bilateral to another, making direct comparisons problematic.

Alongside positive support to democratising agents, public sector reform or the improvement of capacity or competence, a strong coercive element is particularly characteristic of the new aid regime, epitomised in the term 'political conditionality' itself. While some bilaterals set general conditions of a political nature in their individual agreements with recipient countries, the exercise of political conditionality is particularly dramatically enacted at consultative group meetings. The outcome of these meetings ostensibly represents collectively imposed conditions. In practice, however, complete consensus among bilaterals may be elusive. But, whether as an overarching condition in country-to-country agreements or set collectively through the consultative group meeting, the significance of such conditionality lies in its implications for national sovereignty. Though benchmarks may be negotiated, the extension of conditions to the very conduct of government and the organisation of the political process in so open a manner signals the open assertion by the donors of a considerable scope for intervention.

The leverage permitting such agency is the very economic disorder experienced by developing countries – more specifically the debt crisis and the need for foreign aid – which has been used to justify the imposition of economic restructuring. Thus, just as aid has been tied for many years to economic conditions (to guarantees to enact economic liberalisation) so it is now increasingly being tied to political conditions, ranging from an increase in government accountability – in openness and transparency – to the initiation and extension of democratic procedures, with a particular focus in some countries on the holding of multiparty elections. The boundaries between what counts as political and what as economic conditionality are sometimes blurred, as, for example, in cases where progress on privatisation comes under scrutiny; but it is evident that a range of issues now normally on the agendas of consultative group meetings – including drug trafficking and corruption – fall under this rubric.

The rationale for setting specific conditions at any particular time for any given recipient may exhibit only a loose fit with the staging of a democratisation process implied by packages of more positive or benign support. Indeed the reading off of any theory of democratisation at all from the issues thrown up in the setting of political conditions would be a risky business, yielding the suspicion that the approach is more ad hoc than one of deliberation. On this basis the possibility emerges that the political conditionality regime has the potential to undermine the very stability which it is presumably intended to promote, a point perhaps more acutely appreciated by recipient governments than by the donors.

Impact of Political Conditionality

Evaluations of the 'success' of political conditionality or the broader programme of directing aid toward political reform necessarily depend on the way in which this aid regime is conceptualised and its goals defined. In this regard a specific focus on democratisation may be problematic, not least because of the lack of explicit consensus over the inclusion of democracy as a specific goal, but also because of disagreement over (or even lack of thinking through) the staging of democratic transitions and the measurement of 'progress' within the democratisation process. In addition, the specific impact of political conditionality alongside other factors may be difficult to disentangle.

In practice, while there is general consensus among donors about the validity and nature of the good government initiative, specific goals are set with respect to the experience of specific countries. Whereas the holding of multiparty elections may be a primary focus in one case, constitutional reform to safeguard human rights (or to provide safeguards against ethnic rivalry) may be matters of concern in another. How far success is achieved in any case will require close scrutiny.

Robinson (1993a) notes that early predictions concerning the impact of political conditionality varied between cautious optimism and scepticism. His own view is that the truth will be found somewhere in between, but he emphasises that evaluation must be on a country by country basis and suggests that political conditionality is likely to have differential effects at different points in the transition process. His specific comparison of the experience of Kenya and Malawi suggests that variable impact has been related to the relative strength and cohesion of internal opposition forces. Uvin's (1993:76) examination of the limits of political conditionality focuses on a number of barriers to its impact which, first, work against the probability that 'a coherent and coordinated policy of political conditionality will be developed' and, second, promote the scope for resistance by would-be recipients. He concurs with Robinson that political conditionality is most likely to have an impact where internal pressures also point in the direction of political reform.

Burnell's (1994) 'sideways look at aid and political conditionality' focuses on the coherence of donors' intentions, while also emphasising the need for the complexities of the political situation in recipient countries to be fully recognised and taken into account. He argues that if political conditionality is to have any positive impact, it is essential that aims and objectives be clear, that donors' purposes be transparent and credible and that the process of policy implementation reflect the same transparency as the intended outcome. In reference to the more benign end of the continuum describing the new aid regime, involving support for institutional and democratic reform rather than the imposing of conditions, Robinson (1995c:70-80) also focuses on donor practice. Rather than evaluating the specific impact of donor assistance to organisations within civil society, which he refers to as political foreign aid, he sets out a framework through which such evaluation might be conducted. In a brief review of the way in which assistance of this sort has been extended (and its pitfalls), Robinson calls for donors to adopt a cautious approach in order to avoid, first, overextending NGOs which may have a fragile base and lack internal means of evaluating their own activities and, second, forcing the pace of the democratisation agenda to jeopardise democratic consolidation.

Moore (1995) is critical of another component at the benign end of the conditionality continuum, namely support for 'institution building' and 'capacity building' which are important elements of the good government agenda. Expressing scepticism about both the coherence and substance of programmes, he suggests that poor results in past attempts at institution building make it doubtful that this time there will be positive gains. At the very least he calls for more clarity in defining aims. There is also a need to avoid embracing the increasingly fashionable concept of capacity building, since for Moore its ambiguity and lack of analytical precision are even greater than that of the older institution building. As have other commentators, he stresses that an appreciation of the complexity of local political environments is essential. For all that, however, he considers that, for beneficial outcomes to be attained, donors may have to be as interventionist (though perhaps in less emphatic ways) as in the more strident practice of setting political conditions (ibid:95,6).

As is evident, evaluations of programmes of political conditionality or donor assistance toward political reform remain few and partial. In part this is a function of the short time in which such programmes have been in existence. But it may also be an indicator of both lack of clarity of intentions and lack of satisfactory evaluatory tools. In practice, the development of 'impact evaluation' criteria is well underway on the ground; but it is an *ad hoc* process which has not yet become the subject of much official or analytic discourse.

Points of Contention

The advent of political conditionality has elicited and in some cases reinvigorated debate on a number of issues, including the very assumptions upon which this aid regime appears to be grounded. One central area of contention relates to the relationship between political and economic reform. Debate on this issue long predates the new aid regime, but has a new relevance now, not least because some accounts of good government conflate political and economic reform within an overarching account which presumes (without precisely specifying or theorising) their necessary association. When the British Foreign Secretary, Douglas Hurd, officially confirmed the importance to be attached henceforth to good government when extending aid, he listed free markets and property rights as well as an independent judiciary, the rule of law, a neutral military, political pluralism, freedom of speech and association and a free press among its constituent elements.

This inclusion of economic elements and indeed of the defining characteristics of capitalist economics is not unique. A number of academic overviews also incorporate an elision of economic and political objectives in their definition of governance or good government. Robinson (1993a:90) for example lists four components of aid regimes linked to administrative and political reform: sound economic policies – which he further defines as 'adherence to market principles and economic openness'; competent public administration; open and accountable government; and human rights and respect for the rule of law. Archer (1994:7) links 'good political management' more explicitly to 'good economic management' and suggests that, approached from politics via the rhetoric of good governance, they revolve around three axes: 'the role of competitive markets (the economy); government responsibility to manage (the state); and the importance of private rights and individual initiative (civil society)'.

The Relationship between Economic & Political Reform

Yet there continues to be doubt in the literature about the nature of the relationship between political and economic reform and more specifically about whether political reform facilitates economic reform or, alternatively, is capable of frustrating reform efforts. Or, put otherwise, the question remains as to how far certain levels of economic development may serve as preconditions for stable democratic systems.

Early modernisation theorists hypothesised a relationship between the introduction of 'modern' economic forms and 'modern' political structures and practices, and often included economic factors among preconditions for particular political systems, suggesting that a certain threshold of economic development might be required before democracy could take hold. Contemporary literature on democratisation frequently incorporates assumptions about the conditioning role of economic factors. Lancaster (1991:157), for example, lists a high level of per capita income and a sizeable middle class as preconditions often associated with effectively functioning democracies. In turn, the trend toward authoritarianism has been partly (sometimes largely) attributed to the weakness of developing economies, lack of a strong indigenous owning class, high levels of economic dependency, etc. Bangura (1992:39,40,52) counters this with the argument that underdevelopment of itself does not constitute a fundamental obstacle to democratisation. But he concedes that democratic rule is possible in such circumstances only in the context of appropriate social systems, capable of providing welfare and economic support for the deprived majority to exercise their democratic rights. Moreover, for such social systems to be sustainable, changes in the form of accumulation must be put in train. If not an inevitable deterrent, therefore, persistent and widespread poverty can make the practice of democracy problematic.

As well as debate over how economic factors favour political developments, there has also been longstanding concern with the conditioning effect of political systems on economic growth and with identifying political structures which are conducive to development. Analysis of those countries which have been economically 'successful' suggests that there is no particular correlation between open, democratic systems and development, nor for that matter between authoritarian regimes and development. As Decalo comments:

> While globally absence of democracy has not necessarily resulted in economic decline (e.g. Japan, South Korea, Taiwan) 'benevolent' authoritarian rule has also not been that frequently the recipe for economic development and nation building (for instance the Middle East and Latin America) – the bottom line of justification for the single party state (1992:12).

The World Bank's *World Development Report* for 1991 concurred that no specific link between a democracy/authoritarianism dichotomy and rates of growth can be demonstrated. But it also commented that 'dictatorships have proven disastrous for development in many economies' (1991:133). Indeed, and in contrast to Decalo's more moderate assessment, the absence of democracy has been specifically cited as a primary cause of chronic crisis in Africa (Ake, 1991).

What Evans has referred to as the third (and currently dominant) wave of orthodoxy in conceptualising the state has encouraged the resurgence of ideas about the developmental state (Evans, 1992; Leftwich, 1994; Sorensen, 1993; White, 1995) and renewed consideration about characteristics which foster economic growth. Evans (1992:164), for example, regards an 'embedded autonomy' as an essential feature of those states enjoying developmental 'success', and of greater signficance than whether a regime is democratic or authoritarian. By this he means the situation where the state enjoys sufficient autonomy from underlying social forces to pursue its own goals, but is not so autonomous that its goals bear no relation to collective requirements and its incumbents become mere predators on society.

Leftwich (1994:378–9) argues that, whether or not democratic, developmental states in the last three decades have been *de facto* or *de jure* single-party states and have been characterised by a weak civil society and relative autonomy of developmental elites. They are collectively distinguished by their institutional structures and political objectives being developmentally driven and their developmental purposes being politically driven (ibid). Indeed he goes so far as to assert that 'at almost every point the models of good governance and the developmental state are in conflict' (ibid:381). Sorensen (1993:30) rejects any universal applicability of the East Asian model of developmental state as well as any notion that authoritarianism is linked to developmental success, but concedes that merely instituting a 'thin layer of democracy' through multiparty systems will not provide states with developmental strength.

Barya (1993:16,17), on the other hand, turns the question around and argues that economic and political conditionalities are in contradiction, not least because conditions set under the typical structural adjustment programme are incompatible with the development of a democratic system and a strong civil society. The reason is simply that the SAP undermines national sovereignty and indeed strengthens or creates authoritarian regimes.

Participants in a seminar on 'Economic Reform in Africa's New Era of Political Liberalization', sponsored by the USAID in the spring of 1993, rehearsed some of these views, with the proceedings revealing the degree to which the debate remains both cogent and unresolved. One stance was well represented by Callaghy (USAID, 1993:10,11), who argued that the requisites of successful economic reform, which he designated as including technocratic decision-making, sustained government commitment and substantial capability, were difficult to achieve under democratic conditions. Thus rather than requiring a democratic regime, donors should support any regime so long as it continued to engage in economic reform (ibid:11). In contrast, Moyo in his contribution (ibid:18) asserted that economic reform cannot precede democratisation in Africa. Others contended that the question was not which of the two should come first or be primarily supported, but that both should proceed simultaneously, or that the reinstatement or emergence of democratic regimes offered a window of opportunity for pressing forward with economic reform, not least because democratically elected governments enjoyed the legitimacy upon which difficult decisions leading to economic reform could be taken (ibid:12). This latter view points to a more cynical interpretation of donor advocacy of pluralist political systems. To the extent that economic conditions are adopted by a popularly elected government, the image of external imposition of directives and strategies may appear softened. Yet if in this manner facilitating economic reform, there are other respects in which democratic regimes might frustrate adjustment and liberalisation programmes. The argument has been put by Callaghy (1990:264) among others, that transition to democracy – and particularly the holding of elections – may undermine the insulation of the state and hinder the carrying out of economic reforms. Similarly Lancaster (1991:160) has noted that in the short run political liberalisation may lead to a worsening of economic problems and a decline in performance. The widening of debate and expansion of the institutions of civil society may make 'internal negotiations on economic reform lengthy, complex and difficult'.

The question of both the staging of economic and political reform, as well as the more specific issue of how far a democratic system facilitates or impedes what donors judge to be essential economic reforms, thus remains unresolved. To this degree there is a clear irony in their figuring so centrally within the new aid regime, with both market economies and democratic procedures frequently conjoined as pillars among donor objectives.

Imposition of External Agendas

That democracy can be effectively promoted through regimes of aid conditionality is also a matter of contention. Schmitz and Gillies (1992:15) remain sceptical, arguing that democracy cannot be 'retailed, or given, much less imposed, on populations which remain in conditions of economic and political dependency'. Yet at the same time they regard the (frequently) accompanying emphasis on human rights and some of the components of good government as having positive benefit. Sorensen (1993a) argues that political conditionality may be used as a smokescreen covering vested donor interests and notes the contrary (and contradictory) international pressures exerted on developing countries – with an increasing ideological consensus on the virtues of good government/democracy on the one hand and projections of continuing economic crisis on the other.

Throughout, the emphasis on the quality of governance places focus in respect of performance – both economic and political – squarely on internal structures and procedures, rather than on the intricacies of the global economy and the historical construction of highly skewed economies, or the lack of development of local skills or its external seepage. To this degree Sandbrook (1993) suggests that the governance discourse has served as an efficient means of focusing responsibility on governments of developing countries, not just for past ills but also for implementation of reform packages. In a related argument, Schmitz and Gillies (1992:15) emphasise the extent to which the governance models (or rather the political conditionalities associated with them) are tied to dominant relationships, ideologies and orthodox economistic development models. But this is simply to reassert that they are part of the prevailing dominant discourse on the relationship of state and economy. The point is put forcefully by Barya (1993:16,17) who outlines five propositions on the new political condition- alities. Among them is that conditionalities are unrelated to any desire by western donors to promote democracy in Africa, but rather should be viewed as part of a broader scheme to promote a new world order in the aftermath of the cold war. But Barya also questions the underlying assumption that any people can be forced to be democratic or accept democracy and remarks on the contradiction between the intended outcome and the utilisation of coercive means.

Manipulation of Conditionalities? – a Questionable Impact

In spite of scepticism about meaning and intentions, some observers, of whom Sorensen (1993a:29) is an example, regard the good government phenomenon in a generally positive light, because it constitutes a more useful and honest approach to aid than that applied during the cold war era. Bayart (1993) is less generous, partly because he is suspicious of the motives behind the good government rhetoric, but also because he sees it as subject to manipulation and in consequence potentially empty of content. Multipartyism, says Bayart, is merely a fig-leaf, covering up the continuation of clientelist processes associated with what he has termed 'the politics of the belly', now accorded a degree of international legitimacy under the approving eye of the donors. Moreover, he argues, political conditionality, in the form of aid to encourage political reform, is a new form of economic rent: 'aid to help pay for democratisation is always good to have – witness the recent spectacle of Mobutu putting in a bid for it! – and the idiom of multiparty politics is like a pidgin language, which indigenous kings use to parley with the agents of the new world economy trade, that of structural adjustment' (Ibid:xiii). Bayart is particularly concerned to distinguish multipartyism from democracy and to question the extent to which competitive elections constitute a qualitative change. While not insignificant, they can and have been incorporated into an existing 'politics' in such a way as to preserve the advantage of those in power. As Bayart notes:

> ... the most able African heads of state have for a long time understood the use they could make of competitive elections to maintain themselves in power. Today they are able to embrace multiparty politics as a way of weakening their opponents and reducing political pressure where formerly they would have consented to contested elections within the single party in order to undermine the position of the party 'barons' ... (ibid:xii)

Questioning both motives and outcome, Bayart calls for an interpretation of the state in Africa and of political process which is grounded in the 'historicity' of the societies concerned. A focus on the agency of recipients of political conditionality by which cosmetic changes are enacted by incumbent political elites in order to satisfy external monitors, also features in the account of Gills and his colleagues (1993). While not drawing specifically on African cases, they offer a broad critique of the democratic claims of new civilian regimes across the third world. If trappings of western liberal democracies have been adopted, ossified political and economic structures from an authoritarian past have also characteristically been preserved (ibid:3). Contrasted with participatory progressive democratic forms, such regimes are referred to as 'low intensity democracies', involving low intensity conflict and permitting changes acceptable to international capitalism to be put in place with greater ease and less resistance than in a more overtly authoritarian regime. Low intensity democracy, or elite democracy, is treated as essentially a sham, though at the same time little more than can be expected in societies which have extreme levels of inequality and where formal participation is effectively limited to the privileged minority. Multiparty elections are introduced and perhaps other reforms written in, but little more occurs.

Utilisation of the Governance Discourse to Support Indigenous Democratic Struggles

Yet accepting these various possibilities – that the good government discourse merely marks a new phase of surveillance and control on the part of international capital (even if the relationship between democratic forms and political liberalisation may be shaky), that political conditionality has been complied with in only a superficial sense, that aid for political reform has become a new form of economic rent or that multipartyism has been manipulated to the continuing advantage of entrenched political elites – the emphasis on democracy may still have positive ramifications. Bayart (1993) reminds us that democratic initiatives are not new and indeed that the changes in the late eighties should be understood less as a consequence of external than internal pressures. Demands for democracy, he says, are not exceptional: 'the democratic fire has been smouldering for a long time' albeit contained and suppressed. And in any case, if external factors are taken into account, they should include such events as the disturbances in Algeria in 1988, which led to the introduction of a competitive party system there, and the freeing of Nelson Mandela in South Africa (ibid:xi). External factors, of whatever magnitude, merely gave impetus to internal initiatives.

To this extent the discourse on governance and indeed the setting of political conditions for the dispersal of aid may support ongoing struggles permitting movement along a democratic path and thereby creating greater space for manoeuvre. Bangura (1992) points to a contradiction between pressures for democratisation in civil society and a conformist tendency on the part of political actors. While this may lead back to centralisation of power, a regime's democratic claims may alternatively permit articulation of conflicting interests and pressure for continued movement.

Conclusion

The new aid regime, whereby donor assistance is directed toward political reform or where targets associated with good government or democracy become conditions for the release of monies, has been treated here as a multi-layered phenomenon. The increased scope for donor intervention which this new orientation permits has been born of attempts to achieve coordinated monitoring of aid programmes. But it has also been based on a rethinking of the state which acknowledges the need for its being strengthened – and indeed playing a central role – if economic reform is to be achieved. It rests, moreover, on the assumption that African states in particular need shoring up, in respect of competence and efficiency as well as in respect of their claims on the loyalty of the population.

Democracy figures more centrally in some bilateral variants of the new aid regime than others. While in practice decisions to hold multiparty elections have seldom been a direct consequence of political conditionality, donor rhetoric and action in support of democratisation may well be of some significance in setting a favourable context within which such reforms occur. In particular, where there has been strong local initiative toward effecting political change, a concerted donor emphasis on political conditionality may well assist its aims being realised. Bilateral assistance to bolster organisations within civil society, or to strengthen government institutions and competence may well be of benefit, though as Moore (1995) warns, the task is a difficult one, and in some respects no less interventionist than the more dramatic and draconian setting of political conditions on the release of general aid funds.

The irony remains, moreover, that promotion of democracy may undermine rapid and successful enactment of economic reforms. Stringent political criteria, indeed, may be no less difficult for a government to meet than economic criteria. To this degree, in the enthusiasm to ensure compliance with political conditions, the legitimacy of a state may be undermined and its government weakened, especially where the successful enactment of economic reforms results in increased and widespread poverty and is thus a far from popular measure. In such circumstances political conditions may have the potential to undermine democracy, should their pace and content be misconceived.

Bibliography

Ake, Claude (1991), 'Rethinking African Democracy,' *Journal of Democracy*, 2(1): 32-44.

Archer, Robert (1994), 'Markets and Good Government,' in A. Clayton (ed.), *Governance, Democracy and Conditionality: what role for NGOs?*, Oxford: INTRAC: 7-34.

Bangura, Yusuf (1992), 'Authoritarian Rule and Democracy in Africa', in P Gibbon et al. (eds), *Authoritarianism, Democracy and Adjustment, the Politics of Economic Reform in Africa*, Uppsala: The Scandinavian Institute of African Studies.

Barya, John-Jean (1993), 'The New Political Conditionalities of Aid: an Independent View from Africa', *IDS Bulletin*, 24(1): 16-23.

Bayart, Jean-Francois (1993), *The State in Africa, the Politics of the Belly*, London: Longman.

Berg-Schlosser, Dirk (1993), 'Democratization in Africa – Conditions and Prospects', first draft, paper presented at ECPR Joint Sessions of Workshops, Workshop on Democratization in the Third World, University of Leiden, the Netherlands.

Bratton, Michael & Nicolas van de Walle (1993), 'Neopatrimonial Regimes and Political Transitions in Africa', Working Paper No. 1, East Lansing, MI: Department of Political Science, Michigan State University, May.

Burnell, Peter (1994), 'Good Government and Democratization: a sideways look at aid and political conditionality,' *Democratization*, 1(3): 485-503.

Buijtenhuijs, Rob & Elly Rijnierse (1993), *Democratization in Sub-Saharan Africa, 1989-1992*, Leiden: African Studies Centre.

Callaghy, Thomas M. (1990), 'Lost Between State and Market: the Politics of Economic Adjustment in Ghana, Zambia and Nigeria', in Joan Nelson (ed.), *Economic Crisis and Policy Choice, the Politics of Adjustment in the Third World*, Princeton, NJ: Princeton University Press: 257-319.

Carothers, Thomas (1995), 'Recent US Experience with Democracy Promotion', *IDS Bulletin*, 26(2):62-9.

Clayton, Andrew (ed.) (1994), *Governance, Democracy and Conditionality: What Role for NGOs?* Oxford: INTRAC.

Decalo, Samuel (1992), 'The Process, Prospects and Constraints of Democratization in Africa', *African Affairs*, 91: 7-35.

Edwards, Michael (1994), 'International Non-Governmental Organizations, "Good Government" and the "New Policy Agenda": Lessons of Experience at the Programme Level', *Democratization*, 1(3): 504-515.

Evans, Peter (1992), 'The State as Problem and Solution: Predation, Embedded Autonomy, and Structural Change', in Stephan Haggard and Robert R Kaufman (eds), *The Politics of Economic Adjustment, International Constraints, Distributive Conflicts and the State*, Princeton, NJ: Princeton University Press, 139-81.

Gibbon, Peter (1993), 'The World Bank and the New Politics of Aid', in Georg Sorensen (ed.), *Political Conditionality*, London: Frank Cass: 35-62.

Gibbon, Peter, Yusuf Bangura & Arve Ofstad (eds) (1992), *Authoritarianism Democracy and Adjustment, the Politics of Economic Reform in Africa*, Seminar Proceedings No. 26, Uppsala: The Scandinavian Institute of African Studies.

Gills, Barry, Joel Rocamora & Richard Wilson (eds) (1993), *Low Intensity Democracy, Political Power in the New World Order*, London: Pluto Press.

Healey, John & Mark Robinson (1992), *Democracy, Governance and Economic Policy, Sub-Saharan Africa in Comparative Perspective*, London: Overseas Development Institute

Husain, Ishrat & Rashid Faruqee (eds) (1994), *Adjustment in Africa, Lessons from Country Case Studies*, Washington, DC: World Bank, Regional and Sectoral Studies.

Kahler, Miles (1990), 'Orthodoxy and its Alternatives: Explaining Approaches to Stabilization and Adjustment', in Joan Nelson (ed.), *Economic Crisis and Policy Choice, the Politics of Adjustment in the Third World*, Princeton, NJ: Princeton University Press: 35-61.

Lancaster, Carol (1991), 'Democracy in Africa', *Foreign Policy*, 85, Winter 91-92: 148-165; (1990), 'Governance in Africa: Should Foreign Aid be Linked to Political Reform', in *African Governance in the 1990s: Objectives, Resources, and Constraints*, Working Papers from the Second Annual Seminar of the

African Governance Program, The Carter Center of Emory University, Atlanta, GA, 23-25 March.

Larsson, Karl-Anders (1994), *Structural Adjustment, Aid and Development*, Stockholm: SIDA Information Secretariat.

Leftwich, Adrian (1994), 'Governance, the State and the Politics of Development', *Development and Change*, 25: 363-86.

Moore, Mick (1995), 'Promoting Good Government by Supporting Institutional Development', *IDS Bulletin*, 26(2): 89-96.

ODA (1993), 'Taking Account of Good Government', Government and Institutions Department, Technical Note No. 19, October.

Pinkney, Robert (1993), *Democracy in the Third World*, Buckingham: Open University Press.

Robinson, Mark (1993a), 'Aid, Democracy and Political Conditionality in Sub-Saharan Africa', in Sorensen, *Political Conditionality*, 85-99; (1993b), 'Will Political Conditionality Work?', *IDS Bulletin*, 24(1): 58-66; (ed.) (1995a), *Towards Democratic Governance, IDS Bulletin*, 26(2), University of Sussex; (1995b), 'Introduction', *IDS Bulletin*, 26(2): 1-8; (1995c), 'Strengthening Civil Society in Africa: the role of foreign political aid', *IDS Bulletin*, 26(2): 70-80.

Sandbrook, Richard (1993), *The Politics of Africa's Economic Recovery*, Cambridge: Cambridge University Press.

Schmitz, G. J. & D. Gillies (1992), *The Challenge of Democratic Development, Sustaining Democratization in Developing Societies*, Ottawa: The North-South Institute.

Sorensen, Georg (1993a), *Democracy and Democratization*, Boulder, CO: Westview Press; (ed.) (1993b), *Political Conditionality*, London: Frank Cass.

USAID (1991), 'Democracy and Governance', Washington, DC, November; (1993), *Economic Reform in Africa's New Era of Political Liberalization*, proceedings of a workshop for SPA Donors, 14-15 April, Washington, DC.

Uvin, Peter (1993), '"Do as I Say, Not as I Do": the Limits of Political Conditionality', in Sorensen, *Political Conditionality*, 63-84.

Wade, Robert (1990), *Governing the Market*, Princeton, NJ: Princeton University Press.

Wekkin, Gary, D. Whistler, M. Kelley & M. Maggiotto (1993), *Building Democracy in One-Party Systems, Theoretical Problems and Cross-Nation Experiences*, London: Praeger.

White, Gordon (1995), 'Towards a Democratic Developmental State', *IDS Bulletin*, 26 (2): 27-36.

World Bank (1991), *World Development Report*, chapter on 'Rethinking the State', Washington, DC; (1993), *Governance: the World Bank's Experience*, Washington, DC: World Bank, Operations Policy Department, 29 November.

24 BJÖRN BECKMAN
The Liberation of Civil Society:
Neo-Liberal Ideology & Political Theory   [1993]

The state versus civil society debate is an arena where competing class projects confront each other, each seeking to ensure a social basis for its own control over the state. The state plays a central role in the construction of civil society. The neo-liberal project seeks to de-legitimise the state as a locus of nationalist aspirations and resistance, drawing on theories of 'rent-seeking', 'patrimonialism' and 'state autonomy'. The neo-liberal project conceals its own massive use of state power, transnational and local, for the construction of a civil society in its own image while suppressing actually existing civil society which it defines as 'vested interests'.

'State vs. Civil Society' as an Arena for Ideological Contestation

The 'liberation of civil society' from the suffocating grip of the state has become the hegemonic ideological project of our time. The emergence of the new hegemony is dramatised by the collapse of the socialist-oriented states in Eastern Europe, the weak performance of statist and nationalist strategies in much (but not all) of the third world, and the crisis of state welfarism in the West, all linked to the restructuring of class relations in these societies and the related disintegration of state-centred development coalitions.

A range of political forces across the political spectrum think that civil society has been constrained by the state and needs to be liberated. Neo-liberals claim they want to free its entrepreneurial potentials. But also socialists, of many shades, seem to accept that the failure of socialist experiences so far has been due to the suppression of civil society. Also in the social democratic middleground is the retreat from 'excessive statism' argued in terms of more freedom for civil society. In the third world, neo-liberals spearheaded by the World Bank, seek to roll back the state. But forces on the left are also disenchanted with their own statist experiences. They cling to the freedoms of civil society in defence against a hostile state. Organised interests seek to assert their autonomy.

Current arguments, however, are concerned not just with the liberation of civil society but with its very creation, especially in the third world and East European context. Socialism as well as post-colonial statism have not only repressed civil society but prevented it from emerging. It is fatal for the state itself because it has not been subjected to the necessary discipline provided by the forces of civil society and has opened the way for authoritarianism, parasitism, and inefficiency. The road to the creation of a 'proper' state therefore goes via the promotion of a 'proper' civil society.

Is this the 'end of ideology' proclaimed by the victorious cold-war warriors or the coming of a new global consensus as heralded by the World Bank (1989; Beckman, 1992)? Not at all. All sides have their own designs on both state and civil society. Interestingly, all depend heavily on a presumably redundant state in their efforts to develop the right type of civil society. The consensus is a conjuring trick – an attempt to assert hegemony. In the name of consensus, the World Bank, for instance, draws on radical populist positions, incorporating metaphors of the indigenous, the grassroots, and the development from below as against the alien, elitist and anti-civil society practices of the past.

This article is primarily concerned with the role of the state-civil society dichotomy in the ideological strategies of the current neo-liberal offensive. In the effort to de-legitimise the principal ideological rival, economic nationalism, neo-liberals seek to de-legitimise the state, the main locus of nationalist aspirations and resistance to the neo-liberal project. In order to undercut the claims by the state to represent the nation, its alien nature is emphasised. Its retrogressiveness is explained in terms of its separation from civil society. I will also examine some principal elements in this analysis of state separation, the notions of 'rent-seeking', 'patrimonialism' and 'state autonomy'.

The article does not attempt a definition of either 'state' or 'civil society', nor does it attempt to solve the difficult riddles of their interconnectedness which are also actively debated in the African context (cf. Mamdani, 1990b; for the Hegel/Marx/Gramsci attempts in this direction, see Sassoon, 1983). 'State vs. civil society' is treated here primarily as a metaphor that suggests, in a rough manner, a terrain of ideological struggle. I argue, however, that the state plays a central role in the constitution of civil society which is an issue which goes beyond ideology.

The Neo-liberal Project

Why 'neo?' Why not just 'liberal?' While the project is clearly liberalisation, the prefix is justified in order to distinguish current liberal strategies from those which have dominated the agenda of international development institutions since the decolonisation phase. They were also predominantly liberal in as far as they sought to promote capitalist development and world market integration. The World Bank has been involved since the 1950s in support of market forces, foreign investment and local entrepreneurial classes. Because of the weakness of the domestic bourgeoisies, state-sponsored development schemes were treated as nurseries. The state was expected to act as a trustee of a budding capitalism. State enterprises and parastatals proliferated not so much from a commitment to public ownership, as in the absence of alternatives. Partnership with the state gave national legitimacy and the necessary political protection to foreign capital and international development agencies (Beckman, 1977, 1981, 1985). The 1970s witnessed a deepening of state-promoted commercialisation within foreign-sponsored large-scale rural development projects, covering vast parts of national territory and developing foreign-managed administrative apparatuses that often overshadowed existing 'national' state institutions (Beckman, 1987). Agency-encouraged foreign borrowing for such projects contributed to the debt crisis, which in turn opened the way for the current neo-liberal offensive.

The new strategy is therefore neo-liberal, not because it promotes capitalism, commercialisation and markets, which all liberal strategies do, but because of the redefinition of the role of the state in this process. It is neo-liberal not in an abstract orthodox sense but in a specific historical and regional context. This redefinition has taken place, not just or even primarily because of the failure of the previous strategy but because of a shift in the balance of forces, undermining the bargaining power of post-colonial nationalism. The global dimensions of this shift require no further elaboration. It is important to stress that it is also supported at the level of bourgeois class formation within post-colonial society.

This is not to downplay the crisis of the post-colonial statist development model. The neo-liberal option, however, does not emerge as the 'only' or 'natural' response to the crisis. Nor is it necessarily the most capitalist one, in the sense of leading to the most rapid transformation of African societies on capitalist lines. This continues to be contested, for instance, on the basis of the successful statist East Asian experience. The neo-liberal project is promoted in competition with other nationalist and statist options.

The 'liberation of civil society' plays a vital role in the struggle to legitimate the shift in the balance of forces, both internally and globally, and to de-legitimise resistance and contending options. While the shift itself is quite dramatic, it is important not to lose sight of the basic continuities in the commitments of the leading international agencies in their efforts to lay the institutional pre-conditions for world-market integration, both at the level of state and civil society. Nor should we underestimate the centrality of state intervention to the liberal project in its new 'anti-statist' phase.

State vs. Civil Society & the De-legitimation of Post-colonial Nationalism

The post-colonial state emerged in the context of global contradictions between dominant and dominated positions in the world system. It became the focus of national aspirations and of resistance even if neo-colonial and accommodationist forces often gained an upper hand. Yet, post-colonial nationalism provided in most cases a real constraint on the world market integration of the post-colonial world. Nationalist aspirations were reinforced in the 1970s by the military victories of the national liberation movements in Vietnam, Central America and southern Africa. UNCTAD and the Non-Aligned Movement asserted the right of third world economies to protect themselves politically against a world market.

The de-legitimation of the state is central to the ideological de-construction of post-colonial nationalism as the state continues to be the locus of resistance to world market subordination. 'The state vs. civil society' discourse offers an arena for de-legitimation. 'Civil society' is therefore substituted for the 'nation' as the principal locus of legitimation. The contradiction between state and civil society is propagated as the dominant one. The more 'alien' the state can be made to appear, the less legitimate is its pretence to represent the nation.

I have discussed elsewhere how the World Bank plays skilfully on nationalist sentiments in this de-legitimisation exercise. Post-colonial 'statism' is presented as the result of foreign ideologies, not just marxism and socialism but also the statist ideas that had dominated development thinking in the West (Beckman, 1991,1992). The foreign-ness of the state becomes a means of explaining its irrelevance to the needs of civil society and its failure to establish appropriate roots. The international agencies present themselves as the spokesmen of the forces of civil society that have been suppressed. The 'empowerment' of civil society is supposed to lay the foundations of a future more genuine state, more responsive to the requirements and aspirations from below.

Political Science & the Academic Foundations of Neo-liberal Ideology

International intervention on the side of civil society draws on academic theorising about the nature of the African state. Political science has become useful to the 'international development community', having previously been marginalised by economists. The World Bank's (1989) long-term plans for Africa are prepared in consultation with political science scholars (World Bank, 1990). While economists focus on the dysfunctional impact of the state in African development, political scientists offer to explain the weakness of the state itself. Professional organisations such as the US African Studies Association and new institutions, like the Carter Center in Atlanta, have provided fora for a new discourse on African 'governance' (Carter Center, 1989, 1990).

Reviewing the proceedings of one of the Carter Center conferences, Mamdani (1990a) outlines a critique of this new paradigm where polarity between state and civil society is a core feature. He argues that it misrepresents the manner in which 'forces within society penetrate the state differentially, just as the state power reinforces certain social interests and undermines others'. The paradigm fails, according to Mamdani, to address the relationship between social processes and state power. It downplays fundamental differences in the manner in which production is organised and wealth generated in African societies, whether, for instance, the base is large-scale commercial agriculture, small-scale peasant production, or mineral rent. Such differences 'shape the contours of social groups, their demands and their capacities to wage struggle around these' (Mamdani, 1990a:8–9).

In theorising the state its 'class character' is defined in terms of the appropriations ('rent-seeking') of the 'political class' or the 'nomenclatura', not in terms of the role of such appropriations and functionaries in the management of the contradictions of the wider social formation. State and politics is reduced to rent. The logic of rent-seeking is extended to the 'vested interests' which share, directly or indirectly, in the appropriation of political rent. These include wage earners, public sector contractors, and private businessmen whose profits are an outcome of state patronage and preferential treatment. The relationship of these classes to production is seen as essentially unproductive and predatory. Public enterprises are subsidised and thus part of the rent-seeking order. Theories of rent-seeking are firmly linked to 'neo-patrimonialist' theories which stress personal rule and clientelistic relations. Both sets of theories obscure how power relations and appropriations articulate with social forces, reinforcing or modifying the manner in which social contradictions are resolved. Government spending is reduced to the distribution of patronage, favouring some sectional interests and discriminating against others in a pattern of ethnic or clan politics (Beckman, 1988a).

In a recent text, Gibbon (1992) develops the critique of this new political science-dominated paradigm. Like Mamdani, Gibbon demonstrates how patrimonialism and rent-seeking are abstracted from the social and economic relations that define their actual content and the failure to focus on their articulation with other social processes. Patrimonialism, for instance, becomes an 'empty box tied to personal rule', making it difficult to distinguish what it means and the limits within which it operates in different contexts, whether Nigeria, Kenya or Zaire (Gibbon, 1992:4). He also notes that clientelistic relations may be combined 'successfully' with 'free markets' as in Pinochet's Chile or in a state-civil society 'symbiosis' as in Japan. Gibbon shows convincingly how Robert Bates, one of the theoreticians of the new paradigm, separates politics from production relations. The entire focus is on politics as a source of accumulation, neglecting all other forms (Gibbon, 1992:8).

Rent-seeking & the Contradictions of Post-colonial Society

The failure to situate rent-seeking and patrimonialism in relation to the wider dynamics of production serves to conceal the manner in which the neo-liberal project intervenes in these contradictions. For instance, in a mining or oil economy, 'rent' concerns the terms under which mining and oil companies extract these resources, including their access to deposits, the terms on which labour is 'made available' and profits transferred. The function of the state in this context cannot be reduced to the parasitism of rent-seeking classes, however extensive it may be. The relation involves both national and class contradictions. The state represents national territorial interests. The 'political rent' that is appropriated by the 'political class' must be discussed in relation to what happens to this 'national rent'. It is in the interest of the neo-liberal project to blur the distinction between the two and to reduce the issue of rent to that of 'political rent' in a narrow class or 'nomenclatura' sense. It diverts attention from the underlying national contradictions and, in particular, from the way in which the neo-liberal project intervenes in those contradictions on the side of transnational capital. But also, class contradictions are obscured by the focus on rent-seeking. The state acts as gatekeeper for the terms under which local labour is made available to foreign capital. The issue of 'political rent' needs therefore to be related to the manner in which the state performs this role. Does the state collaborate with management in obstructing workers' rights and suppressing wages? Or is it supporting workers' interest? The neo-liberal intervention has implications for this relationship.

Agricultural marketing boards are favourite villains in the neo-liberal world view. Producers are prevented from reaping the full value of their labour. By reducing the boards to rent-seeking, however, it becomes possible to pursue liberalisation without addressing the problems of improving market access, price stability, extension services, access to inputs and so on, which were supposed to engage the boards, apart from their fiscal functions. If the boards are reduced to rent-seeking it also blocks an attempt to relate their functions to dynamics of social forces and contradictions within agrarian society itself. At the one end we merely find an amorphous suffering 'peasantry' and at the other a parasitic bureaucracy. While there may be much truth to such a picture, it blots out the highly differential manner in which board activities involve different strata among the producers, intermediary structures, co-operatives, traders, and village/community power-relations, including the struggle of such local forces to reform the marketing system in their own interest (for a discussion of the politics of Ghanaian cocoa marketing, see Beckman, 1976; on recent Nigerian experiences of liberalisation, see Mustapha, 1992). All this can be brushed aside in the bold neo-liberal sweep. Neo-liberal theory has no need for any knowledge about the demands and aspirations of the particular social groups affected in order to offer its solution. The medicine is supposed to work anywhere anytime. If not now, later.

Radical Reinforcement of the Separation Theories of State & Civil Society

Rent-seeking and patrimonial features are readily identified in most African societies and are dramatically conspicuous in some. Theorising about these features in terms of state-civil society polarity is not necessarily linked to support for the neo-liberal project. Some of it is rooted in concerns with popular emancipation, social movements, and democracy. My argument so far has been to demonstrate how a narrow, seemingly 'materialist' conceptualisation of the state in terms of rent-seeking and patronage abstracts those features from the relations of production with which they are articulated and which will influence their content and meaning. Moreover, as every-thing becomes subordinated to the logic of patrimonialism and rent-seeking, the model also obstructs an understanding of the functions performed by the state where rent is not a significant feature, for instance its actual role in regulating land, property and labour relations.

Radical scholars are of course as disturbed as the neo-liberal crusaders by the venality and parasitism of African ruling classes. In trying to explain the failure of the state to respond reasonably and efficiently to the imperatives of social and national emancipation they also draw on theories about state-society disjunctures. A 'comprador' model of the post-colonial state explains the separation of the state from society in terms of its international dependence. Local ruling classes have been reduced to agents – compradors – in the subordination of their societies to the requirements of neo-colonial or transnational capital. The commission that they collect in this relationship is their rent. I have elsewhere developed a critique of these positions which fail in my view to take the dynamics of local bourgeois class formation seriously enough and underestimate the significance of access to state and territory as a basis for bargaining power (Beckman, 1980, 1981, 1982, 1985). At this point, however, my concern is with the manner in which such radical positions draw on theoretical assumptions which are appropriated by the neo-liberal project (Beckman, 1988a).

One such 'common' assumption is the absence of a 'proper' bourgeoisie. While neo-liberals would certainly not think in terms of a 'national' versus a 'comprador' bourgeoisie, there is common ground both in the rejection of the existing one and the search for a substitute. While some radicals, at an earlier point at least, were preoccupied with finding a more progressive replacement for the missing national bourgeoisie, for example, in patriotic military quarters, neo-liberals have gained the upper hand in their pursuit of an 'enabling environment' in which new entrepreneurial classes will emerge, less dependent on the state, with their own autonomous institutions (for example, Chambers of Commerce), and ultimately destined to trans-form the state from below (with some little help from their foreign friends) into a proper capitalist state (see my critique of the World Bank's long-term perspective for Africa; Beckman, 1992). While radicals find such transnational intervention objectionable, their way of posing the problems in terms of a missing bourgeoisie opens itself for co-optation.

In theorising the separation of the state from society, neo-liberal theory can also draw on the vulgarisations of theories of the 'autonomy of the post-colonial state' borrowed from the radical tradition. An elaborate analysis by Hamza Alavi (1972) of ruling class factions, primarily in Pakistani post-colonial society, was at an early point adopted within radical discourses on Africa, revised out of recognition, and finally incorporated into the 'populist' luggage of neo-liberal ideology. The original argument concerned the relative strength of the state bureaucracy, civilian and military, within the arrangement of ruling class forces, local and foreign, dominating the Pakistani state. This was seen as enhancing the relative autonomy of the state. It was explained in terms of the history of class and state formation in the colonial context, including the crucial role of external forces in imposing a particular state on the society. In its application in the African context, the 'autonomy' aspect of the argument has tended to be drastically inflated. No domestic social forces seem to count in explaining the class character of the state except those who inhabit the state itself, the bureaucrats and politicians, who 'inherited' the colonial state, itself an imposition. To some radicals such special autonomy held out the prospects for struggles within the state apparatuses on primarily ideological grounds and therefore also the possibility that socialist-oriented forces may gain an upper hand, capable of confronting the continued domination by transnational capital (for a review of the debate, see Goulbourne, 1979).

As such radical aspirations waned with the deepening financial difficulties, indebtedness and dependence of the state itself, the autonomy argument was modified and incorporated into the new liberal discourse. Hyden (1983) speaks of 'the existence of a state with no structural roots in society', suspended 'as a balloon' in mid-air. African societies, according to him, lack a social class which is in command of society which is 'an inevitable prerequisite to development and there is no way that Africa, if it is serious about development, can escape taking the challenges therefrom' (Hyden, 1983:19,195). Hyden's argument about the separateness of the state, its lack of roots, is coupled to the 'neo-patrimonial' model. The absence of a genuine class base makes the state wide open to penetration by 'the economy of affection', his euphemism for nepotism and clientelism, which prevents the state from performing its legitimate functions and ruling it out as an agent of development (Hyden, 1988 and my critique, Beckman, 1988b).

The 'autonomy' that is attributed to a state can only be meaningfully defined in terms of the social parameters that delimit and specify its content. Questions must be asked about 'autonomy to do what?' 'autonomy in relation to what?' The original Alavi argument contained some efforts in this direction. Notions of states 'without roots in society' serve no analytical purpose and only help to obscure an understanding of the balance of forces within which they operate. It is essentially an ideological position suggesting that the state lacks the roots which you think it ought to have.

Civil Society & the Construction of the Post-colonial State

The neo-liberal project is able to draw on a radical critique of the state, claiming that the post-colonial state is primarily driven by its own internal 'class' logic (rent and patronage), in separation from the people. Both have good ideological reason for projecting this reductionist image of the state: it serves to prepare the way for their own alternative orders (radicals may be in good faith). It is obvious that the state fails to represent popular and national interests as these are perceived by them. Yet, the radicals are the ones to lose most from the promotion of the myth of the root-less state. If the neo-liberals indulge in self-deception it does not matter much. They currently have good access to state power and can promote their own project with the help of the very state they have declared redundant. In the case of the radicals, self-deception on these lines is bound to obstruct their own projects. In particular, it obstructs an understanding of the popular roots of ruling class politics, past and present.

The analysis of state-civil society relations must start from what has constituted the state historically at the level of civil society. What are the demands that 'society' has made on the state and how has the state developed 'as a state' in response to such demands. The fact that the post-colonial state was 'inherited' from colonialism does not make it any more 'cut off from society' than any other state. While originally having developed in response to the requirements of colonialist interests, transformations at the level of local society internalised these demands. The contradictions generated by the transformations created new sets of demands on the state which it sought to manage, combining promotion, repression and other means of regulation. Colonial capital and other foreign capital had a primary stake in the state and continue to do so. The state offers protection and services. While neo-liberal more than radical theorising can be blamed for obscuring this relation, the latter tends to neglect the manner in which such seemingly external determinants of the state were internalised into local civil society. While Cadbury, the chocolate manufacturers, wanted the colonial state to protect its interests, the cocoa farmers organised in their own defence, pressuring the state. The colonial state, which was very rudimentary at inception, was itself formed – constituted – as part of this process. Some of the interests in the state were of a pre-colonial origin, seeking protection, for instance, for pre-existing relations of power and privilege. Others represented emerging social forces, challenging such 'traditional' relations and their mutations under colonialism, as well as new ones, specific to the colonial economy and society. In its management of these contradictions, the colonial state developed its own 'popular roots'.

The state at an early point became the focus of demand for public services. Local civil society developed largely in the way in which claims on the state were increasingly taking on organised, collective forms. Roads, schools and health services were, and are, basic popular demands. It was natural that the competition for these services came to take on a territorial character, reinforced by the uneven penetration of commercial relations in peasant agriculture and other economic activity. Commercially more advanced areas were usually better placed in the struggle for services because their civil societies were better organised and more articulate (access, information, education, etc.).

One of the most unacceptable aspects of the neo-liberal paradigm is the tendency to reduce the relations which developed on the basis of these demands to questions of state rents and patronage. If instead the point of departure is taken in the legitimate popular aspirations contained in these demands and the genuine conflicts of interest that they involve, the irrelevance of the neo-liberal recipes of rolling back the state and breeding more entrepreneurs should be apparent.

The State & the Construction of Post-colonial Civil Society

The demands along the public service nexus have been central in shaping the state as well as in the construction of post-colonial civil society itself. For the notion of civil society to make sense it must involve some structuring of relations that distinguishes it from just being society. It seems to me that it is the relationship to the state that is this structuring principle. Civil society does not exist independently of the state, it is situated in rules and transactions which connect state and society. Chambers of Commerce, for instance, a popular representative of civil society in the neo-liberal world view, organise and represent the interest of business in a public arena as defined primarily by relations to the state (legislation, taxes, licences, duties, etc.). If we are to look for the institutions of post-colonial civil society we therefore need to pay special attention to the public service nexus. This is where we find a plethora of organised community interests, seeking to ensure that the new road, school, market, borehole, etc. will come their way. This is also where we find the organisations of public service workers, teachers, doctors, nurses, railway workers, etc. who in the neo-liberal world view are the 'vested interests' which obstruct their designs. It is not surprising that such groups play a leading role in the articulation of popular demands on the state (Bangura & Beckman, 1991).

The construction of civil society is centred on the rules that regulate the relations between competing interests in society. Interests demand from the state that it should lay down and enforce rules in their favour. People seek the protection of the state in the pursuit of their productive and reproductive life. They want protection for life, property and contract, access to means of production, rights of employment and tenancy. They want due process. Little of this is natural, which should be apparent when considering, for instance, the ongoing transformation of property and family rights as part of the commercialisation of the social relations of production. Most rights are situated within relations of domination and unequal power. Most relations are contested.

Both state and civil society are formed in the process of this contestation. Law is at the centre of the contest, not just the law of the book and the court room, but in its interpretation and application as determined by social struggles. It is in this contest that the neo-liberal project intervenes, prodding the state to be more responsive to interests of capital and private property. The intervention is made in the name of civil society as opposed to the state, while its consequences are to intensify state intervention in suppressing existing forces of civil society, including those converging within the public service nexus. It is also an intervention on the side of capital within the capital-labour relation. In either case, actually existing civil society is portrayed as 'vested interests' which need to be combated in the interest of a civil society yet to come.

The organised social groups that most actively articulate the defence of the autonomy of civil society vis-à-vis the state can be found within and around the public service nexus, for example, teachers, students, doctors, nurses, lawyers and journalists.

Conclusions & Implications

The state versus civil society debate has been discussed in this article as an arena for ideological contestation. Competing class projects confront each other, each concerned with the promotion and defence of different civil societies, populated by different NGOs, social movements and encapsulating different civil rights. Each project seeks to ensure the long-term social basis for alternative configurations of state power. The state plays a central role in both the construction and the liberation of civil society. The functioning of civil society, also in its autonomy from the state, depends on state intervention, including the enforcement of the rules which constitute and regulate property, markets and other rights. The freedoms of civil society are gained in struggles against inherited constraints, including feudal, patriarchal, religious and other restrictions. The freedom and emancipation of subordinated social groups depend on the ability of the state to restrain the exercise of power in society, based on arms, property, gender, ethnicity and other factors which discriminate between people in access to resources.

This article has been concerned with the manner in which the state-civil society dichotomy has been appropriated by and geared to the neo-liberal agenda. By pretending to be civil society's best friend and by assigning the state the role of the enemy of civil society, the neo-liberal project conceals its own massive use of state power, transnational and local, for the purpose for constructing a civil society according to its own image. In so doing, it is busy suppressing and disorganising much of the civil society as it actually exists, with its aspirations and modes of organisation centred on influencing the use of state power. While pretending to act on behalf of all civil society – NGOs, social movements, grassroots – by a definitional trick, groups which are not supportive of its own project are defined out of civil society. They are 'vested interests', benefiting in one way or other from the state and therefore not truly civil society in the way the polarity has been falsely constructed. The hypocrisy of this ideological construct, however, is that the beneficiaries of neo-liberal state intervention are as profoundly dependent on state promotion and protection, including the state enforcement of their own type of property rights. The neo-liberal project exploits successfully the radical and populist critique of the bad state but ignores that such a critique is based on radically different expectations about what the state could and should do for the people.

How do Third World radicals respond to this ideological challenge? The state was identified as the principal agent of development in most radical development theories, be they primarily socialist or nationalist by orientation. As socialists, radicals sought to turn the state into an instrument of popular class power. As nationalists, they aspired to use it to liberate the nation from its subordination to transnational power that obstructs national development. Faced with the neo-liberal hegemonic thrust, responses from radical democratic and nationalist forces have been ambivalent. While vocal in denouncing the retrogressive and oppressive nature of the existing state, including the parasitism and rent-seeking behaviour of its functionaries, the state is still defended as an instrument of national aspirations. In the past, solutions may have been more commonly thought of in terms of the capturing of state power. The defunct post-colonial state was to be reconstructed under radical leadership. With the likelihood of this happening being even more remote, radical expectations of the state are fading.

The focus of radical democrats has shifted towards the construction and protection of popular democratic power in society. To that venture the state appears as a threat. There is a primary preoccupation with enhancing the autonomy of popular organisations vis-à-vis the state. The liberation of civil society makes sense in that context. A radical retreat into civil society may reflect a sobering of expectations and a more realistic understanding of local and global determinants of state power. It does not necessarily mean an abandonment of the quest for it. Disenchantment with state politics has created new strategies of influencing the exercise of state power from organised and autonomous bases of popular power in civil society. The experience of the Nigerian labour movement, for instance, points to the manner in which the laws, institutions, and practices that define the freedom of the civil society develop in the context of class struggle (Andrae & Beckman, 1992).

A critique of neo-liberal ideology, its hypocrisy, its false consensus, and its hegemonic pretensions, does not exclude, of course, that radical democrats and neo-liberals have areas of common interest in the liberation of civil society. There may be a scope for alliances based on a platform of pluralism and constitutionalism in defence against arbitrary state power. Radical democrats have their own agenda for the reconstitution of state-civil society relations, and not one but many, depending on concrete experiences and openings. In Algeria, for instance, the 1988 events are seen by some as evidence of the final breakdown of state-civil society relations built on an element of social consensus inherited from the liberation struggle and a certain societal acceptance of state violence in the national interest (Bourenane, 1990). In this perspective, the real rupture only occurred as a result of the structural adjustment policies of the 1980s, as linked to the disintegration of the income support and welfare services which both agriculturalists and wage earners had received. It went hand in hand with the intensified enrichment of state and related elites. Other Algerian scholars situate the origin of the rupture much earlier, in the nature of the liberation struggle itself, where the capturing of state power from the colonialists at an early point opened up for the private enrichment of entrenched cadres (Talahite, 1992). Mamdani (1990c), drawing primarily on the Ugandan experience but referring to a wider African one, suggests an even earlier rupture, coupled to the rise of state nationalism linked to the suppression of the popular and democratic elements in the origins of the nationalist movement. Such differences will of course affect radical strategies vis-à-vis the current crisis of the post-colonial state.

At present the primary preoccupation of radical democrats may be to fend off state repression and widen the democratic space. In this there is room for alliances with both liberal and neo-liberal forces, foreign and domestic. Similarly, the rights of labour may be advanced and protected within the context of 'social contracts' with state and capital. The real meaning of such rights to the popular classes, however, depends – as always – on struggle and organised strength.

What about the project of national liberation? Economic nationalism has been retreating in the face of advancing neo-liberalism, causing a dissolution of previous nationalist-dominated radical alliances. Does the retreat into the defence of its own civil society mean that nationalism has been abandoned as the other leg of the radical project? Current experiences suggest that this is not necessarily the case. The resistance to the neo-liberal thrust of 'structural adjustment' as promoted by the international finance institutions has opened up a renewal of alliances which are both national and democratic (Beckman, 1990).

Editors' Note: This paper was presented to a workshop on 'Social Movements, State and Democracy', organised by the Delhi University Group in Politics of Developing Countries and the Indian Statistical Institute Sociology Group, New Delhi, October 1992.

Bibliography

Alavi, H. (1972), 'The State in Post-colonial Societies', *New Left Review* 74.

Andrae, G. & B. Beckman (DATE ?), 'Labour Regimes and Adjustment in the Nigerian Textile Industry', paper to a workshop on 'The State, Structural Adjustment and Changing Social and Political Relations in Africa', Uppsala: Scandinavian Institute of African Studies.

Bangura, Y. & B. Beckman (1991), 'African Workers and Structural Adjustment: A Nigerian Case Study', in Dharam Ghai (ed.), *The IMF and the South: The Social Impact of Crisis and Adjustment,* London, Zed Books.

Beckman, B. (1976), *Organising the Farmers: Cocoa Politics and National Development in Ghana*, Uppsala, Scandinavian Institute of African Studies; (1977), 'Public Enterprise and State Capitalism' in Yash Ghai (ed.), *Law in the Political Economy of Public Enterprise: African Perspectives*, Uppsala and New York, Scandinavian Institute of African Studies and International Legal Centre; (1980), 'Imperialism and Capitalist Transformation: Critique of a Kenyan debate', *Review of African Political Economy* 19; (1981), 'Imperialism and the National Bourgeoisie', *Review of African Political Economy* 22; (1982), 'Capitalist State Formation in the Third World', seminar paper, Uppsala, AKUT 19; (1985), 'Neo-colonialism, Capitalism and the State in Nigeria' in H. Bernstein and B. Campbell (eds), *Contradictions of Accumulation in Africa*, Beverly Hills, Sage; (1987), 'Public Investment and Agrarian Transformation in Northern Nigeria' in Michael Watts (ed.), *State, Oil, and Agriculture in Nigeria*, Berkeley, Institute of International Studies; (1988a), 'The Post-Colonial State: Crisis and Reconstruction', *IDS Bulletin* 19, 4, also at the Centre of African Studies, Edinburgh, *African Futures: 25th Anniversary Conference*, Seminar Proceedings No. 28; (1988b), 'Comments on Göran Hydén's State and Nation under Stress' in Swedish Ministry of Foreign Affairs, *Recovery in Africa: A Challenge for Development Cooperation in the 90s*, Stockholm, MFA, pp. 159–64; (1990), 'Structural Adjustment and Democracy: Interest Group Resistance to Structural Adjustment and the Development of the Democracy Movement in Africa', Research proposal, Stockholm University, Department of Political Science; (1992a), 'Empowerment or Repression? The World Bank and the Politics of Adjustment' in P. Gibbon, Y. Bangura and A. Ofstad (eds), *Authoritarianism, Democracy and Adjustment: The Politics of Economic Reform in Africa*, Uppsala: Scandinavian Institute of African Studies (also in *Africa Development* XVI, 1, 1991).

Bourenane, N. (1990), 'Pouvoir d'état et société civile en Algérie', *Africa Development* XV, 3/4.

Carter Center (1989), *Beyond Autocracy in Africa*, Working Papers, Inaugural Seminar of the African Governance Program, Atlanta, GA, Emory University; (1990), *African Governance in the 1990s*,

Working Papers from Second Annual Seminar, Atlanta, GA, Emory University;

Gibbon, P. (1992), 'Understanding Changing Social Relations in Contemporary Africa', paper to a workshop on 'The State, Structural Adjustment and Changing Social and Political Relations in Africa', Uppsala: Scandinavian Institute of African Studies.

Goulbourne, H. (ed.) (1979), *Politics and State in the Third World*, London: Macmillan.

Hyden, G. (1983), *No Shortcuts to Progress: African Development Management in Perspective*, London: Heinemann; (1988), 'State and Nation under Stress' in Swedish Ministry of Foreign Affairs, *Recovery in Africa: A Challenge for Development Cooperation in the 90s*, Stockholm, MFA; (1990a), 'The Changing Context of Institutional Development in sub-Saharan Africa', Washington, DC, World Bank; (1990b), 'Creating and Enabling Environment', Washington, DC, World Bank.

Mamdani, Mahmood (1990a), 'A Glimpse at African Studies, Made in USA', *CODESRIA Bulletin 2*, 1990; (1990b), 'Social Movements, Social Transformation and the Struggle for Democracy in Africa', *CODESRIA Bulletin 3*; (1990c), 'State and Civil Society in Contemporary Africa: Reconceptualizing the Birth of State Nationalism and the Defeat of Popular Movements', *Africa Development* XV, 3/4.

Mustapha, A. R. (1992), 'Structural Adjustment and Agrarian Change in Nigeria' in A. Olukoshi (ed.), *The Politics of Structural Adjustment in Nigeria*, London: James Currey.

Sassoon, A. S. (1983), 'Civil Society', in T. Bottomore (ed.), *A Dictionary of Marxist Thought*, Oxford: Blackwell.

Talahite, F. (1992), 'Algeria: Democracy under Threat', seminar paper, Uppsala: AKUT.

World Bank (1989), *Sub-Saharan Africa From Crisis to Sustainable Growth: A Long-Term Perspective Study*, Washington, DC; (1990), *Institutional and Sociopolitical Issues: The Long-Term Perspective Study of sub-Saharan Africa*, Background Papers, Vol. 3 (1991), *World Development Report 1991: The Challenge of Development*, Washington, DC.

25

JOHN RAPLEY
New Directions
in the Political Economy of Development   [1994]

This article underlines the changing balance of paradigms over the last decade and argues that the critique of neo-classical theory is gaining new life. What is emerging, though, is a subtler and more sophisticated view of the state than the traditional state-market dichotomy allowed for. It situates the recent African experience within a wider international context and reviews the different roles played by the state in encouraging or discouraging development.

To say that we live in a liberal age, in that neo-classical liberalism dominates contemporary discourse in the social sciences and practice in politics, might seem a truism. Yet it is only half-true, for the neo-classical victory was made possible by the left's inability to provide a sufficient defence against its assault.

The collapse of the left in both the political and academic realms did not result from the rise of the right, but preceded it, though the full extent of its debilitation did not become apparent until the 1980s. Yet by the 1970s, political scientists had uncovered a long-term erosion of the support bases for Western socialist parties, while experts on the Soviet Union and Eastern Europe were pointing to a stagnation in these economies that showed no way of being relieved. Yet leftist theorists and politicians clung doggedly to old orthodoxies. When the neo-classical assault began to accumulate political victories, they spluttered critiques and condemnations, yet seldom offered practical alternatives.

Nevertheless, certainly in development studies, the critique of neo-classical theory is gaining new life. But whether or not leftist theories can rehabilitate themselves in academic circles, it seems difficult at present to conceive of a revived socialism in practice. On the surface, socialism seems well and truly dead. Journalists and right-wing ideologues have seized upon the collapse of socialism in the Soviet Union and Eastern Europe, as well as the failures of and retreat from state control in Africa, Latin America and much of Asia – not to mention the irremediable cleavage between the old socialism of the working class and the new socialism of new social movements like environmentalism and feminism – as evidence that socialism is defunct.

Yet despite what seems to be overwhelming evidence, the conclusion may be premature. The continuing economic success of China, where reform has yet to alter the fundamentals of public ownership and central control, is the strongest reason against rushing into this conclusion. Using China as a model, the descent into anarchy of the former Soviet Union as a contrast, some theorists argue that the reform of socialism may yield more fruit than its abolition (see Nolan 1993). Meantime the collapse of socialism has purged Western socialist theory of its orthodoxies. This has injected an invigorating breath of fresh air into academic debate on the left, even if it has weakened the left politically, at least for the time being. While it may be years before the left reconstitutes itself as a vigorous political force, neo-classical theory does not stand unchallenged.

One of the common themes that has arisen from critiques of neo-classical theory has been that government and the market are often symbiotic rather than conflictual (see, for example, Killick, 1989; Stewart, 1985; Taylor, 1992, 1993a, 1993b; Toye, 1987; Weeks, 1993). In other words, to make the market more efficient one need not so much reduce the state's role in the economy as alter it. Given that structural adjustment has been the practical manifestation of neo-classical theory in the developing world, it is telling that much of the empirical research on structural adjustment points to a similar conclusion.

Structural adjustment programmes (SAPs) aim to remove blockages believed to thwart the efficient operation of markets. Typically, these blockages are seen to result from government intervention. So SAPs have usually included such elements as the removal of price and other controls on enterprises, the removal of quantitative barriers to trade and the streamlining of taxes on imports (import liberalisation), the abolition of marketing boards (market liberalisation), exchange rate devaluation, the privatisation or denationalisation of state-owned enterprises, and the encouragement of new industrial private foreign investment.

Many doubts have been raised about the principle of structural adjustment. Even their supporters admit that while SAPs restore macroeconomic stability, it is not entirely obvious that macroeconomic stability on its own leads to growth (see Frenkel and Khan, 1992; and Doroodian, 1993). Africanists can easily point to countries that have fared badly under structure adjustment (Guillaumont, 1993); while even where the policy has produced more positive results, expectations still remain unfulfilled (on Nigeria, see Oyejide, 1991a; on Tanzania, see Shao, 1992). In the case of Ghana, for example, arguably Africa's test case for structural adjustment, most observers say there have been clear gains, but hasten to add that these gains relied on strong donor backing, unlikely to be repeated elsewhere in Africa, while the long-term sustainability of the programme remains in doubt (see Rothchild, 1991; Loxley, 1990; Kusi, 1991).

The African experience with structural adjustment has generally pointed to one conclusion: while yielding short-term improvements, the policy is apparently jeopardising long-term development. And so, quite apart from the moral and political critique of structural adjustment – the fact that SAPs tend to have concentrated benefits while immiserating a substantial part of the population – a cursory glance at the evidence from Africa, as well as from some Asian economies (see, for instance, Rahman, 1992 on Bangladesh) could lead one to conclude that structural adjustment, and with it the neo-classical approach to development, has generally been an unmitigated failure. That conclusion would be hasty. For turning to Latin America, we find that structural adjustment has yielded some considerable gains, even if the benefits remain unevenly distributed (on Chile, see Ritter, 1990, and Diaz and Korovkin, 1990). This contrast points us towards an emerging consensus in development studies: liberalisation works best in those economies which have first been through a phase of infant industry promotion.

An anatomy of SAPs helps explain why they succeed and why they fail. Different elements of structural adjustment have met with differing degrees of success. Beginning with privatisation, agreement is emerging that such policies have little to commend themselves. Not only does the basic assumption underlying them, that private ownership leads to improved firm performance, not stand to reason, the growing body of evidence belies it.

To begin with, it is questionable that public firms can always be assessed by the same criteria as private ones, the standard measures being financial performance and efficiency. State firms are often created to rectify market failures or deficiencies, or to confer beneficial externalities (spin-offs that enhance the development of the economy, but are not profitable for individual firms to undertake, such as research and development or human capital formation) conducive to the development of the private sector. Or they may embrace difficult subsectors whose development is necessary to the economy, but that private firms eschew (Lesser, 1991:166). In Côte d'Ivoire, for instance, the Banque Ivoirienne de Développement Industriel's unrecovered loans eventually drove the bank into bankruptcy, but not before it had funded the creation and expansion of a large number of successful local private ventures. These ventures would probably not have been funded otherwise, because the foreign-dominated private banking sector avoided Ivoirien entrepreneurs in favour of safe investments in large multinational corporations (Rapley, 1993:135–36). Such a case is scarcely exceptional: research on Taiwan (Crane, 1989–90), Brazil (Faucher, 1991) and Indonesia (Ellis, 1993) has also highlighted public firms whose individual performances were questionable but whose contributions to national economic development were not.

But even ignoring the importance of externalities, there is little if any evidence that publicly-owned firms are intrinsically prone to poor performance or that private firms are necessarily more efficient than public ones (Taylor, 1993a:586; Bardhan, 1992:566; Killick, 1989:26; Toye, 1987:58). In fact, there are many instances of successful public firms in the developing world (for examples see Crane, 1989–90, Harrigan, 1992, Haider and Kemal, 1991; also Cook, 1992:404). Consequently it is not clear that reducing the public sector to expand the private one exercises any significant impact on development (Yoder, Borkholder and Friesen, 1991). As for the inefficiencies of African marketing boards, Gibbon (1992:58) argues that these did not always result from public mismanagement but from external problems like under-capitalisation or mandates beyond the scope of the boards' resources.

Because of such findings, most development theorists, including some who might loosely be described as on the right (see, for example, the cautious stance of Harrell (1993) who is echoing the position of a World Bank study), have moved away from advocating privatisation as an ingredient in a recipe for accelerated development. Not only does it seem neither to improve firm performance nor accelerate economic development, but contrary to popular perception it does little, if anything, to raise money for cash-starved governments (Cook, 1992:406; Haider and Kemal, 1991; Ramamurti, 1993:37–38). It is also arguable that the resources put into privatisation could be better spent elsewhere (Murrell, 1992; Ickes and Ryterman, 1992): luring investors into the purchase of the public firms may 'crowd out' investment in private firms at a time when capital is in short supply. While some still consider privatisation to be useful in certain situations, such as the former Soviet bloc countries (Lee and Nellis, 1991), more and more development theorists are favouring reform over privatisation as a means to improve the performance of public firms.

The results of liberalisation have been more mixed than those of privatisation. Most theorists now agree that liberalisation can have beneficial results, but only if done in a discriminating manner which takes account of both local and international demand and supply conditions. At a general level, there are two types of liberalisation: the liberalisation of domestic markets through the elimination of such things as price controls and marketing boards, and the liberalisation of foreign trade through the elimination of such things as tariffs and qualitative restrictions on imports, and also by devaluing overvalued currencies. In addition, because it raises the price of export goods in local terms, devaluation has often been promoted as a means to 'get the prices right'. In theory, freeing up markets and restoring currencies to something approximating a 'market' value should increase the efficiency of resource allocation. In practice things are not so simple.

Because the world economy is dominated by the highly protected and subsidised producers of the developed world, indiscriminate import liberalisation can lead to deindustrialisation in developing countries (Stewart, 1991; Lall, 1990:66). Nevertheless, while the benefits of liberalisation should not be overstated – the relationships between trade liberalisation on one hand, and exports and economic performance on the other, are at best weak (Adhikari, Kirkpatrick and Weiss, 1992:7–8; Greenaway and Sapsford, 1993; Wade, 1990:15–22) – it has produced positive results in East Asia and Latin America, even if these benefits have sometimes been modest (see Weiss, 1992 on Mexico). This brings us back to the point made earlier: opening onto the market works best after a phase of sheltered development, during which industries are nurtured by the state and strengthened in preparation for future competition (Singer, in Singer and Roy, 1993:21; Lall, 1992; Bienefield, 1987).

This has come to be known as the infant industry model for industrial development. During the early phases of industrialisation, the state can not only mobilise large pools of savings in a short time and build up human capital and technological capability, it can also foster comparative advantage (Lall, 1992). Herein lies one of the weaknesses of the neo-classical approach: its calls for liberalisation are motivated by the desire to realise comparative advantage, but these calls presuppose static comparative advantage and ignore dynamic comparative advantage. In addition, there are cases in which a national economy is unable to realise even its static comparative advantage in the absence of effective government intervention. A study of Lesotho's wool and mohair industry found that while Lesotho enjoyed a clear comparative advantage in the production of these goods, producers were unable to realise it because South African exports benefited from a considerably superior distribution network, something which could only be rectified by the Lesotho government creating its own distribution network (Storey, 1992).

Contrasting the successful East Asian experiences with the more disappointing ones of Latin America and India, where import-substitution industrialisation was used at length, import industry theorists agree on a few simple rules. They accept the importance of export-orientated industrialisation, and tend to agree that there should be a time limit to protection: clearly specified time limits enable plant managers to know how long they have to build up their capabilities before their companies will be thrown onto the world market. In addition, government interventions should be in support of the market, or market-enhancing, rather against the market, or market-repressing (Lall, 1990:60; Lall, 1993; Putterman and Rueschemeyer, 1992; Garnaut, 1991; Killick, 1993).

The idea that the state should shelter and assist domestic industry during the build-up phase, then gradually withdraw from the economy and allow for encroachment by the market, has many supporters. In fact, Peter Nolan attributes the success of the Chinese reforms at producing one of the world's fastest-growing economies partly to the Chinese state's gradual opening onto the market; in contrast, the one-off reforms tried by Russia have yet to promise similar gains (Nolan, 1993). Even those not so wedded to the idea of a strong state are coming to agree that gradual reform of state socialist systems is preferable to the Russian approach (see McKinnon, 1991).

It is therefore important to understand that most who criticise import liberalisation are not suggesting that it not be done at all, but that it not be done too soon. Even in more developed third world countries like Mexico, some contend that too far a retreat by the government will jeopardise future development due to spending reductions on investment and infrastructure (Ramirez, 1993). Thus, an emerging trend in development studies seems to be that import liberalisation is an effective strategy for promoting economic development, but only after a period in which the state has nurtured the development of industry and prepared it for world competition, and even then with continuing government support in the form of such things as infrastructure provision and human capital formation. Yet if the benefits of import liberalisation are now widely accepted, getting the prices right, or domestic market liberalisation, has been an entirely different matter. For the most part, this exercise has produced disappointment. Not because of unsound theory, but because the practice has frequently failed to take account of the realities of third world agricultural markets.

The current fascination with getting the prices right grew out of the 'new political economy', associated with the work of Robert Bates (1981). This school contended that Africa's urban-biased ruling elites overvalued their countries' currencies so as to inflate industrialists' profits (by keeping the prices of imported inputs low) and keep the prices of consumer goods low for the urban working class. Food prices were also kept deliberately low to favour this urban constituency. At the same time, marketing boards were used to skim off resources from the rural sector in order to develop the cities. All in all, there was a net drain of resources from the rural to the urban sector, while low producer prices resulted in sluggish production. This was seen to be especially detrimental in Africa, which relies so heavily on exports of primary goods to fuel its development. The solution, once again, was to roll back the state: abolishing marketing boards would inject competition into the purchase of primary goods, while currency devaluation would cause local prices of primary commodities to leap. It was expected that these price incentives would spur greater exports, and thereby greater revenue and faster growth in the economy.

Among the shortcomings of the new political economy as it has been applied to Africa, critics have noted that the urban interest groups which Bates suggested controlled the state turned out to be less powerful than he had supposed they would be; after all, structural adjustment has hit them hardest. Moreover, given that most urban Africans retain close ties to their villages, rigid urban-rural dichotomies seldom apply (Gibbon, 1992; Mkandawire, 1992:308–9). Nor is it obvious that a net drain of resources from the countryside to the cities always inhibits development. It can, and often does do so, but in East Asia industrialisation often relied on the state transferring resources from agriculture to industry (Jenkins, 1991:214–15). Arguably, this strategy was also used successfully in Côte d'Ivoire (see Rapley, 1993: chapter 4). As for the argument that raising producer prices will lead to increased exports, all other things remaining equal, the logic is fine. The problem is that all other things are rarely equal, especially in Africa.

The moral economists aside, most development theorists currently believe that peasants do in fact respond positively to price incentives. However, the neo-classical emphasis on prices is not being criticised for being too reductionist: in its focus on prices, it neglects the many other incentives or the conditions that must be in place before they will respond to prices. It is now well-established that peasants will respond positively to price increases only if they have access to such things as a good transportation infrastructure, reasonable credit, subsidised inputs, land and labour, as well as the benefits of government-sponsored research and development. They also seek incentives to production: getting a better price is of little value if there is nothing that can be done with the extra income. So, readily available consumer goods are among the important incentives to production. The availability of inputs, incentives and an adequate infrastructure, can be jeopardised by government rollback. Retrenchment in some spheres, such as marketing and price-setting, may need to be accompanied by advances in others like infrastructure, credit provisions, extension and so forth. Thus an emerging consensus seems to be that 'getting the price right' relies on a number of government measures to be made effective.

Using devaluation to raise producer prices presents its own problems. While it may benefit agriculture, devaluation can hurt urban industry since it raises input prices. Moreover, some argue that devaluation has done little to stimulate exports in sub-Saharan Africa due to the low demand elasticities for these commodities and declining demand in developed countries (Mengisteab, 1991; Mengisteab and Logan, 1991:106). Meantime, devaluation and/or the removal of subsidies on inputs lead to inflation because of the jump in import costs. This yields a whole new set of problems, including the possibility that resultant inflation can erode most of the gains in producer prices, as appears to have happened in Kenya, Tanzania and Zimbabwe (Shapouri, Missiaen and Rosen, 1992; Shao, 1992). Once again, the solution to these dilemmas posed by devaluation appears to be not a wholesale renunciation of the strategy, but government intervention to mitigate the effects of inflation or decreased consumption, at least in the short term (see Rhodd's conclusion on the Jamaican experience: Rhodd, 1993).

In addition, it now appears that the new political economy may have overestimated not only the degree of currency overvaluation that prevailed under the old regimes in Africa (Mengisteab 1991), but also its negative impact. While devaluation and producer price increases have led to some significant increases in recorded exports, at least some – and in several cases possibly most – of this increase can be attributed not to new production, but to the re-entry into formal circulation of goods formerly smuggled because of unfavourable official prices (Guillaumont, 1993). Sara Berry (1993) suggests the new political economy overstated the detrimental impact of government policies on agriculture: they may have led not to decreased production, but simply to increased secrecy. The obverse of this is that government retreat may not be as effective as the data seem to suggest it is.

As for liberalising domestic agricultural markets by abolishing marketing boards, the results have been mixed. Nigeria's experience appears to have been good, but elsewhere, the withdrawal of the state has not left in place a free and competitive market. Agricultural markets all over the developing world, especially in Africa, are often fraught with imperfections (Harriss, 1992; Harriss and Crow, 1992; Lesser, 1991; Guillaumont, 1993; Gregoire, 1990). In such cases, small groups may end up absorbing the price gains, perhaps even depositing them abroad (de Alcantara, 1992). Not all African agricultural markets work so badly (Beynon, 1992:8), but when they do, reregulation rather than deregulation appears a better way to increase output (Harriss and Crow, 1992). Again, better rather than less state intervention.

Apart from reducing market distortions, marketing boards can perform other functions. Some subsectors – in Africa, examples include cotton and bulk food crops – rely on public marketing because they are unattractive to private traders (Gibbon, 1992: 58). More important is the role that marketing boards can play in price stabilisation: a completely free market in primary goods will reflect the vagaries of world commodity markets, with their sometimes violent price swings. Peasant producers are often more concerned with risk than with price, and will retreat from production of crops in which the risks of price fluctuation are very high. Many theorists argue for the retention of marketing boards (Guillaumont, 1993; Beynon, 1992:7; Barker, 1989:210), though reform remains an option. This is because 'monolithic' marketing boards may not be necessary, as Indonesia's experience shows. Its rice board has successfully stabilised prices by intervening at the margins of output, buying between 3 per cent and 8 per cent of any year's marketed output (Ellis, 1993).

Finally, in addition to the liberalisation of the markets for primary products, neo-classical theory has advocated financial liberalisation and labour market deregulation. Although financial liberalisation can free up credit, especially that available to small firms (Oyejide, 1991b on the Nigerian experience), it can equally raise rather than lower capital costs if the banks choose to lend money to firms rather than invest in them. A more regulated market, in which banks are required to invest directly in firms – one can add, in long-term bonds rather than stocks, as in Germany – will maximise the efficient use of capital (Taylor, 1993a:585–86). As for labour market regulations, the evidence is weak that minimum wage laws significantly distort labour markets (Haggblade, Liedholm and Mead, 1990:67). Indeed, there are cases where minimum wage rates actually reduce distortions (Azam, 1992). Allowing wage rates to fall too low can erode the gains brought on by increases in comparative advantage if the domestic market becomes so restricted as to reduce sales (Taylor, 1993a:587; Fitzgerald, 1990:385–86).

The growing criticism of liberalisation policies has not gone unnoticed by neo-classical theorists. Among other things, they have recognised that structural adjustment has tended to fall rather hard on the poor. The World Bank itself admits that there is a political element to adjustment: people must be sheltered from its hardest effects if regime stability is to be preserved (Davies and Sanders, 1993:81). With this in mind, the World Bank has come to advocate targeted programmes of assistance to the poor, which are said to have achieved partial if not complete success in Jamaica (Grosh, 1992), Chile (Barrientos, 1993) and India (Chellaraj, Brorsen and Farris, 1992). Yet underlying such programmes is a continuing mistrust of the state; they are designed to alleviate misery until the expected benefits of structural adjustment trickle down to the population. Grudgingly, neo-classical theorists accept that maybe better rather than less state intervention is a good idea, but only for a while. Fundamentally, the neo-classical faith in the market remains unshaken, even if one can detect clear shifts away from earlier radical free-market approaches (see the World Bank's call for an increased state role in its 1991 *World Development Report*).

Yet the state continues to play an important, often essential, role in the development of third world countries, and as the influential work of Lance Taylor has shown, more state does not necessarily entail less market. The two may expand and contract together (though even Taylor acknowledges that state investment can sometimes 'crowd out' private investment: see Taylor, 1993b:5). It is now apparent that there is no firm evidence to suggest that less government leads to faster economic growth. If there is any relationship between the two, it may be that, in the aggregate, more government leads to more growth (Sattar, 1993). Moreover, many of the successes attributed to the increased role of markets may in fact have stemmed from other factors, as Bramall (1993) argues with regards to the decollectivisation of Chinese agriculture.

Structuralist economists and developmental state theorists will hardly be shocked to hear that the state has a vital role to play in the development process. What is perhaps surprising, though, is that many neo-classical economists are now coming around to the view that it is not the size of the state, but rather its role and effectiveness that is the key to development (Singer and Roy, 1993:23). Even the World Bank appears sensitive to the renewed importance of the state in development. What is emerging in the current development debate is a subtler and more sophisticated view of the state than the traditional state-market dichotomy allowed for. It is concerned not so much with the quantity as with the quality of state intervention.

It is all very well to say that better rather than less state is the solution to under-development. The fact remains that the capacities of states to implement development programmes and policies differ widely. As regards Africa, many Africanists are coming to the gloomy conclusion that many states are simply not up to the task of development (Rothchild and Chazan, 1988; Seidman, 1992:10). Some, yearning for the elusive 'governance' that has become the World Bank's Holy Grail, have looked to the recent wave of democratisation as means to improve the functioning of African governments. Half-heartedly, they hope that the increased accountability forced on political leaders by liberal democracy will yield such results as a reduction of corruption (Mkandawire, 1992; Medard, 1990). Unfortunately, a good many Africanists are pessimistic as to what democratisation can achieve. Few see it as a bad thing, but they are not overly confident that it will make much of an impact on the operation of governments (Clapham, 1992; Bratton and van de Walle, 1992; Jeffries, 1993). Some point to the apparent contradiction of the twin processes of state retreat and democratisation: in poor societies, states need to mobilise popular support for both democracy and state legitimacy, and are handicapped by the lack of resources they suffer from retrenchment (Clapham, 1992; Mengistaeb and Logan, 1991:110). Among other results of state retrenchment, people lose faith in the government's ability to render even the most basic of welfare services, turning elsewhere for functions normally performed by government (Rudebeck, 1990). This further undermines the state's ability to play an effective role in development, regardless of whether that prescribed role is minimalist or maximalist. A few Africanists, bewildered by state failure, throw up their hands in despair and say that the nation-state, imported from Europe by colonialism, is inappropriate technology in Africa and cannot hope to fulfill the requirements of development (Davidson, 1992; Darbon, 1990).

This last opinion of the state in Africa remains a minority one. Nonetheless, it epitomises a despondence that has gripped many Africanists over the last decade. Although there have been cases of good, and even outstanding, state performance in Africa, like Botswana and Côte d'Ivoire, there have been many abysmal failures, like Zaïre and pre-Museveni Uganda. This raises a question that challenges development theory even more than does the question of what the appropriate role for the state in the economy is: why is it that some states have apparently been instrumental to development, whereas others have apparently been obstacles to the process? What explains such glaring differences?

There are a number of theories that seek to explain success and/or failure. Attention has inevitably turned to the 'success' stories – the East Asian NICs – in order to identify possible reasons for success. This has given rise to the developmental state school. Originated by Chalmers Johnson, the concept of the developmental state has come to be closely – though by no means exclusively – associated with a group of theorists at the Institute of Development Studies at the University of Sussex. While neo-classical theory has attributed East Asian success to outward-oriented market economies, the developmental state school emphasises the highly interventionist role of the state in East Asian development, particularly in South Korea and China.

Speaking loosely, one can list the features of the developmental state as including the following: a state in which economic development is the top priority, with the welfare of the population being given little importance; a state committed to private property and markets (this allows for socialist developmental states like China, since they are opening onto the market); state guidance of the market, as engineered by an elite or technocratic economic bureaucracy; a bureaucracy that enjoys substantial autonomy, with its autonomy guaranteed by a powerful political authority, typically though not necessarily an authoritarian regime (that autonomy enables the bureaucracy to impose discipline – at times harsh – on the private sector). In directing development, the developmental state plays an interventionist role that goes far beyond the limits acceptable to neo-classical theory. However, its protection of infant industries differs from import-substitution industrialisation in its discrimination: some industries receive little if any protection, and even in healthy industries poorly-performing firms are left to wither on the vine. Finally, developmental states promote the social change necessary to development by redistributing land (if necessary) and repressing labour.

The developmental state model, with its emphasis on the 'strong' state, seems now to be the chief rival to neo-classical minimalism. It may well emerge, in modified form, as the leading explanation for state failure and success. Yet how is it that some states obtain this strength and autonomy while others do not? And why should the governors of a strong state choose to develop an outward-oriented capitalism with such effectiveness? The rulers of many powerful states choose to do otherwise.

Some developmental state theorists have turned to the overdeveloped state model, originated by Alavi (1972) and Saul (1979), to explain state strength. According to this explanation, developmental states are considered strong because they elude capture by societal interests, unlike 'weak' or 'soft' states. This strength is attributed to the fact that such states were colonial legacies suspended above society, rather than being institutions which grew out of domestic social forces. While this model may apply to some cases, Taiwan being a possibility (Wade, 1990), it offers a poor explanation for the behaviour of the state in Africa, where theorists argue that it is precisely because the state is weakly linked to social forces that it can be both rapacious and ineffectual: civil society is so weak in many African countries that it lacks the ability to limit the state's predatory behaviour, while the state is unable to use links to civil society to mobilise support for its development policies (Woods, 1992; Clapham, 1992:13–15; Healey and Robinson, 1992:89–91). Nevertheless, the theory of the overdeveloped state draws our attention to the importance of the colonial legacy. Particularly in East Asia, efficient civil services and centralised power appear to have been products of colonial rule (Amsden, 1993:32; Nordhaug, 1993). In Africa, as we shall see below, the legacy was usually quite different. At one time, the bureaucratic-authoritarian model was a popular tool for explaining state strength. Developed by the Argentinian political scientist Guillermo O'Donnell, this model sought to account for the rise of military regimes in Latin America during the 1970s by attributing it to the advent of the need for difficult economic development policies, and thus for a regime that could ignore or repress popular demands. Subsequently, the model came in for trenchant criticism (Serra, 1979), and experience has shown that authoritarian regimes are not always the best at implementing demanding economic reform or austerity programmes (Remmer, 1986; Haggard and Kaufman, 1992:32–34; Healey and Robinson, 1992:122; Bates and Krueger, 1993:459; Moore, 1990). The thesis that authoritarian regimes are better than democratic ones at implementing reform seems also to assume an enlightened leadership, something which is often lacking. After all, there have been cases of monumental mismanagement by authoritarian regimes in, for instance, Marcos's Philippines, Duvalier's Haiti and Mobutu's Zaïre (Haggard and Webb, 1993:146). Nor are authoritarian regimes immune to societal pressure: they may be able to resist popular pressure, but the result may not be an interest-free state but one in which a single interest monopolises power (Toye, 1992:193). Furthermore, it is apparent that democratic, or otherwise 'weak' regimes can implement difficult reforms, sometimes quite effectively, provided their leaders mobilise popular support for change.

Such findings may lead to a refinement of the developmental state model. It appears that state strength – the autonomy needed to engineer and direct development – arises not so much from authoritarian rule, but from a concentration of power in the executive branch along with the focus of policy-making power in a small circle of technocrats. Even those outside the developmental state school seem to accept this (Krueger, 1993, chapter 7; Bates and Krueger, 1993:462). At key conjunctures in their history, many states have experienced something akin to what Marx called a bonapartist moment: turning points, sometimes crises, in which political power was largely granted to, or usurped by, the executive branch, or even one leader. This can occur in the midst of a political-economic crisis (see Onis, 1992 on the Turkish experience) or result from a military coup (see Haggard, Kim and Moon, 1991 on the South Korean experience). In Africa, where it occurred, it seems to have followed decolonisation, as in Côte d'Ivoire and Botswana, a key feature in each case appearing to be a strong party (an element in state strength emphasised by Haggard and Webb, 1993:150–51).

Côte d'Ivoire presents an interesting case, because the Ivoirien state not only ruled in alliance with capitalists, indeed it was thoroughly penetrated by them. However, through a variety of economic organisation, and via the key agency of the Parti Démocratique de la Côte d'Ivoire, the class was able to articulate a unifying vision which could override the interests of individual members (Rapley, 1993). This gave the presidency, where decision-making power was concentrated, a coherent development strategy with which to work. Meanwhile the technocrats who put it into effect were insulated from political pressures of a patrimonial variety, and developed a high degree of organisation loyalty (Crook, 1988). It is interesting to note, however, that at the height of the political-economic crisis of 1989–90, the president appointed a government consisting largely of technocrats, who set about implementing a strict reform programme. In this experience Côte d'Ivoire may mirror the Turkish transition.

What keeps regimes with highly concentrated power from becoming predatory, like Zaire's government? The answer appears to be twofold. It seems that two conditions, neither sufficient but both necessary, need to be in place before an autonomous regime will become developmental. First, the executive power must have at its disposal a pool of highly-skilled technocrats who enjoy a considerable measure of autonomy; that is, civil servants who do not owe their positions to political or personal appointments. This helps to account for Zaire's failure, since it has been estimated that there were fewer than two dozen trained technocrats in the entire country at the time the Belgians left. Equally, it accounts for Côte d'Ivoire's success, where the regime retained a large French contingent during a transition period in which it built up its own administrative capacity (Crook, 1988). It also helps to account for those African countries in which the weakness of class rule has led to personalised rule based on patron-client networks: official positions are filled not necessarily by the best qualified people, but by political clients (Sandbrook, 1985, 1993; Medard, 1990).

Second, given that there is no such thing as a purely autonomous state, given that every state is embedded in the society it governs, and is closely linked to and penetrated by social forces, given that the state is dependent on the economy for the resources that enable it to function, it is important that the regime be closely linked to the capitalist class, while being comparatively distanced from what Clive Hamilton calls the 'classes which derive wealth from unproductive activities or which are otherwise hostile to industrial development' (Hamilton, quoted in Sorensen, 1993:11). By blending Hamilton's thesis with Evans' conception of 'embedded autonomy', Georg Sorensen develops a useful theory for understanding the relationship between capital and the state: while the governing elite must be closely linked to business, it must at the same time retain sufficient autonomy from it to be able to discipline it (Sorensen, 1993; Amsden, 1993:35). This brings to mind the marxist debate of the 1970s, which generally concluded that the most effective capitalist regimes were those which were able to overlook and even repress the demands of certain fractions of capital in order to govern in the interest of the whole class.

Among other things, the class basis of African states may help to explain why some of them become patrimonial while others become developmental. Independence movements led by urban petty bourgeoisies (e.g. civil servants, teachers) lack a private base of accumulation, and turn to the state as their avenue to upward mobility. Put crudely, the state becomes their cash cow, offering opportunities for taxation and rent-seeking. Moreover, coming largely from state positions, these individuals arguably share an ideology which places faith in the capacities of the state to enact social change. By contrast, independence movements led by bourgeoisies turn to the state as a means to secure and advance their private interests: any improvements in the economy will benefit their interests, so they will seek to keep state predations within limits that the economy can sustain (cf. Brett, 1985). However, to forestall the emergence of what has been called crony capitalism, these business people probably need to be organised into associations. Such organisation enables them to recognise and articulate a common class interest which governs their political behaviour. Otherwise they might act only in their personal interests, and seek or enact policies that advance their businesses to the detriment of other capitalists.

Much of the recent development literature on East Asia concludes that what can be called developmental states are rooted in capitalist power, especially productive capitalist power, with these capitalists enjoying close ties to the bureaucracy (see Islam, 1992:77; Vogel, 1992; Haggard, Kim and Moon, 1991:869). Similar findings emerge in two African states which might be considered developmental, Botswana and Côte d'Ivoire, where indigenous bourgeoisies captured the state at the time of independence (Botswana, it should be noted, presents a nuance to the developmental state model: it has effectively spearheaded development, but in so doing has been much less interventionist than either the East Asian or Ivoirien states). In a similar vein, the recent reform drive in much of the third world has in many cases been attributed not to external pressure but to the rising power of an indigenous bourgeoisie. This meshes with Jonathan Barker's thesis that reform in Africa will be motivated by a triple alliance among international financial capital: the World Bank and IMF; private capital, foreign and domestic; and 'progressive' small farmers (Barker, 1989), which seems to find support in Mozambiques's reform experience (Bowen, 1992). One hastens to add that Barker is not optimistic that such alliances will emerge in most of Africa. His pessimism points to a phenomenon which may lie at the heart of Africa's disappointing post-colonial development record. At the time of independence, indigenous bourgeoisies in much of sub-Saharan Africa were politically weak. Seldom did they play a prominent role in independence struggles. By consequence, independence movements were typically led by urban petty bourgeoisies. These new ruling elites, unconstrained by bourgeois civil societies, were left with surprising latitude to use, and abuse the state.

Thus it is not surprising to find that, while development theorists elsewhere are presently concerned with reinserting the state into development, Africanists are moving in the opposite direction and increasingly calling for state retreat. In the form of decentralisation or devolution, this is seen as a way to improve the delivery of services and mobilise people in support of development efforts, and the chorus in favour of decentralisation is getting ever louder (Wunsch and Olowu, 1990; Klitgaard, 1991; Cornia, van der Hoeven and Mkandawire, 1992; Hyden, 1990; Mabogunje, 1990;

Janvry, Sadoulet and Thorbecke, 1993:573; Stewart, 1993). In keeping with this stance, the World Bank is calling for central governments to continue financing public services like health care, but to leave service delivery in the hands of private sectors and non-governmental associations (Hecht and Musgrove, 1993). It is not an ideal solution, but may be the best of a set of undesirable options. Whether or not decentralisation will improve governance is difficult to say. So far the evidence is mixed, and Ingham and Kalam (1992:377) identify a shift in the decentralisation literature away from cautious optimism towards a view that decentralisation is not self-evidently good. The most optimistic prognosis might be that any change which makes government more responsive will increase its legitimacy, thereby leading to its long-term strengthening (Bratton and Rothchild, 1992:269, 284).

The glum assessment of the state and prospects of bourgeois power in much of Africa dampens hopes of developmental states emerging in all but a few countries. It is not that capitalist development will not occur. While it may be difficult for indigenous capitalists to emerge in small economies (Bayart, 1993:91–92), especially if those economies are dominated by producers and distributors from a neighbouring economy as is the case in much of southern Africa, elsewhere capitalists are prospering. Even in Zaïre, by reputation the predatory, anti-developmental state par excellence, capitalists continue their activities (MacGaffey, 1987). But these activities will remain inchoate – linkage into an emerging capitalist economy will be minimised – and concentrated disproportionately in those sectors which offer fast returns and are most easily concealed from the public eye (for instance, trade). Certainly, entrepreneurs in hostile or unpredictable policy environments will hesitate to move into manufacturing (cf. Forrest, 1994, chapter 9). In the absence of state direction, whether minimalist or maximalist, coordinated national development is unlikely to occur. After years of disparagement, one of the canons of marxist theory may be correct after all: a bourgeois revolution, in some form, may have to precede national capitalist development. And in much of Africa, such revolutions may not be on the horizon.

Bibliography

R. Adhikari, C. Kirkpatrick and J. Weiss (eds) (1992), *Industrial and Trade Policy Reform in Developing Countries*, Manchester/New York, Manchester University Press; Hamza Alavi, (1972), 'The State in Post-Colonial Societies', *New Left Review*, 74:59–81; Alice Amsden (1989), *Asia's Next Giant: South Korea and Late Industrialization*, New York, Oxford University Press; Alice Amsden (1993), 'The Quality of State Intervention and Industrial Development', Berlin, European Association of Development Research and Training Institutes Conference; Jean-Paul Azam (1992), 'The Agricultural Minimum Wage and Wheat Production in Morocco (1971–89)', *Journal of African Economies* 1:171–91; Pranab Bardhan (1992), 'Economics of Market Socialism and the Issue of Public Enterprise Reform in Developing Countries', *The Pakistan Development Review*, 30:565–79; Jonathan Barker (1989), *Rural Communities under Stress*, Cambridge, Cambridge University Press; Stephanie Barrientos (1993), 'Economic Growth versus Poverty and Inequality in Chile: A Dualist Analysis', Brighton, UK, Development Studies Association Conference, 8 September; Robert Bates (1981), *Markets and States in Tropical Africa*, Berkeley, University of California Press; Robert Bates and Anne O. Krueger (1993), *Political and Economic Interactions in Economic Policy Reform*, Oxford, Basil Blackwell.

Jean-Francois Bayart (1993), *The State in Africa*, London, Longman; Sara Berry (1993), 'Understanding Agricultural Policy in Africa: The Contributions of Robert Bates', *World Development*, 21:1055–62; Jonathan Beynon (1992), *Market Liberalization and Private Sector Response in Eastern and Southern Africa*, Oxford, Queen Elizabeth House, Food Studies Group Working Paper No. 6; Manfred Bienefeld (1987), 'Developing

Countries' Prospects in the 1990s and the Crises of Developed Economies', Lecture presented to Programme of Studies in National and International Development, Queen's University, Kingston, Canada, 6 February; Merle L. Bowen (1992), 'Beyond Reform: Adjustment and Political Power in Contemporary Mozambique', *Journal of Modern African Studies*, 30:255–79.

Chris Bramall (1993), 'The Role of Decollectivisation in China's Agricultural Miracle, 1978– 9', *Journal of Peasant Studies*, 20:271–95; Michael Bratton and Donald Rothchild (1992), 'The Institutional Bases of Governance in Africa' in *Governance and Politics in Africa* edited by Goran Hyden and Michael Bratton, Boulder, CO/London, Lynne Rienner Publishers; Michael Bratton and Nicolas van de Walle (1992), 'Popular Demands and State Responses' in *Governance and Politics in Africa* edited by Goran Hyden and Michael Bratton, Boulder, CO/London, Lynne Rienner Publishers; E. A. Brett (1985), *State Power and Economic Inefficiency: Explaining Political Failure in Africa*, Manchester, UK, Political Science Association Conference.

G. Chellaraj, B. Wade Brorsen and Paul L. Farris (1992), 'Effects of Subsidized Wheat Consumption by State in India', *Agricultural Economics*, 7:1–12; C. Clapham (1992), 'Democratisation in Africa: Obstacles and Prospects', ASA Conference, Stirling, September; Paul Cook (1992), 'Privatization and Public Enterprise Performance in Developing Countries' *Development Policy Review*, 10:403–08; Giovanni Andrea Cornia, Ralph van der Hoeven and Thandika Mkandawire (1992), *Africa's Recovery in the 1990s: From Stagnation and Adjustment to Human Development*, New York, St. Martin's Press/London, Macmillan, for UNICEF; George T. Crane (1989–90), 'State-Owned Enterprises and the Oil Shocks in Taiwan: The Political Dynamics of Economic Adjustment', *Studies in Comparative International Development*, 24, 4:3–23; Richard C. Crook (1988), 'State Capacity and Economic Development: The Case of Côte d'Ivoire', *IDS Bulletin*, 19,4:19–25; D. Darbon (1990), 'L'Etat Predateur', *Politique Africaine*, 39:37–45; Basil Davidson (1992), *The Black Man's Burden: Africa and the Curse of the Nation-State*, London, James Currey.

Rob Davies and David Sanders (1993), 'Economic Strategies, Adjustment and Health Policy: Issues in Sub-Saharan Africa for the 1990s', *Transformation*, 21:78–93; Cynthia Hewitt de Alcantara (1992), 'Introduction: Markets in Principle and Practice', *European Journal of Developmnt Research*, 4,2:1–16; Polo Diaz and Tanya Korovkin (1990), 'Neo-Liberalism in Agriculture: Capitalist Modernization in the Chilean Countryside during the Pinochet Years', *Canadian Journal of Latin American and Caribbean Studies*, 15,30:197–219; Khosrow Doroodian (1993), 'Macroeconomic Performance and Adjustment under Policies Commonly Supported by the International Monetary Fund', *Economic Development and Cultural Change*, 41:849–64; Frank Ellis (1993), 'Private Trade and Public Role in Staple Food Marketing: The Case of Rice in Indonesia', *Food Policy*, 18:428–38; Philippe Faucher (1991), 'Public Investment and the Creation of Manufacturing Capacity in the Power Equipment Industry in Brazil', *Journal of Developing Areas*, 25:231–60; E. V. K. Fitzgerald (1990), 'The Impact of Macroeconomic Policies on Small-Scale Industry: Some Analytical Considerations' in *The Other Policy* edited by Frances Stewart, Henk Thomas and Ton de Wilde, London/Washington, DC, Intermediate Technology Publications in association with Appropriate Technology International; Tom Forrest (1994), *The Advance of African Capital: Studies in the Growth of Nigerian Private Enterprise*, Edinburgh, Edinburgh University Press, for the International African Institute; Jacob A. Frenkel and Mohsin S. Khan (1992), 'Adjustment Policies of the International Monetary Fund and Long-Run Economic Development', *Bangladesh Development Studies*, 20, 2–3:1–22; Ross Garnaut (1991), 'The Market and the State in Economic Development: Applications to the International Trading System', *The Singapore Economic Review*, 36,2: 13–26; Peter Gibbon (1992), 'A Failed Agenda? African Agriculture under Structural Adjustment with Special reference to Kenya and Ghana', *Journal of Peasant Studies*, 20:50–96.

David Greenaway and David Sapsford (1993), *Exports, Growth and Liberalisation: An Evaluation*, University of Nottingham Centre for Research in Economic Development and International Trade, Credit Research Paper 93/1; Emmanuel Gregoire (1990), 'L'Etat doit-il abandonner le commerce des vivres aux marchands?', *Politique Africaine*, 37:63–70; Margaret E. Grosh (1992), 'The Jamaican Food Stamps Programme: a Case Study in Targeting', *Food Policy*, 17:23–40; Patrick Guillaumont (1993), 'Politique d'ajustement et développement agricole', *Economie Rural*, 216:20–29; Stephan Haggard and Robert R. Kaufman (eds) (1992), *The Politics of Economic Adjustment*, Princeton, NJ, Princeton University Press.

Stephan Haggard, Byung-Kook Kim and Chung-In Moon (1991), 'The Transition to Export-led Growth in South Korea, 1954–1966', *Journal of Asian Studies*, 50:850:73; Stephan Haggard and Steven B. Webb (1993), 'What Do We Know About the Political Economy of Economic Policy Reform?', *World Bank Research Observer*, 8:143–68; Steve Haggblade, Carl Liedholm, Donald C. Mead (1990), 'The Effect of Policy Reforms on Non-Agricultural Enterprises and Employment in Developing Countries: A Review of

Past Experiences' in *The Other Policy*, edited by Frances Stewart, Henk Thomas and Ton de Wilde, London/ Washington, DC, Intermediate Technology Publications in association with Appropriate Technology International.

Jane Harrigan (1992), 'Review' in *Journal of African Economies*, 1:151–62; Barbara Harriss (1992), 'Real Foodgrain Markets and State Intervention in India', *European Journal of Development Research*, 4, 2:61–81; Barbara Harriss and Ben Crow (1992), 'Twentieth Century Free Trade Reform: Food Market Deregulation in Sub-Saharan Africa and South Asia' in *Development Policy and Public Action* edited by Marc Wuyts, Maureen Mackintosh and Tom Hewitt, Oxford, Oxford University Press, in association with The Open University; John Healey and Mark Robinson (1992), *Democracy, Governance and Economic Policy: Sub-Saharan Africa in Comparative Perspective*, London, Overseas Development Institute; Robert Hecht and Philip Musgrove (1993), 'Rethinking the Government's Role in Health', *Finance & Development*, September, pp.6–9; Goran Hyden (1990), 'Responses from Below: A Tale of Two Tanzanian Villages', *Food Policy*, 15:299–305.

Barry Ickes and Randi Ryterman (1992), 'Credit for Small Firms, not Dinosaurs', *Orbis*, 36:333–48; Barbara Ingham and A. K. M. Kalam (1992), 'Decentralization and Development: Theory and Evidence from Bangladesh', *Public Administration and Development*, 12:373–85; Iyanatul Islam (1992), 'Political Economy and East Asian Economic Development', *Asian-Pacific Economic Literature*, 6,2:69–101; Alain de Janvry, Elisabeth Sadoulet and Erik Thorbecke (1993), 'Introduction to Special Section on State, Market and Civil Organisations', *World Development* 21:565–75; Richard Jeffries (1993), 'The State, Structural Adjustment and Good Government in Africa', *Journal of Commonwealth and Comparative Politics*, 31:20–35; Rhys Jenkins (1991), 'The Political Economy of Industrialization: A Comparison of Latin American and East Asian Newly Industrializing Countries', *Development and Change*, 22:197–231.

Tony Killick (1989), *A Reaction Too Far: Economic Theory and the Role of the State in Developing Countries*, London, Oversas Development Institute; Tony Killick (1993), 'What Can We Learn about Long-term Development from Experiences with Restructuring?', Berlin, European Association of Development Research and Training Institutes Conference; Robert Klitgaard (1991), 'Adjusting to Reality: Beyond "State versus Market"' in *Economic Development*, San Francisco, ICS Press.

Anne O. Krueger (1993), *Political Economy of Policy Reform in Developing Countries*, Cambridge, MA/London, MIT Press; Newman K. Kusi (1991), 'Ghana: Can the Adjustment Reforms be Sustained?', *Africa Development*, 16,3–4:181–206; Sanjaya Lall (1990), *Building Industrial Competitiveness in Developing Countries*, Paris, OECD Development Centre; S. Lall (1992), Lecture, Economics Development Series, University of Oxford, 4 November; S. Lall (1993), 'Promoting Technology Development: The Role of Technology Transfer and Indigenous Effort', *Third World Quarterly*, 14,1:95–108; Barbara Lee and John Nellis (1991), 'Enterprise Reform and Privatization in Socialist Economies', *Public Enterprise* 11:101–17; Barry Lesser (1991), 'When Government Fails, Will the Market Do Better? The Privatization/Market Liberalization in Developing Countries', *Canadian Journal of Development Studies*, 12:159–72; John Loxley (1990), 'Structural Adjustment in Africa: Reflections on Ghana and Zambia', *Review of African Political Economy*, 47:8–27; Akin L. Mabogunje (1990), 'Mobilizing Nigeria's Grassroots for Increased Food Production: Reaching out from the Centre', *Food Policy*, 15:306–12; Janet MacGaffey (1987), *Entrepreneurs and Parasites: The Struggle for Indigenous Capitalism in Zaïre*, Cambridge, Cambridge University Press; Ronald I. McKinnon (1991), *The Order of Economic Liberalization: Financial Control in the Transition to a Market Economy*, Baltimore, Johns Hopkins University Press.

J-F Medard (1990), 'L'Etat Patrimonialisé', *Politique Africaine*, 39:25–36; Kigane Mengisteab (1991), 'Export-Import Responses to Devaluation in Sub-Saharan Africa', *Africa Development*, 16,3–4:27–43; K. Mengisteab and Bernard I. Logan (1991), 'Africa's Debt Crisis: Are Structural Adjustment Programs Relevant?', *Africa Development*, 16,1:95–113; Thandika Mkandawire (1992), 'The Political Economy of Development with a Democratic Face' in *Africa's Recovery in the 1990s: From Stagnation and Adjustment to Human Development* edited by G. A. Cornia, Ralph van der Hoeven and T. Mkandawire, New York, St. Martin's Press/London, Macmillan, for UNICEF; Mick Moore (1990), 'Economic Liberalization versus Political Pluralism in Sri Lanka', *Modern Asian Studies*, 24:341–83; Peter Murrell (1992), 'Privatization Complicates the Fresh Start', *Orbis*, 36:323–32.

Syed Nawab Haider and A. R. Kemal (1991), 'The Privatization of the Public Industrial Enterprise in Pakistan', *Pakistan Development Review*, 30:105–44; Peter Nolan (1993), 'Economic Reform: China's Success, Russia's Failure', Economic Development Seminar Series, University of Oxford, 13 May; Kristen

Nordhaug (1993), 'Late Industrialization and Democracy: The Case of Taiwan' in *Development Theory: Recent Trends. Proceedings of the NFU Annual Conference 1992*, Bergen, Report of the Chr. Michelsen Institute; Ziya Onis (1992), 'Redemocratization and Economic Liberalization in Turkey: The Limits of State Autonomy', *Studies in Comparative International Development*, 27,2:3–23; T. A. Oyejide (1991b), 'Structural Adjustment and its Implications for Financing Small Enterprises in Nigeria', *Small Enterprise Development*, 2,4:31–39; Louis Putterman and Dietrich Rueschemeyer (eds) (1992), *State and Market in Development: Synergy or Rivalry?*, Boulder/London, Lynne Rienner; Sultan Hafeez Rahman (1992), 'Structural Adjustment and Macroeconomic Performance in Bangladesh in the 1980s', *Bangladesh Development Studies*, 20,2–3:89–125; Ravi Ramamurti (1993), 'Privatization as a Remedy for State-owned Enterprises' in *Latin America's Turnaround: Privatization, Foreign Investment and Growth* edited by Paul H. Boeker, San Francisco, Institute for Contemporary Studies; Miguel D. Ramirez (1993), 'Stabilization and Trade Reform in Mexico, 1983–1989', *Journal of Developing Areas*, 27:173–90.

John Rapley (1993), *Ivoirien Capitalism: African Entrepreneurs in Côte d'Ivoire*, Boulder/London, Lynne Rienner Publishers; Karen Remmer (1986), 'The Politics of Economic Stabilization: IMF Standby Programs in Latin America, 1954–198', *Comparative Politics*, 19,1: 1–24; Rupert Rhodd (1993), 'The Effect of Real Exchange Rate Changes on Output: Jamaica's Devaluation Experience', *Journal of International Development*, 5,3: 291–303; A. R. M. Ritter (1990), 'Development Strategy and Structural Adjustment in Chile, 1973–1990', *Canadian Journal of Latin American and Caribbean Studies*, 15,30:159–95; Donald Rothchild (ed.) (1991), *Ghana: The Political Economy of Recovery*, Boulder/London, Lynne Rienner Publishers; Donald Rothchild and Naomi Chazan (eds) (1988), *The Precarious Balance: State and Society in Africa*, Boulder/London, Westview Press; Lars Rudebeck (1990), 'The Effects of Structural Adjustment in Kandjadja, Guinea-Bissau', *Review of African Political Economy*, 49:34–51.

Richard Sandbrook (1985), *The Politics of Africa's Economic Stagnation*, Cambridge, Cambridge University Press; R. Sandbrook (1993), *The Politics of Africa's Economic Recovery*, Cambridge, Cambridge University Press; Zaidi Sattar (1993), 'Public Expenditure and Economic Performance: A Comparison of Developed and Low-Income Developing Countries', *Journal of International Development*, 5:27–49; John Saul (1979), 'The State in Post-Colonial Societies: Tanzania' in *The State and Revolution in Eastern Africa*, New York/London, Monthly Review Press; Ann Seideman (1992), 'Towards a New Vision of Sustainable Development in Africa', Presidential Address to 1990 Annual Meeting of the ASA, *African Studies Review*, 35,1:1–15; Jose Serra (1979), 'Three Mistaken Theses Regarding the Connection between Industrialization and Authoritarian Regimes' in *The New Authoritarianism in Latin America*, edited by David Collier, Princeton, NJ, Princeton University Press; Ibrahim Shao (ed.), *Structural Adjustment in a Socialist Country: The Case of Tanzania*, Harare, Southern African Political Economy Series Books, Monograph Series No. 4; Shahla Shapouri, Margaret Missiaen and Stacey Rosen (1992), *Food Strategies and Market Liberalisation in Africa: Case Studies of Kenya, Tanzania and Zimbabwe*, Washington, DC, US Department of Agriculture; H. W. Singer and Sumit Roy (1993), *Economic Progress and Prospects in the Third World*, Aldershot, Edward Elgar; Georg Sorenson (1993), 'Democracy, Authoritarianism and State Strength', *European Journal of Development Research*, 5,1:6–34.

Frances Stewart (1985), 'The Fragile Foundations of the Neoclassical Approach to Development', *Journal of Development Studies*, 21:282–9; F. Stewart (1991), 'Are Adjustment Policies in Africa Consistent with Long-run Development Needs?', *Development Policy Review*, 9:413–36; F. Stewart (1993), Contribution to EADI Session on Governance, Adjustment and Reform, Berlin, European Association of Development Research and Training Institutes Conference; G. G. Storey (ed.) (1992), *Agricultural Marketing in Lesotho*, Ottawa, International Development Research Centre; Lance Taylor (1992), 'Polonius Lectures Again: The World Development Report, the Washington Consensus, and How Neoliberal Sermons Won't Solve the Economic Problems of the Developing World', *Bangladesh Development Studies*, 20,2–3:23–53; Lance Taylor (1993a), 'The Rocky Road to Reform: Trade, Industrial, Financial, and Agricultural Strategies', *World Development*, 21:577–90; L. Taylor (1993b), *The Rocky Road to Reform: Adjustment, Income Distribution and Growth in the Developing World*, Cambridge, MA/London, MIT Press; John Toye (1987), *Dilemmas of Development*, Oxford, Basil Blackwell; J. Toye (1992), 'Interest Group Politics and the Implementation of Adjustment Policies in Sub-Saharan Africa', *Journal of International Development*, 4:183–97.

Ezra F. Vogel (1992), *The Four Little Dragons: The Spread of Industrialisation in East Asia*, Cambridge, MA/London, Harvard University Press; Robert Wade (1990), *Governing the Market: Economic Theory and the Role of Government in East Asian Industrialization*, Princeton, NJ, Princeton University Press; John Weeks (1993), 'Fallacies of Competition: Myths and Maladjustment in the Third World', London, Professorial Lecture, School of Oriental and African Studies, University of London, 13 October; John Weiss (1992),

'Trade Policy Reform and Performance in Manufacturing: Mexico 1975–88', *Journal of Development Studies*, 29:1–23; Dwayne Woods (1992), 'Civil Society in Europe and Africa: Limiting State Power through a Public Sphere', *African Studies Review*, 35,2:77–100; James Wunsch and Dele Olowu (1990), T*he Failure of the Centralized State: Institutions and Self-Governance in Africa*, Boulder, CO, Oxford, Westview Press; Richard Yoder, Philip L. Borkholder and Brian D. Friesen (1991), 'Privatization and Development: The Empirical Evidence', *Journal of Developing Areas* 25:425–34.

26 CHRIS ALLEN
Who Needs
Civil Society? [1997]

'Civil society' has become a popular concept in both the analysis of the social bases of recent political change in Africa and external policy support for processes of liberal democratic political reform. In the latter case, civil society, as represented by a set of (largely urban) formal organisations and especially by NGOs with external links, is portrayed as the driving force behind and guarantee of democratisation and the containment of the state. Conceptually, however, 'civil society' proves to be diffuse, hard to define, empirically imprecise, and ideologically laden. Analytically it is vacuous, and concepts such as class or gender contribute far more to understanding recent political change than can 'civil society'. Its popularity and continued employment rest on its ideological underpinning, notably on claims that civil society is necessarily distinct from the state, in opposition to the state, and the source of (liberal) democratic values and pressures. It is thus the proponents of liberal democratic reform, notably those external to African polities, that 'need' civil society.

While it has a long history in political theory, use of the concept 'civil society' has only been current in discussion of African politics for a decade (since, e.g., Bayart 1986), and in particular since its close association with the analysis of African struggles for democratisation since 1989 (e.g. Bratton, 1989, 1992). One of the volumes under review (*Civil Society and the State in Africa*, henceforth CSSA) dates from the middle of this latter period, originating in a 1992 conference. Its answer to the question 'who needs civil society?' would be tentative, at least in the eyes of one of its co-editors (Harbeson) and several of the contributors. Ndegwa, completing his doctoral research a couple of years later, is much less circumspect. For him, there is a well-established 'civil society-political liberalisation thesis – that organisations in civil society, including NGOs, are central to opposing undemocratic governments and to furthering and consolidating democracy'; this thesis he associates with Bratton and Chazan, respectively contributor to and co-editor of CSSA. So familiar a part of his intellectual landscape is this thesis that while Ndegwa contests it – on empirical grounds – he does not regard 'civil society' itself as requiring definition, still less discussion.

In a sense, Ndegwa is justified. Since 1990, and despite the carefully expressed misgivings of many of the contributors of CSSA, of political theorists (Gellner, 1991; Kumar, 1993), and of contributors to this *Review* (e.g. Beckman, 1993; Marcussen, 1996; Stewart, 1997), the thesis outlined by Ndegwa has been widely current, especially among NGOs, IFIs and grant-seeking academics, as Stewart has recently made clear. Yet the empirical evidence for the thesis is weak; the concept of civil society is difficult to pin down empirically, and the theoretical arguments with which it is involved are so closely associated with neo-liberal ideological campaigning, as to cast doubt on the value of the concept overall.

The problems with civil society start with its definition, a matter that preoccupies Harbeson and Young in CSSA. The earliest uses of the concept do not so much distinguish 'civil-society' from 'society', as see civil society as a way of conceiving of society when the latter is self-consciously politically active (and creative). For Locke, and several others, society is, or becomes, civil when it seeks to define and establish legitimate political authority. By extension, the processes of establishing the norms that define legitimacy are also an aspect of 'civil' society. In this version – which in Gramsci has become the ideological process by which a dominant class creates and protects its hegemonic grip on the state, and allows that grip to be presented to subordinate classes as legitimate – 'civil' society is essential for the existence of the modern (post-absolutist) state, but also inconceivable without the state. This tradition is reflected in CSSA, primarily by Harbeson, in passages such as these:

> Civil society is treated not as synonymous with the adoption of particular rules of the game but as those behaviours by which different cultures define the rules of the game. (Harbeson, CSSA, 299)

The missing dimension supplied by the idea of civil society is that, in process terms, working understandings concerning the basic rules of the political game or structure of the state emerge from within society and the economy at large. In substantive terms civil society typically refers to the points of agreement on what those working rules should be (Harbeson, CSSA, 3).

> [Civil society] should be used in a very restricted sense relating to the emergence of consensus on norms defining a civil sphere .. In this sense, civil society would be – a space or realm defined by newly constituted norms about what the state should and should not be and by the rules of politics in that space, including politics by non-state actors. (Callaghy, CSSA, 235)

In practice, however, a quite different definition now predominates, claiming a somewhat uncertain descent from Gramsci, and turning not on political processes so as much as on the actors supposed to be (largely) responsible for them. Callaghy, critical of this usage, summarises it thus: civil society consists of 'autonomous societal groups that interact with the state but delimit and constrain its action: here associational life is seen as the core of civil society' (CSSA, 234). This definition is close to Bayart's 'society in its relation to the state ... in so far as it is in confrontation with the state. The process by which society seeks to "breach" and counteract the simultaneous "totalisation" unleashed by the state' (Bayart, 1986:111). It also flourishes, importantly, in Bratton.

Bratton is unfortunate to be thus fingered, in that he is careful in CSSA to root his discussion of civil society in the tradition discussed above: 'civil society – embodies a core of universal beliefs and practices about the legitimation of, and limits to, state power' (52). He frequently reminds readers that it is a 'theoretical concept rather than an empirical one' (57). At the same time, his interest in analysing the relationship between protest and political transitions has led him to argue that 'protest has led to reform in countries where popular forces have an independent material, organisational, and ideological base – that is where there is a strong civil society ... (and) political transition in different countries unfolds at least partly as a function of the institutional characteristics of their respective civil societies' (51–2). Now, instead of society becoming 'civil' – instead of 'civil' society – we are offered entities called 'civil-societies', visible as 'intermediate associations and the institutional linkages among them' (66).

Bratton reached this point (as he did in earlier work; see Bratton 1989, 1992) because he wished to understand the link between the growth of associational life and activity, and the growth of pressures for (viable) political reform. Others have chosen – as Callaghy's curt summary above makes clear – to drop the context within which Bratton uses the term in favour simply of identifying civil society with associational life. Thus MacGaffey:

> I will first define civil society as Michael Bratton does – as an 'arena where manifold social movements – and civic organisations from all classes – attempt to constitute themselves in an ensemble of arrangements so that they can express themselves and advance their interests (CSSA, 169).

Likewise Jane Guyer:

> we understand by civil society those organisations created by non-state interests within society to reach up to the state and by the state to reach down into society (CSSA, 216).

In practice, most of the authors in CSSA, Ndegwa, and the bulk of the contemporary literature use the 'associational life' version of civil society. With its use have tended to come a number of theses:

(a) that civil society is not only distinct from the state, but in conflict with it; Bayart is often quoted (perhaps wrongly) in this context; 'civil society exists only in so far as there is a self-consciousness of its existence and of its opposition to the state' (1986:117);

(b) that civil society is at the heart of the democratisation struggle – or process, as these authors prefer;

(c) that NGOs form a highly significant part of civil society, and thus of forces driving democratisation (Fowler, 1991).

This last is the precise thesis that Ndegwa attempts to test, though he is less concerned with the relevant NGO literature that Marcussen (1996) and Stewart (1997) have recently criticised in the *Review*.

Civil Society, Democratisation & the State: a Critique

Ndegwa's book is a straightforward empirical critique of the last two of the theses above. By examining the activity of Kenyan NGOs collectively (in one instance) and of two of the largest indigenous NGOs over many years, he is able to argue that there is no necessary connection between NGO activity and democratic struggle. An example of close involvement is offered (the Green Belt Movement, an environmentalist group, with tree-planting as a primary activity), as is one of deliberate non-involvement (the Undugu Movement, concerned with urban poverty and especially street children). The case study of collective action – NGO resistance to the 1990 NGO Co-ordination Act which sought to place NGO activity and resources under the control of the Kenyan Interior Ministry – leads him to conclude that this was not an instance of NGOs seeking political reform as a result of their values, structure and dynamic, but of the mounting of oppositional action only after their own existence had been threatened and after the wave of general societal mobilisation was already under way – NGOs did not see their actions as enhancing democratisation; instead they saw the openings achieved by the democratic movement as giving them a right to operate freely in their own development activities (Ndgewa, 1996: 52–3).

Ndegwa concludes that on his evidence

> civil society activity does not cause political liberalisation; the democratic movement is a larger force engulfing the whole of society to which civil society actors respond – NGOs – are not the originators of reform movements. Indeed they are respondents to both the repressive capacities of the state and the reformist backlash against the state from sectors of civil society. The resurgence of civil society and its political activity in Africa therefore reflects a social movement of which it may be only a belated but nevertheless significant sign (111).

Two questions arise, if one accepts Ndegwa's general conclusion. If there is no necessary connection between being a 'civil society organisation' and democratisation, then what does determine whether and under what conditions a given organisation is or is not involved in political transformation? More broadly, one should also ask: what are the boundaries of civil society, seen as associational life? Are any and all associations eligible, no matter what their function, origin or membership? Several contributors to CSSA point out that many organisations are either hostile to democratisation, or encourage tendencies which may undermine it (e.g. ethnic politics). Bratton's own essay in CSSA makes clear, too, that organisations found to be active in democratisation movements are drawn – to an even greater extent than those that contributed to nationalist activity in the post-war period – from urban groups, often with middle-class membership and/or leadership: student groups, churches, trade unions, professional bodies, human/legal rights groups, women's organisations, etc. It is one thing to argue that civil society (as associational creation, growth and life) expands dramatically from the mid-1980s in Africa, quite another to assert that the same 'civil society' lies undiffentiatedly behind democratisation (and yet another to identify NGOs as the quintessence of civil society).

Ndegwa's answer to the first question above is twofold: that involvement depends on the organisation's leadership, and that we are looking in the wrong place for the democratising impact of NGOs (if any). The latter, he argues, lies in the way that the routine developmental activity of NGOs helps empower their grassroots members or clients, and not in their conscious organisational contribution to reform movements. Both arguments are open to doubt, as can be seen from his case studies. The Undugu Society, led by Ezra Mbogori, took no part in political protests, although Mbogori was a key member of the NGO Network that opposed the 1990 Act. By contrast, Wangari Maathai's Green Belt Movement was actively involved, spinning off a civic education campaign to help ensure free and fair elections in 1992 (the Movement for Free and Fair Elections). This contrast Ndegwa attributes to the 'institutionalised' nature of directors, which prevented Mbogori from using its resources for general political goals. The Green Belt Movement was not institutionalised, and did not therefore impede Maathai's use of its resources (Ndegwa, 105). Ndegwa's somewhat inconsistent summary of his argument runs thus:

> the explanation for the two faces of civil society lies in the willingness of the leadership of these organisations to use organisational resources against the repressive state ... This political will stems from a fairly arbitrary element of personal leadership within civil society organisations (111).

Later, in discussing the fluctuating stance in the early 1990s of the leadership of the Central Organisation of Trade Unions (COTU), he remarks, 'where does the trade union movement in Kenya belong – among progressive forces for democratisation, or among reactionary forces for the dominant former single party? This depends very much on the direction that the labour elites choose' (113). Ndegwa confuses the membership with the organisation, and the organisation with its leadership: rank and file trade unionists in Kenya had little doubt about where they 'belonged'.

Perhaps the stress on grassroots empowerment is more promising, seeming to have parallels with Beckman and Jega's careful analysis of the centrality of internal political relationships, and of internalisation of democratic values, in the important role played by student and lecturer organisations in Nigeria's democratic struggles (Beckman & Jega, 1995). Yet the empowerment described in the two Kenyan organisations differs in significant ways. Undugu, which thinks in terms of clients, not members, 'focuses on the individual as the appropriate point of entry for helping a community: the goal is to make that individual self-reliant and conscious of his or her community' (Ndegwa, 61). It distances itself from political actions undertaken by (former) clients, and indeed those actions may as readily reflect as being distinct from Undugu's own close relationship with the Moi regime. One such action – taken in 1990 and described at length in Undugu's 1990-91 biennial report – involved 20 women who had been given leadership training and assistance in building low-cost housing in 1988 by Undugu. In 1990 these women had their trading kiosks damaged in a riot stemming from official destruction of a nearby shanty settlement. The women tried to get a new site, going in turn to the local chief, to the District Officer, and the Provincial Commissioner, and at each step being fobbed off. Eventually a threat to march on Moi's official residence secured an interview with the Commissioner. The report comments: 'the women did confirm that the self-confidence to do what they did on their own resulted from their previous interaction with Undugu' (Ndegwa, 61). This is quite possible, but what they did, on their own, however brave, was to appeal to official structures, and had little or nothing to do with political reform.

By contrast the thousands of rural women's groups associated with the Green Belt Movement (GBM) join as groups, not individuals, and are encouraged to act collectively. Their involvement in tree-planting campaigns 'enhances the women's felt power'; but in addition, educating them on the immediate local and national social, economic and political realities has enhanced members groups' awareness about broader political issues. The environmental movement in Kenya, the GBM believes, cannot ignore the position of women in society. Moreover, the GBM's working philosophy entails a critique of the marginal political position of the masses of citizens in Kenya (82, 94).

According to Ndegwa, group members are 'strongly committed to what Maathai does at national level' even when not directly involved, are actively involved in the government of GBM, and were heavily involved in the voter education campaign (93–102). It is now somewhat easier to understand why it was GBM, and not Undugu, that was involved in the democratic struggle, and to judge to what extent this was merely a manifestation of 'the unfettered drive of Wangari Maathai' (Ndegwa, 105).

Empirically, then, the thesis that civil society 'can become a source of counter-hegemonic social movements that occasionally are sufficiently strong to effect a regime transition' (Bratton, CSSA, 75), or more baldly that 'organisations in civil society... are central to opposing democratic governments' (Ndegwa, 61) is supported only in a vacuous sense. The concept of 'civil society' does not take us far in analysing, or even in describing, struggles for democratisation – something which both Callaghy and Young foresaw in CSSA. Thus the latter asks whether civil society is 'merely a metaphor masquerading as a player' (43), while the former doubts 'whether civil society as commonly defined can do much to elucidate important processes in contemporary Africa, can do more than label them vaguely' (235).

If 'civil society' does not 'behave as a change agent in all circumstances, let alone as a catalyst for a particular kind of change, such as democratisation' (Harbeson, CSSA, 298), then by what means may we identify such agents? While 'the hypothesis of this book (CSSA) is that civil society is a hitherto missing key to sustained political reform'

(1), its texts leave one with either a definition of civil society that is too limited to be a key (norm-setting[1]), or one which is empirically unsustainable. To see civil society as 'associational life' continually requires one to ask what are its boundaries: which associations, when, and under what conditions act in the ways supposedly characteristic of civil society? As Harbeson admits in CSSA (297), this issue arises in most contributions, but – like the question of the ethnocentrism of the concept – is usually sidestepped.

The Dakar-based Council for the Development of Social Science Research in Africa (Codesria), which has encouraged so much valuable work in African social science, is thus rightly cautious in using the term. When it chose to put together a collection on popular protest and democratisation at much the same time as the CSSA collection, it published them under the title of 'African studies in social movements and democracy', with civil society banished to a short but emphatic critical essay by Mahmood Mamdani. This collection, focused largely on Northern African case studies, uses the older concept of 'social movement', together with those of class, gender, ethnicity and the state.

Ali Mari Tripp, in her contribution to CSSA, complains that 'the discussion has yet to fully incorporate and problematise the gender implications of civil society' (150). She argues that the example of the recent growth of small, informal women's organisations in Tanzania, the ways in which they necessarily link 'public' and 'private' domains (state and household, which civil society is supposed to separate), and their contribution to the political awareness, skills and action of women, makes such incorporation essential. What her essay shows, however, is that the values, dynamics and extent of these organisations, and the political values and capacities women get from them, are best understood in terms of gender, as is their contribution to democratisation in Tanzania. Similarly the significance of the Green Belt Movement in Kenya is more fully understood in terms of gender than in Ndegwa's terms of civil society.

Similar arguments can be offered in favour of class and class categories when analysing the role of workers or the urban poor in democratic struggles, though the contributors to Mamdani and Wamba-dia-Wamba are cautious in doing so. Chikhi, for example, uses class concepts largely descriptive in his analysis of workers and democratisation in Algeria, while Zhgal identifies the key role of young women workers in a provincial town in the 1983–84 Tunisian bread riots, but avoids analysis in gender terms. The editors comment that 'neither social forces nor social movements can be presumed to have internal consistency and coherence, or be the agents of a trans-historical agenda' (9–10). What one can presume is that if one tries to identify social forces underlying democratic struggles, whether in specific cases or more generally, then 'civil society' vanishes as a viable analytical tool in favour of older concepts: gender, class, etc.

The Ideology of Civil Society

If 'civil society' has been widely used despite its manifest weakness, why should this be so? One reason for its popularity is its ideological component (or what Mamdani calls its 'programmatic' elements). The 'associational life' version of civil society has carried with it, like bedbugs in an otherwise serviceable blanket, three assertions:

1) civil society is the source within contemporary African political systems of liberal democratic values of pluralism, accountability, transparency, the rule of law, etc;

2) civil society is the prime engine of democratisation (seen in terms solely of liberal democratic models);

3) civil society is necessarily opposed to the state, not simply in the sense of confronting authoritarian regimes, but also – and primarily – in the sense of containing and constraining the scope and action of the state. For it to flourish, and in its flourishing, civil society thus requires a state which is limited, non-interventionary, and which furthers the 'freedoms' of individual citizens, notably their market freedoms.

These three form a neo-liberal package, linked to notions of 'governance' and to contemporary IFI arguments on the links between economic and political reform. Since 1989, the World Bank and the IMF have argued that instances of 'failure' of structural adjustment programmes are linked to the maintenance of authoritarian regimes which serve the rent-seeking interests of those controlling the regime. Liberal-democratic political reforms would weaken – or end – their grip, while also creating means for the constituencies presumed supportive of SAPs (business circles, peasants and others) to influence policy, make regimes accountable, etc. Hence political reform is not just consistent with economic reform, but essential for it.

From such arguments flow the setting of political conditions for loans (Baylies, 1995) and the variety of programmes designed to support civil society and especially NGOs. A key element of policy towards NGOs has been the diversion of resources from the state (seen as bad) to NGOs (seen as civil society, and thus good). 'This preference for NGOs' says Ndegwa 'reflects a fundamental tenet in current development theory and practice that holds in disdain existing official state arrangements and seeks to "get government off the backs of the people" by elevating private and public non-state actors' (20–21). Marcussen, who has discussed such arguments more fully in a recent review, provides us with a telling quotation from Alan Fowler:

> The dominant western concept of socio-economic development based on liberalism and market forces maintains that NGOs must be supported because of their political role within civil society. It is envisaged that people must be empowered to take over some aspects of development from the overbearing, autocratic, inefficient and corrupt states that have commonly ruled in Africa. NGOs must also provide countervailing power to government expansionism; strengthen people's ability to hold public servants and politicians accountable for their actions; and foster democratic change by expanding social pluralism. (Marcussen, 1996: 406)

In this discourse, rooted in US academic and policy practice but by no means limited to that, the 'state' is not only portrayed as inherently overweening, inefficient, bureaucratic, self-interested, etc, but it is sedulously confused with particular political systems, and even particular regimes. Thus the quite valid observation that many 'civil society organisations 'are opposed to (say) the current Nigerian regime is taken as evidence that 'civil society' is opposed to the 'state', and that movements for democratic reform must necessarily also be for a neo-liberal, market supportive, non-intervention state form and development strategy. As the painstaking case studies in Mamdani and Wamba-dia-Wamba make clear, there is no such necessity: although 'social movements in Africa are not just about opposing the state, but also about redefining the form of the state', equally, 'just as there is no single social project characteristic of social movements, there is no one state project that they come to define ultimately' (34, 33). In practice, as Ndegwa points out, there is no single pattern of relationships between regimes and elements of civil society. Not only are there some organisations close to authoritarian governments, but there is a general sense in which civil society as associational life depends on the state, while its growth may depend on material support from government. Past history,[2] too, shows us that organisations that have been actively involved in pursuing democratic reforms – such as trade unions in the late colonial period – may readily fall victim to the incorporation of national and local leaderships into the politics of clientelism and corruption: civil society may ultimately become part of the state. To summarise: the empirical evidence for 'opposition to the state' as an integral part of the programme of civil society is thus as flimsy and ambiguous as that for its role in democratisation; it appears to be merely an ideological construct.

Who Does Need Civil Society?

Who, then needs 'civil society'? It is neither a necessary nor a sufficient condition for democratic struggle to occur; indeed civil society may more often need democratic struggle than the reverse. As a concept, it is too vague, difficult to define, and empirically elusive, to contribute to analysis or description. The significant theses associated with the concept appear not to be derived from a body of empirical evidence and well-constructed theory but from a set of neo-liberal nostrums, incorporated into the argument as assumptions and then proudly presented as valid conclusions. As such, civil society forms part of the 'liberal project' analysed recently by Tom Young (who describes the Africanist civil society as 'absurdly naive' (1995: 533)). As Young himself points out, it is the 'liberal project' that can be seen to 'need' a suitably defined civil society. Writing as part of the project, the process of 'erosion of traditional under- standings by liberal democratic norms', he argues that 'its essential component, as is recognised by the more candid western analysis, is a "civil society" which will marginalise, and if necessary pulverise, groups whose modes of existence and values are not compatible with liberal democracy' (544). Mamdani makes the same point in arguing that civil society is a polar term whose matching term is not 'state' but 'community', and in referring in his final sentence to the 'uncompromising modernism of the "civil society" theorists' (Mamdani and Wamba-dia-Wamba, 1995: 613–14).

Thus apart from the grant-seeking NGOs and the academics, it is proponents of the 'liberal project' who need civil society: western governments, their associated agencies, multinationals, and IFIs. Africanists can dispense with it: 'civil society' forms part of a large body of general concepts that have appeared briefly to illuminate analysis but which are too diffuse, inclusive and ideologically laden to sustain illumi- nation: nation building, modernisation, elite, dependency, disengagement – even, perhaps, ethnicity.

Endnotes

1   It is also worth pointing out that the norm setting has to a large extent been done by external agencies, notably the apparatus of 'democratic institutes' and election and human rights monitoring bodies, acting through local elements of civil society. Even this version of 'civil society' is empirically dubious.
2   The literature on civil society (with the exception of Crawford Young) is oddly ahistorical, making only the most modest references to the growth and activity of 'civil society' under colonial and immediate post-colonial rule, By contrast, many of the essays in Mamdani & Wamba-dia-Wamba have a substantial historical component.

Bibliography

Bayart, J. F. (1986), 'Civil Society in Africa', in P. Chabal (ed.), *Political Domination in Africa*, Cambridge: CUP.

Baylies, C. (1995), '"Political Conditionality" and Democratisation', *Review of African Political Economy* 65: 321–37.

Beckman, B. & A. Jega (1995), 'Scholars and Democratic Politics in Nigeria', *Review of African Political Economy* 64: 167–81.

Beckman, B. (1993), 'The Liberation of Civil Society: Neo-Liberal Ideology and Political Theory', *Review of African Political Economy* 58.

Bratton, M. (1989), 'Beyond the State: Civil Society and Associational Life in Africa', *World Politics*, 41, 3: 407–30; (1992), 'Popular Protest and Political Reform in Africa', *Comparative Politics,* 24, 4: 419–42.

Fowler, A. (1991), 'The Role of NGOs in Changing State-Society Relations: Perspectives from Eastern and Southern Africa', *Development Policy Review*, 9, 1: 53–84.

Gellner, E. (1991), 'Civil Society in Historical Context', *International Social Science Journal,* 129: 495–510.

Harbeson, J. W., D. Rothchild & N. Chazan (eds) (1994), *Civil Society and the State in Africa*, Boulder, CO: Lynne Rienner.

Kumar, K. (1993), 'Civil Society: an Enquiry into the Usefulness of an Historical Term', *British Journal of Sociology*, 44, 3: 375–96.

Mamdani, M. & E Wamba-dia-Wamba (eds) (1995), *African Studies in Social Movements and Democracy*, Dakar: Codesria.

Marcussen, H. S. (1996), 'NGOs, the State and Civil Society', *Review of African Political Economy* 69: 405–23.

Ndegwa, S. N. (1996) *The Two Faces of Civil Society: NGOs and the Politics in Africa*, West Hartford, CT: Kumarian Press.

Stewart, S. (1997), 'Happy ever after in the Marketplace: NGOs and Uncivil Society', *Review of African Political Economy* 71: 11–34.

Young, T. (1995), '"A Project to be Realised": Global Liberalism and Contemporary Africa', *Millennium,* 24, 3: 527–46.

INDEX

Abdullah, Hussaina 9, 157-62
Acheampong, Gen. 113, 204
accountability 9, 166, 220-2 *passim*, 251, 265, 266
accumulation, capital 4, 5, 11, 17, 20, 36-56 *passim*, 61, 68, 71, 72, 76, 78-85 *passim*, 93, 94, 182, 183, 254
Ademola, K. 159
Adhikari, R. 247
adjustment, structural 6-7, 10-13, 160, 170-6, 202-15, 218, 219, 226-8 *passim*, 241, 242, 245, 248, 250, 266
Afghanistan 110, 135
agriculture 6, 7, 19, 24, 38, 39, 46-9 *passim*, 60, 62, 66, 67, 71, 77, 81, 85, 99, 103-4, 171, 183, 184, 199, 218, 236, 248, 249
Ahuma, Attoh 191
aid 6, 11-12, 23, 34, 38, 68, 69, 101 118, 120, 131, 132, 135, 184, 185, 191, 215-30 *passim*; military 118, 131,134-5
Ake, Claude 226
Alavi, Hamza 2-3, 32, 112, 237, 238, 252
Alexander, Jocelyn 9, 195-201
Algeria 105, 229, 241, 265
Allen, Chris 12, 260-8
Althusser, L. 178
Amin, Idi 24, 25, 27-30
Amin, Samir 59, 64, 94, 96
Amsden, Alice 252, 254
Anderson, Perry 96, 181
Andrae, G. 241
Angola 100, 110, 150, 153-4, 188, 193
anthropology 165-7, 182
Archer, Robert 216-18 *passim*, 223
armaments industry 102-5, 137-9 *passim*
army 23, 26-31 *passim*, 107-16, 118, 120-1, 124, 126, 141 *see also* military
Asia 109, 244; East 226, 234, 247, 248, 251, 252, 254; South 3; Southeast 6, 44; Soviet 61

Asians, East African 19, 24, 28, 29
Assiri, A.M. 6
Atieno-Odhiambo, E.S. 163
Austro-Hungarian Empire 188
authoritarianism 2, 8, 11-12, 205-10, 214, 225, 226, 228, 232, 252, 253, 266 *see also* military rule
autonomy, of civil society 240; of state 3, 4, 19, 26, 30, 45, 50, 52, 112, 226, 233, 237-8, 252-4
Ayu, Iyorchia 107-9 *passim*
Azam, Jean-Paul 250

Babangida, Gen. 9, 157-9 *passim*
Babangida, M. 158, 161
Bahro, Rudolf 137
balance of payments 6, 38, 39, 41, 42, 46-50 *passim*, 53, 217, 203-4
Balandier, George 165
Bale, 118, 120, 127
Banda, Dingiswayo 90
Bangladesh 32, 110, 245
Bangura, Yusuf 11, 202-14, 225, 229, 239
banking 71, 76, 246, 250
Bardhan, Pranab 246
Barker, Jonathan 249, 254
Barrientos, Stephanie 250
Barya, John-Jean 226, 227
Bates, Robert 235, 248, 252, 253
Bayart, J.-F. 95, 96, 165-6, 179, 181, 228, 229, 255, 260-2 *passim*
Baylies, Carolyn 11-12, 215-31, 266
Baynham, Simon 148
Beckett, P.A. 9
Beckman, Björn 4-5, 12, 43-83, 93, 107-16, 232-43, 260, 264
Bernstein, Henry 93
Berry, Sara 249
Beynon, Jonathan 249
Bienefeld, Manfred 247

269